This **Mar** first comprehensive study of the women in Ibsen's pla **Tel:** provides a close reading of the texts and a ree xamination of the critical tradition on Ibsen's women, including the much-debated question of the playwright's relation to feminism. Templeton traces patterns of gender throughout Ibsen's work, analyzing the women of the lesser-known early plays, from *Catiline* through *Love's Comedy*, as precursors of later, famous women like Nora Helmer of *A Doll House* and Hedda Gabler. Templeton also reexamines how the women in Ibsen's life influenced the women in the plays, and offers new information on and a new reading of Ibsen's relation with the young women of his later years. The book contains photographs of important women in Ibsen's life as well as of prominent actresses in the major roles.

IBSEN'S WOMEN

IBSEN'S WOMEN

JOAN TEMPLETON
Long Island University

CAMBRIDGE
UNIVERSITY PRESS

PUBLISHED BY THE PRESS SYNDICATE OF THE UNIVERSITY OF CAMBRIDGE
The Pitt Building, Trumpington Street, Cambridge, United Kingdom

CAMBRIDGE UNIVERSITY PRESS
The Edinburgh Building, Cambridge CB2 2RU, United Kingdom
40 West 20th Street, New York, NY 10011-4211, USA
10 Stamford Road, Oakleigh, VIC 3166, Australia
Ruiz de Alarcón 13, 28014 Madrid, Spain
Dock House, The Waterfont, Cape Town 8001, South Africa

http://www.cambridge.org

First published 1997
Reprint 1999
First paperback edition 2001

Printed in the United Kingdom at the University Press, Cambridge

Typeset in 11/12½ New Baskerville

A catalogue record for this book is available from the British Library

Library of Congress cataloguing in publication data
Templeton, Joan.
Ibsen's women / Joan Templeton.
p. cm.
Includes bibliographical references and index.
ISBN 0 521 59039 6 (hardback)
1. Ibsen, Henrik, 1828–1906 – Characters – Women. 2. Women in
literature. 3. Ibsen, Henrik, 1828–1906 – Relations with women. I. Title.
PT8897.W7T46 1997
839.8′226–dc21 96–49141 CIP

ISBN 0 521 59039 6 hardback
ISBN 0 521 00136 6 paperback

BS

For my students in Brooklyn and France, who have taught me much

The glory of Ibsen is that he refused to make certain fatal separations. He refused to separate the individual from the collective, the personal from the social.

Eric Bentley *In Search of Theatre*

Contents

List of illustrations	*page*	xiii
Preface		xv
List of abbreviations		xix
Note on translations		xxi

1	Roots	1

2	The seminal women of the early career	23
	Revising the fatal woman: *Catiline's* "worser spirit"	23
	Moving on: new ingénues, a troll temptress, a woman-centered triangle, and gender	29

3	Love and marriage	40
	The Queen of Iceland and her step-mother	40
	Love's tragedy: *The Vikings at Helgeland*	53
	Love's Comedy: feminist satire	58

4	Love and the kingdom	74
	The feminization of history: *The Pretenders*	74
	Marrying heaven and earth: the his-and-her deities of *Brand*	80
	Troll sex and pure love: Peer Gynt's Manichean theory of woman	90
	Julian's "pure woman": a note on *Emperor and Galilean*	108

5	The poetry of feminism	110
	The *Doll House* backlash	110
	Nora's predecessors in art and life	128
	The death of chivalry: masculine and feminine in *A Doll House*	137

6	Mrs. Alving's ghosts	146

7	A new woman and three housewives	163
	The doctor's disciples: *An Enemy of the People*	163
	Sense and sensibility: women and men in *The Wild Duck*	166

8   Taming wild women   181
  The beatification of Rebecca West: *Rosmersholm*   181
  The acclimatization of Ellida and Bolette Wangel:
   The Lady from the Sea   194

9   The deviant woman as hero: *Hedda Gabler*   204
  The unreal woman in the realistic play: Hedda as anomaly   204
  The defective woman: Hedda as type   206
  The author's right to a subject: Hedda's reality   210
  The *agents-provocateurs*   218
  The closing and the springing of the trap   225
  Hedda's difference   229

10 The glories and dangers of the rejuvenating
 feminine   233
  May loves of a September life   233
  Beloved nemesis: *The Master Builder*   263

11 Women who live for love   278
  Rita Allmers' law of change: *Little Eyolf*   278
  Down among the dead women: *John Gabriel Borkman*   291

12 The revolt of the muse: *When We Dead Awaken*   302

In Conclusion: Ibsen's women and Ibsen's modernism   323

Notes   336
Select bibliography   373
Index   380

Illustrations

1 Marichen Ibsen. Reproduced by kind permission of the Telemark Folk Museum, Venstøp Farmhouse   *page* 2

2 Water-color by Marichen Ibsen. Reproduced by kind permission of the Telemark Folk Museum, Venstøp Farmhouse   3

3 Hedvig Ibsen. Reproduced by kind permission of the Telemark Folk Museum, Venstøp Farmhouse   6

4 Clara Ebbell. Reproduced by kind permission of the Ibsen House and Grimstad City Museum, Grimstad   19

5 Magdalene Thoresen. Photography Collection, Royal Library, Copenhagen   42

6 Henrik Ibsen at the age of thirty-five. Gyldendal Collection, University Library, Oslo   49

7 Suzannah Ibsen at the age of forty. Gyldendal Collection, University Library, Oslo   50

8 Ragna Wettergreen as Hjørdis of *The Vikings at Helgeland*. Courtesy of the Theatre Museum, Oslo   56

9 Camilla Collett on the Norwegian 100-kroner note   69

10 Linn Stokke as Solveig of *Peer Gynt*. Photograph by Frits Solvang. Collection of the National Theatre, Oslo   99

11 Asta Hansteen. Photography Collection, University Library, Oslo   130

12 Liv Ulmann as Nora of *A Doll House*. Photograph by Friedman-Abeles, Billy Rose Theatre Collection, The New York Public Library for the Performing Arts, Astor, Lenox, and Tilden Foundations   144

13 Mrs. Fiske as Mrs. Alving in *Ghosts*. Billy Rose Theatre Collection, The New York Public Library for the Performing Arts, Astor, Lenox, and Tilden Foundations   153

14 Blanche Yurka as Gina and Helen Chandler as Hedvig
in *The Wild Duck*. Billy Rose Theatre Collection,
The New York Public Library for the Performing Arts,
Astor, Lenox, and Tilden Foundations   174

15 Eva Le Gallienne as Hedda in *Hedda Gabler*.
Photograph by Chidnoff, Billy Rose Theatre
Collection, The New York Public Library for
the Performing Arts, Astor, Lenox, and Tilden
Foundations   215

16 Emilie Bardach. Gyldendal Collection, University
Library, Oslo   258

17 Hildur Andersen. Gyldendal Collection, University
Library, Oslo   259

18 Henrik Ibsen at the age of fifty-nine. Gyldendal
Collection, University Library, Oslo   260

19 Margaret Barker as Aline and Joan Tetzel as Hilda
in *The Master Builder*. Billy Rose Theatre Collection,
The New York Public Library for the Performing Arts,
Astor, Lenox, and Tilden Foundations   272

20 Katja Medbøe as Rita in *Little Eyolf*. Photograph by Frits
Solvang. Collection of the National Theatre, Oslo   288

21 Wenche Foss as Ella and Ingerid Vardund as Gunhild
in *John Gabriel Borkman*. Photograph by Siggen
Stinessen. Collection of the National Theatre, Oslo   293

22 Lise Fjeldstad as Irene in *When We Dead Awaken*.
Photograph by Leif Gabrielsen. Collection of
the National Theatre, Oslo   311

Preface

This book began in a Brooklyn classroom. A better Ibsenite than
I, one of my students questioned the standard reading of *Ghosts* as
a tragedy that fixes the responsibility on the protagonist's refusal
to welcome her husband sexually: "Mrs. Alving didn't love the
captain and didn't want to marry him, so . . ." The student could
not complete her idea, her voice trailed off, and I was saved by the
end of the hour, but the fragmented objection teased at me and
sent me back to the text, until, much later, like Helene Alving
examining the outworn moral system that ruled her life, I saw that
what I had been teaching was ghost ridden. *Ghosts* led me back to
A Doll House, the play to which it was a sequel; "After Nora," Ibsen
wrote, "Mrs. Alving had to come" (*LS* 208). And in the critical
commentary on the woman who slammed the door, I found the
same ghostly censure as in the commentary on the woman who
stayed. Like Mrs. Alving, Nora is to blame. I also found a widespread determination to rescue *A Doll House* from the contamination of feminism. Thinking through the terms and arguments of
this claim made me reexamine the relation of *A Doll House* and its
author to the feminism of his day and ours, a study that led me to
conclude that Ibsen's play is the quintessential feminist work
because it does nothing less than destroy the notion of Woman,
the female Other of history.

It seemed imperative to know how Ibsen had arrived at this
contention, and so I went back further, to Nora's predecessors,
and to an examination of another claim: that Ibsen's paradigmatic plot, beginning with his first play *Catiline*, consists of a male
protagonist whose internal conflict is dramatized in his relation
with two opposing representatives of Woman – one aggressive,
masculine, and destructive, and the other passive, womanly, and
nurturing – as though Ibsen believed in a species of She that

consisted of two varieties. I concluded that although Ibsen began, as Brandes put it, "waist-deep in the Romantic period" (B 79), as one of the chief creators of modernism, he transformed the forms, ideas, and ideologies of his cultural legacy, one of which was the centuries-old stereotype of Woman as Angel or Devil. And I discovered that Ibsen created patterns of his own, including a female-centered triangular plot as important in his work as the male-centered one.

It is not possible to write intelligently about "Ibsen's Idea of Women" or "Woman's Place in Ibsen's Ideological Landscape."[1] Long before the post-Freudians, Ibsen questioned the existence of a "female nature," critically examining the exclusiveness of the categories "masculine" and "feminine" both within people and within systems. Ibsen's refusal of Woman allowed him to discover the socialization of sexual identity we now call "gender" and to investigate women as full moral beings struggling against the cultural norms that define and limit them. Taken as a whole, his plays constitute a remarkable literary contribution to feminist thought, whose central tenet historian Joan Scott defines as "the refusal of the hierarchical construction of the relationship between male and female in its specific contexts and an attempt to reverse or displace its operations."[2]

This book is a reading of the women in Ibsen's plays, and thus of the plays, from first to last. Ibsen insisted that his work should be read as a continuous, developing whole, and the rightness of this judgment is nowhere better borne out than in a study of his women. The female characters in the early plays prefigure the famous women of the middle and late plays. My major working method is close textual analysis, accompanied, in the case of three of Ibsen's major plays – *A Doll House*, *Ghosts*, and *Hedda Gabler* – by an argument against the hostility, even condemnation, that characterizes much of the commentary on three of Ibsen's greatest protagonists. I am convinced that such criticism misunderstands Ibsen's purposes and violates his texts.

If Ibsen insisted on the unity of his work, he also insisted that it never reflected experiences he had merely "lived out" (*op*levet), but only those he had "lived *through*" (*gennem*levet) (H 17:402).[3] I have tried to discover what Ibsen "lived *through*" with women and what he made of the private history. I have tried to fill in shadows, near missing persons like Clara Ebbell, Ibsen's early love, and the more substantial, yet still neglected Camilla Collett, the founder of both Norwegian feminism and the Norwegian realist novel, and one of the very few authors whose influence Ibsen acknowledged. With regard to other women – Marichen Altenburg Ibsen, the poet's mother, Suzannah Thoresen Ibsen, the poet's wife, and the young women Ibsen was drawn to in his old age – I have reexamined what has been claimed about their relation to the playwright and his work.

Ibsen was fond of saying that a writer needs models as much as a sculptor, and he drew on both women he knew and on fictional women. I have tried to identify Ibsen's models, literary and living, and to suggest how he used them. As with all artists, of course, Ibsen's models were starting points; "there is a big difference," he said, "between the model and the portrait" (*LS* 91).

Although Ibsen's reticence regarding his work is well known, his letters constitute a rich critical commentary from which I have drawn extensively. I am deeply indebted to two great critical editions of Ibsen's works, the Norwegian "Centenary Edition," the *Hundreårsutgaven*, edited by Francis Bull, Halvdan Koht, and Didrik Arup Seip, and *The Oxford Ibsen*, edited by James McFarlane. I also owe a large debt to Ibsen's Norwegian and English biographers, especially Halvdan Koht and Michael Meyer, although I sometimes disagree with them. Meyer, for example, claims that he has supplied an element missing in Koht's biography, "the truth" about Ibsen's relation with his wife and with the young women of his old age (M xvi); I have reached different conclusions from Meyer on these matters as well as on others.

An abbreviated version of parts one and two of chapter five, "The Poetry of Feminism," appeared in *PMLA*, as did an earlier version of chapter six, "Mrs. Alving's Ghosts." An earlier version of part two of chapter seven, "Sense and Sensibility: Women and Men in *The Wild Duck*" appeared in *Scandinavian Studies*. I thank both journals for permission to reprint.

I owe a great debt to Professors Joseph Duchak and the late Jay Redfield of the Long Island University Library. I also thank Hedvig Vincenot, curator of the Bibliothèque Nordique of the Bibliothèque St. Geneviève in Paris, Turid Eriksen and Grete Lund of the University Library, Oslo, and the librarians of the Central Research Library and the Library for the Performing Arts of the New York Public Library. I am very grateful to Astrid

Sæther, director of the Ibsen Center at the University Library, Oslo, for her generous hospitality. And many thanks to Jarle Bjørklund, director of the Ibsen Museum in Grimstad, Tor Gardåsen, director of the Telemark Folk Museum in Skien and Venstøp, and Gerd Rosander, director of the National Henrik Ibsen Museum in Oslo.

This book could not have been written without the generous support of the National Endowment for the Humanities of the United States. I am also grateful to the American Scandinavian Foundation and to the Long Island University, Brooklyn Campus, Released Time Committee. I thank the Long Island University administrators who have facilitated my work: David Cohen, Dean of Conolly College of Arts and Sciences, Edward Clark, former President of the Brooklyn Center, and Gale Stevens Haynes, Provost.

I owe special thanks to Rolf Fjelde for his support and encouragement over the years. I also thank Leif Sjøberg and Robert Spector for their encouragement and for writing grant recommendations crucial to this project. Ross Shideler's appreciation of my work has meant a great deal to me. Other friends and colleagues whose support I gratefully acknowledge are Asbjørn Aarseth, Ann-Charlotte Gavel Adams, Alma Adcock, Nina and Karsten Alnæs, Roger Asselineau, Kenneth Bernard, Pål Bjørby, Marilyn Johns Blackwell, Marvin Carlson, Jan Dietrichson, George Economou, Irene and Fredrik Engelstad, the late Maurice Gravier, Otto Hageberg, Ellen and Terje Hartmann, Bjørn Hemmer, Margaret Higonnet, Annie Hubert, Esther Hyneman, Irene Iversen, Barry Jacobs, Seymour Kleinberg, John Kronik, Maurice Lévy, Jerome Loving, Terence and Kathleen Malley, Sue Montgomery, Mary Kay Norseng, John Northam, Helge Rønning, Sandra Saari, Mark Sandberg, Howard Silverstein, Steven Sondrup, James Yeldell, and Vigdis Ystad. Special thanks go to my colleague Cynthia Dantzic for the idea for the book-jacket design. My deepest gratitude goes to my good friend and fellow Ibsen enthusiast Thomas Van Laan, who read the manuscript, made valuable suggestions, and saved me from errors. Any that remain are mine. My most essential debt is the one I owe my physicians, Drs. S. Huh, Benjamin Payson, and Bernard Weiss. *Et, finalement, bien que tu ne sois plus là, mon cher Jean-Claude, je te remercie de tout mon coeur.*

Abbreviations

References to works in the Select Bibliography are cited by author or short title in parenthesis. For other works, I give the full citation in a note, and in subsequent references, the name of the author or a short title; in the few cases of widely spaced references, I repeat the full citation. Following is a list of abbreviations for references I employ frequently.

A   Ibsen, Henrik. *The Works of Henrik Ibsen*. Ed. and trans. William Archer. New York: Scribner's, 1917. 13 vols. References to the monographs on Ibsen by Edward Dowden, Edmund Gosse, and James Huneker are to volume 13 of this edition.

B   Brandes, Georg. *Henrik Ibsen and Bjornstjerne Bjørnson*. Trans. Jesse Muir, rev. William Archer. London: Heinemann, 1899.

BI   Ibsen, Bergliot. *The Three Ibsens*. Trans. Gerik Schjelderup. London: Hutchinson, 1951.

F   Fjelde, Rolf. "Introductions." *Ibsen, The Complete Major Prose Plays*. Trans. Fjelde. New York: New American Library, 1978.

H   *Hundreårsutgave. Henrik Ibsens Samlede Verker* [*Centenary Edition. Henrik Ibsen's Collected Works*]. Ed. Francis Bull, Halvdan Koht, and Didrik Arup Seip. 21 vols. Oslo: Gyldendal, 1928–57.

K   Koht, Halvdan. *Life of Ibsen*. Trans. Einar Haugen and A.E. Santaniello. New York: Blom, 1971.

LS   Ibsen, Henrik. *Letters and Speeches*. Ed. and trans. Evert Sprinchorn. New York: Hill, 1964.

M   Meyer, Michael. *Ibsen*. Garden City: Doubleday, 1971.

N   Northam, John. *Ibsen: A Critical Study*. Cambridge
      University Press, 1973.
OI   *The Oxford Ibsen*. Ed. James Walter McFarlane and
      Graham Orton. Trans. McFarlane et. al. 8 vols. London:
      Oxford University Press, 1960–77.
P   Paulsen, John. *Samliv med Ibsen* [*Living with Ibsen*]. 2 vols.
      Christiania: Gyldendal, 1906, 1913.
Z   Zucker, A.E. *Ibsen the Master Builder*. 1929. New York:
      Farrar, 1973.

Note on translations

References to Ibsen's plays and prefaces from *Catiline* through *Emperor and Galilean*, except for *Peer Gynt*, are to the first four volumes of *The Oxford Ibsen*, ed. James McFarlane and Graham Orton, trans. McFarlane et. al. (London: Oxford University Press, 1960–70). The Oxford translations render the frequent dashes in Ibsen's early manuscripts as spaced dots; to avoid confusion, I have regularized the punctuation. References to *Peer Gynt* are to Rolf Fjelde's translation, second edition (Minneapolis: University of Minnesota Press, 1980). References to Ibsen's plays from *Pillars of Society* through *When We Dead Awaken* are to Fjelde's *Ibsen: The Complete Major Prose Plays* (New York: New American Library, 1978), except for *Ghosts* and *The Wild Duck*, for which I have used my own translations; references to these two plays are to the original texts in the "Centenary Edition," the *Hundreårsutgave*, ed. Francis Bull, Halvdan Koht, and Didrik Arup Seip, 21 vols. (Oslo: Gyldendal, 1928–57). Unless otherwise noted, translations of Ibsen's poems are mine and references are to the *Hundreårsutgave*.

Translations from Camilla Collett's works are mine; references are to the *Samlede Verker. Mindeudgave* [*Complete Works. Commemorative Edition*]. 3 vols. Christiania: Gyldendal, 1913.

When available, I have used reliable English versions of biographical and critical material; otherwise, all translations are mine.

CHAPTER 1

Roots

Some turn to brandy, others to lies,
And we – well, we took to fairy tales
Of princes and trolls and strange animals.
Peer Gynt 2:2 (43)

On the wall at Venstøp farmhouse, near the town of Skien, in
Norway's Telemark region, hang two water-color landscapes. The
artist is identified as "Henrik Ibsen's mother." Marichen Cornelia
Martine Altenburg was an avid painter; more important for literary posterity, she was in love with the theatre. She worried her
upright parents by attending every performance of the travelling
Danish troupes, and by continuing to play with her childhood
dolls when she was grown. More outrageous was her ambition to
go on the stage. Accompanying herself on the piano, she loved to
sing the old Telemark folk songs, performing them so well that
people suspected her of a hidden connection with theatre people,
a rumor she did nothing to discourage. Marichen Altenburg was
small, brunette, and dark-complexioned, and the only existing
likeness of her, a silhouette, bears out the tradition that she was
beautiful.[1]

On December 1, 1825, when she was twenty-six, and he twenty-
eight, Marichen Altenburg married Knud Ibsen. There is a strong
tradition in Telemark that Marichen loved a man called Tormod
Knudsen, but that her family had destined her for Knud Ibsen.
Whether this is true or not, the marriage was an excellent family
arrangement. Marichen's mother and Knud's step-father were
sister and brother, and the bride and groom, who had grown up
together, were practically regarded as sister and brother themselves. Marichen Altenburg was a fine catch, the daughter of one
of the wealthiest merchants in the prosperous lumber town of
Skien, where the enterprising Knud Ibsen ran a general store.

1. Silhouette of Marichen Altenburg Ibsen (1799–1869), Ibsen's mother, as a
young woman. Artist unknown.

2. One of two surviving water-colors by Marichen Ibsen.

Ten months after her marriage, Marichen Ibsen gave birth to her first child, a boy, and eight months later was pregnant again. Henrik Ibsen's birth, on March 20, 1828, was followed three and a half weeks later by the death of his older brother. During the next seven years, Marichen Ibsen would on the average bear a child every other year, and Henrik would grow up the oldest of five children.

The young Ibsen couple lived very well in "Stockmann House" in the center of Skien, and when Henrik was three years old, they moved up the street to Marichen Ibsen's family home, "Altenburg Manor," where they lived even better. The two-storied house of ten rooms was flanked by outbuildings, including a stable that housed Marichen's and Knud's saddle horses. Knud Ibsen was socially as well as financially ambitious, and to this end "enjoyed dispensing reckless hospitality," as his famous son would later comment to Georg Brandes (*LS* 212). Altenburg Manor was known for its sumptuous dinners and holiday festivities that lasted for days. Knud Ibsen also entertained lavishly with drinking par-

ties and wolf hunts at an old farmhouse he bought at Venstøp, a
few miles outside Skien.

Marichen's father, a ship-master and timber merchant, had
died before her wedding and left a large private fortune.
Marichen had one sister and no brothers, and thus Knud Ibsen
became the "man of the house." The records of his business
transactions show that by 1830, five years after his marriage, he
had taken over almost all his wealthy mother-in-law's property in
and around Skien, including a brewery and a profitable schnapps
distillery. He no longer troubled about his general store, and
began to speculate heavily in salt and timber. When his risky
investments failed, he mortgaged the Altenburg properties to
banks and private lenders, and by 1834, he had run out of money
and was unable to pay his taxes. The authorities sealed the distillery, and the following year, the brewery was auctioned to pay
Knud Ibsen's debts, and following it, Altenburg Manor. In May
and June of 1835, thirty-six-year-old Marichen Ibsen, pregnant
with her sixth child, saw her family home fall under the hammer,
along with its "copper, brass, tin, ironware, wooden goods, bed-
clothes, two rare carpets together with assorted furnishings and
two large looking-glasses" (Mosfjeld 69). The distillery was set to
be sold at the end of the year, and the Ibsens moved in disgrace to
the sole property Knud Ibsen's creditors had left them, the
Venstøp farmhouse.[2]

Devoted to horses and hunting and his place in the world, the
man who kept Christmas open house with a groaning sideboard
was humiliated by his ruin. He had neither the integrity to accept
the blame for his failure nor the force to start over. His love of
drink, which in his palmy days was regarded as an aimiable weakness, now took the form of a destructive passion for alcohol.
Always an authoritarian, Knud Ibsen became a family tyrant, visiting his bitterness and resentment on his wife and children. The
Ibsen biographers who had first-hand accounts of the Ibsen
household hint that Knud Ibsen was physically violent; Oskar
Mosfjeld, the biographer of Ibsen's boyhood, writes that his conduct "bordered on brutality" (20), and Halvdan Koht, the author
of Ibsen's definitive Norwegian life, notes that "Henrik had ample
opportunity to feel his father's heavy-handed insistence on obedi-
ence" (K 29).

We do not know what Marichen and Knud Ibsen's marriage was

like before they moved to Venstøp farm, but afterwards, it was one of total estrangement in which the children took the side of their mother against their father. Marichen Ibsen, whom acquaintances had consistently described as "full of life," "merry," and "outgoing" (Mosfjeld 27–28), was emotionally devastated by the disaster and thoroughly cowed by the man who had lost her family's money. One neighbor who knew the Ibsens well said that Knud Ibsen "frightened [his wife] to death, so much so that she became like a changeling" (Mosfjeld 27). Bearing her husband's abuse as best she could, Marichen Ibsen worked desperately to make ends meet and sought solace in her children, her pietist religion, and her easel.

Marichen Ibsen's love of painting and theatre has been characterized by Hans Heiberg as a mere reflection of the times, "when refined young ladies were expected to be able to play the piano, recite, embroider, take part in amateur dramatics and also perhaps paint and draw a little" (*Ibsen* 22). Other biographers of Ibsen, including Koht and Michael Meyer, have seen in Marichen Ibsen's drawings and water-colors the evidence of talent. We cannot know whether Marichen Ibsen might have developed as an actress or a painter if she had had the opportunity. But whatever one believes about Marichen Ibsen's talent, or about hereditary influence on talent, what we do know is that Henrik spent hours by the side of his mother as she drew and painted, then began to draw and paint himself. Marichen Ibsen also taught the son who was said to be her favorite the pleasures of imaginary beings; Henrik passed countless hours making dolls, painting pictures of well-dressed people, glueing them on to pieces of wood and arranging them in groups. Imagining what this "cast of characters" might do, he would shake with silent laughter. From these embryonic plays, it was a small step to a puppet theatre, which people came from miles around to see. Behind a curtain, Henrik manipulated the strings of his scarlet-clad stars Fernando and Isabella. He also delighted in performing as a magician and ventriloquist, which he accomplished with the aid of his brother Nicholas, bribed for the occasion and hidden in a chest.[3]

If Henrik had his mother's tastes, he also resembled her in another important way. No longer the oldest child of one of Skien's reigning families, but of a socially degraded family banished to a rundown farmhouse, Henrik took the family disgrace

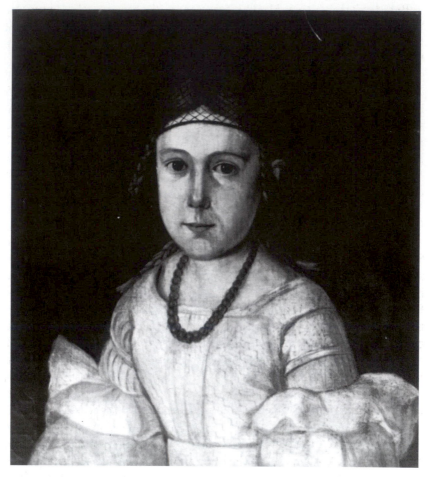

3. Oil painting of Hedvig Ibsen Stousland (1832–1920), Ibsen's sister, as a girl. Artist unknown.

hard. "Closed as an oyster" (Heiberg 29), he distanced himself from other children and from his schoolfellows, and is even said to have paid the country boys not to accompany him on the two icy miles to the schoolhouse. At home, he took refuge in a special space he claimed as his own; visitors to Venstøp farmhouse can see the little room off the back porch, a sort of closet, where he locked himself in with his dolls and paint-box. When invaded by his brothers and sister, he would drive them away in a rage. Their games bored him and interrupted his serious play.

Besides his mother, Henrik felt a close tie to one other person, his sister Hedvig, four years and eight months younger. One day he confided in her: "You know, there's a lot in the bonnet of this little Henrik Ibsen" (Mosfjeld 94). Brother and sister shared the same taste for dolls and books, including the treasure trove of volumes they had discovered in the Venstøp attic. The books had belonged to the house's former owner, a gratifyingly mysterious sailor known as "The Flying Dutchman." Most of the books were in English, but it was the illustrations that fascinated Henrik and Hedvig. A favorite volume was *A New and Universal History of the Cities of London and Westminster*, with a hundred large copper plates.[4]

Henrik loved learning, and dreamed of a university education. Unfortunately, to prepare himself properly for the entrance examination, he would have to attend Skien's expensive Latin School. Koht notes that Knud Ibsen could have obtained a scholarship for his talented son, but that he decided otherwise (K 33); instead, Henrik attended a cheaper school and only until he was fifteen, when he left to earn his living. The Ibsens were so poor that they often had nothing to eat but potatoes, and with Henrik gone, there would be one less mouth to feed. Knud Ibsen learned of an apprenticeship at an apothecary shop in Grimstad, and sent his son away, a hundred miles down the coast.

It is a commonplace that Knud Ibsen's financial ruin left a lasting impression on his famous son. Even as a successful author, Ibsen lived frugally, investing all the money he could. He was determined that his own son would never experience the penury and disgrace he himself had suffered. The necessity of money – its crucial connection to both respect and self-respect – figures importantly in *Peer Gynt, Pillars of Society, A Doll House, Hedda Gabler*, and *John Gabriel Borkman*.[5]

Equally formative for Ibsen was his mother's oppression. Ibsen's sympathy with women came from his understanding of their powerlessness, and his education began at home. From the age of seven to fifteen, when he left Skien for good, Ibsen saw his father intimidate and bully his mother, who became, in the words of contemporary witnesses, more and more "taciturn," "withdrawn," and "melancholy" (Mosfjeld 26). Constant financial worries coupled with her husband's domination made Marichen Ibsen "so weighed down with sorrow and so cowed that she almost dared not speak to people, but rather hid herself away to be as unnoticeable as possible" (Mosfjeld 26–27). Sentimentalizing her mother's depression and her submission to Knud Ibsen, Hedvig Ibsen Stousland later admiringly told Henrik Jæger, Ibsen's first Norwegian biographer, that in spite of her mother's suffering, "it was not in her to be bitter or reproachful" (Jæger 16). Hedvig's brother Henrik reacted differently. He neither forgot nor forgave his father's abuse of his mother. Bergliot Bjørnson Ibsen, Ibsen's daughter-in-law, records that even late in life Ibsen recalled with anger his father's smallest injustices and could not bear to remember his mother "succumbing to her husband's tyranny" (BI 12).

In Ibsen's very brief reminiscences of Skien, he wrote that the air "was filled all day long with the subdued roar of Long Falls, Cloister Falls, and all the many other rapids and waterfalls. And the roar was pierced from morning till night with a sound like that of shrieking and moaning women" (*LS* 2). Edmund Gosse, Ibsen's first English biographer, remarked that the poet's "earliest flight of fancy seems to have been this association of womanhood with the shriek of the saw-mill" (A 13:9). If Marichen Ibsen was mute, her son heard women screaming as the quintessential sound of his boyhood town.

Marichen Ibsen's pain would echo through her son's work in unremitting portrayals of suffering women: Margit of *The Feast at Solhoug*, Hjørdis of *The Vikings at Helgeland*, Helene Alving of *Ghosts*, the protagonist of *Hedda Gabler*, trapped in loveless marriages; the women of *The Pretenders*, instruments of male ambition; Agnes of *Brand*, martyred by her husband; Aase of *Peer Gynt*, impoverished and abandoned by a profligate husband; Rita of *Little Eyolf*, Ella and Gunhild Rentheim of *John Gabriel Borkman*, and Irene in *When We Dead Awaken*, deceived and utilized by ambitious men eager for fame.

Ibsen's Skien boyhood, Bergliot Ibsen comments, was the poet's "Achilles heel" (BI 94). Not long before he died, Ibsen told his niece, "It is not easy to go to Skien" (Mosfjeld 59), and in fact, Ibsen's last visit to his family was the brief trip he made at the end of his Grimstad apprenticeship. He went home only because his sister had begged him to come. He was undoubtedly reluctant to rewitness the family scenes, and he must certainly have wanted to avoid his mother's and sister's increasing devotion to an evangelical pietism he despised and to which his sister had tried to convert him in letters she sent him in Grimstad. Several days before Ibsen's arrival, the evangelist G.A. Lammers began a revival that challenged the Lutheran State Church, and Marichen and Hedvig Ibsen joined his following. We have no record of what transpired during Ibsen's visit, but it marked a complete break with his family. Almost twenty years later, when Hedvig wrote him the news of their mother's death, he waited four months to answer her, and when he did, he asked her to believe that it was not indifference that had kept him silent "all these long years." He admonished her, "Make no attempts at converting me," and had this to say about the event that had caused her to write: "So our dear old mother is dead. Thank you for having so lovingly carried out by yourself the duties which the rest of us should have shared" (*LS* 87). Ibsen closes with an admission followed by a plea: "This letter is short, and I have avoided what you perhaps wished most that I should write about. It cannot be otherwise at present. But do not think that I lack that warmth of heart which is the first requisite for a true and thriving spiritual life" (*LS* 87). Although Ibsen wants his sister to read between the lines and understand that he possesses both family feeling and human kindness, he is unwilling to give her even the partial solace of shared pain. Perhaps he knew that after twenty years of silence, expressions of grief at his mother's death would ring false. He offers the following explanation of his behavior: ". . . there is so much that stands between us, and between me and my old home" (*LS* 86).

Five years later, on the occasion of his father's death, Ibsen claimed in a letter to his uncle, whom he had not seen in twenty-seven years, that he had not written home because he could not help his parents financially. He asks his uncle to thank those who fulfilled "the duties and obligations that I myself should have carried out" (*LS* 171–72). In a clear reference to his mother's and sister's pietism, he further explains that in spite of a real desire to visit Skien, "I felt strongly disinclined to have any contact with certain tendencies that prevail there, tendencies with which I do not sympathize. A clash with them might have led to unpleasantness, which I preferred to avoid" (*LS* 172).

Ibsen's claim that his silence came from his poverty seems a poor excuse. The truth was that it was easier to be a purist of the affections, regarding separation as preferable to partial communication, than to expose himself to his mother's humiliation and his mother's and sister's pietism. Ibsen had in great supply both a reticence to display his feelings and an ability to distance himself from other people. He lived intensely, but within himself. Three years after his mother's death, Ibsen wrote to Bjørnstjerne Bjørnson: "Do you know that I have entirely separated myself forever from my own parents, from my whole family, because being only half understood was unendurable to me?" (*LS* 68).

Hedvig Ibsen Stousland took her brother as he was, reconciled with him, and eventually took an interest in his plays. Ibsen wrote her an occasional and affectionate letter, and when they became old, they exchanged visits. In his seventieth year, Ibsen sent her a photograph of himself with the following note: "Dear Sister, With this picture my most heartfelt greetings. I think the two of us have stayed close to each other. And so it will continue between us" (*H* 19:292). Excusing her brother's long silence, Hedvig Stousland explained to Koht, "It was just that it was always so difficult for him to put his feelings into words . . . That was why he could never get himself to write home."[6]

But putting his feelings into words was Ibsen's great gift. In a letter to Danish critic Peter Hansen on the autobiographical origins of his plays, Ibsen wrote: "For Aase [of *Peer Gynt*] my own mother – with necessary exaggerations – served as model (as she also did for Inga in *The Pretenders*)" (*LS* 102). Marichen Ibsen's ordeal is refigured in Inga's trial by fire. Inga undergoes the test to prove her son Haakon's right to the throne, only to be banished afterwards by the son she made a king. Both Francis Bull and Koht suggest that Ibsen's guilt is reflected in Haakon's for having "closed his heart to his mother" ("Henrik Ibsen" 273; K 54). If this is so, then Ibsen wishfully pardoned himself at the same time, for he has Inga declare: "No one who has so great a son can complain of being badly treated" (*H* 2:266). Marichen Ibsen's neglectful son's projection of her understanding response after he had achieved fame and fortune seems especially grievous since Ibsen, unlike his protagonist, would never reunite with his mother.

Four years after *The Pretenders*, living in Italy in self-imposed exile from Norway, Ibsen wrote one of his greatest and most autobiographical works, *Peer Gynt*, whose early scenes between Peer and Aase constitute a memorial to Marichen Ibsen written

two years before she died. "Being so far away from one's future
readers makes one reckless," Ibsen confessed to Peter Hansen.
"This poem contains much that is reminiscent of my own youth"
(*LS* 102).[7] In Peer's and Aase's recollections, the poet commemo-
rates the joy his lively mother gave him as a child:

> Peer: Remember the evenings you sat
> By my bedside when I was young
> And tucked me under the coverlet
> And sang me ballad and song?
> Aase: Of course! And when your father
> Was out, then we played sleighs.
> The spread was a lap robe of fur,
> And the floor was a sheet of ice.   (84–85)

The offending father is gone (Jon Gynt, absent from the play, has
deserted his wife and child), and a compensatory bond between
mother and son allows them to bear the troubles he brought
them. Aase, the woman in whom W.H. Auden saw a classic portrait
of the artist's mother, the "playmate who stimulates and shares his
imaginative life" ("Genius and Apostle" 336), fortifies Peer
against life's pain by schooling him in make-believe: "Oh, we've
had to stick close in misery. / Because, you know, my man – he
drank, / Roamed the parish with a line of bluff, / Scattered and
trampled our goods to dust – / While back at home my Peer and
I sat . . . / Some turn to brandy, others to lies, / And we – well we
took to fairy tales / Of princes and trolls and strange animals"
(43).

The most important of the "necessary exaggerations" that transformed the mother of the poet into the mother of Peer Gynt was
making the fictional woman voice what the real woman did not.
Ibsen replaced his mother's passive suffering with active
complaint:

> Aase: What have we got now from the days
> When your grandfather's fortunes rose?
> Those sacks of coin that Rasmus Gynt
> Willed us – you know where they went?
> Your father! Him, with his open hand,
> And the money running through like sand,
> Buying property right and left,
> Driving his gilded carriages –.   (8–9)

In the scene of Aase's death, in the cold, poor hut, stripped by
the creditors as bare as Marichen Altenburg's family home, Ibsen

returns to his mother both what she gave him and what his father took away. Transforming Aase's bed, his own as a boy, into a sleigh, Peer tucks in the coverlet and sings his mother "ballad and song" as he drives her east of the sun and west of the moon to Soria Moria castle, a heaven resembling Altenburg Manor before the disaster. The dishonored Aasa is restored to her rightful place as St. Peter pours her out "the sweetest wine" and the bishop's wife serves her "the finest cakes" (87). Peer eases his mother's death and restores her honor through the saving art of the imagination.

Blotting out the beaten-down Marichen Ibsen he could not bear to remember, Ibsen let his young mother grow to old age as full of life as ever in the irrepressible Aase. Seventeen years after *Peer Gynt*, in another of his greatest works, Ibsen performed another feat of suspended animation. In giving his sister's name to Hedvig Ekdal, the loving young girl of *The Wild Duck*, Ibsen "stopped" Hedvig Ibsen; Hedvig Ekdal's death as the victim of a crusading idealist marks the death of the Hedvig Ibsen her brother loved, transformed by the zealots. Now she would be fixed forever in the Venstøp attic, with the picture book of their childhood: "There's one just enormous book called *Harryson's History of London*; it must be a hundred years old, and it's got ever so many pictures in it. At the front there's a picture of Death with an hourglass and a girl" (437).

Ibsen's way of acknowledging his feelings toward his mother and sister was the buried way of the artist. He knew this, and it haunted him. In the masterful scene six of the last act of *Peer Gynt*, the procrastinator and emotional coward walks through the ashes of a burned out wasteland, coming home to face himself in the withered leaves, "watchwords you should have spoken," the sighing air, "songs you should have sung," the dewdrops, "tears that were never shed," and the broken straw, "deeds that you should have done" (179–81). The last accusing voice calls out: "Ai, what a driver! / Hoo, I'm upset / in the new-fallen snow – / I'm chilled and wet – / Peer, where's the castle? / You've turned the wrong way. / The devil misled you; / He's guided the sleigh" (181). Peer's conscience tells him that all his fine talk could not get his mother into heaven after all. But the self-deceiver's faithful protective mechanism rescues him: "It's time a poor fellow picks up and runs. / If I had to carry the devil's sins, / I'd soon be flat on the ground for sure – / One's own are heavy enough to bear"

(181). Beneath the irony of Peer's self-pitying rationalization lies his creator's self-recognition, an illustration of his celebrated definition: "To *live* is – to war with trolls / In the holds of the heart and mind; / To *write* – that is to hold / Judgment Day over the self" (*H* 14:461).

Marichen Ibsen died at the age of seventy, in 1869, two years after the publication of *Peer Gynt*. Ibsen was by then famous in Scandinavia, and she undoubtedly heard of his success, but there is no evidence that she had read a line of his work.

In January of 1844, a little more than two months before his sixteenth birthday, Ibsen arrived in Grimstad with no money, one suit of clothes, and a trunk full of books. He would later write of the six years he spent in the little shipbuilding town: "I found myself at loggerheads with the small community in which I lived, cramped as I was by private circumstances and by conditions in general" (*OI* 1:110). By "conditions in general," Ibsen doubtless meant the religious, social, and political conservatism that governed what he termed the "little provincial Philistine town" (*LS* 101). And his grinding poverty would have been "private circumstance" enough to distance himself from his fellow citizens even without the accompanying stigma that resulted from his fathering of an illegitimate child.

When Hans Eitrem visited Grimstad in 1909, three years after Ibsen's death, people who remembered the apothecary's apprentice described him as short and thin, well built, and very strong (*Ibsen and Grimstad* 18). He looked older than his years, had his mother's dark hair and complexion, and cultivated a full, almost black, seaman's beard. One Grimstad resident remembered that his face was "uncouth" (*Ibsen and Grimstad* 18), but like many people of strong personality, Ibsen had a way of repulsing people he did not like or respect, which was a considerable number of those he met; to Christopher Due, the first close friend of his life, Ibsen's face was "full of vitality," and altogether he gave the impression of "a good-looking, well-built young man" (*Reminiscences* 20). What impressed Due most was the glint in the apprentice's grey-blue eye, the bright, searching gaze that Ibsen would keep undiminished all his life and would become his most famous physical characteristic. To the casual observer, Ibsen seemed aloof, if not hostile; as he had done in Skien, Ibsen was reacting to his penury by withdrawal and silence. But even if Ibsen had had the money necessary to mix with the good citizens of Grimstad, and he certainly did not, earning a mere pittance, he would have had no time to do so, since he was expected to do virtually all the work of the indifferent apothecary Reimann and take care of the town's mail into the bargain, his employer being the postmaster. Besides the hardship of the gruelling hours of work, from dawn to late in the night, there was often not enough to eat.

Ibsen put on a brave front in his letters home. In a letter to a Skien acquaintance, in the first extant letter we have from his hand, he asks for news of a girl whose young man has just died and of "the lucky fellow . . . who has taken his place – because I know her too well to believe that she is still mourning him," remarking also that the Grimstad "ladies, although not as flirtatious as in Skien, are quite acceptable; and you can be sure I do everything possible to win their favor, which isn't too difficult" (*LS* 6–7). This cavalier comment from the impoverished apothecary's drudge is pure adolescent bravado.

One of the memories from Skien that lingered on in Ibsen's mind was an old rumor that Knud Ibsen was not his father. Ibsen once told Due that he was the son of Tormod Knudsen, the man Marichen Ibsen was said to have loved. There is no evidence that Marichen Ibsen and Tormud Knudsen were lovers; moreover, that Knud Ibsen was indeed the playwright's father is borne out by their striking physical resemblance.[8] Ibsen was taking advantage of the Skien rumor to disassociate himself from his father.

Mosfjeld believes that Ibsen had grave, preoccupying doubts about his paternity, and notes the high incidence of illegitimate children in his plays; similarly, Meyer argues that because Ibsen had no respect for his father, he accepted the false rumor as true, and that his supposed illegitimacy "was something from which he was never to escape . . . Hardly a play he wrote, from *The Pretenders* to *Rosmersholm*, but has its illegitimate or supposedly illegitimate child: Haakon and Peter in *The Pretenders*, Gerd in *Brand*, the Ugly Brat in *Peer Gynt*, Regine in *Ghosts*, Hedvig in *The Wild Duck*, Rebecca West in *Rosmersholm*" (M 15–16).

The only time we know that Ibsen spoke of Tormud Knudsen as his father was when he had been drinking heavily, and if on this occasion he preferred to think that he was not his father's son, it seems difficult to argue that he was overcome by the shame of it.

It is more probable, perhaps, that the recurrence of illegitimacy in Ibsen's work is his own fathering of an illegitimate child, a result of what was in all likelihood his first sexual experience.

The terrible history of Else Sofie Jensdatter seems the stuff of a Hardy novel. One of two servants in the Reimann pharmacy, she slept in a room through which Ibsen had to pass to answer the night bell. She became pregnant two years after his arrival in Grimstad, when he was not yet eighteen and she was twenty-eight. She left Grimstad to have the baby, to whom she gave the last name of Henriksen, and did not return. Ibsen, who had to pay paternity support until his son was fourteen years old, never saw her again. The few facts about her remaining life more than suggest that the experience destroyed Else Jensdatter. She was desperately poor, and although Hans Jacob Henriksen eventually earned a meager living as a blacksmith, their home was taken from them, and his mother moved to a hut on a hillside, where she died a pauper at the age of seventy-four. There is no reason to suppose that Ibsen (who by then was a famous author) heard of her death. Hans Jacob outlived his father by ten years, dying in 1916, penniless and alcoholic.[9]

Neither her own time nor posterity has been kind to Else Sofie Jensdatter. The early writers of Ibsen's life, doubtless out of deference to Ibsen, never mention her. His later biographers are quick to sympathize with the young man who became the great playwright and to slight or blame the woman he slept with. For A.E. Zucker, who devotes three sentences to the matter, the unnamed Else Jensdatter is simply "a servant girl for whose support [Ibsen] had to pay for fourteen years" (Z 23); for Koht, she is equally nameless, seems to have been solely responsible for the baby, and was embarrassingly old: "These years [in Grimstad] brought many humiliations to the young man, but worst of all was the shame he felt when a servant girl, fully ten years older than he, bore him a child" (K 38). Meyer, the first Ibsen biographer to discuss Else Jensdatter, wants to correct her reputation: "Else was not, as many commentators have taken for granted, a kitchen slut; her ancestors had been gentleman farmers, and the family had become impoverished in an honourable cause. Her grandfather, Christian Lofthus, had led a rebellion of the Norwegian peasants against their Danish overlords in the preceding century, as punishment for which his farm had been burned . . . and he himself chained to a block in the [Oslo] fortress of Akershus, where, ten years later, he died" (M 31). One would like to know whether Meyer would classify Else Jensdatter as a "kitchen slut" if her social class and her grandfather's courage had been less noble. Unfortunately, Else Jensdatter's proud lineage was of no help to her.

So poor that he had neither overcoat nor underpants, and at one point, no stockings, the close-mouthed Ibsen never complained of his support payments to Else Jensdatter. The second half of his stay in Grimstad, even though he was still wretchedly poor, was a period of intellectual and personal flowering, and the impression he made was that of an energetic, ambitious, and rather cynical young man of high, if somewhat bitter, spirits and great personal determination. Reimann had had to sell his business to pay his debts, and the new owner moved it to a better part of town in a larger house close to the sea. It was here that Ibsen made the first, and among the only, close friends of his life in Due and Ole Schulerud. Bound together by literary interests and poverty, the three young men talked literature and philosophy, discussed the startling new feminist movement, and drank punch, when they could afford it, out of ointment jars (Due 37–41). Due and Schulerud were Ibsen's audience for radical religious and political harangues, stinging poems satirizing the town dunces, and what Ibsen later termed "crazy, riotous pranks that brought down upon me the ill will of all the respectable citizens" (*OI* 1:101). It was during this time that Ibsen also met a kind Scottish woman, Georgiana Crawfurd, who guided him in his reading from her considerable private library; he read the Romantic tragedies of Adam Oehlenschläger, the most important Scandinavian dramatist of the first half of the nineteenth century, who would influence his early work, Voltaire (whose radicalism delighted him), Dickens and Scott, and the Dano-Norwegian playwright Ludvig Holberg, the "Molière of the North," for whom he developed a lifelong love. In spite of his heavy work schedule, he had not given up his dream of entering the university and worked furiously to prepare the entrance examination. He was profoundly stirred by the European upheavals of 1848, which confirmed his growing radicalism and spurred him to write revolutionary poems.

Whatever Ibsen did not say about his illegitimate child, the "dark secret," writes Francis Bull, "gnawed at him and tormented him," continuing "to remain a dark spot in his life" ("Henrik Ibsen" 276). Bull notes that Ibsen drew directly on this experience for the plots of *Lady Inger of Østråt* and *The Pretenders,* and the presence of hidden, illegitimate children in these plays may be less significant than the curious excess of brutality in their fates. In *Lady Inger,* Inger's son is stabbed to death, and in *The Pretenders,* Skule's son is hacked to pieces. Hans Jacob Henriksen floats like an incubus over *Peer Gynt.* The child component of the repulsive troll duo the Woman in Green and her bastard son, the deformed "Ugly Brat" haunts his father Peer.[10] In Ibsen's middle and late plays, illegitimate intruders, even sympathetic ones, continue to suffer harm, maiming, or destruction. At the end of *Ghosts,* Regina begins a career in Engstrand's sordid "sailors' home," and in *The Wild Duck* and *Rosmersholm* the girl and woman of suspicious birth destroy themselves. Disease, maiming, or death also occur to legitimate children who are unwanted – Hedda Gabler's unborn baby dies when she shoots herself, lame Eyolf falls into the fjord and drowns – and to the offspring of misalliances: in *Ghosts,* Oswald Alving inherits syphilis, in *The Lady from the Sea,* the Wangels' baby son dies, in *The Master Builder,* the Solness' twins die. The large number of child deaths in Ibsen's work is so striking that James Kerans has commented that "one cannot but believe that it is forced into [Ibsen's] fictive structures by some irresistible imaginative energy,"[11] and it may be that underneath Ibsen's varied examples of *kindermord* lies a compulsive urge to remove Hans Jacob Henriksen over and over again.

A curious footnote to Ibsen's short-lived relation with Else Jensdatter is the brief fragment of a novella he wrote at Grimstad about two and a half years after her departure. *The Prisoner at Akershus* was to be the story of the great political rebel Christian Lofthus, and one wonders what made Ibsen want to commemorate Else Jensdatter's famous grandfather and why he abandoned the project. It is tempting to speculate, as Meyer does, that "some re-kindled flicker of affection" prompted Ibsen to begin the work (M 50), and that afterwards, stronger feelings of guilt made him abandon it; it is also possible that *The Prisoner at Akershus* is less the product of a man's fleeting wish to give the mother of his child something more than cold paternity payments than of a young radical's genuine interest in a martyred patriot. Ibsen may have even thought better of the project because of his own disreputable connection with the woman who was Christian Lofthus' granddaughter.

In any case, Ibsen now had another woman on his mind. His friend Due had persuaded him to buy an evening coat on credit so that he could attend the local balls, where he fell unsuitably in love with one of his dancing partners. Nineteen-year-old Marthe Clarine Ebbell belonged to the prosperous Ebbell clan, one of Grimstad's reigning families. She lived on "Main Street" in a large house with tall English windows. The photograph of her in Grimstad's "Ibsen House," a museum lodged in the former apothecary shop, shows a serious face with regular features. "Clara," as she was called, was considered not the prettiest of Grimstad's young women, her granddaughter Clara Thue Ebbell records in a memoir, but rather the most unusual.[12] She was intelligent, spirited, and a talented pianist with professional ambitions. Her favorite authors were Oehlenschläger and Norway's great lyric poet Henrik Wergeland. Sociable, she was fond of balls and theatricals, and was known for her recitations at Grimstad "evenings." Altogether, Clara Ebbell was the little town's most brilliant young lady.

Ibsen and Clara Ebbell read and discussed poetry together, including Ibsen's. He was delighted by the attention of this literary young woman, who inspired him to write a series of conventional lyrics in the best Petrarchan-romantic manner. Clara becomes "Stella" (after a poem by Wergeland), the heavenly star who draws the poet upward to light and truth. In "To The Star," in a pun on her name, she is "Klare Stjerne!" ("Bright/Clara Star!"), inhabiting "High Eternity" and worshipped from afar: "Joyful in the silent night / Will I gaze upon my Star!" (*H* 14:58–59).

Ibsen must have known that this daughter of Grimstad pillars of society was not for him – a penniless, disreputable outsider and the town's *enfant terrible*. Due wittily termed his friend's adoration of Clara Ebbell "Love Without Stockings," a reference to J.H. Wessel's comedy and Ibsen's lack of legwear (*Reminiscences* 35). Ibsen fell in love in the summer, and saw his hopes dashed in the autumn when Clara Ebbell became engaged to the successful Hemming Bie, a ship's captain twice her age. Bie was also Clara's maternal uncle. Ibsen read *Werther* and wrote nostalgic poems about memories and death. In "Memories of a Ball," dedicated

4. Clara Ebbell Bie (1830–97), Ibsen's early love.

"To Stella," the poet brings his love a "Bouquet of fresh flowers /
Sprouted in last summer / Out of Memory's garden bed," which
turn out to be a "bunch of faded, autumn asters / Sprouted from
a tomb" (*H* 14:71–72).

Clara clearly had misgivings about her engagement to her uncle, for she broke it less than a year after she had made it, in the
summer of 1850. She then went to Christiania (now Oslo), where
Ibsen was now a student, to take piano lessons, and they saw each
other. Ibsen showed her his writing and promised to send her a
sampling of his new verses. When he did, he noted that the poems
would explain his state of mind; he also asked Clara's forgiveness
"for having been unable to keep myself from adding these words,
probably the last that I will ever address to you" (Ebbell 131). The
six poems contained private allusions to Ibsen's and Clara's relation and were contrived, as Eitrem has shown, to make Clara
Ebbell "see what [Ibsen] wanted her to see: a soul torn to pieces,
a restless brooder, a young man with high abilities and great
dreams, but whose hopes were crushed."[13] Ibsen's "last words" to
Clara Ebbell would turn out to be penultimate. News of her
performance as a troubadour at a masquerade ball spurred him to
send her a poem "To A Troubadour," in which the speaker asks
his love to "Whisper only to Nature's breast / What your heart
would hide" so that he, "like a silent echo," can listen (*H* 14:114).
Whether Clara answered the poet's plea is not known, but "The
Troubadour" is the last direct record of their relation.

Skipper Bie was a patient man. On Clara's twenty-second
birthday, two years after she had broken their engagement, he
gave her a collection of Oehlenschläger's tragedies with the
following inscription carefully copied in each volume: "To Clara
Ebbell, July 31, 1852, From Uncle Hemming", which shows,
as Clara Thue Ebbell writes, "that *he* was still mad for her, and
that *she* was still mad for Oehlenschläger, and that they had
not renewed their engagement" (129). Hemming Bie waited six
years for his niece to marry him, a month after her twenty-fifth
birthday.

Clara Bie and her uncle had several children who were born,
her granddaughter writes vaguely, "with some physical infirmity"
(Ebbell 130) and who died in infancy. Hemming Bie became
more and more respected, becoming the town's alderman.
Eventually, Clara's mother brought her husband to live in her

brother's and daughter's house. The two families were conservative in politics and devout in religion.

Ibsen's "troubadour" remained silent about her relation with him, but although Clara Bie kept Ibsen's love poems a secret, she also kept them. Before her death in 1897, nine years before Ibsen's, she entrusted the poems to her firstborn daughter and only surviving child, Inga Bie, along with her copy of *Catiline*, Ibsen's first play, with the dedication removed.

Clara Ebbell continued to linger in Ibsen's memory. Eleven years after he last saw her, he wrote *Love's Comedy* (1862), in which Svanhild's refusal of a young, penniless poet in favor of a middle-aged, moneyed pillar of society, seems a direct echo of Ibsen's thwarted love affair. Four years later, Ibsen wrote a tender lyric, "Album-Rhyme," about his and Clara's relation. When he collected his poems for publication in 1871, he excluded the "Stella" poems, probably because he knew that they had little merit and because he did not want to make public his prior private life. But he included "Album-Rhyme," thus according Clara Ebbell a discreet place in his official literary posterity:

> Joy's harbinger, my name for you;
> the star of my existence.
> And truth to God, just such you grew,
> joy's harbinger that came – withdrew; –
> a star – yes, shooting-star it's true,
> that died out in the distance.[14]

The life of Ibsen's first love seems a copy, even a parody, of his mother's. Marichen Altenburg married her mother's brother's step-son, and Clara Ebbell married her mother's brother. After marriage, Marichen Altenburg gave up her theatrical ambitions, and Clara Ebbell, who had had professional training, gave up her ambition to become a pianist. Both women found life easier to bear as converts to evangelical pietism.[15] Marrying within their families, abandoning their vocational aims, devoting themselves to child bearing and child rearing, the two most important women in Ibsen's early life were paragons of proper feminine behavior, models of selflessness and servitude. Marichen Ibsen endured her husband's abuse, year in, year out, and Clara Ebbell, bowing to her family's wishes, married and bore children to her own uncle.

It is this paradigm of dutiful feminine submission that Ibsen would repeatedly subvert: in the bitterness of the conveniently married Margit (*The Feast at Solhoug*); in the frustrated Hjørdis' hatred of shuttered domesticity (*The Vikings at Helgeland*); in the anguish of Inger, forced to choose between her child and her vocation (*Lady Inger of Østråt*); in Svanhild's unhappy capitulation to her society's demand that she marry suitably (*Love's Comedy*); in Agnes' wifely submission to her husband's moral authority (*Brand*); in Martha's long-suffering service to her family and in Lona Hessel's blasts against male egotism (*Pillars of Society*); in Nora Helmer's refusal of the servicing identities conferred on her by her husband (*A Doll House*); in Helene Alving's fatal compliance with her Christian duty as a wife (*Ghosts*); in Rebecca West's submission to Rosmer's dogma of self-sacrifice (in *Rosmersholm*); in Ellida and Bolette Wangel's marriages of reason and in Ellida's realization that she possesses an autonomous self (*The Lady from the Sea*); in Hedda's rage against her powerless woman's condition and in the self-denying servitude of her foils Julie and Thea (*Hedda Gabler*); in Aline Solness' poisonous devotion to her mother's duty (*The Master Builder*); in Rita Allmers' discovery that she has a self apart from her relation with a man (*Little Eyolf*); in Gunhild and Ella Rentheim's self-consuming obsessions with their identities as wives and mothers (*John Gabriel Borkman*); and in model Irene's censure of her servitude to the male artist (*When We Dead Awaken*). The lives of the women in Ibsen's plays protest against the lives of the first two women Ibsen loved.

Meyer comments on the importance of Ibsen's early sorrows: "The humiliations of life have a different effect on different people. They drove Knud Ibsen to drink and illusions, and turned his son into a dramatist" (M 23). What is certain is that Ibsen's boyhood and young manhood in Skien and Grimstad definitively marginalized him. Koht appraises his subject succinctly – "In Ibsen there lived an eternal rebel" (62) – and nowhere is this essential truth more evident than in the playwright's revolutionary representation of the gendered construction of the world.

CHAPTER 2

The seminal women of the early career

REVISING THE FATAL WOMAN:
CATILINE'S "WORSER SPIRIT"

In the middle of the chamber stands a curious pair;
both are women, one is tall and dark as night is she,
and the other fair as evening when the daylight fades
. . .
one of them was smiling gently, with a look of peace;
from the other's haughty glances savage lightning
    flashed.
Terrible, and yet with pleasure I observed this sight.

Catiline (1:87)

Like the clumsy but auspicious play in which they appear, Ibsen's first women characters are interesting less in themselves than in their promise. Reading Ibsen backwards, we find in Furia and Aurelia of *Catiline* the prototypical pair of contrasting women that will figure prominently in the plays to follow, in Francis Bull's phrase, "the sexually exciting, dangerous, and demanding Furia, and the gentle, pale, and weak Aurelia" (*H* 1:36). For William Archer, Ibsen's early champion in England, the most noteworthy aspect of Ibsen's first play was "the fact that it already shows Ibsen occupied with the theme which was to run through so many of his works – the contrast between two types of womanhood, one strong and resolute, even to criminality, the other comparatively weak, clinging, and 'feminine' in the conventional sense of the word" (A 1:6).

A strong critical tradition maintains that Ibsen's treatment of the contrasting pair is conventional, i.e., that the forceful woman and her submissive opposite are, respectively, malevolent and benevolent. In 1867, twenty-five-year-old Georg Brandes wrote in his first appraisal of Ibsen of the playwright's habit of placing a man "between two women, one fierce and the other mild, one a mannish valkyrie or fury, and the other tender, lovable, and of womanly gentleness. Thus, he placed Catiline between the terrible Furia and the gentle Aurelia, his wife and guardian angel" (B 10). Shortly after Ibsen's death, writing retrospectively of the canon, James Huneker noted: "From the start, certain conceptions of woman took root in [Ibsen's] mind and reappear in nearly all his dramas. Catiline's wife Aurelia, and the vestal Furia, who are reincarnated in the Dagny and Hjørdis [of *The Vikings at Helgeland*], reappear in *A Doll House, Hedda Gabler,* and at the last in *When We Dead Awaken.* One is the eternal womanly, the others [sic] the destructive feminine principle, woman the conqueror" (A 13:280). For Janko Lavrin, writing in 1950, Ibsen's women neatly belong to one of two types: "the self-reliant, aggressive and often destructive 'Valkyrie,' on the one hand, and her devoted, self-sacrificing opposite" (*Ibsen* 29). Commenting on the pervasiveness of this motif, James McFarlane writes that in *Catiline* Ibsen

was at pains to emphasize a pattern that continued to absorb him throughout most of his later career: the pattern of the man juxtaposed between two women who – here, as in innumerable guises in the later plays – represent Ibsen's conception of the two basic kinds of Woman: the terrible and the gentle. So insistent does this become in the play – and by extension, presumably, for Ibsen – that the struggle in the play between the two women for possession of the man becomes sheerly allegorical, with the women becoming unambiguously allegorical forces of Good and Evil. (*OI* 1:10)

The same critical tradition that views Ibsen as a profoundly radical thinker, possessing a "deep-seated revolutionary cast of mind," in McFarlane's apt phrase (*OI* 1:10), excludes his women characters from this habit of thought, segregating them as "female types" in an otherwise probing text. The assumption is that when Ibsen created characters of the female sex, he put aside his radical mind, temporarily abandoning his habit of questioning scrutiny to substitute the centuries-old stereotype of "Woman" as angel or demon, man's "savior" or his "demonic destroyer," to quote a recent restatement of the critical position.[1] Presumably, Ibsen returned to his essential, reforming spirit when he had finished off the women. But while Ibsen drew on the ubiquitous cultural tradition that divides women into "subversive feminine symbols" and "feminine symbols of transcendence,"[2] he did not leave the tradition as he found it. What is characteristic in Ibsen's handling of the pattern he inherited, from his first plays to his last, is his testing of it. It is when Ibsen is most unorthodox that he is most himself, and already in *Catiline,* in his treatment of the dark, demanding woman and the fair, passive woman who is her foil, the future creator of Hedda Gabler and Thea Elvsted is too critical a judge of his culture's ideals and values to accept its conventional wisdom on women.

Ibsen encountered the story of Catiline when he was required, as preparation for his university entrance examination in Latin, to read Cicero's orations against Catiline and Sallust's *Catilinae Coniuratio* [*The Conspiracy of Catiline*]. It was a fortuitous obligation. Ibsen found in the thwarted and ambitious rebel a mirror, on the grand scale, of his own position, and the frustrated Grimstad apprentice, despising his neighbors' provincialism and dreaming of fame, in a pardonable self-dramatization, identified with the great conspirator and was thus inspired to write his first play.[3]

The plot of *Catiline* is constructed on a resemblance between author and protagonist that Ibsen makes the basis of his action – an illicit sexual past. Transforming Sallust's passing mention of Catiline's liaison with a nameless priestess of Vesta, Ibsen makes his Catiline a seducer whose victim drowns herself, invents an avenging sister "Furia," a dark-eyed, dark-haired vestal whom Catiline loves passionately, and the straightforward tale of a failed political conspiracy becomes a drama of female vengeance.

After declaring her love for Catiline and making him swear revenge against her mortal enemy, Furia learns that Catiline is the man she is seeking; in providing him with the mettle he lacks to head the rebellion, she goads the hero to his destruction. In a paradox that will later take on more interesting forms in *The Master Builder* and *When We Dead Awaken,* the fatal woman of Ibsen's first play is the hero's genius and alter-ego. In Furia's vilification of her dreary vestal prison, no outlet "for all the wealth of proud and lofty plans within my breast!", Catiline recognizes "sounds which seem to come from my own breast" (1:46).

Taking only the name of Catiline's wife from Sallust, in whose account she seems as debauched as her husband, Ibsen creates Furia's foil in the gentle Aurelia. Begging Catiline to renounce his lofty plans and quit Rome, Aurelia pleads the virtues of the private life, reproaching Catiline for wanting more than her: "Is your Aurelia not enough for you?" (52).

Divided between the two women, Catiline loves them both, "but what a world of difference in my love – / Aurelia is so kind . . . / while Furia –" (45). Interrupting Catiline's contrast to let Furia make a Promethean denouncement of "These hateful halls that witness all the pain / and agony to which I am condemned!", Ibsen then creates a development in which the protagonist, vacillating between his "better spirit" (63), who is worried for his physical safety, and a "child of darkness" (79), who tempts him to follow his ambition, chooses the way of the latter and in so doing obeys the valiant part of himself. Bored and frustrated by his wife, and fortified by Furia's scorn for Aurelia's plans for existence *à deux* – "a life which is part death, part lethargy" (67) – Catiline summons the strength to lead the conspiracy, declaring an "eternal bond" with the woman whom he recognizes as "the genius and image" of his soul (69). Even after losing the battle, Catiline rejoices that he has chosen "honor and eternal fame" (96), and in the last, confused scene of the play, as Aurelia attempts to persuade the defeated hero to flee with her to safety, he rejects her version of life – "Would you once again / clap me in chains?" (105) – and stabs her. He then begs Furia to kill him, now that his revolution has failed, and she obliges by thrusting a dagger into his breast, promising to follow him beyond the grave. Aurelia, however, drags herself back onstage to disrupt the brutal union of Furia and Catiline in a last proof of conjugal power. Following the Romantic drama's convention of redemptive death, Ibsen gives Catiline, in Thomas Van Laan's phrase, "a salvation beyond catastrophe,"[4] and husband and wife die together in the calm of mutually acknowledged love.

To claim that in *Catiline* the struggle for the hero's soul is between two women who are unambiguous symbols of good and evil is to invent a morality play at odds with Ibsen's text. If Ibsen's pattern of the hero caught between a light, passive woman and a dark, powerful woman constitutes "the most striking reflection of Ibsen's thorough absorbing of the conventions of Romanticism" (Van Laan, *Catiline* 60), more striking still is that Ibsen's use of the pattern startlingly departs from it. For while *Catiline* is permeated with the conventions and clichés of Romantic tragic drama, the play's treatment of the dark and light woman is in direct opposition to the Romantic pattern, which privileges the weak woman and condemns the strong. Ibsen may have encountered the pattern in the German Storm and Stress drama. Although he told his first Norwegian biographer Henrik Jæger that the only dramatist besides Oehlenschläger whom he remembers reading before writing *Catiline* was Holberg, Koht believes that Ibsen's comment reflects less his reading than his aversion to admitting other writers' influence, and notes that Ibsen had in fact read Schiller's *William Tell* and very probably had read the reknown *The Robbers* (K 45). Neither play contains the pattern of the dark and light woman. But even if Ibsen had read Storm and Stress plays that do contain it, like Schiller's *The Conspiracy of Fiesco at Genoa,* or Goethe's famous *Götz von Berlichingen,* nothing in the German dramas' schematic treatment of the pair looks forward to Ibsen's version.[5] As Andreas Huyssen has shown, the powerful woman of Storm and Stress drama is unredeemingly evil and often comes to a bad end;[6] Ibsen's Furia seeks and achieves vengeance and escapes unharmed.

Whether or not Ibsen was familiar with the pattern of the light and dark woman in German Romantic drama, he encountered it intact in the plays of his early master Oehlenschläger, a follower of Schiller.[7] Oehlenschläger's *Stærkodder* (the protagonist's name) and *The Vikings at Byzantium* contain the conventional Romantic triad of a man caught between two opposing women; in the first play, the contrast is undeveloped, in the second it is more complete, with the dark/evil and light/good women in direct conflict. There is nothing in Oehlenschläger's conventional treatment of the women, however, that suggests Ibsen's.[8] Catiline conspires against Rome to restore liberty to a corrupt state, and in urging Catiline on, Furia inspires him to follow his calling. The claim that Catiline is caught between two women, "one the embodiment of unselfish love and the other representing heedless and destructive ambition,"[9] ignores the center of the play's dramatic action – the hero's developing allegiance to the demands of the dark woman. In the first example of Ibsen's paradigmatic triad of a man caught between two women, Ibsen turns one of Romanticism's and Western literature's favorite truisms on its heels as he makes the powerful woman the hero's conscience and the gentle

woman the representative of moral cowardice. The hero's vocation is linked to a passion that propels him to risk; Catiline prefers
destruction to the half-life Aurelia holds out to him.[10]

Ibsen would link eros and calling again in *The Vikings at
Helgeland* and *Peer Gynt,* in which Sigurd's and Peer's refusal of
erotic love signals their failed vocations, and in his late plays. In
Rosmersholm, the passionate Rebecca West helps to remove her
gentle rival and establishes herself as Rosmer's genius; in a reversal of *Catiline*'s action, the weak protagonist fails to carry out
the great mission he has envisioned with his *âme soeur* and demands her death as proof of her love. Both *The Master Builder*'s
plot and its sexual ethos look back to *Catiline*. Solness is tormented
by a sense of failed mission and by guilt at having sacrificed his
protective wife to his ambition; enticed by a nemesis in a hiking
skirt, he performs his great and fatal climb. In *Little Eyolf,* it is the
erotic Rita who teaches her moral philosopher husband the
meaning of his own vocation. In *When We Dead Awaken,* artist
Rubek is jolted out of his self-tormenting lethargy by the passionate Irene, who leads him to epiphany.

Like her descendants Rebecca West, Hilda Wangel, Rita
Allmers, and Irene, Furia is strongly attached to a man, yet she
exists in her own right and has her own purposes. She uses
Catiline's ambition to serve her own ends, and nothing could be
less like the "natural" evil of the traditional fatal woman than
Furia's reasoned vengeance. While Furia, like much else in the
play, belongs to Romanticism's Gothic mode, to identify her as
"merely incarnate fury and revenge"[11] is to use the time-honored
neutralizing technique as old as Biblical exegesis, whose practi-
tioners, as Joan Ferrante has shown, divested the strong women of
the Bible of their character and force by ignoring their human
qualities and allegorizing them into abstract principles.[12]

In contrast to Furia's individual identity, Aurelia, who believes
that women exist to provide maternal service to world-weary men
– "A woman's role is to console and comfort" (52) – is an exemplary version of a stereotype, woman the warrior's repose. Object,
Aurelia lives only in relation to a man, while Furia, subject, possesses an identity of her own. Ibsen would return to this pattern
that absorbed him: Aurelia and Furia are the ancestors of Dagny
and Hjørdis in *The Vikings at Helgeland,* Betty and Lona in *Pillars of
Society,* Beata and Rebecca in *Rosmersholm,* Aline and Hilda in *The*

Master Builder, Thea and Hedda in *Hedda Gabler*, Asta and Rita in *Little Eyolf*, Maja and Irene in *When We Dead Awaken*.

Following critical tradition, Meyer categorizes Furia as "the first of those domineering and destructive women whom Ibsen was to portray at intervals throughout his work: Margit in *The Feast at Solhoug*, Hjørdis in *The Vikings at Helgeland*, Rebecca West, Hedda Gabler, Hilda Wangel, Rita Allmers" (M 42). At the same time, he suggests that *Catiline* reveals Ibsen's guilt at "having shrugged off his responsiblity towards a woman with whom he had had an affair" (M 44). If the relation between Catiline and the dead vestal reflects Ibsen's guilt, then Ibsen's avenging fury would seem less a domineering and destructive woman that the agent of merited punishment. In any case, it is also worth noting here that in both *Catiline* and in the sub-plot of *Lady Inger of Østråt*, written a few years later, the seducer is so sexually appealing that the wronged woman's sister falls in love with him. The young Grimstad apprentice, struggling in dire poverty to meet paternity payments and longing for a love of his own, readily imagined Don Juans who were irresistible to beautiful, passionate women.

MOVING ON: NEW INGÉNUES, A TROLL TEMPTRESS,
A WOMAN-CENTERED TRIANGLE, AND GENDER

MARGIT: This is more than a woman can bear! *The Feast at Solhoug* (1:420)
HEDDA: Oh, I'll die – I'll die of all this! *Hedda Gabler* (767)

Ibsen wrote his next five plays, over a period of seven trying years, as a poet of National Romanticism, the compulsory artistic mode of the day that vigorously lauded the recently discovered Norwegian past. The uncritical acceptance of all things Norwegian was basically uncongenial to Ibsen, who, although his own taste was not yet formed, was already distrustful of platitudes. It is characteristic of him that his essential investigative spirit manifested itself even as he tried to be conventional. The subject of gender appears for the first time in an Ibsen play in *Lady Inger of Østråt*; in *The Feast at Solhoug*, Ibsen reversed the traditional Romantic triangle of a man caught between two women by inventing a female-centered triangle of a woman caught between two men; in the same play, and in *St. John's Night*, he foregrounded female sexuality. Like

Furia and Aurelia, the women of the five, flawed plays Ibsen wrote between *Catiline* and *The Vikings at Helgeland* are crude ancestors of the mature portraits to follow.

Ibsen wrote the one-act *The Burial Mound* shortly after his arrival as a student in Oslo, in the spring of 1850. It was a revision of *The Normans*, written in Grimstad in the autumn of 1949, while Ibsen was courting Clara Ebbell, and its protagonist Blanka is partly a young man's compliment to his love. In its principal meaning, *blank* (bright, clear) is very close to *klar* (clear), and Blanka possesses Clara's spirited character. She is the raisonneur for the didactic drama's argument that the North possesses cultural and scenic beauties equal to those of the South, a conviction she has acquired from an old Viking stranded in Normandy. Her dreams of a hardy Norseman who will make her his bride are answered by the arrival of Viking King Gandalf. Although sentimentality and melodrama pervade *The Burial Mound*, the intelligent, strong-minded, and naive Blanka, Ibsen's first woman protagonist, is, as Koht notes, "the only character in the play who is a living person" (K 58). Artless, yet perceptive, she is a knowing ingénue, like her successor Anne, the protagonist of *St. John's Night*: both women are the ancestors of Dina Dorf in *Pillars of Society* and Nora Helmer in *A Doll House.*

When *The Burial Mound* was performed with success at the Christiania Theatre, Ole Bull, the founder of the new Norwegian National Theatre in Bergen, offered Ibsen a position as "dramatic author." It was a momentous chance, and he leapt at it. His inadequate preparation had caused him to fail major parts of his university examinations, and he was desperately poor. On November 6, 1851, at the age of twenty-three, he signed his contract in Bergen and began his profession in earnest.

It was *de rigueur* that for Ibsen's first offering to the National Theatre he should return to the National Romantic well; this time, however, he had the temerity to let loose his critical spirit, and *Saint John's Night* failed to please. Like her predecessor Blanka, the play's protagonist–raisonneur Anne is the spokesman for Norway's virtues; unlike *The Burial Mound*, however, *St. John's Night* approaches National Romanticism satirically. In opposition to Anne's honest love for the log houses and fairy lore of old Norway Ibsen places the affectations and pretentions of the ridiculous Julian, president of the trendy "Society for the Restitution of Old Norse" (as Norway's national language). Accompanying this distressing irreverence was Ibsen's treatment of the female creature dear to National Romanticism's apologists, the bewitching fairy "hulder" of the Norwegian mountain forests. Playing on her horn, the hulder inspires the skalds, the bards of Norway's heroic past. Ibsen pays lip service to the hulder as virtuous muse in the "Prologue" to the play ("the plaintive melodies of the hulder are heard on the mountain scree" [1:204]), but he was more interested in the less idealized view of her, firmly established in popular tradition, as a particular variety of female troll, a vulgar inland siren who lures men into her mountain home. The Norwegian folk version of the archetypal female monster, the hulder reflects what Sandra Gilbert and Susan Gubar have termed "the male ambivalence about female 'charms'" that underlines the archetype (*Madwoman* 34). Like the mermaid, and, in English literary tradition, Spenser's Error and Duessa and Milton's Sin, the hulder is deformed below the waist. She can be distinguished from mortal women by an essential identifying appendage, a fat cowtail, which has a way of sliding out from under her skirts to betray her animal purposes; when hulders marry Christian men, their threatening tails fall off at the altar. Ibsen was plainly fond of what one of his offended biographers has primly called "the really quite unaesthetic Norse fairy of the woods" (Z 110), and he liked to insist on this piquant example of folk symbolism. In *Saint John's Night*, Julian painfully confides to Juliane the most distressing event of his life, his disillusionment with "the most national creature that ever existed": "that adorable, evanescent creature who sits under the linden tree in the dark forest and sings her delightful songs . . . I loved her and I was happy in my love . . . And then one day I got hold of a collection of folk tales. Oh, the monster who wrote that book! . . . I discovered that the *hulder* had – had – a tail!" (1:230). Behind Paulsen's dewey-eyed calf love and National Romantic cant lie the realities of female sexuality and Norway's bawdy folklore.

In a play he had begun and abandoned a few years earlier, *The Grouse in Justedal*, intended to be as sterling an example of National Romanticism as *The Burial Mound*, Ibsen suppressed the hulder's sexuality by burying her in her opposite, the fey heroine of a folk tale. Alfhild ("Alf" is a variant of "Elf," i.e., fairy), is a human hulder without a tail, a childlike female creature whose companions are elves, flowers, and lambs. Ibsen would return to the earthier hulder of *Saint John's Night* in *Peer Gynt*, putting her cowtail to good use in the Walpurgnisnacht troll scene. His most original use of the musical mountain siren would be the baroque version in *The Master Builder*. The fairy has disappeared, "Alfhild" has become the erotic, demanding "Hilde" whose "long alpen-stock" (800) and magical harps signal her hulder ancestry.

According to Ibsen, the dark *Lady Inger of Østråt*, which followed *St. John's Night*, was "the result of a love affair – hastily entered into and violently broken off" (*LS* 103). The young women's name was Henrikke Holst, and she was not yet sixteen, ten years younger than Ibsen. Like the woman he would later marry, Rikke Holst was attractive, intelligent, and uncommonly unrestrained; tradition has it that their acquaintance began when she tossed a bouquet of flowers in Ibsen's face. She was "the girl next door," living very near Ibsen's boardinghouse, and after lunch, when she saw him taking his café and cigar on the stoop, she would call out, "Hello, Ibsen, will you give me a penny's worth of candy?" She liked the elegantly dressed theatre man (Ibsen now sported a frock coat and yellow kid gloves) who invited her to take chocolate in his room. They went on long walks along the sea and in the moun-tains, and the friendship became romance.[13]

Ibsen's early love life was destined to be thwarted by upstanding ship captains. He met Rikke in the spring, and when he proposed marriage in June, Skipper Holst considered the poor theatre man and political radical an unsuitable candidate for his daughter's hand. The couple continued to meet secretly, using Rikke's five-year-old brother Lars as their watchdog, and one day, following tradition, they pledged their troth by joining their rings and throwing them into the fjord. Unfortunately, the romantic idyll was broken when Skipper Holst surprised them; Lars Holst later told Koht that he remembered his father, livid with anger, chasing after them with clenched fists (K 83). Ibsen's reaction exhibited a characteristic physical cowardice – he ran away – and that was the end of that. Not long afterwards, Rikke Holst, like Clara Ebbell, agreed to marry a more solid member of society, a respectable Bergen merchant, to whom she eventually presented eleven children.[14]

The end of his love affair devastated Ibsen. He expressed his pain in a series of poems, but was unable to write a play, and *faute de mieux*, he revised *The Burial Mound*. The first night was a disaster, and the playwright was faced with his second Bergen failure. Coming in the same year as his loss of Rikke, the disappointment was a great blow. Feeling that both his private and professional life had gone to pieces, he wrote "Building Plans":

> I remember as though it had happened today
> When I saw in the paper my first poem in print . . .
>
> A cloud castle I built; it went quickly and well;
> I set myself two goals, a small one and a great.
> The great was to become an immortal man,
> The small to possess one lovely maid.
>
> It seemed to me a plan of purest harmony;
> But then confusion entered in.
> As I grew sane, the plan itself grew mad.
> The great goal came to nothing, the small was all I had.
>
> (*H* 14:208–9)

It is sometimes assumed that the young woman in "Building Plans" is Rikke Holst,[15] but since the poem's action takes place on the day in Grimstad when Ibsen saw his first poem, "To Autumn," in print, in the autumn of 1849, she can only be Clara Ebbell; Ibsen's second failed love affair led him to think back to his first. Ibsen regretted Rikke in other poems, and plodded on, and in the end, as he noted, his dark mood led him to write the somber *Lady Inger of Østråt*.[16]

Lady Inger treats the most oppressive period in Norway's long subjugation by Denmark, commonly referred to as the "four-hundred-year night." Basing his drama on ahistorical, National Romantic accounts that speculated that Lady Inger may have played a part in a short-lived anti-Danish intrigue, Ibsen made his protagonist the head of a full-fledged rebellion. And he made the protagonist's dilemma not merely that of a political leader, but that of a female political leader. Ibsen's first fully developed protagonist is a woman called upon to act like a man.

At fifteen, "with fire in her eyes and steel in her voice" (1:288), Lady Inger was destined to be "the instrument of heaven" (329) in the Norwegian people's struggle. For ten years she led the fight and lived a man's life: "When I was twenty-five everywhere my childhood friends were wives and mothers; I alone was in the fight, in danger. Mine was not the normal lot of woman." Inger's dilemma began when she fell in love with a Swedish knight and gave birth to a son; "It was then I learned there are other longings, other dreams in a woman's soul than those I had so far cherished" (329). Since Norway's cause would have suffered if the liaison were known, the father returned to Sweden with the baby, who was given to the Swedish chancellor to rear until "better times." For Inger, her "child of love" was all she had "to remind me of the time when I was really and truly a woman" (330).[17] When her lover died, she begged the chancellor to return her son, but he would agree only if she joined an open revolt against the Danes. Terrified for her son's life if her cause failed, Inger withdrew from the nationalist struggle and agreed to an arranged marriage with a Dane in which her "conjugal duties were sheer slavery." Thus began twenty years of dissimulation, in which Inger kept alive her Norwegian retainers' hopes of throwing off the Danes and at the same time formed alliances with the oppressor. Now she is once again called to lead a rising rebel movement. Bitter at the Norwegian male nobility's cowardice – "Not one of them has the courage to be a man, yet they reproach me for being a woman!" (288) – yet aware of her patriotic duty, Lady Inger assumes her task. But she also determines to protect her son. Caught between her country and her child, she tries to save both and ends by saving neither; intriguing with her enemies, she orders the murder of the man she believes to be heir to the throne, only to learn afterwards that it is her son she has killed.

Lady Inger's conflict between protecting her son and leading her country is presented as a struggle between a woman's and a man's traditional priorities, between love and duty, between the personal and the public life, and the soul of Ibsen's play is the pathos in the protagonist's divided allegiance: "Fate made me a woman, but burdened me with a man's work" (284).[18] The play's implied criticism of the gendered, binary division of the world into women's and men's priorities and spheres of action looks forward to the direct challenge in *The Vikings at Helgeland, Love's Comedy, The Pretenders,* and *Brand,* and the repudiation in *Pillars of Society* and *A Doll House.*

In *Lady Inger*'s futile maternal sacrifice lies the kernel of the grimmer and greater *Ghosts.* Like Lady Inger, Helene Alving, though wanting to live honorably, determines at all costs to protect her son from a dangerous truth. Both women live twenty years in deceit and fear; suffering through loathsome marriages, sending their sons away, they make monumental attempts to hide the past only to see their honor lost and their efforts hideously wasted. The crude irony of the intrigue drama, in which the son is murdered by his mother's mistaken order, becomes in the tragedy subtly brutal: Helene Alving is forced to recognize that in the very act of conceiving her son, she condemned him to a living death of imbecility. Both plays end in horror, with a mother screaming over the body of the son for whom she sacrificed her life.

Writing *Lady Inger*, Ibsen immersed himself in the history and literature of the Norwegian Middle Ages. He then turned, as he later wrote, to the "saga times proper" (*OI* 1:372), and influenced by the recently translated Old Norse sagas, began to plan *The Vikings at Helgeland*. At the same time, he became fascinated by the recently collected Norwegian ballads, and decided to put off the Viking piece to write a ballad drama *The Feast at Solhoug*. But as he explained, he kept the women characters he had already sketched, and thus "the foster-sisters Hjørdis and Dagny in the originally projected tragedy became the sisters Margit and Signe in the completed lyric drama" (373).

Margit – passionate, rebellious and intelligent – and Signe – gentle, passive and simple – look back to Furia and Aurelia of *Catiline* and constitute Ibsen's second version of the pattern of the strong and weak woman.[19] Again, both women love the same man, and the spirited woman of the pair, unlike her mild opposite, functions not merely as the man's possible partner, but possesses a story of her own. This triad, however, as Åse Lervik has pointed out, is subordinate to the play's principal action ("Between Furia and Solveig" 71); *Catiline*'s triangle of a man and two women has given way to one of a woman – the protagonist Margit, the only individual in a case of stock characters – flanked by two men.

The Feast at Solhoug is Ibsen's third successive work in which a marriage of convenience figures prominently. Loving the impecunious Gudmund, the equally poor Margit has married the doltish but rich Bengt. On a mission to escort to Norway the French princess who is to marry Norway's king, Gudmund surprises her with a lover, who, upon arrival in Norway persuades the king to banish his discoverer. When Gudmund flees to Solhoug, Margit longs to leave her despised husband for her old sweetheart, but

Gudmund falls in love with her younger sister Signe, the simple girl–woman in whose blue eyes he can still see "the innocent child" he used to carry in his arms (1:398). In despair, Margit poisons her husband's wine, Gudmund and Signe chance on the goblet, from which they almost drink, and Margit is horrified by her attempted crime. A *deus ex machina* in the person of the King's Messenger arrives to announce the execution of Gudmund's enemy, who has "offended against the Queen of Norway" (425), the stage is suddenly sunlit,[20] and the chastened Margit announces her decision to enter a convent.

The Feast at Solhoug is a curiously divided work, for alongside its superficialities and clichés it dramatizes the authentic story of Margit's frustration: "Just imagine it, Signe, to have to wither and die without having lived!" (408). The mere presence of her well-meaning but loutish husband is torture to her: "When I see him . . . / it feels just as though my blood had stopped flowing" (381). Margit likes to imagine herself as a hulder, free to satisfy her desire: "How I would lure the bold young man / past green forest slopes to my mountain den; / . . . there with my darling I could burn in love's fire!" (405). Forced to listen to her uncomprehending husband speak of the happy foursome to come – "in the winter we will sit indoors the whole day long, each with his wife on his knee" – she announces in an aside, "This is more than a woman can bear!", and promptly pours in the poison: "Your goblet is full!" (420).

The raging Margit is overwhelmingly out of place in her drama's safe, cardboard world, in which the romantic lead marries the ingénue and the ardent French princess becomes the holy "Queen of Norway" and her lover is beheaded. In the end, Ibsen tries to make the play's two conflicting parts come together, turning Margit into the wicked sister and sending her off repentant to a nunnery, an old remedy for troublesome females. This happy ending fools no one (except for Ibsen's Bergen public, who were charmed), for Margit's transformation remains inexplicable, and there is no reason why the French princess should be any happier in her arranged marriage with the king than Margit was with Bengt. And thus the denouement, which would silence the disturbing questions raised by the development, leaves us dissatisfied, as the protagonist, whose deviant story clashes with the conventional frame enclosing it, escapes, revealing the play's essential schizophrenia.

The Feast at Solhoug constitutes the first example of a plot as paradigmagic in Ibsen's work as that of the male-centered triangle of *Catiline*: a female-centered triangle in which the woman's choice represents either rebellion from or allegiance to her woman's duty to marry suitably. Trapped and frustrated in a marriage of convenience and loving another man, Margit is the antecedent of Hjørdis of *The Vikings at Helgeland*, married to the passive Gunnar and loving the aggressive Sigurd; Svanhild of *Love's Comedy*, the reluctant bride of the respectable, successful businessman rather than the marginal, poor poet; Helene Alving of *Ghosts*, who against every prompting of her heart obeys the weak man she loves and returns home to her vile arranged marriage; the properly married Ellida of *The Lady from the Sea*, haunted by a prior, passionate love; and the protagonist of *Hedda Gabler*, the play that looks back most explicitly to *The Feast at Solhoug* in its desperate, impecunious protagonist who has married beneath her a bumbling man she despises.[21] The "Ha! ha! ha! Margit!" of the fourteenth-century landowner becomes the equally maddening "Uh, Hedda?" of the nineteenth-century academic. "To have to live here with him! Oh God! Oh God!" (419) is Margit's line, but it could as well be Hedda's. "Oh, it drives me mad having to endure all this!" Margit rages (390); Hedda *"moves about the room, raising her arms and clenching her fists as if in a frenzy"* (705). Living with Tesman – "Oh, I'll die – I'll die of all this! . . . Of all these – absurdities" (767) – is like living with Bengt: "Oh, to have to suffer all this scorn and ridicule!" (413). Driven to distraction by keeping up the pretense of a happy marriage, feeling such disgust for their husbands that any allusion to sexual intimacy is unbearable, the women are pushed to violent acts by the return of the "other man." But while Margit's story is a simple tale of acknowledged error, Hedda's is one of unavowed conflict. The rebellious Margit announces her mistake and confronts her plight, but the respectable Hedda will admit nothing. A constant reminder of why she married him, Bengt's riches disgust Margit; Tesman, Hedda would like to think, is not rich enough. Margit has everything she could wish for, including "a mount ready saddled whenever she feels so inclined" (388), but Tesman's income will not permit

Hedda to have her coveted saddle horse. In the conflict between the self and the world, Margit tries to choose the self, but her young creator, writing for the public, takes it back. In *Hedda Gabler*, the mature playwright's protagonist mistakenly believes that she can live for the conventions of the bourgeois world, but in the end, she flaunts them utterly.

For his next, and, as it turned out, last play for the Bergen theatre, Ibsen took the ballad of "Olaf Liljekrans" and joined it to his earlier, unfinished *The Grouse at Justedal*. Engaged to Ingeborg, a rich farmer's daughter, the impecunious Olaf is in love with the fey Alfhild of the *Grouse* fragment, and they determine to marry against his mother's wishes. This does not worry Ingeborg, the frank, forthright precursor of Petra Stockmann of *An Enemy of the People*: "If Olaf is in the mountain, bewitched, then let her who did it take him. I don't intend to share my husband's heart and mind" (1:478). When the weak Olaf capitulates and agrees to marry Ingeborg, the spurned Alfhild becomes mad with jealous rage; using a favorite method of the feuding Icelandic saga families, she sets fire to her enemies' house to burn the marriage party alive. Miraculously, all escape, and the play ends happily as Ingeborg elopes with the unsuitable man she prefers to Olaf, and Olaf and Alfhild are allowed to marry when Olaf's mother, in a touch of characteristic Ibsenian irony, learns that Alfhild is an heiress. On the whole, the melodramatic *Olaf Liljekrans* may be the slightest of Ibsen's plays, but in it lies the kernel of one of his most justly praised scenes. Although the abrupt transformation of Alfhild from an angelic child into a bitter woman is incongruous, her torch-throwing and its motive – "If I'm to be banished to blackest night, / In the bridal chamber at least there'll be light! / . . . Within the house there is fear and alarm, / The bride is burning on the bridegroom's arm!" (528) – are the precursors of a later burning scene, this one psychologically masterful, in which another woman possessed by jealous hatred would like to burn her rival's hair off and settles for burning to death the fruit of her rival's love: "Hedda: Now I'm burning your child, Thea! You, with your curly hair! (*Throwing another sheaf in the stove.*) Your child and Eilert Løvborg's" (762).

Ibsen would remain for a while longer a half-hearted advocate of National Romanticism, but *Olaf Liljekrans* is his last attempt to satisfy the public's sentimental taste. Returning to his plans for a saga drama, as he was creating his indomitable hero Hjørdis of *The Vikings at Helgeland,* a woman who resembled her entered his life, the surprising Suzannah Daae Thoresen. At last, both parts of Ibsen's cloud castle seemed to be realizing themselves, as work and love miraculously merged.

CHAPTER 3

Love and marriage

THE QUEEN OF ICELAND AND HER STEP-MOTHER

SIGURD: . . . the finest of all, because she was clever and full of spirit.
The Vikings at Helgeland (2:76)

Ibsen met his wife Suzannah Thoresen through her step-mother, his extraordinary colleague at the Bergen theatre. Anna Magdalene Kragh Thoresen (1819–1903) was one of Scandinavia's first women of letters. She translated the French farces Ibsen was obliged to stage, and also wrote plays of her own, choosing anonymity rather than a masculine pen name. Her two-act historical drama *A Witness* was one of the first plays Ibsen staged after his arrival in Bergen; when the public called for the author, the director had to announce that he desired to remain anonymous. Many people knew "his" identity, however, for Magdalene Thoresen, who ran Bergen's only *salon* in the parsonage where she lived with her husband, kept her passion for literature no secret.

Magdalene Thoresen had already lived a singular life. The daughter of a Danish boat pilot, she had spent her young years on the Jutland coast. When her father was implicated in a shipwreck and forced to give up piloting, he opened a sailors' tavern in Fredericia, where he sank into drunkenness. Magdalene's grand-mother took her in and she was able to escape the squalor of her father's home until she was fourteen. She learned to read and write, but otherwise was given no education, and at her grand-mother's death she returned to her parents' tavern, where, in her own later analysis, she lived "like a wild animal . . . forgetting the world, or rather not understanding it," becoming the prey to "disappointments, vileness, and abuse."[1] At twenty – "despised, rejected by everyone" (*Letters* 18) – she was rescued by a magnani-

40

mous Copenhagen factory owner, who sent her to school. She worked long and hard at her lessons, learning French and German and preparing to become a teacher. At the same time, she had a disastrous love affair with a fellow student, Icelandic poet Grímar Thomsen, who abandoned her. Humiliated and despairing, she decided to leave Denmark to forget him, and at the age of twenty-two, she became governess to the children of the twice-widowed, forty-year-old Norwegian pastor Hans Conrad Thoresen.[2] A year later, they married, and eventually added four children to the five he already had.

Pastor Thoresen encouraged his wife to write, and to complete her education he gave her a "grand tour" in Germany, France, and England. Magdalene grew to love her adopted country, considering herself more Norwegian than Danish, and developing a passion for the magnificent landscape of the Norwegian west coast and for the sea; physically fearless, she swam out beyond the fjord daily, from spring to late summer, a habit Ibsen would later make use of in *The Lady from the Sea*.

After the death of her husband, Magdalene Thoresen took on the difficult task of earning her living as a woman author. Her *Poems of A Lady* (1860), with its frank treatment of female sexuality, an astonishing refusal of the dominant romantic tradition, has been called the "first modern Norwegian poetry" (Engelstad, *History* 1:109). The volume made a reputation for its "anonymous" author, and two years later, Gyldendal, the great Copenhagen publishing house that would later be Ibsen's, accepted Magdalene Kragh Thoresen as one of its first women authors. Now published under her name, her novels, short stories, and non-fiction appeared steadily during the 1860s and 70s. A curious blend of romanticism in the fashion of George Sand (whose work she much admired) and realism, Magdalene Thoresen's works gained her great popularity. She was most admired for her two-volume *Pictures from the Land of the Midnight Sun* (1884, 1886), an original blend of documentary and fiction, and most criticized for her novella *My Grandmother's Story* (1867), termed by scandalized critics "the most immoral product of Norwegian literature" (Engelstad, *History* 1:111), an ironic, feminist portrait of conventional feminine happiness that became a *cause célèbre*.

So it went on year after year. I was a brave man's sweet, brave wife. No one offended me, and my calm, even temper prevented people's envy; I

5. Magdalene Kragh Thoresen (1819–1903), Ibsen's mother-in-law. One of Scandinavia's first women of letters.

was set apart, inviolate, a self with its own thoughts. And hadn't I everything I wanted? A comfortable home, a pretty garden – a blue silk dress, a porcelain vase with artificial flowers, a canary bird in one cage, a parrot in another – Oh yes! I was happy, not only in others' judgement, but also in mine. (*Livsbilleder* [*Life Images*] 65)

Because Magdalene Thoresen later developed a deep attachment to Bjørnstjerne Bjørnson,[3] twelve years younger than she, and Georg Brandes, twenty-two years younger, Meyer assumes that at thirty-six, she wanted the sexual attention of her colleague

Ibsen, eight years younger. He accepts the supposition of Ibsen's daughter-in-law Bergliot Bjørnson Ibsen that it "must have both amazed and annoyed popular Magdalene Thoresen, when young Ibsen gave all his attention to her step-daughter [Suzannah] instead of to herself" (BI 17). Meyer also writes of Magdalene Thoresen's return to Denmark after her husband's death, "where the sorrows of widowhood do not seem greatly to have inhibited her" (M 158), and where Bjørnson and Brandes barely escape from her "clutches" (M 320). But Bergliot Bjørnson Ibsen, who refused to admit the truth of her father's extra-marital affairs, and who disapproved of Magdalene Thoresen, is on this matter an unreliable source. Moreover, neither Bjørnson, whom Meyer rightly characterizes as an "intensive and successful womanizer" (M 153), nor Brandes, whose affairs with women both unmarried and married were notorious, needs defending against woman's wiles. One would also hope that at thirty-eight, the widowed Magdalene Thoresen would be held back from a new relationship by the "sorrows of widowhood" no longer than the good pastor her husband, who had married three women in rapid succession.

Magdalene Thoresen was an extravagant and passionate woman, rather like Mme. de Staël, and she habitually tried to charm interesting men. This hardly means that she desired the sexual attention of her younger colleague, whom she wittily and pitilessly described, in a phrase that became known, as "a small, shy marmot"; "there was," she added, "something clumsy and worried in his manner and he seemed afraid of being laughed at" (P 2:50). And although she later became a great admirer of her son-in-law's work, she did not like – and not without reason – Ibsen's early plays, which she described to Brandes as "flat as mere sketches."[4] Magdalene Thoresen intimidated Ibsen; seven years after she became his mother-in-law, he confessed, in a letter to her from Italy: "I was never able to be myself with you . . . My innermost thoughts and feelings always sounded false when I expressed them" (*LS* 48). Timid and admiring, Ibsen was drawn to this invincible woman from the beginning; after his marriage, they became good friends, and for many years, until she angered him by repeating to his wife gossip about his infidelity, she was an important person in his life. They corresponded regularly, and he poured out his bitterness toward Norway in his letters to her from

Italy. On June 3, 1899, four years before her death and seven years before his, Ibsen sent her the following formal message: "Dear Magdalene Thoresen, On your eightieth birthday I send you this wreath with thanks for everything, both what you have been for our literature, and for me personally. Yours, Henrik Ibsen" (*H* 18:430).

Magdalene Thoresen and Ibsen were colleagues for three years, during which time he stage-managed four of her plays, before she invited him to her home. After the successful premiere of *The Feast at Solhoug*, Ibsen attended one of her literary evenings at the parsonage, and it was there, on January 8, 1856, that he met and fell in love with her step-daughter, nineteen-year-old Suzannah Daae Thoresen, whom Magdalen Thoresen had raised and educated from the age of six.[5]

As a child, Suzannah Thoresen planned to be Queen of Iceland when she grew up. She loved the sagas, which she read aloud to her brothers and sisters, and invented theatrical games based on them, in which Marie, her gentle, self-effacing younger sister, played the victims, and Suzannah, the heroes. Schiller was another favorite source, and Pastor Thoresen liked to tell the story of one occasion on which *The Robbers* was the text of the day. Hearing shrieks from the nursery, he rushed in to find the children, including the boys, in tears, except for Suzannah, who although clearly hurt, declared, "Since I have been worthy of wearing a beard, I shall not cry!" (Z 69). At nineteen, Suzannah was outspoken and irrepressible, and although very serious-minded, she was also a great storyteller and lover of jokes. She had a flair for the dramatic, and regaled her siblings and friends with embellished versions of her experiences. Like her step-mother, whom she adored and imitated, she was intellectual and independent. She had the reputation of a bookworm, and her favorite author was George Sand. She spent hours reading novels on a bench back to back with her best friend Karoline Reimers; they promised each other that when they married and became mothers, if one had a girl and the other a boy, their children would marry, a girlhood fantasy that would be realized when Suzannah Ibsen's son Sigurd married Karoline's Bjørnson's daughter Bergliot. Suzannah had a plump figure, large, clear features, fine eyes, and long, glowing chestnut hair that reached to the ground, so heavy that it was once weighed at the Bergen fair.

Suzannah Thoresen's overwhelming vitality acted on Ibsen like a miraculous tonic, and he was smitten. He was not merely in love, however, but saw and valued Suzannah's character – her integrity and strength of will – from the beginning; one of the first things she told him was how much she had liked *Lady Inger,* to which he replied: "At present you are 'Eline' [Lady Inger's spirited young daughter] but one day you will be Lady Inger" (BI 17). Twenty years later he would give her a copy of the German translation of the play with the following dedication: "To this book you have the strongest claim / Your spirit and Østråt's are the same" (BI 17). Their second meeting was at a ball given by the Bergen Philharmonic Society, at which they did not dance, but talked through the evening, and shortly afterwards Ibsen sent Suzannah a writer's proposal of marriage, the poem, "To the Only One," in which he declared that if he chose her as the "bride" of his "thought,"

> Ah, then what fair songs upspringing
> Should soar from my breast on high;
> Ah, then how free I'd go sailing
> Like a bird toward the coasts of the sky!
> Ah, then should my scattered visions
> To one single harmony throng;
> For all of life's fairest visions
> Would mirror themselves in my song.[6]

Dressed in his best, Ibsen came to the parsonage and waited in the parlor. Time passed, and no one came; the forlorn poet was running for the door when he heard Suzannah's bright laughter, and turning, he saw her rising from behind the sofa, her answer in her eyes.

Ibsen's conception of his betrothed as his private muse would turn out to be both naively romantic in one sense and insufficiently visionary in another. Suzannah would briefly and partially serve her husband as inspiration and model, in the conventional way of a poet's beloved, for Hjørdis of *The Vikings at Helgeland,* the play of their engagement, and, less conventionally, for Svanhild of *Love's Comedy,* the play that followed. For the forty-eight years of their married life, Suzannah Ibsen would serve her husband as cleaning woman, cook, beer-maker, nurse, seamstress, and housekeeper. But besides these conventional wifely occupations, she was also a voracious reader who served her writer husband as a

clearing house of literary and intellectual news. And most importantly, she was and remained an essential example of the uncompromising mind.

The Ibsen marriage was based on a particular kind of partnership. While the division of labor was carried out according to the
traditional socio-sexual pattern, there was no discrimination in
matters of opinion. Suzannah Thoresen, who like her mentor
step-mother considered herself an ambassador for her sex, was as
independent a spirit in marriage as before. Wife and husband had
their own ideas, and when they differed, they were not ashamed
to argue in public. An Oslo physician who visited the Ibsens in
Dresden reported a conversation in which Ibsen said to his wife:
"Would you be kind enough to be silent for a moment while I tell
one little story [?]; after I have finished with it you shall have the
floor again as long as you wish" (Z 138). The Ibsen family quar-
rels, in which Suzannah refused to give in to her husband in her
strong, declamatory voice, led people to believe that they were
unhappy together.[7] But Ibsen loved and appreciated his strong-
minded wife, whom he liked to call by the nickname her sisters
and brothers had given her in childhood, "the eagle." He was
fond of presenting her with "bank notes," decorated with eagles'
heads, on "Ibsen's National Bank," which he "cashed" when he
received a publisher's bank draft. He knew that he was hard to live
with, and let Suzannah know it; she was decorated with "The
Order of the House of Ibsen" in recognition "of her help and
support in times of stress" (BI 92). After Ibsen's death, sketches of
Suzannah's decorations, with crosses, stars, and eagles' heads,
were discovered in the margins of his papers. The hard taskmaster
Brand explains to his wife what she and his son have meant to
him: "It was as if all that tenderness I had borne / Within me, in
secret and in silence, / I had treasured up for him, and for you,
my dear wife" (3:129). And Ibsen could be a romantic husband;
besides "the eagle," Suzannah was, less formidably, "my cat," and
she cherished the private poems she called "my cat poems," which
she burned before her death, along with her husband's love
letters. "Our relationship does not concern anyone but ourselves,"
she said (BI 17).

At nineteen, Suzannah Thoresen saw what Ibsen had in him
and joined him in a battle of two against the world, a pledge she
kept to the end. It took seven years before Ibsen earned a living

wage, and Suzannah did not complain, not even during what must have been the hardest period, in Italy, before the publication of *Brand* gave her husband his first financial success. Living in a foreign country, off the charity of Norwegian friends, with a six-year-old child, she nursed Ibsen through his delirium-ridden malaria, suffered the worry and humiliation of bounced bank drafts, and lived from hand to mouth, counting soldis to buy bread and waiting for the mail.

Ibsen wrote *Brand* in near exaltation, rising at dawn and finishing the 270-page five-act verse drama in three months. Remarking to her daughter-in-law that the frugal circumstances in Ariccia were those of *Brand* – "when [Ibsen] makes Brand describe his home, he draws from life – it was so like the way we were living there" – Suzannah described the Ibsen mealtimes with a good touch of Norse understatement: "Sigurd [the Ibsens' son] can tell you how he went every evening and bought three soldis worth of bread and three soldis worth of Caceotto cheese; with half a carafe of red wine, this was our evening meal. I used to cook our midday dinner down in the kitchen, which had a baker's oven, and this in a temperature of thirty degrees centigrade so that there was no fear of my being cold" (BI 26). Bergliot Ibsen comments that it was her mother-in-law's determination to keep the struggles of daily existence away from Ibsen that made it possible for him to write to Bjørnson (who had kept the Ibsens from starving by taking up collections in Oslo): "I was indescribably happy, even in the midst of all my pain and misery. I felt the exultation of a Crusader; I would have had the courage to face anything on earth" (*LS* 53).

Ibsen wrote of his uncompromising protagonist, in a phrase often quoted, "Brand is myself in my best moments" (*LS* 102). But Brand was also Ibsen in his worst moments, an example of the driven "great man," determined to live for his calling at the expense of everything and everyone else. Although Ibsen not only had no means of supporting his wife and son, but not even enough money to buy postage for the desperate letters in which he pled for money, he refused the post of Director of the Christiania Theatre to stay in Italy and write. The play that in bringing Ibsen recognition solved the Ibsen family finances has as its protagonist a man so devoted to his work that he chooses the deaths of his son and wife rather than compromise his calling.

Typically, Ibsen, who knew what he demanded of his family, was, on paper, his own severest judge.

Even after *Brand* assured the family of decent food on the table, it would be years before the Ibsens were comfortably off. Suzannah lengthened her growing son's pants, which she made out of his father's worn-out ones, and lengthened them again. Like her husband, however, Suzannah was frugal, and may have disliked spending money even more than he; against his protests, she insisted (and won) that they travel third-class on the Italian trains. What was certainly harder than the constant penny-pinching was living with Ibsen's writer's egotism. When he was into the actual writing of a play, Suzannah's conversation with her husband often did not exceed a "good morning" and a "good night." And one wonders if Suzannah was annoyed by Ibsen's physical cowardice. Danish novelist Vilhelm Bergsøe, Ibsen's companion on Ischia and in Sorrento during the writing of *Peer Gynt*, cites repeated examples of Ibsen's terrors: of dogs, of steep mountain walks, of the possible theft of his manuscript, of a trip to Capri for fear the boat would capsize. One incident must have left Suzannah feeling at least disappointment. Ibsen appeared at Bergsøe's window shouting: "She is sick!" "What she?" asked Bergsøe. "My wife, of course. She has cholera, and I don't know what to do." "Well, go get the doctor." "No, I won't go down [to the town]. I might catch it. Then what would happen to us – and Sigurd?" Bergsøe obligingly fetched a doctor, and, luckily, Suzannah did not have cholera and recovered in a few days. Intent on his fame, Ibsen was terrified that something, or someone, would cheat him of it: "If you rob me of Eternity," he told Bergsøe, "you rob me of everything!"[8]

Suzannah made it posssible for Ibsen to work in total concentration in a routine that never varied. He got up, breakfasted frugally, washed, and went to his desk. He worked all morning, took a walk, ate the main meal of the day, following Norwegian custom, in mid-afternoon, napped, then copied over what he had written. Suzannah was servant and watchdog; meals were provided punctually, all visitors sent away, and Ibsen was disturbed by no one.

But there were compensations. We have only to look at a photograph of Ibsen in 1863, taken five years after his marriage, to see his attractiveness (see page 49). It shows a face full of character, with a high forehead, a head of swept-back dark brown hair and a

6. Henrik Ibsen at the age of thirty-five (1863).

7. Suzannah Thoresen Ibsen, Ibsen's wife, at the age of forty (1876).

luxuriant beard; the most striking feature is the piercing gaze. Even if Ibsen was not conventionally handsome, it is impossible to agree with Meyer that he was "physically unattractive" (M 153), "ugly" (M 176). And Ibsen was not only enormously quick-witted, but exceedingly amusing; although one might be put upon by such a husband, at least one wasn't bored. And Ibsen was a domestic creature, for while he enjoyed drinking with his cronies in taverna and biergarten, he preferred the company of his wife and son to that of all other people, and spent most of his evenings at home with them, reading, talking, and playing chess. Ibsen's habit of writing, in which he spent months, usually well over a year, thinking about his characters, "living with them," as he liked to put it, making notes, and ruminating, before he put pen to paper, made him a good companion for the long walks and excursions that Suzannah Ibsen loved. And quite apart from her husband, Suzannah had her own interests, which, once she had her house in order, she pursued with gusto. She read unceasingly – German, French, Italian, English, as well as Scandinavian classics and contemporary fiction and poetry – and, before she became old and crippled by arthritis, was an inveterate tourist who had a great love for scenery and the Mediterranean landscape. Here is her description, in a letter to her daughter-in-law, of Sorrento, where she had lived over thirty years earlier, while Ibsen was writing *Ghosts*:

How carefree one lives there in the warmth and cools oneself every day in the sea. Take Tancred and little Irene [Bergliot's and Sigurd's children] with you one day and show them where we lived, don't forget. Every day I climbed up the cliffs in the scorching heat. It was a long climb, but I was lissom and good at climbing then and up there were grasses and wild flowers. The road to Deserto passes by and there is a strange, perfumed atmosphere there. To this day I can smell the scent of roots, herbs and flowers on that road to Massa. (BI 167)

Like the strong women of her beloved sagas, Suzannah Thoresen was determined to link her destiny to that of a great man. Ibsen had a lazy streak, and when he was depressed by hostile criticism and lacked the will to write, she sent him to his desk; what did he, "Ibsen," as she called him in the fashion of the day, care about small-minded journalists? "I couldn't endure these men of jelly who lack both will and ability," she wrote in a letter to her brother. "The first prerequisite of manliness is energy

he had to free himself from by writing *Love's Comedy* is the same as that of his preceding play, *The Vikings at Helgeland* – the relation between love, marriage and vocation – but whereas in *Vikings* the three are interdependent, in *Love's Comedy* they seem not only separate but contending.

Virtually plotless, *Love's Comedy* consists of tirades and conversations whose subjects are a series of antitheses constructed on the central Romantic opposition of freedom versus constraint: love/marriage, vocation/security, the present/the future, the self/the world. A lodger in the boarding house of Svanhild's widowed mother, whose life's aim is to marry off her daughters, Falk is a misanthropic outsider, "the serpent in our little Eden," as businessman Guldstad ("Gold City") calls him (2:145). Fond of making sweeping proverbial pronouncements such as "Romance, like varnish, wears away in time" (101), Falk serves Ibsen as scourger of idols; as Ibsen wrote unabashedly in the preface to the play's second edition, "I cracked the whip as best I could over love and marriage" (*OI* 2:359).[13]

But Falk, as Svanhild comments, is "like two different people that can't agree" (117); Ibsen turns the tables on himself and makes Falk, a portrait of the artist as fledgling poet, mercilessly parrot his creator while Svanhild-Suzannah takes over the role of raisonneur. In his Bergen days, alone and floundering as a writer, Ibsen had had, "ridiculously enough," he wrote to a friend, "a burning desire for – I almost prayed for – a great sorrow that might round out my existence" (*LS* 26). "Give me," Falk proclaims, "a harrowing, overwhelming, crushing sorrow, / and all my poems would palpitate with joy" (106). Svanhild, modelled on the longed-for bride who had shared the unhappiness so ardently desired by poet Ibsen, warns Falk: "Good; I shall pray for you, that you may be / granted the fate that you desire; but when / it comes to you – endure it like a man." Falk, like Ibsen, will get more than he bargained for: "Wait till sorrow comes / and withers the green summer of your life – / torments you waking, harrows you in your dreams" (107). But Falk's true salvation as a poet would be the woman he married: "Or best of all, let me but find a bride, / to be my all, my light, my sun, my God! . . . / I need a course of spiritual gymnastics, / and perhaps that would be the way to get it" (106). In Falk's insistence that Svanhild link her destiny to his for the sake of his art, Ibsen reexamines what he had desired and expected from Suzannah Thoresen six years earlier. He parodies his proposal poem, in which he had declared to Suzannah that if she agreed to marry him, then "fair songs upspringing" would soar from his breast as he rose "like a bird toward the coasts of the sky!"[14] Falk's version is less romantic: "I am a falcon, as my name implies; / and, like a falcon, I must fight the wind / if I'm to reach the heights; you are the gust / to carry me aloft" (134). "*Violently,*" he insists on Svanhild's feminine destiny as the inspirer of his creativity: "It is your simple duty / to give me what God granted you so freely!" Svanhild gives Falk a hard lesson on Woman as Muse as she speaks to him of selfishness and of childish dependency: "I was the breeze that was to bear you up – / and without me you couldn't rise at all / ... / I saw you as a kite, not as a falcon, / a paper kite, fashioned of poetry, / which in itself is and remains a trifle / while the important feature is the string" (135–36). Svanhild completes her lesson to the poet by explaining the proper source of his power: "Go onwards by the strength of your own wings, / let them sustain you, or else let you down" (136). She will be neither his salvation nor his well of inspiration: "I've sung my last song from the leafy bough. / I have no more; that was my only one" (136–37).

Stripped of the illusions of his "childish project," Falk determines to do nothing less than marry the woman who in refusing to be his "flute" has, he notes, "whistled me to shame" (166). The union of Falk and Svanhild will "show the world" that love "can face the dull and grimy weekday round / and still remain stainless and undismayed" (167). In a *volte face*, Ibsen's verse turns from bitter pronouncements and sharp exchanges to the lyricism of an ecstatic love poetry: "Svanhild: My heart was empty, when you came in triumph / and entered with your thousand and one / songs; / ... Falk: I'll be a sentry in the camp of light; / we'll be together, and our life shall be / a hymn to celebrate love's victory!" (171)

But the lovers' betrothal is brief, for in the third and final movement of the play businessman Guldstad makes short work of their exalted plans. Arguing Falk's earlier point – that marriage is "a veritable ocean / of obligations and demands and claims / that haven't very much to do with love" (188) – Guldstad maintains that Svanhild should marry him for emotional and financial security. When Falk answers Svanhild's question whether their love will last a lifetime with "It will last a long, long time" (193), she determines that they must part; thus, their "glad, triumphant love, shall never / be paled by age and riddled by disease" (194). Throwing her engagement ring into the fjord, she then makes a Kierkegaardian declaration of the necessity of renouncing Falk in this life to gain him "for eternity" (195), and decides to marry Guldstad.[15]

This resolution resolves nothing, for the play's development has simply reversed itself as Guldstad repeats to Falk "the truth" he told "but a few hours ago" (189). And since the passion of Falk and Svanhild is too strong to be summarily dismissed, the question arises whether it would not have been wiser to risk rather than renounce marriage for such a love. Moreover, the marriage of Guldstad and Svanhild fails to convince as a preferable alternative to a love match. Guldstad attempts to justify the "solid foundation" of such a union: "It is a sense of happiness in duty, / . . . the even temper that outlasts the years, / the arm that gives safety and firm support" (191). This paternalistic and rather sentimental vision of domestic contentment seems as naive as the ecstatic vows of Falk and Svanhild, a woman singularly unfitted for dependency. A young, passionate, and strongminded woman will not easily be satisfied with a middle-aged, fatherly protector, whose magnanimity, in any case, in John Northam's terms, "strikes us more as that of a fairy godfather than as that of a man who has evolved a practical morality through intimate experience of life" (N 29). And renouncing a man one loves is one thing, marrying a man for whom one has no feeling is another; the play's end shows a reluctant bride who requests that her wedding be put off until autumn, "till the leaves have fallen" (199). As Guldstad approaches and bows, Svanhild *"gives a start, but soon collects herself and gives him her hand"* (202).

As Northam has pointed out, *Love's Comedy* does not "explore the full dimensions" of the conflict it has raised, and thus it is "impossible to be sure where the irony stops" (N 28). But what the play suggests will be Svanhild's future seems more than equivocal, for her decision is presented as capitulation. In the husband-supply depot that is her boardinghouse, Mrs. Halm is moved to tears by her daughter Anna's betrothal: "that makes the eighth / to find a husband underneath this roof" (125); only Svanhild

remains to make it nine. "You know," her moth(
"which way your duty lies" (199).

Svanhild's surrender to society's essential demand
a suitable marriage – is the conclusion both of *Love's*
of its important feminist leitmotif, Ibsen's first explic(
of feminist issues. A precursor of *Pillars of Society* and *A*
Love's Comedy owes much to the feminism of Magdalene ..noresen
and Suzannah Ibsen, but Ibsen's feminist education had begun
earlier, in Grimstad, where the aspiring writer read the work
of the Swedish feminist author Fredrika Bremer, and read and
discussed with his friend Due the sensational *Twelve Letters* by
Danish author "Clara Rafael" (Mathilde Fibiger), whose argument
for female emancipation created a scandal (Due, *Reminiscences*
38).

And Ibsen also read, and would continue to read, the works of
one of his favorite authors, the great Dano-Norwegian playwright
Ludvig Holberg (1684–1754), one of the earliest and most vocal
of the European feminists.[16] In a classic enlightenment text, *Intro-*
duction to the Science of Natural Law and the Law of Nations (1716),
Holberg argues the equality of women with men as a natural,
given condition. The poem "Zille Hansdotter's Defense of the
Female Sex" (1722) maintains that women should have the right
to all employments currently reserved for men, and points to
examples of outstanding women in government, in learning, and
in arts and letters. In the preface to *Comparative Histories of Heroines*
(1745), a companion volume to *Comparative Histories of Heroes*
(1739), Holberg explains that his book's purpose is to prove that
women are as worthy of education and political enfranchisement
as men. Holberg's comedies *Jean de France* (1723) and *The*
Weathercock (1723) contain an important feminist strain in their
satire on accepted notions of feminine weakness and folly;[17] his
last play, *The Transformed Bridegroom*, in which all the characters
are women, wittily concludes: "A merry play has been performed
/ With actresses alone. / By this and many other things / We hope
that we have shown / It's not so hard to carry on without a single
man, / For girls and women play their parts / As ably as men
can."[18]

Holberg's most famous feminist text is his best-selling science-
fiction novel *The Journey of Niels Klim to the World Underground*

(1741).[19] Klim travels through the earth's center to various animal
and plant kingdoms, through whose customs Holberg satirizes the
foibles of human society. In Utopia, or "Potu," the realm of the
tree people, Klim discovers to his astonishment that there exists
no moral, cultural, or legal distinction between male and female
trees. He remarks on the wisdom of the female president of the
senate, which leads him to wonder whether on earth, in Bergen,
for example, there would be any harm done if the daughter of a
famous lawyer pled cases in the place of her obtuse father. When
Klim travels to the kingdom of Cocklecu (Cock-A-Doodle-Do),
Holberg reverses the traditional earthly division of labor according to strict sexual lines in order to show its perfect arbitrariness.
In Cocklecu, the men perform all the household duties, as well as
all the onerous physical work, while the women hold the professional occupations and rule the country. This division of labor is
justified on the ground that since nature gave men stronger bodies, they are obviously created to perform physical work. The
women court the men they are enamored of, writing them love
poems and sending them gifts, and brag among themselves of
their lubricity and the number of men they have enjoyed. When
Klim claims that only the male sex is capable of great things, he is
told that he confuses custom with nature; that women's "weaknesses" are a result of their poor education is proven by
Cocklecu's women, who are serious, prudent, and taciturn, while
its men are frivolous, slow-witted, and garrulous, behavior which
has resulted in the Cocklecuan expressions for an absurd story –
"That's a manly trifle" – and for a rash action – "That's only manly
weakness" (92). Returning to Potu, Klim tells its citizens that his
Cocklecuan experiences have taught him the grave dangers of a
country's allowing women to perform public functions, for this
arrogant and ambitious sex always works to extend its own power.
When he presents to the senate a law that would forbid women
from holding any position of authority, it is refused on two
grounds: because women form half the citizenry of the country
and because they have talents that enable them to contribute to
the public weal. Klim is exiled for his pains.

Holberg's feminism is part of his enlightened rationalism, a
conviction that as human beings women have the same natural
rights as men. To oppress them is to deny them these rights on the
basis of foolish cultural superstition. Holberg's conviction that sex

is an absurd basis for discrimination against people anticipates Nora Helmer's argument, a hundred and forty years later, in the third act of *A Doll House.*

In 1852, Ibsen was plunged into the contemporary debate over feminism when the board of the Norwegian Theatre of Bergen sent its newly hired "dramatic author" on an educational tour to Copenhagen and one of the nineteenth-century's great houses, the Royal Theatre, where it was Ibsen's delight to meet the Heibergs, the tastemakers of Scandinavia: Johanne Luise – director, writer of comedies and memoirs, and Scandinavia's greatest actress – and her husband Johan – writer of vaudevilles and comedies, drama theorist, the most important man of letters in Scandinavia, and the theatre's director. The Heibergs were ardent, active feminists, and had helped Mathilde Fibiger to publish *Twelve Letters.* Ibsen was disappointed by the conversation of Johan Heiberg, but captivated by his wife. He saw her play several roles, including one of her most famous, the protagonist of *The Weathercock,* Holberg's exuberant parody of the stereotype of the capricious woman. Luise Heiberg befriended Ibsen, and would later become one of his most ardent supporters, performing the important task of introducing him to the Danish stage, directing *The League of Youth* at the Royal on February 16, 1870. She complained that his great women characters had arrived too late for her; she would especially have liked to play the "New Woman" Lona Hessel in *Pillars of Society.* In 1870, eighteen years after their first meeting, Ibsen visited Copenhagen again, and was once more received by Luise Heiberg. He thanked her for this, and for her earlier kindness to him, in one of his greatest poems, the intricately rhymed "Rhyme Letter to Fru Heiberg," which merges a lyrical description of the time they spent together with a tribute to the great actress, a woman who turned her "own substance rich and free" into art.[20]

One of the plays Ibsen saw at the Royal and would later put on in Bergen was *Bataille de Dames,* a comedy by Scribe and Ernest Legouvé that pled the feminist cause. Legouvé, now virtually forgotten, was an important figure in French intellectual life; he gave lectures on feminism at the Collège de France and collected them as *L'Histoire morale de la femme* (1848), whose central argument was the necessity for women's education. The book was an important influence on the feminist movement in Scandinavia.[21]

Legouvé's most ardent disciple was Ibsen's friend Camilla Wergeland Collett (1813–95), who launched both Norwegian feminism and the modern Norwegian novel with *The District Governor's Daughters*.[22] Deciding against a masculine pen name like that of her admired "George Sand," Collett brought out her novel anonymously in two parts in 1854 and 1855, fifteen years before Mill's *The Subjection of Women*. She became widely known as the author and famous overnight. The book, she later said, was "the first swallow" (Aarnes, *Searchlight* 7), and this was true in several senses: the novel was the first attempt at realism in Norwegian literature, its author was a woman, and its theme was society's systematic oppression of women.

Collett's novel, which ushered in the first, "utopian" phase of Norwegian feminism, so-called because of its lack of interest in direct political reform,[23] pleads implicitly that women should have the right to educate themselves and to marry whom they please. In the world of *The District Governor's Daughters*, it is masculine success and family propriety that matter. In parallel stories, the two eldest daughters, raised to be ornaments, housewives, and mothers, make loveless and disastrous matches with men deemed suitable by their parents. The main plot of the novel concerns Sofie, the youngest daughter, an intelligent and unhappy misfit who is tormented by her sisters' misery and torn between her own longings for education and independence and her duty to marry well. When her father's secretary George takes an interest in her and becomes her tutor, she falls in love. In this feminist version of the Pygmalion myth, the teacher undergoes a metamorphosis along with his pupil, whose intellectual flowering undermines his notion that women are unfit for education; as Sofie learns, George falls in love. But in the end, the power of the world is too strong, the lovers are separated, and Sofie makes a good match, marrying a wealthy middle-aged widower and devoting her life to his and his children's well-being.

Collett's novel was violently objected to on the same grounds as *Love's Comedy* eight years later: "Camilla Collett exaggerates! There are also happy marriages!" (Aarnes, *Searchlight* 8). And it was read and discussed as no other work of its time in Scandinavia.

Collett was forty-one when she published *The District Governor's Daughters*. Left a widow at thirty-eight, she devoted her remaining forty years to the women's cause. "Now I will speak!" she cried out

9. Camilla Wergeland Collett (1813–95) on the Norwegian 100-kroner note. Novelist, essayist, and founder of Norwegian feminism and the Norwegian realistic novel.

in *From the Camp of the Dumb* ([1877] *Works* 2:376), and she spared no one. In her essay "Women in Literature," a striking anticipation of twentieth-century feminism's analysis of the literary representation of women, Collett takes on Goethe's "eternal feminine," the French Romantics and Realists, the writers of "Young Germany," and the English Victorian novel. Nowhere does Collett find real women, only men's constructions of Woman: "Half teasing demon, half saint; half siren, half merciful sister – fire in a crust of ice, or the other way around; in short, here are our prototypes for the whole 'sphinx-and-frou-frou' genre" (*Works* 2:386–87).

Inexhaustible, Collett travelled incessantly, lecturing and writing on the feminist movement. She met the Ibsens in Europe some years after *Love's Comedy*, when Ibsen had become an established author. It was natural that she and Suzannah Ibsen should become fast friends and mutual admirers. Accompanying the antique filigree brooch Collett once sent her friend was a poem of tribute to Suzannah's "mind, spirit, and strong will" that provided a model for the modern woman (*Works* 2:491).

And it was natural, too, that the rebel Ibsen should find in Collett a kindred spirit. On her seventieth birthday, January 23,

1883, Ibsen wrote to his friend to congratulate her, promising her that he and Suzannah would drink her health, and to praise her: "The Norway now being developed will bear traces of your spirit and of your pioneer work. To coming generations, you will be regarded as one of the fighters without whom that progress could not conceivably have taken place" (*LS* 215–16). On her eightieth birthday it was Ibsen who took Collett to table at the official dinner honoring her; she was not used to such ceremony, she said, and compared herself to the old Viking ship that had just been unearthed at Gokstad.

Collett was one of the very few writers whose influence Ibsen would admit to. He goes out of his way to signal *Love's Comedy*'s indebtedness to *The District Governor's Daughters* by appropriating one of the novel's metaphors, a comparison of love to tea. In the novel, the diary of Margrethe allows the author to record her own opinions on love and marriage. In a passage on the brutalization of love, Collett warns:

Do not carelesssly tamper with the fragile leaves at [love's] heart, in the foolish belief that afterwards the coarser leaves will do as well – No, they will not do. The difference between the two is as great as that between the tea which we ordinary mortals call by that name, and the tea which only His Celestial Majesty [the Emperor of China] drinks, and which is the *real* tea; it is gathered first, and is so delicate that the harvesters must wear gloves, after having washed their hands, I think it is, twenty-four times. (*Works* 1:333)

Ibsen extends Collett's metaphor into an elaborate conceit; Falk contrasts the unopened buds of love's "celestial kingdom" with ordinary black tea, "as different from the first as silk from sisal." There is even, as there is "beef tea," "beef love"; just as tea must cross the desert by caravan, taxed and stamped at every frontier, love must exhibit the "seals and documents" of marriage until the "celestial kingdom" becomes a fairy tale and love itself is forgotten (157–58). The language of Margrethe's pleading, and of Collett's novel in general, that of sentiment, has been transformed into the language of irony, but the metaphor of love's destruction in Falk's cynical speech remains that of its gentler source.[24]

The main debt of *Love's Comedy* to *The District Governor's Daughters* lies in the story of Svanhild, whose name itself, Falk comments, "carries with it the idea of sacrifice for the sins of the age" (*OI* 2:213).[25] Svanhild's namesake is the unlucky Svanhild of the

Volsung Saga, daughter of Sigurd and Gudrun, trampled to death by horses as expiation to the gods for her family's arranged marriages. Ibsen makes the victimization of his Svanhild, a "second Svanhild," Falk analyzes cruelly but accurately, more direct; an "innocent [who] must bleed to expiate the nation's guilt" (132), she is sacrificed to her own marriage of convenience. Like the women of *The District Governor's Daughters*, Svanhild does not marry, but is married off. And like Collett's protagonist Sofie, Svanhild is an outsider in marriage-obsessed bourgeois society, bored and unhappy in the tea-party world of her mother's boarding-house. Falk describes his first sight of her: "A fashionable crowd sat round the table; / the tea was fragrant; conversation buzzed / . . . / They set great store by morals and religion, / those worthy matrons and mature old maids, / and the young wives praised domesticity; / while you sat silent, utterly apart / like a bird on a roof" (132). Guldstad foolishly interprets Svanhild's apartness as ineptness in the ways of polite society; "socially," he says of the woman he has targeted to be his wife, "she is still a little gauche" (126). This crass and superficial measure of Svanhild's worth leads Falk to begin what becomes a duet on "The Making of Ladies":

> FALK: [*gaily*] They're rather like the seed of winter rye;
>   they sprout unnoticed in the frost and snow.
> GULDSTAD: At Christmas, they're transplanted to the
>   ballroom –
> FALK: A rich, nutritious soil, where they acquire
>   an ear for scandal, and a taste for splendor –
> GULDSTAD: Until in early spring, they all emerge –
> FALK: As tiny, little ladies, green and tender! (127)

Svanhild has struggled against married ladyhood, in whose "gilded cage," Falk laments, the "fine lady will thrive" but "the woman dies" (133). Ibsen gives Svanhild his own mother's dreams of being a painter and, less respectably, an actress. Svanhild tried painting, she explains to Falk, but believing that she had no talent, she lost confidence and decided to go on the stage. "But then the aunts came round with their advice – / they all discussed, and worried, and considered" (131). The matter was settled when the eldest aunt forced her to take a governess' post, the only proper job for an unmarried woman. Naturally, the family kept secret this shocking story of rebellion: "My 'future,' don't you

know, might be endangered / if young gentlemen got to hear of
it." Svanhild's story is one of failed courage and thwarted hopes; "I
wanted to break free, and stand alone." Her surrender to her
aunts has broken her for good, and the brief engagement to the
unsuitable Falk, banished from the boardinghouse for his criticism of its idols, marks a last, momentary revolt in her life's
capitulation. Like Collett's Sofie, Svanhild makes a proper loveless
marriage with a prosperous older man. "Now both my girls are
going to be wed," Mrs. Halm cries triumphantly, leading the pack
of relatives who at the play's end *"rush toward [Svanhild and
Guldstad] and surround them with high glee"* (201–2). The spirited,
intelligent woman whom Falk once described as "minted silver /
amidst the copper" (132) has dutifully settled for marriage without love, crushed, like her namesake, by the sins of the age. Like
the well-married wife of Magdalene Thoresen's *My Grandmother's
Story*, Svanhild, too, will have "a comfortable home, a pretty garden – a blue silk dress, a porcelain vase with artificial flowers, a
canary bird in one cage, a parrot in another" (*Life Images* 65).

Love's Comedy caused a literary and personal scandal that damaged Ibsen's already bad reputation. The uncomprehending public was deeply shocked that the playwright's wife of four years
approved of a work whose overriding theme they took to be the
castigation of marriage. Later, Ibsen wrote that when he refused
to make his fellow countrymen his "father-confessors," he was
"excommunicated" (*LS* 101). The Ibsens, maddeningly, were not
to be had.

The Oslo gossips could not understand that Suzannah Ibsen
had no reason to dislike *Love's Comedy*. On the contrary, she
undoubtedly agreed with Falk and his creator that marriage was a
hard awakening after the romantic pleasures of courtship. She
had, after all, lived through four years of poverty and worry, had
experienced a difficult childbirth, and had lived with a husband
struggling in deep depression. And she must have been pleased to
see herself in the intrepid Svanhild who teaches the poet the
falsity of Woman as Muse. *Love's Comedy*, in which Ibsen wrote
himself free of his naive expectations about love and feminine
inspiration, and in which, for the first time, he lashed out unabashedly against a social evil, namely the marketing of women as
wives, was a play after Suzannah Ibsen's own heart.

But the Svanhild who sends the poet away, afraid to test their love against the realities of marriage, is Suzannah Ibsen's foil. For Suzannah Thoresen had married the poet; they had not lived happily ever after, as Falk and Svanhild temporarily anticipated, but they had lived, happily and unhappily, and had come through together. Guldstad warns: "Love chooses not a wife / but a woman; and if she wasn't made / to be a wife for you – ?" (188). But Ibsen did not have this disappointment. When he wrote that *Love's Comedy* was the full expression of the urge toward freedom his marriage had given him, he was undoubtedly referring to the influence of Suzannah Thoresen's distrust of conventional thinking, her hatred of lies and cant, in short, her exemplary freedom of mind. *Love's Comedy* was a tribute to the strong, free spirit of its author's wife, and this was, no doubt, one of the reasons that she approved of it.

CHAPTER 4

Love and the kingdom

Oh, life – ! No second chance to play!
Oh, dread – ! *Here's* where my empire lay!
Peer Gynt 5:5 (178)

THE FEMINIZATION OF HISTORY: *THE PRETENDERS*

A year after the hostile reception of *Love's Comedy*, Ibsen experienced his first critical and popular success with *The Pretenders*. The last of Ibsen's works to be based on Norwegian history and saga, *The Pretenders* treats the thirteenth-century civil wars. In a version of the traditional psychological opposition famously characterized by Schiller as the *naiv* versus the *sentimentalisch*, Ibsen imagined in Haakon Haakonsson a self-confident fortune's child who knows himself born to glory and in Earl Skule a tormented self-doubter. A conflict between two notions of ruling accompanies the psychological opposition; Skule's policy of divide and conquer, whose goal is to maintain the king's supremacy, opposes Haakon's mission to forge Norway's warring kingdoms into one nation.

From its appearance, *The Pretenders* has been read as a psychological and ideological duel between its two antagonists.[1] Yet alongside the Haakon/Skule antithesis Ibsen creates an equally important parallel conflict in which the two men belong to the same side. Despite their differences as human beings and as rulers, both Haakon and Skule reject the personal life for reasons of state, shutting out everything but their rivalry for the throne. Opposing their bloody enmity are the women they use and abuse, who are at once victims of the men's power struggle and agents of their transformation from warriors to peacemakers.

Ibsen begins his history play with a woman's ordeal by fire.

74

The rival factions of Haakon and Skule anxiously wait in a church-yard while Queen Inga, Haakon's mother, undergoes the test of the glowing iron to silence her son's enemies' charge that he is illegitimate. As the choir sings a Gloria, the church doors open and Inga holds out her unburned hands to the crowd, speaking her only words in the scene: "God has judged. Look at these hands; with these I bore the white hot iron" (2:222). As though she were a living icon, Haakon embraces this "most blessed among women" (222) whose intercession has assured his political future, and sends her away, joyfully anticipating his election as king.

Scene two presents a female counter-world to the male world of politics and violence. Hidden in darkness, Ragnhild, Margrete, and Sigrid – Skule's wife, daughter, and sister – observe through a window the men's frenzied assembly. The marginalized, inner world frames and measures the outer as the women, free to speak their minds, express their grief over past bloodshed and their terror of more to come.[2] Margrete and Ragnhild describe how hate is transforming the faces of Haakon and Skule into those of fiends. Sigrid, who became a Cassandra on her wedding day, when her husband was slaughtered and "blood and iron seemed to shut out the world around us from my eyes," prophesies that Skule "will lose his soul" if he gains royal power (258). Divided between her loyalty to her father and her love for Haakon, Margrete flatly announces Haakon's triumph, and her shaken mother leaves, weeping less for her husband's disappointment than the general suffering she knows will follow.

The young king confirms the women's fears as he begins his rule by making himself a paradigm of masculine imperviousness to sentiment: "Everything that the king holds dear must be re-moved" (233). He orders his mother's immediate departure, and with similar dispatch, arranges a politically expedient marriage to Margrete, who notes sadly that "it will be long before you need send me away" (236).

The crisis of Haakon's coveted kingship – Skule's rebellion – leads the king to discover his folly. The act-three recognition scene moves from an idyllic portrayal of maternal love to a drama-tization of the virulent rivalry of two powerful men, to a second dramatization of maternal love, and finally to an affirmation of the primacy of love and human ties in the affairs of men. The scene begins with one of the tenderest passages in Ibsen's works, the "Cradle Song" which Margaret, alone with her baby, sings:

> Now roof and rafter merge with
> The starry sky above;
> My baby Haakon rises
> On dreamless wings of love . . .
>
> God's angel host is watching
> The babe the whole night through;
> God bless you, little Haakon,
> Your mother watches too. (278)

Upon Skule's arrival, the young mother proudly shows her father the baby and prays: "May peace at last unite our family!" (279). But Skule looks at the continuation of Haakon's royal line and dreams of stealing his own grandson. In the confrontation that follows, Skule demands of Haakon half the kingdom. Sure of his kingly purpose, Haakon declares the true goal of Norway's ruler in a passage now famous in Norway as a set speech: "The men of Trondelag fought the men from Viken. The men of Agde fought the men of Hordaland . . . now all must be united . . . *That* is the task which God has lain upon my shoulders" (283). Too much a man of his time, the uncomprehending Skule leaves in anger to declare himself king.

Responding to the catastrophe with his usual hard single-mindedness, Haakon calls for his wife, tells her the news – "Two kings in the land!" (286) – and asks her advice on how he can have Skule killed. Margrete implores her husband, *"sinking in agony to the bench and kneeling before him*: Have you forgotten that he is my father?" (287). Admitting that he has, indeed, forgotten, the king lifts his wife up and tries to comfort her with words that show he misunderstands her misery: "Courage, do not cry; you are not to blame in this." His real object of pity is himself: "God, God, why do you strike me so hard, I who have done nothing against you!" (287).

This appeal – the zenith of Haakon's callousness to his wife – is followed by his recognition of error. Something more important than the throne stops his preoccupation with the threat of its loss. The agent of change is his mother, unable, in spite of her son's command, to stay away. "My mother! Sitting like a dog outside her son's door! And I have been asking why God has afflicted me!" (287). Inga's love melts the king's heart, and he confesses:

"Margrete – Mother – I have sinned deeply. I have shut my heart against the two of you – both of you so generous in your love." Drawing his mother and wife close, the warrior who was once insensible to everything except his national task makes light of what he despaired of minutes before: "Even if there are two kings in Norway, there is only one in Heaven – and I dare say *He* can take care of things!" (288).

Haakon's conversion transforms his notion of kingship, abolishing the exclusively gendered categories of *feeling/feminine* and *action/masculine* that have ruled his conduct. To stop the bloodshed, he pleads with Skule to accept what he himself had earlier rejected in horror, the sharing of the kingdom between them. When Skule refuses, Haakon is forced to put a price on his head, but privately, he instructs a follower to persuade the earl to flee.

As Haakon's leniency comes from the influence of women's love, Skule's newfound resolve results from the proof of his male power to destroy his adversary, in the person of a son. "But you have a daughter, Sire – a gentle, lovely daughter" (300), reminds the skald Jatgeir when Skule bemoans his lack of sons. "If my daughter were a son I would not ask you what gift I needed [to become king]," Skule responds. The earl's wish is fulfilled when Ingebjørg, his long discarded mistress, arrives to offer him the son whose existence she has kept hidden. Reared by monks, the well-named Peter, father-worshipper and unquestioning disciple, is the perfect lieutenant for a man unsure of his own capacities: "My father, my great and splendid father . . . Let your cause be mine and whatever be your cause, I shall know that I am fighting for the right" (306–7). Wishing to appear a visionary leader to his son, Skule presents Haakon's dream of Norway's unification as his own, and with Peter as inspiration, his insecurity transforms itself into its alter ego, fanaticism. Bolstered by the borrowed force of the male offspring, he rises to challenge Haakon's appeal to divide the kingdom in an outburst of hysterical hate:

HAAKON: Think of my Queen, your daughter!
SKULE: I have a son! I have a son! I think of him alone.
HAAKON: I also have a son – if I fall the kingdom will be his!
SKULE: Kill Haakon's child wherever you find him! Kill him on the throne; kill him before the altar; kill him, kill him in his mother's arms! (311)

Skule's freneticism conceals inadequacies for which Peter's male allegiance cannot compensate. Ibsen markedly dramatizes Skule's inability to love and incapacity to lead in the sexual impotence and physical cowardice of his most grotesque cleric, the nihilist bishop Nicholas. Consumed with ambition and envy, the scheming *eminence grise* has spent his life hatching plots to perpetuate war among the superior men he hates. It is he who revives the civil war by secretly ordering Ingebjørg to produce Skule's son. Urging Skule to acts of violence, Peter, fresh from the monastery, is the tool of the old churchman, whose deathbed confession contains his own psychosexual analysis of his crimes: "I hated because I could not love . . . Eighty years old I am, and still this desire to kill men and embrace women – But it was the same for me with women as in battle; only longing and desire, impotent from birth" (274).

In the bloody conflict that follows his refusal of peace, Skule's military blunders turn the townspeople against him. His last hope is to prove his legitimacy by appearing at the side of St. Olaf's shrine. Rejoicing when Peter announces that the shrine awaits him, Skule then listens appalled as the young zealot proudly describes how he tore the shrine from the high altar and dragged it from the church under the monks' curses. Horrified by the sacrilege, Skule sees his son transformed into the meanest church robber, his loyalty into mortal sin. He abandons his futile struggle and flees, despairing for his son's soul.

Skule confronts his misdirected life at the Elgeseter convent, where Sigrid is abbess, and where Margrete and Ragnhild have taken sanctuary. Like Haakon before him, Skule begs forgiveness as he praises what he has repudiated: "Gentle, loving women! Oh, how good to live! . . . My wife, my daughter; I have found peace and light" (335). But the sudden reappearance of Peter, the poisoned gift, still following orders and screaming of death, is a fateful reminder of the enormity of Skule's error. Wildly demanding the whereabouts of Haakon's son, Peter announces that he has rallied a group of Skule's supporters who are on their way to kill the child. Uncomprehending, Skule's wife and daughter confront Skule with the precious son he preferred to them. Ragnhild shouts out, "Can this be he whom you have loved so dearly?", and Margrete chastises her father: "How could you forget all of us for his sake?" (336). Hearing Peter scream his own command – "Kill it, kill it in its mother's arms!" – fills Skule with horror and remorse. Knowing that if his men arrive before Haakon's he cannot stop them from killing Margrete's child, Skule announces his decision to go to his death at the townspeople's hands. And thus the man who has repudiated his daughter dies to save her happiness, the man who has commanded the death of his grandson dies to save his life. It is not Margrete's son who will die, but Skule's; the fanatic arm of Skule's crusade for power will expiate his father-worship at his father's side. The play comes full circle in Sigrid's rhetorical question: "Have not we frightened women stood long enough in secret rooms, terror-stricken and hidden in the darkest corners, listening to the marching feet of war and death tramping through the land from end to end?" (339). As the bells ring, the women enter the chapel to sing thanks for the end of bloodshed, no longer constrained to watch helplessly the "spectacle of [men's] bloody struggles for power over other men, their implicit sacrifice of human relationships and emotional values in the quest for dominance."[3] As Haakon arrives to begin a reign of peace and unity, a follower pronounces: "At last you can begin your royal task with free hands. In there are those you love" (341). The curtain comes down as the "*song of the women swells more loudly from the chapel*" (341).

The significance of the women of *The Pretenders* lies not in their "unslaked thirst for love" (K 162), but in the power of this love to affect the world.[4] Like the women of Shakespeare's history plays, who, in Juliet Dusinberre's phrase, stand "for permanence and fidelity against shifting political sands,"[5] the women of *The Pretenders* constitute a feminine counter-world of love and stability in opposition to the masculine sphere of violence and struggle. But if Shakespeare's women can only "undercut the gains of the male world" by their losses (Dusinberre 297), the women of *The Pretenders* impose their values on the struggling claimants for power. As Atle Kittang has shown in a valuable essay, *The Pretenders* is permeated with the teleological Christian–romantic view of history, in which Haakon Haakonsson's "majestic thought" of transforming a "Rike" into a "Folk," a kingdom into a nation, expresses the divine plan for Norway.[6] In Ibsen's version of the nationalist fable, Haakon is willing to share Norway with Skule for the sake of human ties and human life. As first the king and then his rival for power embrace the values of mother, wife, and daughter, the personal influences the political, the temporal the teleological. The women of Ibsen's history play, who begin as objects – prizes and tools of politics – emerge as subjects, and thus do not function outside history, but rather help to make it.

In the autumn of 1863, about the same time that he sold *The Pretenders* for publication, Ibsen received a piece of happy news: the government had at last awarded him a writer's grant. The small stipend was to prove among the most important of all the prizes and honors that Ibsen would win in his long career, for it allowed him to do the two separate but related things that constituted the watershed of his life as an artist: to leave Norway and to experience the Mediterranean world.

In May of 1864, Ibsen crossed the Alps, released, in Gosse's lovely phrase, into "the glow and splendor of Italy" from his "prison house of ice" (A 13:83–84). His first months in Italy were a time of culture shock resembling stupefaction. He spent days basking in the Italian sun and drinking in the art and monuments of old Rome. To escape the blazing summer heat, he moved out to the Alban Hills and Genzano, where he joined a Scandinavian colony and spent the summer enjoying *far niente*. Mediterranean culture's delight in pleasure and in the joy of living profoundly affected him, and like the Southern sun, would put its imprint on everything he wrote, beginning with *Brand*.

The frame of *Brand*'s dramatic argument looks back to *Catiline*'s triangle of a man caught between two opposing women; Gerd, the play's "Furia," appears at key moments to goad the protagonist on in his mission, and the gentle Agnes, like Aurelia, is the protagonist's wife, and is associated with the personal life. But in *Brand*, the gentle woman is not opposed to, but rather a follower of, the hero's mission; it is because of Brand's devotion to his calling that Agnes loves him. What Hjørdis in *The Vikings at Helgeland* longs for with Sigurd, Agnes has with Brand: a marriage of love dedicated to a great endeavor. Gradually, however, Agnes becomes Brand's chief antagonist in the female/male oppositional pattern of *The Pretenders*. For if the iconoclastic pastor is, in a sense, Ibsen's most heroic male character, his perfect devotion to his vocation renders him inhuman. Ibsen gave his protagonist a calling like his own, which he defined as "the work of arousing the people of our nation and urging them to think great thoughts" (*LS* 57). But in creating his inspired moral leader, Ibsen exhibited what from now on would be a characteristic *modus operandi* – the relentless examination of a theory of life or a mode of conduct down to its ultimate implications – and the uncompromising idealist becomes the fanatic.[7] Ibsen himself noted what has now become a commonplace: "*Peer Gynt* is the antithesis of *Brand*" (*LS* 124). And as *Peer Gynt* followed *Brand,* as Ibsen said, "as though of itself" (*LS* 102), so *Brand* followed *The Pretenders.* Like Haakon, Brand considers himself divinely called to his life's work, denying his feelings and sacrificing those of others to his vocation; in opposing Brand's absolutism, Agnes, like the women of *The Pretenders,* stands for compassion and tolerance. But whereas in *The Pretenders,* the feminine and masculine worlds unite, in *Brand* they remain separate and contending, for unlike his predecessor, Brand will not allow feelings to moderate his moral imperative.

Agnes, whose sign is the sun, appears in the first act of *Brand* singing her way down a sunlit mountain with her fiancé Einar, "true children of joy" (3:87). They meet the solemn prophet Brand, who derides their frivolity and delivers a Kierkegaardian pledge to bury the "God of hacks and time-serving drudges . . . [who] has been ailing / These three thousand years" (88).[8] Sapped of energy by Brand's harangue, Agnes is too tired to continue her games with Einar; the pathetic fallacy prophecies her future as the sun disappears and the wind grows cold. Seduced by Brand's dark gravity, she muses: "Did you see . . . *speaking softly, as if in church*: As he was speaking – how he seemed to grow?" (94). She has fallen in love with the moral life.

Meditating in the mountains, Brand meets his like-minded nemesis in Gerd, a solitary inhabitant of the heights.[9] As Agnes' chief symbolic attribute is warmth, Gerd's is coldness. Contemptuous of the mean valley church, Gerd invites Brand to the mountain top and its "Ice Church," a natural formation of snow and ice. Although Brand dismisses Gerd as mad, their meeting reaffirms the dichotomous symbolic categories that inform his thought: "There's the valley – and the mountain – / Which is right?" (99).

As Gerd is identified with the heights, Agnes is established as the voice of the valley. When the villagers plead with Brand to remain as their pastor, the world's prophet refuses. But as he leaves, he sees Agnes "listening as if to some / Music in the air," and her ecstatic recognition – "This is the world that thou must people!" (113) – transforms Brand's conception of his life-work. The man who needed "the open ears of all the world" (111) will remain in the remote valley to perform the humble labor of a country pastor.

For Brand, Agnes is merely God's instrument, and when she has revealed His plan, His servant discards her: "Take her," he says to Einar (125). But Agnes, who has learned to speak like Brand, denouncing her days with Einar as "false frivolity" (123), has decided differently. In the operatic trio which ends act two she affirms her commitment to the sacrificial life against the warnings of the priest and his opponent:

> BRAND: Remember, my demands are severe and stern.
>   I shall require All or Nothing . . .
> EINAR: Give up this madness! Reject this grim suitor
>   And his dark demands! Live your own life! . . .
> AGNES: (*rises, and says slowly*):
>   I choose the night. Through the way of death.
>   Beyond them shines the crimson dawn of day. (126)

In giving herself to Brand, Agnes is pledging an absolutism for which she is ill-fitted. For in scaling down Brand's grandiose plan to temporal size, she has implicitly favored an ethic of compromise that opposes Brand's philosophy of "All or Nothing." In Agnes' first act of solidarity with Brand – the journey to the bed of a dying man who has killed his child because he could not bear to see it starve – Ibsen provides a premonitory measure of comparison; Brand will choose to let his and Agnes' son die not to save him from a life worse than death, but to sacrifice him to Brand's vocation, a motif that weighs gruesomely against the prior one of kindness.

Brand's treatment of his mother prefigures what he will demand of his wife. Another in Ibsen's long line of unhappy women who make marriages of convenience, Brand's mother was persuaded by her father to forget the man she loved and marry a more promising "money-maker" (120). In a union that looks forward to the Alving marriage in *Ghosts*, the good party turns out to be a bad investment, and the wife, finding herself with neither love nor money, becomes a businesswoman, amassing a tidy fortune after her husband's death. Brand grants his mother no compassion for her emotional suffering, giving her instead a sermon on her greed.

Agnes protests against Brand's resolve not to go to his dying mother's bedside: "Brand, how hard you are!" (127). Even his love for her is "still hard. It has a touch that hurts" (130). Agnes' word *hard*, in Northam's phrase, "begins to chime in the dialogue like a refrain" (N 48) as messengers arrive from Brand's mother. The voice of mercy, Agnes chides: "You drive too hard a bargain. / . . . Can any man on earth accept such terms as yours?" (136). Brand's mother dies alone.

While Brand's mother is lying on her deathbed, Brand's and Agnes' two-year-old son Alf lies ill, a foreboding counterpoint that Ibsen develops into the crisis of his action. What Agnes fears and conceals in metaphor is that Brand will destroy their child: "Wherever you shoot the arrow / Of your thought – it flies to him!" (137). Letting herself be persuaded by Brand's reassurances, she "*looks up at him happily and says*: One thing God cannot demand of us!" Leaving Brand to watch over her sleeping son, Agnes does not hear his dire rejoinder: "The Lord can test me / As he tested Abraham" (138). Brand's sacrifice of his ambition to human need, a choice identified with Agnes, has proven a paltry offering, "no sacrifice in that"; only the apotheosis of willed suffering can satisfy Brand's notion of salvation: "To suffer death in agony upon the cross – / That is no martyrdom, no sacrifice at all. / But to desire, to *will* that death upon the cross, / . . . *that* / Is martyrdom!" (133).

For Alf to live, Brand must take him away from the freezing mountain valley and thus abandon his parishioners. Practicing what he preaches was easier when Brand despised the person in question, his mother; now the choice falls on his dear son. As he vacillates, and as Agnes waits with Alf in her arms, the priestess of the Ice Church enters to assure Brand's decision: "The priest has flown! / From the mountains and from the hills / The goblins and the trolls are swarming" (152). Brand at first refuses to acknowledge this accusatory description of the moral relapse of his parishioners after his departure, seeing in Gerd only a mad girl raving about "heathen idols." But Gerd throws back his word: "Idols? Well, you see that woman? / Can't you see beneath the shawl / The shape of baby hands and feet . . . / Idols! Idols!"

Brand takes this characterization of his love for his son as the voice of Abraham's god: "Some Greater Power has sent her to us" (153). He seeks Agnes' complicity in his decision, and although she at first refuses in horror, she then wavers, taking refuge from responsibility in her powerless status: "I am your wife. Command me. I shall obey" (154). In the end, it is as Brand's disciple that Agnes seals her child's death, re-affirming the ultimatum her master needs to hear: "You must take the path your God has bidden you to take." When Brand replies, "Then let us go – for now it is time," Agnes asks "(*tonelessly*): Which way are we going?", but she knows the answer; her "That way?" as she points to the garden gate is wholly wishful. Brand's response, as he points to the house door – "No. This way!" – inspires an outburst both accusatory and suppliant as lifting Alf high, Agnes cries: "The sacrifice Thou cravest / I dare raise up towards Thy Heaven! / Lead me through the terrors of this world!" (155).

Because he has another life besides the personal, Alf's father is better able to bear his death than Alf's mother. Almost crazed with grief, Agnes looks out on her child's grave as Brand, newly returned from a pastoral duty, exults in his masculine striving: "Oh, out there I was a man. / The sea went surging over the rocks. / . . . The sharp hail drummed on the planks / . . . I stood exultant at the helm, and felt myself / Grow tall and strong, like the hero of a legend. / For I was the man who took command" (158). Brand's self-satisfaction angers the gentle Agnes, who rebels against Brand's male prerogative in a speech that could have been spoken by Hjørdis of *The Vikings at Helgeland*: "Oh, it is easy to stand against a storm, / Easy to live a life of action, / But what about me, left here all alone, / . . . What about me? / However much I want to, I cannot / Kill my time as men are able to do."

Brand responds to Agnes' question with an exalted lecture on woman's servicing role in marriage that looks forward to similar, blunter versions voiced by Bernick in *Pillars of Society*, Helmer in *A Doll House*, and Lyngstrand in *The Lady from the Sea*. In making Brand appeal to what Goethe famously called the "eternal feminine" – the notion of woman as the source of man's spiritual enlightenment – Ibsen invents an ingenious theological base for his priest's rendition, a theory of his-and-her deities: "I must see Him great and very strong – / As great as Heaven itself. / . . . Oh, but *you* can see Him face to face, / Can look upon him as a loving father, / And lay your weary head within his arms" (159). Because woman is the weaker vessel, she has the right to a milder god, from whom she receives consolation which she then brings to her man. Although men must have, appropriately, a hard god, they are entitled to a gentle one through their wives: ". . . You can come / From his divine embrace refreshed and healed, / With the radiance of his glory in your eyes, / A radiance and a glory you can bring to me / As I labor here in suffering and strife." Brand summarizes for his uncomprehending wife: "You see, Agnes, to be able to share like this / Is the very heart of marriage" (159).

Brand's argument for his-and-her deities proves Agnes' contention that he, like her, needs warmth and love, and in so doing, it makes a mockery of his exclusive worship of Abraham's god. Seizing upon the notion of the weaker sex, the man who claims to refuse all compromise in following the commandments of the stern god splits Jehovah in two to partake of a gentler god as well. Man must worship the rigorous patriarch, but at the same time, through woman's ministrations, he can be saved from His judgment.

Ibsen ends Brand's lecture with a last thrust at woman's role as the warrior's repose: "I must fight on to victory or defeat, / Fight on in the heat of the day, / Stand guard in the frosts of night – / And your task is to hand to me / Your brimming cups of sweet, refreshing love, / And wrap the cloak of tenderness beneath my breastplate of steel – / That is no little task, my love" (160).[10] Agnes' simple reply – "Any task would now be too much for my strength" – constitutes a devastating rebuttal of this grandiose description of her wifely duty. Brand has spoken into the wind. His demand that Agnes comfort him as he suffers for having sacrificed Alf is both monstrously egotistical and utterly futile, for Agnes, beyond all theory, sees only her freezing child: "He toddled with faltering baby steps / . . . Stretched out his arms for his mother, / And with a pleading smile seemed / To be asking me to warm him back to life!" Alf's pains are real, while Brand's doctrinaire comfort – "Only the body lies beneath the snow" – is the inhuman theory of a despot: "What you so unfeelingly call 'the body'/ To me is still my little boy / . . . The God you have taught me to know / Reigns like a conquering tyrant" (161). Remembering the "light, and warmth, and sun" of her pre-Brand days, Agnes renounces her discipleship in a flood of condemnation: "Your kingdom is too great for me – / Everything here is too much for me – / You, your calling, your aims, the lonely / Furrow you plough, your almighty will / Only your church is too little" (161– 62). Misunderstanding, Brand obtusely decides to build a bigger tabernacle.

A visit from the village's mayor provides Brand with some theological ballast in his defense of his decision to let Alf die. The mayor reveals that the man Brand's mother rejected took up with a gypsy, Gerd's mother, and his "offspring thus exists / By virtue of her from whom you sprang" (177). The uncompromising priest and the priestess of the Ice Church are, metaphorically, brother and sister. Brand can now reaffirm Gerd as God's agent in Alf's death and justify the death itself as the atonement for his mother's marriage: "Even thus does the Lord above employ the fruits / Of guilt to feed the roots of sanity and justice" (178). This Panglossian reasoning,[11] however, proves satisfying only as theology; despairing of God's comfort, he characteristically demands his wife's: "My dearest – Bring me light!" (180). Agnes enters with the Christmas candles that will light the dark stalemate that follows, in which Brand's disciple, wavering between protest and submission, finally lives out her master's doctrine of "All or Nothing."

Determined to make Agnes renounce her grieving as idolatry, Brand makes her close the shutters that open onto Alf's grave. He justifies his severity in a description of his relation with his wife that imitates the one his god enjoys with him, that of the highminded tyrant and his inferior, powerless dependent: "You are my wife. I can demand / That you give your life entirely / To this calling. It is my right" (183). In the three-page soliloquy that follows, Agnes addresses her dead child through the closed shutters. The pathos rises to a pinnacle of grotesqueness in her misplaced plea that Alf lie to the other children in heaven to protect his father's reputation: "Tell them it was *he* who picked / Those pretty leaves to make your wreath" (184–85). Brand eavesdrops on Agnes' solitary celebration of Christmas as she catalogues her treasures, spreading out Alf's christening dress, scarf and jersey, mittens, stockings, and finally: "Embroidered with the pearls of tears, / Dyed with my anguish, stitched / With the dreadful threads of destiny and terror! / Oh, holy! This is the coronation robe / He wore to his sacrificial baptism!" (186). This passage, which has been condemned as both sentimental and sadistic,[12] is psychologically masterful, as the votary bears her pain through catechizing Alf into a baby Christ the King.

The arrival of a gypsy woman and her freezing child allows Brand to accomplish what pity keeps him from being able to do outright: "destroy / These last vestiges of [Agnes'] idolatry" (186). Agnes protests the "sacrilege" against her dead child, but then relents, agreeing to share Alf's clothes. Brand says to her as he said to his mother: "Share, Agnes – *share?*" (189). Taking Alf's cap from her dress, where she has worn it next to her heart, Agnes holds out to Brand the last earthly relic. "Willingly?" "Willingly" (190–91).

Agnes' giving her treasured remembrances of Alf to a gypsy child, the kin of Gerd, signals Gerd's victory over Agnes, the triumph of religious absolutism over human love; Agnes makes the leap of faith and conquers: "I have won the battle of the Will!" (191). Thanking Brand for his "guiding hand," Brand's disciple throws back his words: "On *you* now falls the burden / Of this 'All or Nothing'!" (192). Brand denies the impossibility of living his doctrine, promising to take Agnes away from her painful memories, but she reminds him: "Are you forgetting that the baptism / Of your calling binds you *here –* " (193). Agnes exits to die: "Thank you for *All*. Now I can sleep" (193).

Auden undoubtedly speaks for many readers in commenting that the effect of the scenes between Brand and Agnes is "to turn Brand into a self-torturing monster for whose sufferings we can feel pity but no sympathy"; Brand "has to drag Agnes after him" ("Genius and Apostle" 343). But Agnes insisted on going, and her destruction is the fulfillment of her original pledge: "I choose the night. Through the way of death" (126). The consummate female follower performs the consummate sacrifice, obliterating herself to satisfy her master's principles. She dies a Saint of the Will, her own as well as Brand's creation, their relation a relentless portrait of the hierarchical ideal famously summarized by Milton: "He for God only, she for God in him."

Brand must justify Agnes' death as he justified Alf's, and thus nothing becomes everything in the ultimate paradox of the fanatical mind: "My soul, be steadfast to the end! / . . . The loss of *All* brought everything to you" (194). But this theory of renunciation, like Brand's other theological principles, proves empty, and the denouement shows the hero in despair, doubting the rightness of his big, new church and missing his dead wife: "If only Agnes had lived, how different it had been! / She could see great things in small; she alone / Could free me from the pain of doubt, / Could marry earth and heaven for me, / As a tree roots itself in its own leaves" (202). Marrying earth and heaven is what Brand forbade Agnes to do; refusing the organic relation represented in the tree's growth, Brand demanded that she abandon the things of this world. Having renounced the joys of the earth, Brand now reclaims them, blaming Agnes for dying: "Oh, Agnes, how could you fail me so!" (206).

Brand's despair is temporarily eased by the arrival of Einar, *"pale and emaciated, dressed in black"* (216), a startling parody of Brand. A convert to fundamentalist pietism, the former advocate of earthly joy asks for news of that "young girl / Who held me in the toils of lust" (218). Einar dismisses Brand's proud exclamation that although Agnes died, she held unshakeable faith "in her God," with a bit of nonsense theologizing that out-Brands Brand: "Ah, only in Him. Then she is doomed!" (219). Consigning Agnes and Brand to the pit, the mad Einar is literature's consummate portrait of puritan self-righteousness: "I have thrashed my Adam's linen clean / Upon the river rocks of vigilance. / I am as unspotted as a perfect altar-cloth / Starched and laundered with the irons of prayer" (220).

Brand learns the wrong lesson from the passage of his double. Spurred on to apotheosis, he harangues his congregation from the church's steps like a Luther gone mad. Throwing the keys of the church into the fjord, he leads the people up to the mountains and the true church, whose "floor is the green earth, / Mountain, meadow, sea and fjord" (225). But Brand's new church lasts but a day. Hungry and exhausted, the people demand of their prophet when their victory will come and receive the answer of martyrdom: "The prize of victory shall be a crown / Of thorns round each man's and woman's head" (230). The village authorities convince the people to turn on their pastor, and although they are cowards and philistines, the Dean's parting summary judgment of Brand – "A bad son, a bad father, and a bad husband! Could you find a Christian worse than that?" (235) – rings true in missing the larger context.

The penultimate scene of *Brand* consists of a coda of the Brand/Agnes conflict that prepares for the hero's destruction in the Ice Church. Its heavenly chorus and female figure from on high recall the "Chorus Mysticus" and the appearance of Gretchen at the end of *Faust.* The "Choir Invisible" speaks to the despairing Brand: "Never, never will you be like Him / For of flesh are you created" (241). Brand thinks of his wife and son, whom he "exchanged for conflict and grief" (242), and his self-doubt summons the figure of Agnes. In bright light she confirms the choir's message: "All these horrid, harried visions / Are evoked by *three words* only" (244). While Gretchen leads Faust heavenward, away from the dross of earth, Agnes draws Brand down to the comfort of the body and the salvation of human love: "Brand, be kind! My flesh is warm. / Your arms are strong – hold me again – / Let us seek the sunlight and summer lands." Brand rejects Agnes' song of the earth, reaffirming his decision to let Alf die, and in her regretful homage to the joys of life, Agnes shows him his murderer's face: "And kill me too? Tear me / Bleeding from the trap? Flog me to death / With the scourge of sacrifice?" (245). Brand struggles to shake off the spirit his doubts have raised and remembering the bird in Gerd's taunting metaphor – "The priest flew off on the hawk's back" – he makes his last stubborn stand, identifying Agnes with the hawk and condemning her voice as "the spirit of compromise!" (246). Making her last on-cue appearance, the angel of the absolute enters with a rifle. Brand's only remaining parishioner, the mad Gerd welcomes Brand to icy, treeless Black Peak: "So you came to *my* church after all" (249).

But in the end, Brand's will is unable to banish Agnes, whose images return in his admission: "Oh, how I long, oh, how I yearn / For light and sun and gentleness, / . . . For the summer kingdoms of this life!" (249). The iron hero breaks down and experiences grace: "The crust of ice is breaking now – / I can weep – I can kneel – I can pray." But Brand has no time to live a changed man, for Gerd's shot at the hawk loosens an avalanche. Confusing the falling snow masses with the hawk, Gerd describes him growing larger and whiter until he becomes "white as any dove" (250). The allusion to the holy spirit prepares the play's last line; as he is crushed, Brand shouts out his great question – "Answer me, God, in the jaws of death: / Is there no salvation for the Will of Man?"

– and "A Voice" from above replies: "He is *deus caritatis!*" (250).
Ibsen used the Latin phrase, as he explained, because in modern
Church Latin, *caritas* is used "to express heavenly love, with the
idea of mercy included" (*LS* 58–59).[13] And thus the corrective
definition Brand gave to Agnes of her deity – "What the world
calls love I neither need / Nor know. I recognize the love of God;
/ That is not weak, or mild, but hard" (130) – is itself corrected as
the woman's god, "more loving father than stern taskmaster"
(159), declares himself the man's as well.

Ibsen insisted several times that *Brand* was not a play about
religion; "I could just have easily constructed the same syllogism,"
he wrote to Brandes, "about a sculptor or a politician as about a
priest" (*LS* 84). The synthesis of Ibsen's syllogism at the end of
Brand lies in the complementarity between womanly feeling and
masculine rigor dramatized in *The Pretenders*. Brand's opposition
of his-and-her deities corresponds to Haakon's division of the
world into masculine (vocational/superior) and feminine (per-
sonal/inferior) spheres. As the king's idealist notion of his calling
yields to the claim of human ties, Brand's demanding patriarch
gives way to Agnes' god of mercy and the "frozen tundras of the
law" melt in the "summer sun" (249). But in the history play,
Haakon experiences epiphany in time, and thus can possess both
love and the kingdom, while in the tragedy Brand must lose both,
destroyed in an ice church, a temple without congregants in a
world without people.

TROLL SEX AND PURE LOVE:
PEER GYNT'S MANICHEAN THEORY OF WOMAN

Brand made Ibsen famous throughout Scandinavia and brought
him a modest government writer's pension. Buoyed by his critical
success and delivered at last from financial worry, Ibsen under-
went his famous sartorial transformation, replacing his thread-
bare garments for the ultra-bourgeois costume he would wear to
the end of his life: a frock coat, waistcoat and trousers, and an
imposing top hat. He then wrote one of his wickedest plays, a
freewheeling realist–expressionist–phantasmagorical masterpiece
about a great rogue who owes much to his impeccably clad creator. Ibsen liked to call his works his "galskaper," his "devilry,"
"tricks," "follies." If he was the highminded Brand, he was also the

rascal Peer, about whom he discovered much, he wrote, "by analyzing myself" (*LS* 102).

Rolf Fjelde has comprehensively defined Peer Gynt in his speculation that in fashioning Brand, "Ibsen's mind must have played with the possibility of creating his counterpart, the man with no ruling passion, no calling, no commitment, the eternal opportunist, the mirror of surfaces, the charming, gifted, self-centered child who turns out finally to have neither center nor self" ("Foreword" *Peer Gynt* xiii–xiv). As he had done with Brand, Ibsen characterizes his contrary largely through his relations with women; the idealist denies his mother and destroys his wife, the opportunist neglects his mother and deserts the woman he loves. But while Brand errs on the side of principle, and Peer, of non-commitment, in matters of love Peer's absolutism matches Brand's. Like Agnes, Solveig, whose name suggests both "Sun Way" and "Sun Woman,"[14] is associated with warmth and light and represents human, temporal love; nowhere do Brand and Peer reveal themselves more clearly to be different sides of the same extremist coin than at the end of their antithetical lives when both the absolutist and the equivocator cry out for comfort to the woman whose love they have refused.

As Brand's intransigence toward his mother looks forward to his demand of Agnes, Peer's irresponsibility toward Aase anticipates his desertion of Solveig. The n'er-do-well has abandoned the family farm at its busiest season. But Peer is irresistible to Aase, whose attitude toward her son alternates between anger and admiration. Furious at Peer for brawling, Aase insists that he vanquish his adversaries; lecturing him on his tall tales, she is enthralled by them herself. Abandoned by the profligate Jon Gynt, who ran off after squandering the family's money, the grass widow and her son have formed a couple. The prized, well-loved male knows how to take advantage of his mother's weakness for him, and his attitude toward her is one of flirtatious condescension: "You pretty little mother, you / Every word you say is true; / So give us a happy smile – " (8).[15]

Peer charms Aase with his talent as raconteur of tall tales. The play opens with the well-known "Peer, you're lying!" (3) as Aase tries to stop her son's account of a magic reindeer, then demands to hear the story. Poetry is a kind of lying, and Norwegian, as is commonly noted, is a language that can make this point power-

fully; *dikt* means both poem and lie, *dikte* means both to compose
or write and to fabricate, dream, invent. In relating the reindeer
ride on Gjendin ridge, his embroidered version of a well-known
folktale, Peer is the folk artist carrying on and enriching oral
tradition. Peer's capacity to trick Aase is that of the poet, who can
make us suspend our disbelief for the time it takes to read or hear
the "lie." Aase's fury when she recognizes Peer's spiel as a version
of the old folktale spurs her to give, unwittingly, a mordant definition of the poet's craft: "Yes, give a lie a new disguise, / Twist it,
turn it out so fine / The bony carcass can't be seen / Spruced up
in the fancy dress" (7–8).

Peer's tales – new versions of old "lies" – set him above his
unimaginative, callow fellows, and it is with such a "lie" that Peer
comforts his mother in the celebrated scene of Aase's death.
Reversing their former roles, Peer drives the fantasy horse and
tells the marvellous tale, as his mother closes her eyes and becomes a rapt child in her son's boyhood bed. The veiled tenderness in Peer's prior teasing emerges as he persuades his mother
that the glimmering light she sees issues from Soria-Moria castle,
transformed into a pagan heaven of earthly delights equipped
with Christian trappings; unable to resist his own imagination,
Peer produces a reluctant gatekeeper in Saint Peter whom he
admonishes "you'll get yours today!" and plays God for the time it
takes to get his mother into heaven, as the saint's superior, "*in a
deep voice*," announces: "Mother Aase can come in free!" (89).

Peer's mother's gift to him – his love of make-believe – possesses
multiple meanings. To the extent that poet/liar Peer's fanciful
journey to Soria-Moria castle denies reality, it is escapist, but our
overwhelming sense of his evasionary strategy is that it soothes his
mother's death, and in so doing poet/creator Peer's invention
bears witness to the power and the compensatory value of the
poetic imagination. At the same time, it is a fine example of Keats'
notion of the poet's basic amorality; the delighted Peer laughs
aloud at his creation, not noticing that Aase has died while he was
spieling. Even in his tender leavetaking, Peer cannot resist pretending, stealing a kiss from his mother's corpse: "Here's thanks
for all of your days, / For the blows and the kisses I had – / But
give me back some little praise – / (*Presses his cheek to her mouth*.) /
There – that was thanks for the ride" (89). And having sung his
mother into heaven and had himself thanked for it, Peer departs

on his wanderer's life, leaving to someone else the task of burying her.

A condemned outlaw, Peer risks his life to see his mother, and both this action and the compassionate sleigh ride redeem, if only partially, his prior negligence. No such mitigating action tempers his treatment of Solveig, for he answers her freely given love with a rejection that remains irrevocable.

Solveig enters the play leading by the hand her younger sister Helga. Ibsen may owe this means of establishing Solveig's maternal tenderness to his admired Goethe, whose Gretchen tells Faust the pathetic story of the little sister to whom she was a mother. Like Faust with Gretchen, Peer loves at first sight Solveig's fair innocence; Gretchen, "past fourteen," comes from confession (*Faust* 91), and Solveig, "just confirmed," and thus about fifteen, comes from church, carrying her prayer book, as was the custom, in a kerchief (28).[16] Peer's "How fair! Who's ever seen one like this! / Eyes on her shoes and snow-white apron – !" (27) directly echoes Faust's "This girl is fair indeed! / No form like hers can I recall. / . . . Her downward glance in passing by / Deep in my heart is stamped" (*Faust* 90). But Solveig, however modest her glance, has noticed Peer, and although she follows her parents into the farmhouse, she soon exits to seek him out. "Aren't you the boy that wanted to dance?" (28). The dutiful daughter has a mind of her own.

Peer's courtship of Solveig is a counterpoint to the Bridegroom's difficulties in persuading the unhappy Ingrid to unlock the storehouse where she is hiding. The shy, whining boy pulling at his mother's sleeve – "Mother, she won't" (29) – contrasts with the assertively masculine Peer, who seizes Solveig by the wrist and plays the troll in a bravura performance whose bluff is revealed by the plea at its end: "I'll come to your bed at midnight, I will / . . . It's me, child! I'll drain off your blood in a cup; / And your little sister – I'll eat her up; / Because, you know – I'm a werewolf at night – / I'll bite you all over the loins and back – / (*Suddenly changes his tone and begs, as if in anguish.*) / Dance with me, Solveig!" (35–36). The frightened Solveig refuses, and Peer, feeling his status as pariah confirmed by this rejection, puts on a grandstand performance, responding to the bridegroom's plea for help with an audacious trick; Ingrid opens the door to the man she has always preferred, and Peer carries her off in the best

kindred spirits chant a troll love duet: "Black looks white, and vile looks fair / Great looks small, and foul looks pure" (53). The princess' call for her "bridal steed" is answered by an *"enormous pig [that] comes running in, with a rope end for a bridle and an old sack for a saddle."* While Peer carried Ingrid "like a pig," the simile takes on direct expressionist life as Peer swings up onto the pig's back and puts the Woman in Green, Ingrid's troll incarnation, in front of him. Where before he walked, now he rides, and on his way to the Dovre King's Hall, Peer proves himself apt for trolldom, transforming the pig into a prancer: "You can tell great men by the style of their mounts" (53). In the troll way of thinking, it's the car that makes the man.

As Peer's ride with the Woman in Green parodies his abduction of Ingrid, the Walpurgisnacht troll scene parodies its aftermath. Like the villagers who hunt him for absconding with Ingrid, the trolls greet Peer with threats of destruction for having lured their king's "most beautiful girl" (53). But the Troll King, who, like Old Hegstad, needs to marry off his daughter, will save Peer if he agrees to a grandiose version of "Hegstad farm, and a lot more too" (40): half the kingdom after the marriage and the other half after the king's demise.

The "princess and half the kingdom" is the hero's stock reward in the *eventyr*, in whose normal course the hero vanquishes the trolls that plague the king. The *eventyr*'s hero is the modest "Askelad," "Ash Lad," a male Cinderella; as Cinderella wins the prince because she possesses the passive virtues of exemplary femininity – goodness and beauty – Askelad wins the princess because he possesses the active virtues of exemplary masculinity: intelligence and enterprise. He triumphs through willing initiative and an ability to make much of small things. The princess in the stock "the princess and half the kingdom" has a shadowy existence outside the phrase, but by implication represents feminine perfection; the actively present princess of the *eventyr* is the ill-tempered, greedy, and physically grotesque troll princess who is destroyed through the hero's clever exertions (a favored technique is to make her so angry that she bursts). Peer, whose only resemblance to the fairy-tale hero is that he spends his time "loafing in the chimney corner / Home, and poking up the fire" (10) is a mock Askelad whose strength, as Aase says, "is all in his mouth" (43). And the trolls, instead of being the obstacles the hero must vanquish in order to win the-princess-and-half-the-kingdom, become the objects of the hero's quest as Peer falls in love with their princess and is promised the kingdom by their king. Once she enters the mountain, The Woman in Green takes on an ugliness that surpasses that of any troll princess as she becomes the pig indicated by her royal mount.

The troll novice eagerly agrees at the outset to "renounce day, deeds, the things of light," for Peer wants the easy victory: "If I can be king, there's nothing to that" (54). Continuing his daughter's lecture on troll culture, the king explains to his newly recruited son-in-law the essential differentiating characteristic of trolldom: "Among men, under the shining sky, / They say: 'Man, to yourself be true!' / While here, under our mountain roof, / We say: 'Troll, to yourself be – enough!'" (55). Refusing to consider the difference between self-realization and self-sufficiency, Peer submits to an initiation rite in which he eats and drinks food served by pig-headed trolls. He then must remove his "Christian dress," i.e., his clothes, and take on the trolls' essential physical trait, a tail. The trolls' tails, Logemann explains, link them "to the family of Old Nick himself" (*Commentary* 108), and the idea of putting one on shocks Peer at first – "Lay off! You think I've lost my mind?" – a momentary rebellion quickly quelled by the upstanding father of the bride: "You can't court my daughter with a smooth behind" (56).[21] A comic forked animal, the naked Peer relents – "Tie away!" (57) – and the king announces with great flourish the royal marriage festivities. But Peer, tail and all, still appreciates human women too much to view the entertainment with troll eyes, and his description of the dancing Woman in Green – a "sow in stockings" – and her accompanyist sister – a "bell cow strumming a catgut lyre" (58) – parodies of Solveig and Little Helga, forces the king to insist on the eye operation that will give Peer unhampered troll vision: "Then you'll realize your bride is beautiful, / And your eyesight will never again confuse / Her charms with pigs or musical cows" (59). Peer's hesitation, which corresponds to his refusal of Ingrid's offer of Hegstad farm, displays a few shreds of integrity: "But *this* – to know you can never be free" is "what I'll never put my consent in" (61). The troll king, like Old Hegstad, rails against this insult to the honor of his now pregnant daughter and hands Peer over to the troll children. Viciously attacked by the biting pack, Peer calls out to his mother, and as church bells ring out, the trolls, who like vampires can not withstand Christian symbols, flee shrieking.

Since Peer's refusal to agree to the ultimate criterion of trolldom proves that he possesses some remaining humanity, one can only conclude that his dreamwork cooperates in exonerating him. Similarly, like the eternal bad boy that he is, Peer calls out to the person on whose aid he knows he can always count – "Help, Mother, I'll die! (63)" – and thus makes Aase, one of literature's most unlikely representatives of feminine intercession for men's follies, into an agent of salvation.

In a coda to the great troll scene, the collapse of the mountain propels Peer to the bottom of his nightmare, where he meets the Great Boyg, the "Great Bender," an enormous and invisible troll. The taunting, ubiquitous Boyg traps Peer in slime and grey air: "Go roundabout, Peer! The heath is wide" (64). This hellish, ungraspable image of entrapment and defeat – "The great Boyg wins by all easy stages" (66) – has at his call a host of great-winged birds, troll harpies. Peer calls on Solveig to use her Christian magic: "The prayer book! Fling it straight in his eye!" (67). Another fairy-tale rescue takes place as churchbells ring out and the Great Boyg "dwindles to nothing," gasping out the reason for his defeat: "He was too strong. There were women behind him" (67). In Peer's wishful subconscious, Solveig's virgin power saves him from the biggest troll of all.

Waking up with a hangover and longing for the traditional herring remedy, Peer discovers Solveig hiding behind his hut. Her excuse for the visit is to bring the outlaw a food basket. Catching sight of her, Peer engages in his usual sexual bragging: "Know where I was last night? / The Troll Princess went after me like a bat" (68). "It's a good thing, then, that we rang the bells," replies the unimpressed Solveig before running away. Overjoyed that she cares, Peer gives the last pitiful treasure of the House of Gynt, a silver button, to Helga to take to his love. "Ask her not to forget me!" (68).

Solveig answers Peer's longing for her with great simplicity and a superb disregard for the world, arriving at his forest hut in the winter dusk, skimming over the snow on skis. The formerly shy girl who clung to her mother's skirts responds to Peer's stupefaction with a moving declaration of love: "Your call reached out in my sister's voice; / It came on the wind and in silences. / In your

10. Solveig (Linn Stokke) arriving at Peer's hut in the National Theatre's production of *Peer Gynt*, Oslo, 1985.

mother's words I felt it flame; / And it echoed out of my waking dreams. / The heavy nights, the empty days, / Kept calling me, telling me, 'Go where he goes'" (74–75). Unable to believe in Solveig's unthinkable act, Peer responds with a series of incredulous questions: "You did this for me? . . . You know the judgment read last spring? . . . You've heard the sentence?" (75). But what Solveig loves in Peer is the rebel who flaunts the good people who pursue him, the man Aase described as "like no one else" (43) and "above their like" (45). In choosing Peer, Solveig has given up the people she loves most for Peer ("Yes, for you alone; / You must be all to me, lover and friend"); disdained material comfort ("You think I cast off the ones I love / Just for some property you might have?'); and come to join the outlaw in a union of two kindred souls: "I asked my way here with each turn of the climb; / They said, 'Why go there?' I said, 'It's my home.'" (75). Solveig's explanation of why she left the valley, couched in stock Romantic dichotomous categories of valley and mountain, establishes her as a rebel whose "home" lies not "down there" but "up here," above law and convention: "Down there it was stifling, closed like a trap; / That was partly what drove me up. / But here, where the firs cut the sky like gems, / What stillness and song! Here I'm at home" (76).

But while Solveig has come to join Peer's outlaw life, his spontaneous expression of joy at having won her constitutes a refusal to take her: "If you can dare live in my hunter's house, / This ground will become a holy place" (76). Solveig's arrival found Peer fastening a bolt on his door "against trolls, and women and men" who "come with the dark," and in identifying Solveig as his protection against the "merciless goblin thoughts" that plague him (74), Peer damns his own sexual desire and denies hers; "Not too near! / Only to look at you! Oh, how pure and fair!" (76). Peer takes Solveig in his arms only to hold her at arms length: "These arms, Solveig, / Will hold your lovely, warm body from me!" Peer's guardian angel, Solveig is to act as the house icon against his baser nature as she threw the prayer book at the Boyg. While Solveig has renounced the valley for the mountain, Peer has fixed her as the feminine ideal of the valley world, Pure Woman, the angel in the hut.

Solveig enters Peer's cabin, but instead of warming her with his body, Peer leaves to hunt firewood to warm the abstraction at the end of a fairy tale: "My princess! At last, she's found and won! / Now my palace will rise on a true foundation!" (76). As Peer picks up his axe, *presto*, out of the dark woods appears the good princess' foil, the Woman in Green. "Good evening, Peer Lightfoot!" (77), calls the troll princess. Peer's vision of his sexual past is a puritan's delight with its fallen woman – the Woman in Green – her illegitimate child – the limping Ugly Brat – and the demon drink – a flask of beer. Trolls grow quickly, and the nightmare offspring is already a toddler. "Give Daddy a drink; he suffers from thirst," taunts the Woman, who explains to Peer the symbolic value of their son's deformity: ". . . he's lame / In his leg as you're lame in your mind" (78). Peer curses the "troll snout" – "Get away, you witch!" – but then allows the sexual, and thus dirtied woman to provide him with an obstacle to making love to the pure woman waiting in his hut: "I'll squint through the door and spy on you both; / And if you sit with your girl by the fire – / And start to caress – and put off your clothes – / I'll slip in between and take my share" (79). Transforming him into Philosopher Troll, Peer produces the Boyg, and Hamlet-like, turns his unwillingness to make love to Solveig into a moral issue: "Roundabout, lad! There's just no way / Straight through to her – no, not for you / . . . / Repentance? It could run on for years" (80). The philandering playboy who sneered at pietism summons the weight of his guilty sexual past: "Ingrid! And the three who danced on that crest! / Would they appear too?" (81). In Peer's puritan conscience, sexual desire belongs to devil trolldom: "Go in after this? So foul and coarse? / Go in, with all this odor of troll?" Peer would remove Solveig from the act of love, from the "mud and filth" of the seter girls. His vulgar metaphor – "If you want a field green, keep it free of your heel" (80) – supposes that an unvirgin Solveig would be valueless. Peer refuses the sexually desiring Solveig whose life was "cut short" by his absence, who passed "heavy nights and empty days" longing for him (74–75). For Peer, women are either the "holy and pure" Solveig or the sexual "witch" the Woman in Green, the good princess or the bad, the virgin or the temptress, only Mary or only Eve.[22]

Peer's refusal of Solveig's sexuality reflects his refusal to become an adult man. It is easier to have an idea of Solveig, to "idealize" her, than to confront the full humanity of this intrepid girl. "Wait, I'll help you," she begs. "We'll share to the full." "No,"

he commands her; "stay where you are!" (81). But although Peer
refuses to love Solveig, he demands that she love him in her mind.
Like a princess under a spell, Solveig must lie dormant until she is
set in motion by the return of her prince: "Be patient, my sweet;
/ Far or near – you must wait" (81).

Peer's evasion of erotic love, like Sigurd's in *The Vikings at
Helgeland*, is an evasion of self; his refusal to go "straight through"
to Solveig signals Peer's whole (non)adult life of "roundabout"
behavior that constitutes his post-Solveig existence. We meet him
thirty years later, a self-made, middle-aged millionaire spouting
the troll motto to his business associates: "What should a man be?
/ I say *himself* and nothing more. / All for *himself* and *his*!" (92).
Relating his youthful love life in aggrandizing troll language, he
transforms the bridestealing into "a trap that Cupid laid," himself
into "a gay and salty dog," and Ingrid/Woman in Green into "the
lady that I coveted – / She was born of royal blood" (92–93).

Desert sheik Peer's male vanity is deflated by dancing girl
Anitra, the love interest of his middle years. Having chanced on
the necessary trappings, Peer has naturally turned prophet, but of
a non-ascetic sort, and like the hero-lover of the seter girls, he is
the god of multiple idolatrous women. Reclining on cushions
before a company of dancing girls, the master of the troll art of
accommodation changes his taste to fit the available woman. The
grubby charms of Peer's handmaiden, whose feet "are not entirely
clean; / Same with the arms; especially the one" (that she uses
for toilet purposes), constitute "one morsel of her appeal" (119).
When Anitra explains that she has no soul, Peer measures her
brain case and decides that a small soul will do nicely. Anitra,
however, prefers the opal on Peer's turban, a choice that so
enraptures him that he is moved to cite Western literature's most
spiritual definition of womanhood: "Anitra! Child! Eve's own
daughter! / Like a magnet drawing me – for I'm a man; / And just
as he said, that well-known writer: / '*Das Ewig-Weibliche zieht uns
an!*'" (120). In Peer's most famous misquotation, Goethe's "The
eternal feminine draws us upward" has been massacred to read
"The eternal feminine leads us on." For Peer, the daughters of Eve
can be counted on to be vacuous, vain, child-like, and sexy.[23]

Galatea/Anitra, who plays to perfection the grateful pupil and
devoted votary – "Lord, from your lips diversion flows / Like
beads of honey" (123) – receives a lesson on male–female rela-

tions from her master: "You must be mine, and mine alone. / I'll be always there to guard / Your charms like a jeweled cameo" (125). Male protectorship, however, is not eternal; Peer instructs Anitra on what he has already put into practice with Solveig: "If we should part, then life is over – / *Nota bene*, that is, for *you!*" (125–26). In a burlesque version of Brand's lecture to Agnes on the eternal feminine, masterful male Peer explains to Anitra her dual function as vessel of his ardor and distraction from his cares: "I want your every inch and fiber / Drained of will and, utterly / Past resistance, filled with me. / Your nest of midnight hair, your skin, / Everything lovely one could name, / Will, like the gardens of Babylon, / Beckon me to my sultan's realm" (126). Anticipating Torvald Helmer of *A Doll House*, Peer concludes with a comment to his natural inferior on the value of stupidity in women: "So it's lucky, after all, / You've kept your head so vacuous. / Those who entertain a soul / Get swallowed in self-consciousness" (126).

Peer's assumptions about women turn out to be dangerously superficial. "Little one," Peer criticizes his acolyte, "You, like other girls, appraise / Only the surfaces of great men" (123). But Anitra has appreciated the prophet from the beginning, for if she lacks a soul, she has a brain. And unlike that of her predecessors in abduction, Anitra's interest in Peer is purely temporary and strictly mercantile; anticipating the tone and technique of Mae West, she cajoles: "You're sweating, prophet; I'm afraid you'll melt – / Throw me that heavy bag at your belt" (129). Peer's careful restriction of his worshippers to women – "Men, my child, are a slippery batch" (118) – proves insufficient protection as the experienced fleecer, slapping him sharply with her riding whip, gallops away with the booty, proving into the bargain that the slave is as good an ironist as her master: "Anitra obeys the prophet! Farewell!" (130).

In the typical stocktaking that follows, Peer advances Boyg philosophy – "The gist of the art is to grope in mist" – and blames his difficulties on female nature: "And the women – pah, they're a scrubby lot!" (133). But Peer has not quite forgotten the woman he left behind, and as if in answer to his verdict on Eve's daughters, a tableau appears, Ibsen wrote Grieg, "like a distant dream picture" (*LS* 146), of Solveig, spinning in the sunshine and singing the poem now known as "Solveig's Song": "The winter may pass, and the spring disappear, / And next summer too, and the whole of the year – / But one day you'll come, I know that you will; / Then, as I promised, I'll wait for you still" (133).

Peer's vision of the faithful, spinning Solveig inevitably recalls her weaving, waiting prototype, Homer's Penelope. But Peer's dream woman shares only sewing with the proud and broken-hearted Penelope, who longs for her husband, outwits his rivals, and grows old alone and miserable. The Solveig of Peer's vision has not even missed the man the earlier Solveig loved. It does not matter to this Solveig whether Peer is absent or present, not even whether he is dead or alive. The girl of acts one through three, who was torn between her family and her lover and who one fine day put on her skis to join him, has disappeared. The earlier Solveig was a human being, but the Solveig of "Solveig's Song" is pure symbol. In Peer's Manichean theory of woman, considera-tion of the "Eternal Feminine who leads us on" naturally leads to thoughts of the "Eternal Feminine who leads us upward," Peer's antidote to Anitra.

As Peer approaches the end of his life, Solveig haunts him to a short-lived epiphany. In the asylum (where Aase prophesied he would end), he wildly recalls Solveig's prayer book as the madmen crown him "Emperor of Self." In the mental landscape of act five, "Peer's Homecoming," the ragged old man at Hegstad farm puts up for metaphorical auction "One dream of a silver-clasped book" (173). In the celebrated "onion scene," with Solveig's hut in the background, Peer picks wild onions and ponders his life. Slowly peeling an onion, he arrives at his coreless career: "Shouldn't it give up its kernel soon? / Damned if it does! To the innermost filler, / It's nothing but layers" (177). Hearing Solveig singing from within the hut, Peer, "*hushed and deathly pale,*" confronts his error: "Oh, life – ! No second chance to play! / Oh, dread – ! *Here's* where my empire lay!" Refusing Solveig, Peer has not developed what Solveig loved in him, the individual self that set him apart, the core that made him "Peer." Terrified by his realization, the old Peer runs away down the same forest path the young Peer took long ago.

Peer stops running on a charred and misty moor, where he contemplates the meretricious empire of his life. In the burned, blurred landscape, the tormented old man hears his dead mother calling: "Peer, where's the castle? / You've turned the wrong way" (181). A reminder of his irresponsibility and failure, Aase's voice, like Solveig's, makes Peer run harder away from himself. But he is stopped by the Button-Moulder, who wields a giant casting ladle and draws the moral conclusion of Peer's onion lesson: Peer's failure to be himself consigns him to be melted down: "Now *you* were planned as a shining button / On the vest of the world, but your loop gave way; / So you'll have to go into the rubbish carton / And merge with the masses, as people say" (185). Peer wasted his talents, his imagination, his difference: "Yourself is just what you've never been" (186).

Obtaining a reprieve to prove that he has been himself all his life, Peer runs now as hard as he can and meets with a person eminently qualified to judge, the Troll King. The king receives Peer's request with hurt shock, for Peer has been so good a troll that he is a model in the Ronde. Forced to abandon his claim of self-realization, Peer gains another reprieve, this time to demonstrate that he has been wicked enough to go to hell. Again he meets the person most qualified to judge, in the person of the Lean One, Ibsen's busy Devil, unimpressed by his confessions of slave-trading and idol-shipping: "I wish you'd tell / Me who's going to waste expensive fuel, / In times like these, on such poppycock?" (201). Peer beats the devil momentarily by sending him off to the Cape of Good Hope, but he knows his reckoning is near.

Desperate, Peer grasps at saving himself through the testimony of the person he has wronged most. Running toward the hut, Peer throws himself down before Solveig, crying "Lay judgment on a sinner's head! . . . Cry out how sinfully I've gone astray!" But this most undemanding of women, now blind, gropes for Peer to embrace him, expressing deep gratitude to the man who abandoned her: "You've made my whole life a beautiful song. Bless you now that you've come at last!" (207–8). Since this exoneration deprives Peer of the confirmation of sin he needs to save him from the casting ladle, the ever versatile rogue grasps at the argument that he has been himself all his life: "Tell me where / Peer Gynt has been this many a year? . . . With his destiny on him, just / As when he first sprang from the mind of God!" (208). But he rejects in consternation her reply – "In my faith, in my hope, and in my love" – because it reaffirms his erotic cowardice: "What are you saying – ? Don't play with words! / To the boy inside, you are the mother."[24] The compliant Solveig now defines her love not only as strictly maternal, but as that of the Mother/Intercessor, Mary: "I am, yes – but who is his father? / It's He who grants the prayers of the mother." A light breaks over Peer, who cries out: "My mother, my wife! You innocent woman – ! / O, hide me, hide me inside!" (209).[25] Clinging to Solveig, Peer buries his face in her lap as the sun rises and his wife/mother sings her soothing lullaby: "Sleep, my dear, my dearest boy, / Here in my arms! I'll watch over thee – / The boy has sat on his mother's lap. / In play, they've used their life's day up. / The boy's been safe at his mother's breast / His whole life's day. May his life be blessed!" (209).

This famous reunion has earned for Solveig a high place in literary womanhood, "the quintessence of the ideal woman."[26] To interpret Solveig in this way is to read her as a modern version of the redemptive woman of European Romanticism, "a new variety of Gretchen" (Lavrin, *Ibsen* 57). But while Ibsen drew directly on Goethe's heroine for the Solveig of acts one through three, Peer's crime against Solveig is the opposite of Faust's against Gretchen, for while Faust seduces Gretchen, Peer refuses Solveig sexually. Faust's love for Gretchen includes passion, while for Peer there exist only *sexus* or *caritas*. In a persuasive argument that *Peer Gynt* is Ibsen's *Anti-Faust*, Patricia Merivale has noted that Peer "needs both Solveig and Ingrid to provide what Faust's Gretchen combines into one figure: Solveig is the pure and later the redemptive Gretchen . . . [while] Ingrid is the sensual part of Gretchen, the fallen woman and sexual being" ("Peer Gynt" 129).

If Faust can be saved because his striving life warrants it, Peer, who merits the casting ladle, demands to be saved by someone else. In comparing Peer to the conventional Romantic hero, Brian Downs has pointed out that Faust, Byron's Don Juan, and Schiller's William Tell "enjoy their creators' moral support much more powerfully than Peer, whose career is, at best, followed with good-humored, half-sardonic amusement, generally with impassibility and never with unmistakable benevolence" (*Six Plays* 96). And to examine Romanticism's paradigm of the questing hero/redemptive bride is to see how ill Peer and Solveig fit it; M.H. Abrams has distilled the pattern from Novalis' romances:

an educational journey in quest of a feminine other, whose mysterious attraction compels the protagonist to abandon his childhood sweetheart . . . to wander through alien lands on a way that rounds imperceptibly back to home and family, but with an access of insight (the product of his experience en route) which enables him to recognize, in the girl he has left behind, the elusive female figure who has all along been the object of his longing and his quest. (*Natural Supernaturalism* 246)

Unlike the traditional Romantic protagonist, Peer does not quest, but merely travels, his journey remaining non-educational to the end as he continues to resist his brief moments of recognition. The meeting with Solveig constitutes an anti-consummation as Peer adamantly rejects the beloved's love. The opposite of the bride who resolves the dramatic conflict, Solveig is a *deus ex machina* who puts an end to conflict, a miracle worker who vanquishes the trolls at sunrise and saves Peer from his kernelless self. In creating a Solveig who exonerates him from the great sin of his life – the one he committed against her and against himself – the adroit Peer escapes both the hell he claims is preferable to the mediocrity of the casting ladle and the ladle as well; in Solveig's assurance that his self has remained intact in her safekeeping, Peer is able to avoid the truth and to take, as usual, what could have been for what is. A last-minute Maryologist, Peer creates a Solveig whose intercession with the Father allows him to dispense with self-examination and save him from the Lean One.

The ending of *Peer Gynt*, like that of *Brand*, leaves us with a striking image of its protagonist's essential character; the man of principle perseveres in his quest as he is crushed by an avalanche, and the great evader dies in hiding, burying his face in a woman's lap. It is sometimes claimed that Ibsen has given Peer more than he deserves in a conciliatory ending that fits uneasily with what has preceded it. And yet that hardminded existentialist the Button Moulder, for whom only acts matter, is waiting; he has interrupted Solveig's song to warn: "We'll meet at the final crossroads, Peer; / And *then* we'll see – I won't say any more" (209). Moreover, to have made Peer confront his life would have been to force him *in extremis* into the tragic mold, and we know him too well to believe in such a transformation. Although Ibsen's eternal little boy running home to mother/wife, will, like other mortals, have to face the Button Moulder in the end, meanwhile, his creator rounds his life with a sleep in the all-forgiving lap of a fantasy woman.

Ibsen would be harder on his later male characters' erotic failures; Peer's refusal of Solveig looks forward to similar evasions in *Rosmersholm, Little Eyolf, John Gabriel Borkman,* and *When We Dead*

Awaken, in which the erotic life is also emblematic of the whole life.

JULIAN'S "PURE WOMAN": A NOTE ON *EMPEROR AND GALILEAN*

Although the two women characters of *Emperor and Galilean*, the final play of what is sometimes called Ibsen's "Epic Quartet," have minor roles, they illustrate in a conspicuous way what would now become for Ibsen an essential, preoccupying subject: man's refusal of woman's full humanity, his objectification of her into an idea. Central to *Peer Gynt*, the male reification of women into notions of Woman will be crucial to all the plays that followed *Emperor and Galilean*, which provides us with a stark parable of such transformations.

Sickened by the corruption within both ruling Christianity and a surviving paganism, *Emperor and Galilean*'s protagonist Julian envisions a new world order in which he and his half-brother Gallus will govern, respectively, the spiritual and temporal realms. He determines that his empire demands what Moses, Alexander, and Christ lacked, a perfect female consort, the "pure woman" incarnate with whom he can found a new race "in beauty and harmony" and thus establish "the empire of the spirit" (4:254). When the emperor Constantius has the powerful Gallus murdered and names Julian his heir apparent, he also hands over to the new Caesar his sister Helena, whom Julian ecstatically receives as the "pure woman." Helena, however, despises both her slight, bookish husband, and her role, longing instead for her dead lover Gallus, a virile man of action and the model of classical male beauty. Returning home after a long absence, Julian exclaims on the dark circles around his wife's eyes; her explanation – "sleepless nights and worrying about you; fervent prayers to the Blessed One on the Cross" (272) – is grotesquely parodied in the death speech she utters after having eaten poisoned fruit. Pushing her monkish husband away in disgust, she calls out, "Oh, my Gallus . . . How proudly your thick hair curls round your neck," and laughingly derides the philosopher: "Now he's going to look into things again – ink on his fingers; dust from his books in his hair, – unwashed; ugh, ugh, how he stinks" (290). Crying out for her "fine suntanned barbarian," Helena mocks her saintly husband: "Women he cannot conquer. How I loathe this virtuous impotence." Mad with pain, she reverses her allegiance, and in a Gothic mingling of sexuality and Christian fervor dies glorying in the "sweet secret" that she has spent her nights in the oratory making love with Julian "in the shape of Thy servant," a priest, who has gotten her with child "in the darkness, in the air, in the concealing clouds of incense" (291). Helena's sexuality savagely and obviously destroys her husband's notion of her as "pure woman," an identity made more ironic by her afterlife; useful to the corrupt priests, she is made a martyred saint, her tomb a shrine for thousands.

The notion of the "pure woman" is exploded in the opposite way through Helena's foil Macrina, an etherealized Agnes who belongs to the group of Christians the apostate Emperor Julian persecutes. Julian greets Macrina's traditional Christian justification for her refusal of sexual love – "My lord, I have renounced life that I may truly live" – with a denunciation of her "delusions": "You sigh for what lies beyond, and which you know nothing about for certain; you mortify the flesh; you repress all human desires. Yet this may be vanity like anything else" (416). Macrina is the "pure woman" only because she has become dead to life, a condition which makes it impossible for her to be Julian's, or anyone else's earthly partner.

Julian's notion of the "pure woman," an illustration of the absolutism that makes him attempt to be a perfect Christian and then a perfect Anti-Christian, looks backward to Brand's and Peer's "eternal feminine" and forward to other self-serving identities that Ibsen's later male theorists force on women: Bernick's and Rørlund's "servant" (*Pillars of Society*), Torvald's and Pastor Manders' "wife and mother" (*A Doll House* and *Ghosts*), Dr. Stockmann's "housewife" (*An Enemy of the People*), Hjalmar's "virgin bride" (*The Wild Duck*), Rosmer's "sacrificial woman" (*Rosmersholm*), Dr. Wangel's "weak vessel" (*The Lady from the Sea*), the Tesmans' "wife of a great man" (*Hedda Gabler*), Solness' "rejuvenation" (*The Master Builder*), Allmers' "mother of our child" (*Little Eyolf*), Borkman's "emotional female" (*John Gabriel Borkman*), Rubek's "inspiration" (*When We Dead Awaken*). These reductionist categorizations of women prove to be as foolish and false as Julian's reification of Helena, whose brutal exposure of her husband's error prefigures the failures to follow.[27]

CHAPTER 5

The poetry of feminism

Peer Gynt is coming home again after his long trip. But Solveig is not exactly the same. She is bored to death in the seter hut and getting tired of waiting. And when Peer arrives, she does not like him as much as she did before.

Camilla Collett, "Letter to Mrs. Laura Kieler" [essay] (*Works* 3:415)

THE *DOLL HOUSE* BACKLASH

A Doll House is no more about women's rights than Shakespeare's *Richard II* is about the divine right of kings, or *Ghosts* about syphilis, or *An Enemy of the People* about public hygiene. Its theme is the need of every individual to find out the kind of person he or she really is and to strive to become that person (M 457).

As strange as it may seem to the uninitiated, it is standard procedure in Ibsen criticism to save the author of *A Doll House* from the contamination of feminism. It is customary to cite a statement the dramatist made on May 26, 1898, at a seventieth-birthday banquet given in his honor by the Norwegian Women's Rights League: "I thank you for the toast, but must disclaim the honor of having consciously worked for the women's rights movement... True enough, it is desirable to solve the woman problem, along with all the others; but that has not been the whole purpose. My task has been the description of humanity" (*LS* 337). Ibsen specialists like to take this disavowal as a precise reference to the dramatist's purpose in writing *A Doll House* twenty years earlier, his "original intention," in Maurice Valency's phrase (*The Flower and the Castle* 151). Meyer urges all reviewers of *Doll House* revivals to learn Ibsen's speech by heart (M 774). James McFarlane, the editor of *The Oxford Ibsen*, the standard English edition of Ibsen's complete works, excludes the subject of feminism from the historical and critical material on *A Doll House*, but includes Ibsen's speech (*OI* 5:456).

Whatever propaganda feminists may have made of *A Doll House*, Ibsen, it is argued, never meant to write a play about the topical subject of women's rights; Nora's conflict represents something other than, or something more than, woman's. In an article commemorating the half-century of Ibsen's death, in 1957, R.M. Adams explained: "*A Doll House* represents a woman imbued with the idea of becoming a person, but it proposes nothing categorical about women becoming people; in fact, its real theme has nothing to do with the sexes."[1] Over twenty years later, after feminism had resurfaced as an international movement, Einar Haugen, the doyen of American Scandinavian studies, insisted that "Ibsen's Nora is not just a woman arguing for female liberation; she is much more. She embodies the comedy as well as the tragedy of modern life."[2]

The notion that Ibsen's objective in *A Doll House* was non-feminist or suprafeminist has become so widespread that even feminist critics feel obliged to mention it. Elaine Hoffman Baruch, in her authoritative "Ibsen's *Doll House*: A Myth for Our Time," terms the drama "the feminist play *par excellence*" and at the same time refers to "the speech in which [Ibsen] denied being a feminist in *A Doll House*" (374; 387). Miriam Schneir includes the last scene of the play in her anthology *Feminism: The Essential Historical Writings*, explaining its presence there as justifiable "whatever [Ibsen's] intention and in spite of his speech."[3]

Critics who deny that *A Doll House* is a feminist play often present their work as part of a corrective effort to rescue Ibsen from an erroneous reputation as a writer of thesis plays, a wrongheaded notion usually blamed on Shaw, who, it is claimed, mistakenly saw Ibsen as the nineteenth century's greatest iconoclast and offered that misreading to the public as *The Quintessence of Ibsenism*. Ibsen, it is now fashionable to explain, did not stoop to "issues." He was a poet of the truth of the human soul. That Nora's doll house and exit from it have long been principal international symbols for women's issues is irrelevant to the essential meaning of *A Doll House*, a play, in Richard Gilman's phrase, "pitched beyond sexual difference."[4] Ibsen, explains Robert Brustein, "was completely indifferent to [the woman question] except as a metaphor for individual freedom."[5] Koht authoritatively summarizes

A Doll House's relation to feminism: "Little by little the topical controversy died away; what remained was the work of art, with its demand for truth in every human relation" (K 323). And thus it turns out that the *Uncle Tom's Cabin* of the women's rights movement is not really about women at all. "Fiddle-faddle," pronounced R.M. Adams (416), dismissing feminist claims for the play. Like angels, Nora has no sex. Ibsen meant her to be Everyman.[6]

The demon in the house

The *a priori* dismissal of women's oppression as the subject of *A Doll House* insists that in Ibsen's timeless world of Everyman, questions of gender can only be tedious intrusions. But for over a hundred years, in another kind of backlash entirely, Nora has been under siege as exhibiting the most perfidious characteristics of her sex; the original outcry of the 1880s is swollen now to a mighty chorus of blame. Ibsen's protagonist is denounced as an irrational and frivolous narcissist; an "abnormal" woman, a "hysteric"; a vain egotist who abandons her own children. The proponents of the last view treat Nora as a kind of bourgeois Medea, whose cruelty Ibsen tailored down to fit the framed, domestic world of realist drama.

When Betty Hennings, the first Nora, slammed the door in Copenhagen's Royal Theatre on December 21, 1879, her contemporaries were not, in what we have come to identify as the usual Victorian way, "shocked"; they were deeply shaken. *A Doll House* was not received as a "play" but as so real that Betty Hennings, identified in the public mind with the woman she played, became *the* "Ibsen Woman." Gosse reported: "All Scandinavia rang with Nora's 'declaration of independence.' People left the theatre, night after night, pale with excitement, arguing, quarrelling, challenging" (A 13:132–33).

From his home in Munich, Ibsen wrote to his publisher: "*A Doll House* has excited as much controversy [in Germany] as at home. People have taken sides passionately" (*H* 17:398). Somerset Maugham's Heidelberg professor in *Of Human Bondage* is a barometer of German burgher outrage; he would prefer his daughters "lying dead" at his feet to "listening to the garbage of that shameless fellow."[7] The first German Nora refused to play the ending on the grounds that she would never leave *her* children. Ibsen held out as best he could, but in order to have the play put on, he agreed to an alternative ending, insisting on writing it himself in order to avoid what he called a "barbarous outrage" (*LS* 183).[8] But the new "happy ending" of *A Doll House* is less than happy; when Torvald pulls Nora to the doorway of the children's bedroom, she sinks to the floor and cries: "Oh, this is a sin against myself, but I cannot leave them" (*OI* 5:288).

Ibsen's grudging conciliatory effort went unappreciated. A new German version of the play appeared, in which in a new, fourth act, added to Ibsen's three, the penitent Nora returns with a baby Helmer in her arms. In answer to her plea for forgiveness, Torvald produces an enormous bag of macaroons and pops one in her mouth. She chews, swallows, and pronounces "The Miracle" to a slow curtain.

The first performance of *A Doll House* in English, in Milwaukee, Wisconsin (June 2 and 3, 1882), was an equally sentimental, if less silly, emasculation. Entitled *The Child Wife*, the melodrama was billed as "An Emotional Domestic Drama – Heroic Wifely Devotion Pictured in Strong Relief." Unlike the original Torvald, this Nora's husband appreciates his wife's forgery to save his life, they happily reconcile, and Nora stays home.[9]

The most notorious of the *Doll House* bowdlerizations was English playwright Henry Arthur Jones' *Breaking A Butterfly*, performed in London in 1886. Harley Granville-Barker called his account of it "*A Doll House* with Ibsen left out": "Torvald-Humphrey behaves like the pasteboard hero of Nora's doll-house dream; he *does* strike his chest and say, 'I am the guilty one.' And Nora-Flora cries that she is a poor weak foolish girl, 'no wife for a man like you. You are a thousand times too good for me,' and never wakes up and walks out of her doll's house at all."[10]

It took ten years for the real *A Doll House* to reach British shores, but finally on June 7, 1889, in the seedy but propitiously named Novelty Theatre, brilliant Janet Achurch made theatrical and social history as Nora. Ibsen exploded on the English stage like an alien rocket. The witty title of Granville-Barker's essay "The Coming Of Ibsen," suggesting the "coming of doom," perfectly characterizes the apocalyptic effect of *A Doll House* on the English Victorian mind. Ibsen was accused not merely of advocating the destruction of the family, and with it, morality itself, but of a kind

and the Castle 151–52). Valency's reading conforms to the diagnosis of the turn-of-the-century European physicians, male students of "female hysteria," for whom Nora was a favorite example. According to Charcot disciple Dr. Robert Geyer, in his 1902 *Etude médico-psychologique sur le théâtre d'Ibsen*, quoted approvingly by Evert Sprinchorn in a 1980 essay, there can be no doubt of Nora's diagnosis: "definitely the hysterical type, who lies pathologically, suppresses her emotions, and suffers from bad traits inherited from her father."[19] Carol Tufts has recently used a report of an American Psychiatric Association task force to show how Ibsen went "far beyond the issue of women's rights" to write a play about a woman driven by narcissism.[20]

Much has been made of Nora's relationship with Doctor Rank, a sure proof, it is argued, of her dishonesty. In 1891, Nora was deemed a "heartless flirt up to the point of endeavoring to extract money from a friend of the family; her conversation, moreover, with this friend is of an equivocal and prurient character" (Crawford, "The Ibsen Question" 732). A hundred years later, in 1980, Nora is still the sexual tease as she "flirts cruelly with Dr. Rank and toys with his deep affection for her, drawing him on to find out how strong her hold over him actually is" (Sprinchorn, "Actors" 124).

Nora's detractors have often been her husband's defenders. Determined to rescue Nora and Torvald from "the campaign for the liberation of women" so that they "become vivid and disturbingly real," Sprinchorn pleads: "[Torvald] has given Nora all the material things and all the sexual attention that any young wife could reasonably desire. He loves beautiful things, and not least his pretty wife . . . And since he is fundamentally an aesthete he tends to treat Nora as a pretty object" ("Actors" 121). Nora is incapable of appreciating Torvald because she "is not a normal woman. She is compulsive, highly imaginative, and very much inclined to go to extremes." And because Nora has earned the money to save her husband's life, it is Torvald who is really "the doll" and "the wife in the family" although he "has regarded himself as the breadwinner . . . the main support of his wife and children, as any decent husband would like to regard himself" (122).[21] In another defense, John Chamberlain argues that Torvald deserves our sympathy because he is no "mere common or garden chauvinist."[22] Ibsen is never tiresomely "relevant" except for those who prefer to read *A Doll House* as "melodrama." If Nora were less the actress Weigand has proven her to be, "the woman in her might observe what the embarrassingly naive feminist overlooks or ignores, namely the indications that Torvald, for all his faults, is taking her at least as seriously as he can – and perhaps even as seriously as she deserves" (85).

All female or no woman at all, Nora loses either way, qualifying neither as a heroine nor as a spokeswoman for feminism. Her famous exit embodies only "the latest and shallowest notion of emancipated womanhood, abandoning her family to go out into the world in search of 'her true identity.' "[23] And in any case, it is only naive Nora who believes she might make an independent life for herself; the play's audience, argues a 1970 essayist in *College English*, "can see most clearly how Nora is exchanging a practical doll's role for an impractical one."[24] Austin Quigley chides: "The process of social moulding is unavoidable. Nora is exiting through a door that can only lead her back to the problem she wishes to escape. And there is much in the play that might make us wonder whether it would be a good thing to avoid such moulding even if one could."[25]

In the first heady days of *A Doll House*, Nora was rendered powerless by substituted denouements and sequels which sent her home to her husband. Bowdlerization, of course, has passed out of fashion, and Nora's twentieth-century critics take the superior position that all the fuss was unnecessary since Nora's deficiences destroy her claim for authenticity. And yet in the twentieth-century case against Nora, whether she is judged childish, neurotic, or unprincipled, and whether her accuser's tone is one of witty derision, clinical sobriety, or moral earnestness, the purpose behind the verdict remains that of Nora's frightened contemporaries: to destroy her credibility and power as a representative of women. The demon in the house, the modern "half-woman" Strindberg complained about in the preface to *Miss Julie*, who, now that she has "been brought out into the open, has taken the stage, and is making a noise about herself,"[26] must be silenced, her heretical forces destroyed, so that *A Doll House* can emerge a safe classic, rescued from feminism, and Ibsen can assume his place in the pantheon of true artists, unsullied by the "woman question" and the topical taint of history.

Bowdlerization, however, is not quite dead. In 1976, *An Anthol-*

ogy of Norwegian Literature appeared, a joint effort of the University
of Cambridge and University College, London.[27] Claiming to be a
"full and representative anthology of Norwegian literature" (xi),
the book substitutes another new ending for *A Doll House.* Here is
Ibsen's:

HELMER: But I'll believe. Tell me! Transform ourselves to the point that
— ?
NORA: That our living together could be a true marriage. (*She goes down
the hall.*)
HELMER (*sinks down on a chair by the door, face buried in his hands.*) Nora!
Nora! (*Looking about and rising.*) Empty. She's gone. (*A sudden hope
leaps in him.*) The greatest miracle — ? (*From below, the sound of a door
slamming shut.*) (196)

Here is the ending in *An Anthology of Norwegian Literature*:

HELMER: But I'll believe. Tell me! Transform ourselves to the point
that — ?
NORA: That our living together could be a true marriage. (*She goes down
the hall.*)
HELMER: Nora. She's gone.
NORA: The miracle. (1:214)

Are we meant to believe that Nora, lingering in the hallway,
expresses in her curtain line a hope that Torvald will experience
the transformation that will save the Helmer marriage? In any
case, the editors have purged the offending door slam, and, as in
earlier "improvements" of Ibsen's ending, pushed Nora back in
the doll house.

Critical reasoning and her master's voice

Universalist readers of *A Doll House* make the familiar claim that
the work in question can be no more about women than men
because the interests of both are the same "human" ones; sex is
irrelevant, and thus gender non-existent, in the literary search for
the self, which transcends and obliterates mere sexual and social
determinations. Faced with a drama whose protagonist rejects the
non-self she defines as a "doll" and describes as the plaything of
her father and husband, we must be cautious not to let feminism,
the proper concern of pamphlets, or thesis plays, perhaps, get in
the way of art. Nora's drama can be poetry only if it goes "beyond"
feminism.

The first point to make here is that this argument is an example of begging the question: the overwhelmingly deductive reasoning, while never laid out, is that since true art is not polemical and thus cannot be feminist, and since *A Doll House* is true art, then *A Doll House* cannot be feminist. The conclusion rests on the assumption that women's struggle for equality, along with, one must suppose, all other struggles for human rights in which biological or social identity figures prominently, is too limited to be the stuff of literature. Feminism is suitable to flat characters in flat-heeled shoes who spring fully armed with pamphlets from their creators' heads in works as predictable as propaganda. Women's equality with men is a subject that lies outside the realm of art, which treats universal, non-polemical issues of human life, whose nature is complex and evolutionary.

Secondly, implicit in the argument that would rescue *A Doll House* from feminist ideology is an emphatically sex-linked ideology whose base is tautological. Women's struggle for equal rights, it is claimed, is not a fit subject for tragedy or poetry because it is insufficiently representative to be generally and thus literarily human. Now if this is so, it can only be because those human beings who are not women, i.e., men, already possess the rights that women seek, and are thus excluded in the other sex's struggle, which is, precisely, a struggle for equality with *them*. In other words, woman's desire to be equal cannot be representative *because* she is unequal. The non-sense of the tautology is doubled when its reasoning is applied to a literary text; for if the lives of Nora Helmer and other female protagonists are worthy of our critical and moral attention only insofar as they are unrelated to the women's inferior status, and if the works themselves are art to the extent that what their protagonists are seeking transcends their sexual identity, then what happens to them is significant literature only to the extent that it can happen to men as well.[28] This means that Nora Helmer, and, to choose among other famous female protagonists of drama – Shakespeare's Cleopatra, Racine's Phaedra, Strindberg's Julie, Shaw's Candida – could just as well be men – except for their sex, of course. And, as Dorothy Sayers reminds us in another context, in her essay "The Human-Not-Quite-Human," women are, after all, "more like men than anything else in the world."[29] Apart from this, however, to say that Nora Helmer stands for the individual in search of his or her self,

tarentella: "...you can imagine then that I'm dancing only for you – yes, and of course for Torvald, too – that's understood" (164). It is not surprising when Rank at the piano proves to be a perfect accompanyist for Nora's frenzied practice session, which shocks and perturbs Torvald: "Rank, stop! This is pure madness" (174). It seems clear that Rank, unlike Torvald, would not want, or need, to reimagine Nora as a virgin as he makes love to her. Through the silk stocking scene, Ibsen shows the sexual side of the Helmer misalliance. And its ending does not prove Nora's dishonesty, but rather her essential honorableness: about to ask Rank for the money she desperately needs, Nora is confronted by his moving confession of love, and rather than make use of his feelings she categorically refuses his help: "After that?...You can't know anything now" (166).

The claim that Nora cannot be a feminist heroine because she is flawed is an example of question-begging similar to the argument that *A Doll House* is not a feminist play because feminism is *ipso facto* an unworthy subject of art. Nora's detractors use unnamed, "self-evident" criteria for a feminist heroine that Nora does not meet, among which would seem to be one, some, or all of the following: an ever-present serious-mindedness; a calm, unexcitable temperament; an unshakeable conviction to obey the letter of the law, even if it means the death of a husband; perfect sincerity and honesty; and a thoroughgoing selflessness. For *A Doll House* to be feminist, it would, apparently, have to be a kind of fourth-wall morality play with a saintly Everyfeminist as heroine, and not this ignorant, excitable, confused – in short, human – Nora Helmer.

But while Nora's flaws keep her from representing women, the argument stops short and the case is curiously altered in the claim that she represents human beings. Nora's humanity disallows her from representing women, but not, magically, from representing people, i.e., men, and women to the extent that what happens to them can happen to men as well, surely as fabulous an example of critical reasoning as we can imagine.

This illogical stance has its parallel in a knotty critical conundrum: if Nora is a frivolous and superficial woman who leaves her husband on a whim, then *A Doll House* qualifies as a piece of shoddy *boulevardisme*; if Nora is "abnormal" or "hysterical," then *A Doll House* is a case study, an example of reductive laboratory naturalism; if Nora is a self-serving egotist whose unbridled thirst for power destroys her marriage, then *A Doll House* is melodrama, with Nora as villain and Torvald as victim, and act three is either an incomprehensible bore or the most ponderously unsuccessful example of dramatic irony in the history of the theatre. But Nora's critics have not claimed that *A Doll House* belongs to any inferior sub-genre. Applauding it as a fine drama, they engage in side attacks on its protagonist, sniping at Nora to discredit her arguments and ignoring the implications of their own.

The incompleteness of this attack, while never acknowledged, is easily explained. To destroy Nora's identity as wife and woman her critics would have to "deconstruct" the play; in the words of Jonathan Culler's useful definition, they would have to show how the text "undermines the philosophy it asserts, or the hierarchical oppositions on which it relies."[31] They would have to examine what Ibsen has Nora say in act three about her husband, her marriage, and her life, and demonstrate that her unequivocal statements are contested by the text. Since the text in question is a play, deconstructing Nora would mean arguing the significance – the interest, worth, and importance – of the part of the dialogue Ibsen gives to Nora's foil, i.e., her husband. Not surprisingly, no one has yet risen to this challenge, for while Torvald Helmer has had his sympathizers, as we have seen, none of them has suggested that Ibsen was of Torvald's party without knowing it, or that Torvald could be Ibsen's, or anyone else's raisonneur in any modestly enlightened universe of the Western world. It would be an intrepid critic indeed who could uphold the position of a man who says to his wife, "Your father's official career was hardly above reproach. But mine is" (160), or "For a man there's something indescribably sweet and satisfying in knowing he's forgiven his wife . . . In a sense, he's given her into the world again, and she's become his wife and his child as well" (190). A charge frequently levelled against *A Doll House* is that Ibsen made the husband too vain to be true, "an egoist of such dimensions," in Koht's phrase, "that we can hardly take him seriously" (K 319). And yet the accusations against Nora are restatements of Torvald's own, from the charges of frivolousness – "What are those little birds called that always fly through their fortunes?" (127) – to deceitfulness – "a hypocrite, a liar – worse, worse – a criminal" (187) – to selfishness and unwomanliness – "Abandon your home, your husband, your children" (192–93). Amused or angry, the husband's accusing voice is so authoritative that Nora's critics, in a thoroughgoing, and, one supposes, unconscious identification, parrot his judgments and thus read her through his eyes. Their Nora is Torvald's Nora.

What Ibsen intended

Anyone who claims that in Nora Ibsen had in mind a silly, hysterical, or selfish woman is either ignoring or misrepresenting the plain truth that Ibsen admired, even adored, Nora Helmer. Among all his characters, she was both the most real to him and his favorite. While working on *A Doll House*, he announced to Suzannah: "I've just seen Nora. She came right over to me and put her hand on my shoulder." Suzannah replied: "What was she wearing?'. Ibsen answered: "A simple blue woolen dress" (P 2:60). After *A Doll House* had made him famous, Ibsen was fond of explaining that his protagonist's "real" name was "Eleanora," but that she had been called "Nora" from childhood. Bergliot Ibsen tells the story of how she and her husband Sigurd, on one of the last occasions on which they saw Ibsen out of bed in the year he died, asked permission to name their newborn daughter "Eleanora." Ibsen was greatly moved. "God bless you, Bergliot," he said to her (BI 157). He had, in fact, christened his Nora with a precious gift, for both "Nora" and "Eleanora" were names given to the sister of Ole Schulerud, Ibsen's Grimstad comrade and one of the few close friends of his life; in the early years of grinding poverty, Schulerud believed in Ibsen's genius when no one else did, tirelessly hawking the manuscript of *Catiline* to bookseller after bookseller and finally spending his inheritance to finance its publication. Schulerud died young, and Ibsen never forgot him.

A year after *A Doll House* appeared, a Scandinavian woman came to Rome, where the Ibsens were living; she had left her husband and small daughter to run away with her lover. The Norwegian exile community considered this unnatural and asked Ibsen what he thought. "It is not unnatural, only it is unusual," was Ibsen's opinion. The woman made it a point to speak to Ibsen, but to her surprise he treated her offhandedly. "Well, I did the same thing your Nora did," she said, offended. Ibsen replied quietly: "My Nora went alone" (Z 166).

A favorite piece of evidence in the argument that Ibsen was uninterested in women's rights is his aversion to John Stuart Mill.[32] It is popular to quote Ibsen's remark to Brandes about Mill's declaration that he owed the best things in his writing to his wife Harriet Taylor: "'Fancy!' [Ibsen] said smiling, 'if you had to read Hegel or Krause with the thought that you did not know for certain whether it was Mr. or Mrs. Hegel, Mr. or Mrs. Krause you had before you!'" (B 76–77) But Brandes, whom Ibsen regarded as both his mentor and spiritual brother, reports Ibsen's *mot* in a discussion of Ibsen's support of the women's movement. He notes that Mill's assertion "seemed especially ridiculous to Ibsen, with his marked individualism" (76), and explains that although Ibsen may have had at first little sympathy for the women's cause, perhaps, Brandes guesses, because of "irritation at some of the ridiculous forms the movement assumed," this initial response gave way "to a sympathy all the more enthusiastic" when he saw that it was "one of the great rallying points in the battle of progress" (77).[33]

Something that is never brought up in discussions of Ibsen's claimed indifference to feminism is that when Ibsen made the banquet speech in which he declined the honor of having consciously worked for the women's rights movement, he was primarily interested in young women and annoyed by the presence of the elderly feminists who surrounded him. During the seventieth-birthday celebrations, he constantly exhibited his marked, and as Meyer has it, "rather pathetic longing for young girls" (M 773).[34] Surely it is pertinent to ask which better represents Ibsen's intention in *A Doll House,* a disingenuous remark made in irritation at a banquet twenty years after he wrote the play or what he wrote when he was planning it?: "A woman cannot be herself in contemporary society, it is an exclusively male society with laws drafted by men, and with counsel and judges who judge feminine conduct from the male point of view" (*OI* 5:436). *A Doll House* is not about Everybody's quest to find Him-Or-Herself, but, according to its author, Everywoman's struggle with Everyman.

Nor is it true that "there is no indication that Ibsen was thinking of writing a feminist play" when he began to work on *A Doll House* (Valency 150). In the spring of 1879, while Ibsen was planning his play, a scandalous incident occurred (easily available in the biographies), that proves not only Ibsen's interest in, but his passionate support of the women's movement. Ibsen had made two proposals, filling over seven book-sized pages, to the Scandinavian Club in Rome: that the post of librarian be opened to women candidates, and that women be allowed to vote in club meetings. In the debate on the proposal, he made a long speech, part of which follows:

Is there anyone in this assembly who dares to claim that our women are inferior to us in culture, intelligence, knowledge, or artistic talent? I don't think many men would dare to suggest that. Then what is it men are afraid of? I hear that it is accepted tradition here that women are such clever intriguers that we keep them out because of this. Well, I have met with a good bit of male intrigue in the course of my life . . . What I am afraid of is men with small ambitions and small thoughts, small scruples and small fears, those men who devote all their ideas and all their energies to obtain certain small advantages for their own small and servile selves (*H* 15:402–3).

Ibsen's first proposal was accepted, the second not, failing by one vote. He left the club in a cold rage. A few days later, he appeared at a gala evening. People thought him penitent, but he was planning a surprise. Facing the dancing couples, he interrupted the orchestra to make a terrible scene, haranguing the celebrants with a furious tirade. He had tried to bring them progress, he shouted, but their cowardly resistance had refused it. The women were especially contemptible, for it was for them he had tried to fight. A Danish countess fainted, and had to be removed, but Ibsen continued, growing more and more violent. Gunnar Heiberg, who was present, later remembered: "As his voice thundered it was as though he were clarifying his own thoughts, as his tongue chastised it was as though his spirit were scouring the darkness in search of his immediate spiritual goal – his play [*A Doll House*] – as though he were personally living out his theories, incarnating his characters. And when he was done, he went out into the hall, took his overcoat, and walked home" (M 450). Two months later, Ibsen began writing *A Doll House*.

For Ibsen's contemporaries, the sophisticated as well as the crude, *A Doll House* was the clearest and most substantial expression of the issues composing the "woman question." From the 1880s on, the articles poured forth; "Der Noratypus," "La représentation féministe et sociale d'Ibsen," "Ibsen as a Pioneer of the Woman Movement,"[35] are a small sampling of titles from literary essayists who agreed with their more famous contemporaries Lou Andreas-Salomé, Alla Nazimova, Georg Brandes, and

August Strindberg,[36] along with every other writer on Ibsen, whether in the important dailies and weeklies or the highbrow (and low) reviews, that the subject of *A Doll House* was the subjection of women by men.

Havelock Ellis, filled with a young man's dreams and inspired by Nora, who he proclaimed held out nothing less than "the promise of a new social order," summarized in 1890, eleven years after Betty Hennings first slammed the door, what *A Doll House* meant to the progressives of Ibsen's time: "The great wave of emancipation which is now sweeping across the civilized world means nominally nothing more than that women should have the right to education, freedom to work, and political enfranchisement – nothing in short but the bare ordinary rights of an adult human creature in a civilized state."[37]

In 1884, five years after the publication of *A Doll House*, the Norwegian Women's Rights League was founded. Ibsen joined with its President, H.E. Berner, and with his fellow writers Bjørnson, Jonas Lie, and Alexander Kielland, to sign a petition to the Storting, the Norwegian parliament, urging the passage of a bill making obligatory separate property rights for married women. When Ibsen returned the petition to Bjørnson he wryly commented that the Storting ought not to be interested in men's opinions: "To consult men in such a matter is like asking wolves if they desire better protection for the sheep" (*LS* 228). Ibsen also spoke of his fears that the current campaign for universal suffrage would come to nothing. The solution, which he despairs of seeing, would be the formation of a "strong, resolute, progressive party" that would include in its goals "the statutory improvement of the position of woman" (229).

Ibsen, then, was not only interested in women's rights, but engaged in the battle. Ibsen was fiercely his own man, refusing all his life to be claimed by organizations and campaigns of many sorts, including the Women's Rights League and the movement to remove the mark of Sweden from the Norwegian flag. And he had a deeply conservative streak where manners were concerned (except when he lost his temper), for he was acutely suspicious of show. Temperamentally, Ibsen was a loner. But he was also, as Brandes declared, "a born polemist" (47). While it is true that Ibsen never reduced life to "ideas," it is equally true that he was passionately interested in the events and ideas of his day. He was as deeply anchored in his time as any writer before or since. Six months after the publication of _A Doll House_, he made the following self-appraisal in a letter to his German translator: "Every new work has served me as emancipation and catharsis; for none of us can escape the responsibility and the guilt of the society to which we belong" (_H_ 17:402). A little over a year later, in August of 1881, Ibsen wrote a letter of support to his friend Camilla Collett, who had dedicated her life to the feminist cause:

> The ideas and visions which you have given to the world are not of the sort destined to live a barren life in literature. The real world will seize them and build upon them. That this may happen soon, soon, I, too, wish with all my heart . . . I beg you to believe in my warm, complete sympathy with you and your life task. Let no one persuade you to doubt that you have this sympathy (_H_ 17:434).

NORA'S PREDECESSORS IN ART AND LIFE

LONA: This society of yours is a bachelors' club. You don't see women.
  Pillars of Society (117)

Nora appears first as Selma Brattsberg of _The League of Youth_, the creaky but landmark play, Ibsen's first to be written entirely in colloquial speech, that followed _Peer Gynt_ in 1869. When Selma responds to her husband's announcement of his financial ruin, both her argument and metaphor are Nora's: "How I've longed for even a little share in your worries! But when I asked, all you did was laugh it off with a joke. You dressed me up like a doll. You played with me as you might play with a child . . . Now I don't want any of your troubles . . . I'm leaving you!" (93).[38] The conflict between wife and husband, happily resolved, is a minor matter in _The League of Youth_. But the disparity between Selma's three-dimensionality and the flatness of the other characters is striking. Brandes remarked in his review that Selma, far too interesting for the small role assigned her, represented something new in literature and deserved a play to herself.

This suggestion is surely one of the most brilliant that critic ever made to author, and Brandes can be pardoned for taking credit for _A Doll House_ (B 76). But Ibsen hardly needed to think back to Brandes' remark when he set about writing his drama. _A Doll House_ is a natural development of the strong feminist thread in Ibsen's earlier work, beginning with _Lady Inger of Østråt_, in which the subject of the gendered division of the world into two spheres first appears, and continuing with the critical examination of this division in *The Vikings at Helgeland, Love's Comedy, The Pretenders, Brand,* and in the play that followed *Emperor and Galilean* and directly preceded *A Doll House,* the unabashedly feminist *Pillars of Society.*

For the history of drama, *Pillars of Society* is arguably the most important play of the nineteenth century, for with it Ibsen introduced on the European stage what is now known as modern theatrical realism and committed himself for the rest of his career to the prose drama of modern life. Except for *Emperor and Galilean,* three times longer, he lavished more time on *Pillars of Society* than on any other work as he struggled with the technical problems of the new form.

Camilla Collett, who regularly saw the Ibsens abroad, visited them during the writing of *Pillars of Society,* and Ibsen prodded her to talk about the contemporary feminist movement in order to get material for his dialogue. Collett deeply admired Ibsen, and was one of the few people discerning enough to recognize the greatness of the hybrid *Peer Gynt,* which she termed a "colossal work" (*Works* 3:412) and championed in the press. But she was annoyed by the character of Solveig, and voiced her disapproval in print and to Ibsen himself; a less passive woman, she told him, would have shown Peer his misspent life. In the years immediately preceding *A Doll House,* when feminism had become one of the main topics of the day, Collett joined with Suzannah Ibsen in urging Ibsen to take up the feminist cause directly, and *Pillars of Society* owes much to the conversations in the Ibsen household.[39]

But the pioneering feminist who most directly influenced *Pillars of Society* was Asta Hansteen (1824–1908), the most notorious woman in Norway, on whom Ibsen based his fearless raisonneur Lona Hessel. Hansteen's "enduring popular image," notes Janet Rasmussen, "has been of an impassioned, eccentric, umbrella-wielding reformer" ("'Best Place on Earth for Women'" 245). In fact, Rasmussen points out, Hansteen had the distinction of being Oslo's first woman portrait painter, the first Norwegian woman to publish in "Nynorsk," "New Norwegian,"[40] and the first Norwegian woman to lecture in public. Hansteen's speeches, in which she denounced traditional theological and social views about women, called forth a storm of abuse. She was also eccentric and practical

11. Asta Hansteen (1824–1908). Painter and militant feminist, the most notorious woman in Norway during the 1870s.

enough to wear men's boots when it rained, and sometimes carried for symbolic purposes a whip to protect herself against the oppressor. Ibsen read about Hansteen, a popular item in the press, in the Norwegian newspapers he daily devoured from cover to cover. *Pillars of Society*'s association of feminism, and progressive thinking in general, with America, echoes Hansteen's widely expressed view that America was the natural home of women's liberation; American feminism pre-dated the Norwegian movement by forty years and also helped to inspire it. But Lona Hessel's main debt to Asta Hansteen lies in her deliberately unfeminine behavior and her outspoken criticism of woman's lot.

Ibsen's play opens with a biting satire on woman's place in the world: in the home of chief pillar of society Karsten Bernick, eight ladies, members of the "Society for the Morally Disabled," are participating in the most quintessentially female literary activity since antiquity – they are "busy sewing" (15) – as they listen to schoolmaster Rørland read aloud from *Woman as the Servant of Society*. The most unctious of Ibsen's conservative males, Rørland lectures the women on the danger of America and other "modern societies": "What matters, ladies, is to keep our community pure. We have to stand firm against all this experimentation that a restless age would like to foist on us" (17). The women's gossip prepares the entrance of Lona Hessel, the scandalous misfit who left for America with her equally scandalous half-brother Johan. Lona, who "cut her hair short and walked around in the rain in men's boots" was "a character!" (26). And Johan, everyone knew, had been surprised in flagrante delicto with a disreputable woman – an actress. Returning unexpectedly with Johan from the wicked new world, where she has sung in saloons, lectured, and written a book, Lona is the "New Woman" with a vengeance: she values independent thinking, she earns her own living, she is progressive in politics, she is single.[41] Bursting into Bernick's stuffy garden room like a fresh sea wind, she comments: "But you all look so lugubrious. And here you sit in the shadows, sewing these white things" (38). Pulling open the curtains, opening the door and windows onto the garden, Lona, Rørland chastises, has destroyed "the proper atmosphere" for a ladies' gathering. Breaking up the sewing bee, he asks Lona what *she* can do for the society for the morally disabled, and receives in reply one of Ibsen's sharpest curtain lines: "I can air it out – Reverend" (39).

Lona had loved Bernick, who rejected her to marry her half-sister Betty, an heiress, whereupon Lona slapped him publicly and packed her bags. Secretly engaged to Lona, Bernick was embarrassed by her outspokenness; he abandoned her, she accuses him, when he "heard the ridicule that rained down" as she tried "to shock all the prigs in this town out of their britches and petticoats" (63). Johan has confessed to Lona that Bernick, and not he, was the guilty party in the actress scandal; emigrating to America, he had agreed to take the blame for his friend. Bernick also confirms Lona's suspicion that although he loved her, he married Betty to get the money to save the Bernick family business.

Bernick the self-confessed hypocrite describes himself unwittingly as Bernick the prig in his explanation of how he successfully de-eroticized his wife. In spite of her passion for him, their marriage has not turned out badly; anticipating John Rosmer's complaint about his wife Beata in *Rosmersholm*, Bernick explains that at first Betty "had any number of exaggerated notions about love [and] couldn't get used to the idea that, little by little, it has to subside into a quiet, warm companionship" (64). Now, however, she has accepted this correct view of connubiality "perfectly": "Of course her daily contact with me could hardly fail to have its tempering influence" (65). Bernick, it is clear, devotes his energy to Bernick and Company. The woman Lona remembers as "lovely, blossoming" Betty (63), now a seamstress for the Society for the Morally Disabled, has made the Bernick household "a model for our fellow citizens" (65).

As Bernick has reduced his wife to an obedient, sexless cipher, he has made a personal servant of his sister Martha, whose story is a paradigm of that of the good spinster who devotes her life to others. The closeness of Martha's story to that of Collett's Margarethe suggests that it may have been inspired by *The Governor's Daughters*. Like Margarethe, Ibsen's Martha loved a young man – Johan – but too modest to declare it, suffered in silence. Martha confesses to Lona her Solveig-like existence: "I loved him and waited for him . . . My entire life has been lived for him ever since he went away" (100). But while Martha has spent her young years doing what Peer demanded of Solveig, i.e., living for a man in her mind, Johan, she now realizes, was living: "Over there he'd been thriving in the bright, vibrant sunlight, drinking in youth and health with every breath; and meanwhile, here I'd been sitting indoors, spinning and spinning." Martha devotes herself to the family of her brother, who is most insufferable when he speaks of her: Martha is a "non-entity, really," good to have around because she will "take on whatever comes along" (57). For Bernick, Johan's "But what about *her*?" is incomprehensible: "Her? What do you mean? Oh yes; well, she has interests enough of her own. She has me, and Betty, and Olaf [his son], and me." It is in explaining Martha's selfless role in life that Bernick speaks one of Ibsen's most brilliant feminist lines: "People shouldn't always be thinking of themselves first, especially women" (57).

This happy maxim is disregarded by lively Dina Dorf, *Pillars of Society*'s modern ingénue. Daughter of the scandalous actress whom Bernick discarded, Dina was taken in by Martha after her mother's death. Made to feel her base origin by the good ladies of the town, Dina has greatly suffered and is as much a misfit in bourgeois society as Svanhild in *Love's Comedy*. Like Svanhild, she forces herself to conform, i.e., to find a suitable husband, and has become secretly engaged to schoolmaster Rørland, who, like Bernick, prefers to keep his engagement to a less than respectable woman secret. Attracted to the frank, unstuffy Johan, Dina confesses to him that her great hope is to go to America, where, she thinks, people are not "so respectable and moral" (52–53). When Johan announces his hope of marrying her, Rørlund decides to announce their engagement to the community "for Dina's well-being" (89). Confronted with the real prospect of marriage to this moralistic, self-satisfied bore, Dina expresses for the first time what she really feels: "I'd throw myself into the fjord before I'd be engaged to him!" (97). Anticipating Nora's mingled feelings of humiliation and anger when Torvald condescends to save her, she bursts out: "Oh, the way he patronized me . . . with his high-flown talk! The way he made me feel he was raising a little nobody up to his level! I won't be patronized anymore. I'm getting out" (97). Dina will emigrate to America with Johan, who vows to wait on her "hand and foot." But Dina has had enough of chivalry: "Oh, no, you won't. I can take care of myself" (97). If Lona is the "New Woman," Dina is the "New Young Woman," who in promising Johan that she will marry him, tells her husband-to-be: "But first I want to work, become something myself the way you have. I don't want to be a thing that's just taken along" (98).

Little known and played outside Scandinavia and Germany,

Pillars of Society is one of the most radically feminist works of the nineteenth century. Using his customary triangle, Ibsen flanks Bernick with two opposing women, the self-effacing, dutiful Betty, the "womanly woman," and her contrasting half-sister, the brash, "masculine" Lona; long-suffering, silent spinster Martha, living on Bernick's crumbs, and the lively, outspoken Dina, who refuses Rørland's, stand on either side of Johan. Rejected as unfit to marry, the play's raisonneur Lona Hessel has not sacrificed herself to a surrogate family, but escaped to the new world, where she has led an independent, authentic life. Under Lona's influence, Bernick sees what he has made of his own life, thanks her for showing it to him, and confesses his wrongdoing: "It's as if I were coming back to my senses now after being poisoned" (117). Recalling Haakon and Skule of *The Pretenders*, he recognizes his neglect of the women who love him and asks their pardon: "And you, Martha – it seems as if all these years I've never really seen you" (117). Lona explains why: "This society of yours is a bachelors' club. You don't see women." Gathering Betty, Martha, and Lona around him, Bernick sentimentally announces that "it's you women who are the pillars of society." But Lona quickly disabuses him, for idealization is the other side of contempt: "Then it's a pretty flimsy wisdom you've gained, Karsten. (*Sets her hand firmly on his shoulder*). No, my dear – the spirit of truth and the spirit of freedom – *those* are the pillars of society" (117–18).

And thus old maid feminist Asta Hansteen, the butt of society's ridicule, becomes, in Lona Hessel, the victorious scourge of the society that traduced her. Vilified by her countrymen and caricatured unmercifully in the newspapers, Hansteen, who later wrote that she felt the ground "burning beneath her feet" (Rasmussen 246), emigrated to America at the age of fifty-five, a year after the publication of *Pillars of Society* (which she greatly enjoyed). Perhaps, Rasmussen suggests, Asta Hansteen "was influenced as much by Lona Hessel as the other way around."[42] Finding in Boston the organized feminist movement that Norway lacked, Hansteen had the momentous experience of meeting Julia Ward Howe, Lucy Stone, and Mary Livermore. She attended women's suffrage congresses and reported back to Norway on "this flock of impressive pioneers who have shown the world true womanhood, genuine femininity – so different from the pitiful model which for such a long time was forced upon us as the correct female posture" (Rasmussen 261–62). Hansteen spent nine years in the

United States, mostly in Boston and Chicago, eking out a living painting portraits and writing journal articles for Norwegian papers. Encountering the sunflower as a feminist symbol of women's right to the light and air Lona Hessel introduces into the meeting of the Women's Society for the Morally Disabled, Hansteen introduced it to Scandinavia, where it was adopted as the official symbol of the Norwegian Women's Rights League. During Hansteen's years in America, Norwegian feminism made great strides; the league came into being, along with Gina Krog's *New Ground*, the first Norwegian feminist journal. Although Hansteen had declared America to be "the best place on earth for women" (Rasmussen 264), in the end, like Lona Hessel, she decided to fight her battle on her home ground and returned to Norway to help "air it out."

The original Nora

Ibsen was directly inspired to write *A Doll House* by the terrible events in the life of his protégée Laura Petersen Kieler (1849–1932), a Norwegian writer who had a long and successful career. When she was nineteen, she wrote a sentimental sequel to *Brand* called *Brand's Daughters* and sent it to Ibsen. Touched by her interest, and always ready to perform kindnesses for admiring young women, Ibsen replied with a letter in which he encouraged her to continue writing. Thus began a long friendship that was to prove momentous for both of them.

The Ibsens welcomed Laura Petersen in their home. They grew fond of her, and it is hard not to resist the speculation that she was, for a time, the daughter they never had. Ibsen was uncommonly affectionate with her, calling her pet names like "my skylark," which he would later put to good use.

Laura Petersen married a Danish schoolmaster called Victor Kieler. When he fell ill with tuberculosis, his doctors prescribed a warmer climate. The Kielers could not afford to travel, so Laura secretly took out a loan, afraid that her volatile husband, who had a phobia against owing money, would refuse to go if he knew. They had their southern journey, and Victor Kieler's health returned, so splendidly, in fact, that he lived another forty years. On the way back from Italy, the Kielers stopped off at the Ibsens' in Munich and Laura confided her secret to Suzannah.

Laura thought she would be able to repay the debt with money earned from newspaper articles once she returned home, but she badly miscalculated; pressed for payment and desperate, she wrote Suzannah from Denmark early in 1878 to ask her to ask Ibsen to read an enclosed manuscript and, if possible, to recommend it to his publisher Hegel. Suzannah replied at once: "Believe me, I feel the deepest worry and sympathy for you, who have to bear such a heavy burden on your poor shoulders, and believe me, also, that I have spoken on your behalf with all my power to Ibsen. God help you!" (Kinck, "Henrik Ibsen og [and] Laura Kieler" 507).

In fact, Suzannah had not only spoken to Ibsen, but had shown him Laura Kieler's letter, which, he tactfully noted at the beginning of his reply, was "naturally . . . meant to be read by me as well" (Kinck 507). Ibsen's letter is both protective and perplexed, like that of any father who cannot understand his daughter's loyalty to an undeserving man. He begins by saying forthrightly that he cannot recommend her book. But even if it were published, it would ruin her reputation, for it is plainly a rush job. He cannot understand what possible circumstances there could be in her marriage that force her to send out her material before it is finished. "In a family where the husband is still living, it can never be necessary for the wife to spill her heart's blood as you are doing. I do not understand, either, how he can allow you to suffer this. There must be something you omitted from your letter that would change the whole story." Ibsen ends his fatherly letter with this advice: "Whatever is troubling you, put everything in your husband's hands. He must bear it" (Kinck 507–8).

Ibsen could not know how futile, even irrelevant, were his well-meaning words. Writing to her mentor had been Laura Kieler's last, desperate measure to stave off disaster. Pregnant and ill, when she received Ibsen's reply she became frantic, burned her manuscript, and forged a note to repay the loan. When the forgery was detected, she was forced to tell her husband what she had done. His reaction was proof that Ibsen had been right in guessing that Laura had omitted something important from her account: a description of her husband's character. Victor Kieler demanded a legal separation on the grounds that his wife was an unfit mother, gained custody of the children, including the newborn baby, and had his wife committed to an asylum, where she was placed in the insane ward.

The Ibsens learned this news from Victor Kieler himself in a brief note. Ibsen immediately wrote to his publisher to ask him to find out Laura's circumstances. In the meantime, Laura had been released from the asylum, after a month. It was not until two years later that Victor Kieler agreed to take back his wife, who returned home to live with her children.

Laura Kieler's story weighed greatly on Ibsen. He brooded on the harrassed wife forced to sacrifice her "heart's blood" to pay back the money she borrowed to save her husband's life, and on the oblivious husband, allowing his wife to slave away on hack work. Laura Kieler had done "all for love" and was treated monstrously for it by a husband obsessed with his standing in the eyes of the world. In Ibsen's working notes, we find: "She has committed a crime, and she is proud of it; because she did it for love for her husband and to save his life. But the husband, with his coventional view of honor, stands on the side of the law and looks at the affair with male eyes" (*OI* 5:437).

Ibsen softened the unusual and sensational aspects of the Kieler story to meet art's demand for plausibility. His protagonist he made a housewife, not a writer, and the hack work not novels but mere copying; her antagonist is transformed from a cruel brute to a possessive guardian: rather than put her into an asylum, he denounces her as an unfit wife and mother, and then, once his reputation is safe, he forgives her and wants to take her back on the spot. The Helmers, in other words, are normal. But in the end, it was Ibsen's stroke of genius to create in his little *husfru* a rebel who throws normality to the winds. Career woman Laura Kieler begged her husband to take her back, but housewife Nora Helmer is tired of begging; in *A Doll House* it is the husband who pleads to be taken back and the wife who refuses.[43]

THE DEATH OF CHIVALRY:
MASCULINE AND FEMININE IN *A DOLL HOUSE*

NORA: I was the one who raised the money. (135)

A Doll House is the greatest literary argument against the notion of the "two spheres," the neat, centuries-old division of the world into his and hers that the nineteenth century made a doctrine for living. The home, the woman's place, is a make-believe world fit for dolls; the chivalric ideal, the old credo of male *noblesse oblige*

the bourgeois century resurrected to justify the cloistering of the
female, proves, when put to the test, pure humbug: "But there's
no one who gives up honor for love" (194), the outraged husband
explains to the stunned wife, who has expected him to shield her
from infamy. And she, who has secretly saved his life and paid for
it through years of hard work, all the while playing the silly doll to
his wise man, recognizes the enormous significance of her folly
born from love: "Millions of women have done just that." The
power of *A Doll House* lies not "beyond" but within its feminism; it
is feminist Bildungspiel *par excellence*, dramatizing the protagonist's realization that she might, perhaps, be someone other than
her husband's little woman. No other work illustrates as powerfully the truth rediscovered by recent feminist scholarship that the
conception of the two spheres reflected neither "natural" compe-
tencies nor the reality of men's and women's lives, but was an
ideological construct that masked inequality and forced segregation on the basis of sex;[44] no other work insists so explicitly on the
hypocrisy, waste, and sheer foolishness of isolating women from
the work of the world as it reduces to nonsense the psychosexual
rationale poeticized for posterity by Ruskin: "[Man] is eminently
the doer, the creator, the discoverer, the defender ... By [wom-
an's] office and place, she is protected from all danger and temptation. The man, in his rough work in the open world, must
encounter all peril and trial."[45]

Ibsen's man-and-wife, the couple in the doll house, is a parodic,
bourgeois version of the pan-cultural ideal of marriage as a relation of natural superior and inferior, in which the wife is a creature of little intellectual and moral capacity whose right and
proper station is subordination to her husband. Faithfully pronouncing this doctrine – "Yes, whatever you say, Torvald" (126);
"Yes, Torvald, I can't get anywhere without your help" (151) –
Nora is the secular, natural (but finally unnatural) descendant of
Milton's Eve, piously repeating the lesson of female subservience:
"God is thy law, thou mine; to know no more / Is Woman's
happiest knowledge and her praise."[46] Torvald, Nora's guardian
and consultant on everything, even to the proper dancing of the
Neopolitan tarentella, knows best. In scene one, the put-upon
breadwinner calls his weaker half a "lark" three times, a "squirrel"
three times, a "featherbrain" once, and a "spendthrift bird" three
times, teasingly regretting, "It's incredible what it costs a man to

feed such birds" (128). Wasting her husband-provider's money is
one of Nora's most important functions in the household. She is
an excellent example of Veblen's useless, improvident little wife,
ornamenting the home and prettily demonstrating both the pecu-
niary mastery of her spouse and "an acquired facility in the tactics
of subservience" (60): "Oh, thank you, Torvald; I can manage no
end on this" (127). In inventing the metaphor of the doll house,
Ibsen captured the quintessential nature of the "woman's sphere,"
described twenty years later by Charlotte Perkins Gilman:

The man, spreading and growing with the world's great growth, comes
home, and settles into the tiny talk and fret, or the alluring animal
comfort of the place, with a distinct sense of coming down. It is pleasant,
it is gratifying to every sense, it is kept warm and soft and pretty to suit
the needs of the feebler and smaller creature who is forced to stay in
it. (*Women and Economics* 263).

A Doll House, like its successor *Ghosts*, is in the ironic mode;
playing pet wife to Torvald's kind keeper, Nora conceals an integrity of purpose and a redoubtable will underneath the silly talk.
Her first word, the first word of the play, is "Hide," and actresses
playing Nora are successful to the extent that they suggest the sub-
text's witty counterpoint: "Hm, if you only knew what expenses
[years of slaving away to pay back the money I got to save your life]
we larks and squirrels have, Torvald" (128). *A Doll House* is that
typical Ibsen play, a drama of disguise and concealment, in which
the past, whose suspenseful revelation reveals character by exposing appearances and lies, will out. Buried in Nora are an intelligence, a courage, and a pride in accomplishment that make her
doll-identity absurd and demeaning, that prove that her brain is
not an organ of her sex. And if Torvald, content with his child-
wife, can be pardoned for not seeing the person Nora hides as she
follows household convention, the reader / viewer cannot, as
Ibsen juxtaposes Nora with Torvald and Nora without: playing the
babyish spendthrift, she begs in scene one: "Oh, yes, Torvald, we
can squander a little now. Can't we? Just a tiny, wee bit" (126); in
scene two she tells the mean truth to the confidante: "I've paid out
all I could scrape together" (137); in scene three, with Torvald,
she reverts to type, flattering him that the job-hunting Kristine
Linde "is terribly eager to come under a capable man's supervi-
sion" (142); in scene four, with the loanshark, she defiantly,
proudly confesses: "*I* signed Papa's name" (148).

Marginalized by society because of her sex, Nora cannot partici-
pate in it; her criminality is thus both a result and a defiance of
her exclusion. Ibsen has the plot turn on money, as Nora, who as
married woman cannot borrow without her husband's consent, is
forced to go outside the law. To acquire money on her own is to
reject her lowly status, for it means operating in the world, although not, of course, on the correct terms; Nora's criminality is
a silent, covert rebellion that looks forward to the final, noisier
one.

Paying back the money was harder than Nora had expected, she
explains to the confidante, for, straightforwardly, "Torvald has to
live well" (137). So she bought cheap clothes for herself, which
she hated, loving fine things, and skimped on everything else,
spending her nights doing copy work. Getting the money and
working to pay it back have been her "joy" and her "pride" (146),
for it made her feel as though she counted for something. "It was
almost," she says, "like being a man" (137).

Ibsen overturns the sexual tables as the sheltered, feeble wife
proves to be a resourceful "masculine" life-provider in the most
literal way, saving her husband from dying, and the protective,
strong husband, the household interior decorator and dancing
master, turns out to be a fainthearted, "feminine" weakling, who
"with his sensitivity ... [and] sharp distaste for anything ugly"
(163) must be protected from the reality of Dr. Rank's sickroom,
from his own romping, noisy children, even from the unaesthetic
sight of his wife knitting. Not only will this false protector not
"save" Nora in the moment of truth, but he will declare *himself* to
be her victim and her his persecutor. His stance of protective
chivalry is exposed as ludicrous posturing as he attacks Nora
between moans of distress: "I'll be swept down miserably into the
depths on account of a featherbrained woman ... They might
even think that I was behind it – that I put you up to it. And all that
I can thank you for – you that I've coddled the whole of our
marriage. Can you see now what you've done to me?" (188).
Upon the arrival of the saving letter, Torvald's cry of relief is
worthy that of any trapped damsel: "I'm saved. Nora, I'm saved!"
(188). And Nora replies in two words which, as Yves Chevrel
notes, summarize the play in expressing "the fundamental cry of
the unrecognized": "And I?" (*Maison de poupée* 93).[47]

Torvald's announcement of his salvation forces Nora to face the truth of his character, the essential moral weakness that results from a sublime regard for his reputation, which he calls "honor." Faced with the loss of this, he views Nora's love as merely the exasperating reason for his diminished position. His betrayal constitutes less a revelation than a final, unavoidable proof of the ugly truth Nora has consistently denied. When he explains that his objection to hiring the disreputable Krogstad is the embarrassing fact that as former schoolfellows they still use the familiar "du," Nora responds that he cannot be serious because his objection is too petty. And her blithe explanation to the confidante of her reason for keeping the loan a secret analyzes her marriage perfectly: "Torvald, with all his masculine pride – how painfully humiliating for him if he ever found out he was in debt to me. That would just ruin our relationship" (136). Finally, when the loanshark turns blackmailer, Nora's frightened anxiety, her desperate self-assurances that Torvald will defend her, reveal that in her heart of hearts she is terrified that he will not. In her sad fantasy of his chivalry, she has named his deed of rescue "det vidunderlige," "the miracle," "the miraculous thing."

After he is "saved," Torvald, profoundly unaware of his wife's pain, and clinging, against all reason, to the idea of her as weak and dependent, quickly reverts to his role of chivalrous protector, lugubriously indulging in his favorite bird metaphors: "You can rest easy now; I've got wide wings to shelter you with . . . I'll keep you like a hunted dove I've rescued out of a hawk's claws" (189). But Nora, who was leaving in costume to drown herself to prevent her husband's self-sacrifice, now sees the absurd and futile generosity of her own: men expect women to live for love while they themselves would never do so. Swindled but enlightened, she leaves the room to change her tarentella garb for an ordinary dress. She has given her last performance as the dancing doll.

To argue that *A Doll House* is not a feminist play because it lacks banners and a bluestocking is to deny the very source of its power: its dramatization of the flowering of one woman's consciousness. Ibsen understood, both in the play and in the world, for Nora and for her audience, that what we live through individually creates our principles and forms our allegiances, that, in what historian Joan Kelly has termed "the essential feminist perception," "the personal is political" ("The Doubled Vision" 60). In the last scene of *A Doll House* it is her own husband's betrayal that forces Nora to examine their marriage, pronounce it counterfeit, and transform her relation to "the world out there" (192); it is her own pain that leads her to the momentous conclusion that "millions of women" (194) have lived as she has. Enlightenment brings difficult admission as Torvald's horrified reaction to the crime she committed to save his life, the one accomplishment she is proud of, makes her acknowledge what her father and husband have made of her.

Patriarchy's socialization of women into servicing creatures is the major accusation in Nora's painful account to Torvald of how first her father, and then he, used her for their amusement, "played with" her (191); how she had no right to think for herself, only the duty to accept their opinions. Excluded from meaning anything, Nora has never been subject, only object. Sexual property, in marrying Torvald, she now sees that she merely passed "from Papa's hands into yours" to live "by doing tricks." Her husband cannot love her, for like her father, he does not know her; he only likes "to be in love" with her. Nora reminds Torvald bitterly that when she needed his understanding, he cared only for what might damage him; the danger over, "I was exactly the same, your little lark, your doll, that you'd have to handle with double care now that I'd turned out so brittle and frail" (195).

In 1908, the great Russian actress Alla Nazimova played Nora in New York in performances that became legendary. In the audience was Halvdan Koht, who describes Nazimova in the last scene acting "with a passionate intensity that made Nora's transformation at the end completely an inner reality, conveyed in low-pitched, emotion-laden words" (K 323). Koht recalls his horror when members of the audience, mistaking "the work of art" for "a collection of ideas," began to applaud Nora's every line "as though it were a political harangue" (K 323). But while not a harangue, Nora's words are nevertheless resoundingly political, for in representing the "inner reality" of an obscure Norwegian housewife, they constitute a discourse of recognition for every woman who has ever lived her life for a man, and by Nora's count, there are "millions." Displaying what the modern theatre condemns as bad manners, the 1908 audience was responding to Ibsen's powerful feminist poetry, the exhilarating promise that on the other side of the doll house, women, no less then men, could learn to take themselves seriously: "I believe that, before all else, I'm a human being, no less than you – or anyway, I ought to try to become one" (193). The universality of *A Doll House* does not come from "its demand for truth in every human relation" (K 323), but in its demand for equality in the relation between women and men.

In their discussion of female protagonists "trapped by architecture," "literally confined to the house," Sandra Gilbert and Susan Gubar maintain that "dramatization of imprisonment and escape are so all-pervasive in nineteenth-century literature by women that we believe they represent a uniquely female tradition in this period" (*Madwoman* 60). If this is so, then *A Doll House* is the great male exception. And while the female heroes of the women writers flee the confining house through the vicarious acts of an imagined double, Nora exits in her own flesh and blood through a very literal door, slamming back in its lock to provide an exclamation point for her departure. Perhaps, in 1879, only a man could imagine such freedom.

Those who dismiss *A Doll House* as dated would do well to reexamine what Nora left behind her. To shut the door on a husband was insufficiently audacious; Ibsen gave Nora three young children as well. Elizabeth Hardwick comments: "Ibsen has put the leaving of [Nora's] children on the same moral and emotional level as the leaving of her husband and we cannot, in our hearts, assent to that . . . He has taken the man's practice . . . that where self-realization is concerned children shall not be an impediment."[48] If "we" cannot approve Nora's leaving, it is because "we" have not caught up with Ibsen, who consistently refuses to make the children a separate issue. Torvald's plea is always that Nora consider her duties to her "husband and children" as though the three words were a compound noun. Ibsen does not separate Nora as mother from Nora as wife because he is identifying the whole source of her oppression, the belief in a "female nature," an immutable thing in itself whose proper sphere is domestic wifehood and whose essence is maternity. Nora's leaving is, in her husband's words, "outrageous" and "insane" (192) because it denies the purpose of her existence, a reproductive and servicing one: "Before all else, you're a wife and a mother" (193). A hundred years before Adrienne Rich's *Of Woman Born* and Elizabeth Badinter's *Mother Love: Myth and Reality*,[49] Ibsen demythologizes motherhood by separating it from childbearing. "And I – how am I equipped to bring up children?" Nora asks

12. Nora (Liv Ulmann) confronting Torvald in the Vivian Beaumont
Theatre's production of *A Doll House*, New York, 1975.

rhetorically (192). Limiting women to domesticity yet simultaneously holding them responsible for raising children is absurd. Nora's old nurse can bring up her children as well or better than she; "I'm not up to the job" (192).

Nora is able to see the emptiness of Torvald's appeals to authority because she possesses her own, that of her own experience: "I was the one who raised the money" (135). Even in the toy world of her marriage she has counted for something; the intelligence and determination that allowed her to save her husband's life will help her to take on the world outside. "You don't know anything of the world you live in," her husband reminds her; "No, I don't," she agrees. "But now I'll begin to learn for myself. I'll try to discover who's right, the world or I" (193).

The poetry of Nora's leavetaking lies in the hint of strength and the certainty of struggle as she shuts the door on the doll house to enter the night of the open world. The famous last stage direction is the final flourish in the play's consummate destruction of the ideology of the two spheres through its systematic exposure of the foolishness of the chivalric ideal and the notion of a female mind. Upon finishing *A Doll House*, Ibsen wrote to his publisher: "I cannot remember any work of mine that gave me so much satisfaction during the working out of the details as this one has" (*LS* 180). He had remained the painstaking artist as he took the woman's part.

CHAPTER 6

Mrs. Alving's ghosts

What is a ghost? Stephen said with tingling energy. "One who has faded into impalpability through death, through absence, through change of manners."

James Joyce, *Ulysses*

It is commonly known that *Ghosts* was Ibsen's riposte to the furious attacks on *A Doll House*. "*Ghosts* had to be written," Ibsen wrote to his champion the Swedish feminist Sophie Adlesparre; "After Nora, Mrs. Alving had to come" (*LS* 208). And yet the standard reading of *Ghosts*, as pervasive as the anti-feminist readings of *A Doll House*, is that Ibsen's answer to the outraged critics of Nora Helmer is a play about a woman who wronged her husband. One of the cornerstones of the modern theatre, the play that proved the possibility of tragedy in modern dress, is a play about a woman who failed as a wife.

That readers of *Ghosts* are to blame Mrs. Alving is the lesson Lionel Trilling teaches in his well-known short story "Of This Time, Of That Place." When Professor Howe puts the question to his class – "At whose door must the tragedy be laid?" – his student Casebeer identifies the culprit as heredity and quotes: "The sins of the fathers are visited on their children" (86). Student Johnson claims that the fault is Pastor Manders' for sending Helene Alving back to her husband. Student Hibbard objects by pointing out that it was the captain who did "all the bad things." Only Professor Howe's favorite student Tertan is equal to the challenge, rising to his feet and coming "brilliantly to the point": "'Your father never found any outlet for the overmastering joy of life that was in him. And I brought no holiday into his home, either. Everything seemed to turn upon duty and I am afraid I made your poor father's home unbearable to him, Oswald.' Spoken by Mrs. Alving" (87–88). The brightest boy in the all-male class sees what

146

the less intelligent ones miss: Ibsen was blaming the woman. Tertan, who gets "the literary point of almost everything," has once again satisfied his teacher by reciting "the summation of the play" (88). Had Mrs. Alving been less driven by duty, had she not obliged Captain Alving to seek his pleasure elsewhere, she could have prevented the catastrophe, the son's madness, a result of the inherited syphilis that infected the father outside the cold home. The wife's lack of sexual responsiveness causes the husband's philandering. Professor Howe patiently explains to his naive students: "We have been assuming that Captain Alving was a wholly bad man, but what if we assume that he became bad only because Mrs. Alving, when they were first married, acted toward him in the prudish way she says she did?" (88).

The most eloquent statement of Mrs. Alving's blame belongs to Una Ellis-Fermor, who marshalls Wordsworth's womanly paragon in the "Ode to Duty" to explain Ibsen's vision of a wife's true duty. In recognizing that she "had starved the joy of life in another person, in the husband whom nature had endowed with that joy," Mrs. Alving "comes within measurable distance of recognizing another 'duty,' to joy, to gladness and to love, a duty akin to Wordsworth's 'Stern daughter of the voice of God' of whom nevertheless he could also say 'Nor know we anything so fair As is the smile upon thy face.'"[1] In other, less lyrical versions of the argument, the uniform point is clear: Helene Alving's failure to perform lovingly her conjugal duty brings on the husband's ruin.[2]

Blaming Mrs. Alving has fitted in conveniently with the stock comparison of *Ghosts* to *Oedipus the King*. The action of Ibsen's play, it is argued, is the protagonist's growing awareness of her complicity in her husband's destruction. Like Sophocles' tragedy, *Ghosts* is a quest drama that exposes the truth about the past to identify moral responsibility. Mrs. Alving confesses her guilt in the recognition speech she makes to her son in act three: "Your poor father never found any outlet for the overpowering joy of life that he had. And I'm afraid I couldn't make his home very festive, either . . . Everything resolved into duties – my duties and *his* duties, and – I'm afraid I made this home unbearable for your poor father" (*H* 9:122).

No demand seems less likely on the part of the author of *Brand*, *Pillars of Society*, and *A Doll House* than requiring human beings to fulfill unwanted, unfelt obligations. And yet critics maintain that

Ghosts is a play about a woman who, had she had different instruction or somehow developed other ideas on her own, would have known better how to love a man she had married for convenience. In McFarlane's explanation, the story of Mrs. Alving, unlike that of Nora, "is the career of one who also slammed the door on her husband and ran off into the night, but who was persuaded to return to the path of duty, with all its alarming consequences"; once she returned, however, "the warmth of charity was lacking, [and] she had left no room for 'joie de vivre' " (*OI* 5:3, 5). In other words, Helene should not have married Alving, or returned to him, but once she did, it was her duty to desire him sexually. That she did not makes her responsible for the tragedy.

While no critic would contend outright that Ibsen believed that wives have a duty to make passionate love with unloved husbands, the claim that Helene should have been sexually warm to Alving is nevertheless the time-worn principle of the "marriage debt" masquerading as sexual liberalism. Helene owed it to Alving to want him. What this suggests about the relation between duty and desire and about Ibsen's view of the relation seems grotesque. It also ignores Ibsen's exposition, which establishes indisputably that Helene Alving loved another man, so much that she committed the unspeakable act of leaving her husband for him. It would thus seem both illogical and cruel to demand that she feel sexual desire for her husband. But even her love for Pastor Manders has been used against her; it is the husband she should have loved and not this ecclesiastic of "doubtful potence" (Davis "Reappraisal" 377). While the play does not offer sufficient information to render judgment on Pastor Manders' "potence," it establishes beyond a doubt the clergyman's earthly love for Helene. However priggish Manders is now, thirty years ago he was a different man; sending Helene home, he tells her, was "the hardest battle of my life" (93). As for the demand that Helene should not have loved the man she ran to crying, "Here I am: Take me!" (93), but rather the one she had unwisely married, it seems germane to make the point Ibsen himself would later make, perhaps better than anyone else ever has, in *The Wild Duck*: the "claims of the ideal" die hard.

Looking back

Francis Fergusson explained in a well-known essay, "The Plot of *Ghosts*: Thesis, Thriller, and Tragedy," how he was forced to give up his effort to read Ibsen's play as tragedy because its protagonist never achieves an epiphany. He concludes that Ibsen abandoned his attempt to write a tragedy to construct a *pièce à thèse* to prove that Helene Alving "should have left home twenty years before" (150).[3] Helene's leaving home twenty years ago, when her son was six or seven, would not have cured his syphilis;[4] but the reason that *Ghosts* does not contain the epiphany necessary to Fergusson's conception of tragedy is that it is not a Sophoclean quest drama. It is a different kind of tragedy, whose shape is not the protagonist's search for self-truth, but rather the revelation of the consequences of her rejecting that truth in favor of the world's demands. *Ghosts* is no truncated Sophoclean tragedy, but one of the tightest plays in drama. What Helene Alving does not know is neither what she is – a coward – nor what she has done – led a life of lies for twenty-eight years – but the results of her being and doing. The tragic action of *Ghosts* is not the quest of a woman who discovers that she should have been more loving to a man she did not love, but rather the revelation of the pollution caused by her surrender to that man – not once, but twice.

The past is more profoundly present in *Ghosts* than in any other Ibsen play. In the complicated chronology of the exposition, Ibsen is very precise about his figures, odd numbers like nineteen and twenty-seven carefully dropped in the casual dialogue. When his wife returned to him, Alving "turned away from his depravities" (78), Pastor Manders summarizes common knowledge, to live a blameless life ever after. He became something of a model citizen, like Bernick of *Pillars of Society*, a "benefactor to the community" (79), and died ten years ago in an odor of sanctity. No one knows about the real Alving except his widow, who reveals to the pastor that after nineteen years of marriage, her husband "died just as dissipated as he had lived all his days" (81). After barely a year of marriage, Helene ran away to Manders, whom she loved and who loved her, but he sent her home to Alving because it was a wife's duty to remain with her husband. She bore the son Oswald, hoping that with a child things might improve, but they only worsened, and when her husband had his way with the housemaid, Helene became terrified that her little boy would see what his father was. So she sent him away to school, bought off the maid, and became a closet businesswoman, supervising the estate and handling the money while her husband lay on the sofa or holed up in his room drinking. The liaison between Alving and the servant produced a bouncing daughter Regine, who has grown up unaware of her father's identity and whom Mrs. Alving has taken in as her maid. All this has been kept secret. Oswald, now "twenty-six, twenty-seven," a painter home from Paris for the dedication of the Captain Alving Memorial Orphanage, has been brought up to believe that his father was a model of respectability. The orphanage, the ultimate falsehood in Mrs. Alving's great life-lie, will be a final seal on the sordid past and cover up the truth once and for all. "It will be as though the dead had never lived in this house" (85), Mrs. Alving ends the exposition to the horrified pastor.

But the important exposition is yet to come, and Mrs. Alving herself shortly begins to hear it in the ingenious offstage curtain business of act one. The dead man comes back startlingly to life through his son's unwitting imitation – in the pop of a wine cork, the scrape of an overturned chair, the squeal of a maid surprised by her master's embrace. The events of the thin, surface plot – the preparations for the dedication of the sanctimonious orphanage – are reduced to so much blather by the counterpoint nastiness slowly forcing its way up through the tight bourgeois rigor of Mrs. Alving's parlor, making a mockery of her endless efficiency, hinting at its presence in the night firelight of the act-two curtain as the orphanage burns to the ground, finally declaring itself vividly in the glare of day when the diseased son meets his inherited fate and the act-three curtain comes down on the mother's screams.

The seeming offhandedness of Manders' "twenty-six, twenty-seven" buries an important truth: whichever is the correct number, Helene's diseased son was conceived *after* his mother's return. If Mrs. Alving had been more welcoming to her undesirable husband, it is possible that she might have kept him home more, but her son would still have been born with his terrible malady, rather sooner, perhaps, than later. Ibsen does not tell us when Alving caught the disease, and considering the extent of the captain's philandering, he would have been hard put to do so; among Ibsen specialists only Joyce seems to have appreciated what Mrs. Alving's detractors like to call her husband's "joy of life": "Weak, wanton, waster out and out," Joyce's captain brags.[5] But Ibsen does have Helene tell her son, when she decides to tell him "everything," that "your father was a ruined man before you were born" (122). Clearly, then, the "confession" of act three is irrelevant to the horrible secret slowly disclosing itself. For no matter how "joyful" Mrs. Alving had made her husband's home, Oswald's condition would not have changed a whit. The argument that the captain caught the disease after she rejected him, and that she is therefore responsible for it, is not only a fallacious *post hoc* argument in itself, but one impossible to maintain on textual grounds. Ibsen, the painstakingly careful writer Knut Hamsun called a "bookkeeper," whom no one would accuse of random plotting, did not locate the crisis of his action in a speech irrelevant to the tragedy's catastrophe.

Looking forward and in

Ghosts begins with its sub-plot, hatched by two ambitious schemers in a secret, sordid conversation. The deformed Engstrand, "out on a spree" the night before (53), whining about how his wife always rejected him, is the dead captain's double. He enters dragging his lame leg and "dripping wet." "You slut" (55), says the false father to his "daughter" Regine, as he encourages her to follow her mother's example and try to sell herself to a rich foreigner. The rustics' discussion of the profitable dive, the "seamen's home" this lowlife satyr plans to open, is perfect preparation for the proper business between their betters, the discussion of the Alving foundling home, that follows just ahead. The lewdness of the hidden talk also reflects on the nature of the much greater secret the play will uncover, Master Oswald's loathsome sickness. After hurrying her disgusting "father" to the door, Regine puts more refined plans into action as she makes overtures to the newly arrived pastor, explaining that she would like to be taken in as his "housekeeper": "You see, if it was in a good house and with a really correct gentleman" (61). But this scheme to escape boring Rosenvold comes to naught as the nervous pastor, painfully aware of how Regine has "grown" ("filled out" [60] she corrects him in her inimitable vulgarity), and as terrified of compromising himself as he was twenty-eight years ago, leaps to his feet and cuts the conversation short. Corruption, mendacity, hidden sexuality are announced as the leitmotivs of the "Family Drama in Three Acts" promised by the play's sub-title.

Helene Alving is in high spirits as she enters to greet the pastor, for her beloved son has come home again and promised to stay the winter. Uninterested in the business details of the orphanage, she wants the affair settled immediately, even acceding to the pastor's wish not to insure the buildings, an extraordinary decision for a good businesswoman. Her holiday mood shows in her avowal to the disapproving clergyman that the radical books he sees on her table "are books *I'm* reading" (64), and in her defense of her son, who shocks the pastor with tales of free love in Paris art circles.

A hint of the real Alving comes when Oswald speaks of the only memory he has of his father: as a small child, he was made to suck on Alving's pipe until he vomited, making the captain shake with laughter.[6] Helene, true to form, lies to protect her son from the truth: Oswald must have dreamed the incident. But he is quite certain ("Don't you remember?"), and in a flashing image Ibsen gives us Helene as Young Mother: "Then you came in and carried me to the nursery. I got sick then, and I saw you crying" (73).

When Oswald leaves to join Regine in the dining room, it is the pastor's lecture to Helene on her duty to this husband that provokes the truth telling – the long recounting of the Alving marriage that begins here, breaks off when interrupted by the curtain business in the dining room, and continues in act two. Moved to the quick by the pastor's sermonizing, Helene, summoning her self-control, announces the arrival of the truth about her marriage. And then she gives the nasty details: how she had to become Alving's drinking companion to keep him home, listen to his dirty jokes, even "fight him" to get him to bed. While he lay "prostrate in sniveling misery" (83), she ran the estate. Dismissing as an *idée reçue* the pastor's insistence that children should love and honor their parents, she demands, "Why don't we ask if Oswald should love and honor Captain Alving?" (90). Implicit here is another question, about wives and husbands: "Why don't we ask if Helene should have loved and honored Captain Alving?", a question as rhetorical as the protagonist's.

In the revelation of the squalid truth about the Alving marriage, we discover not a "dashing young husband," in Evert Sprinchorn's words, driven "back to the taverns and brothels" ("Science and Poetry" 361), but a sad, drunken wreck of a man who abused his wife and son. "And it is to this man that you are building a memorial!" (84) exclaims the stunned pastor, understandably

13. Mrs. Alving (Minnie Maddern Fiske) confronting Pastor Manders in the Mansfield Theatre's production of *Ghosts*, New York, 1927.

confounded. But Mrs. Alving's explanation is lucidity itself. The money for the orphanage has been carefully determined; it is, she says, her "purchase price," the exact amount that made the lieutenant such a good catch. She has calculated the precise figure so that from now on she and Oswald will have only the money she herself has earned. And finally, she explains with immense naivete, "My son will inherit everything from me" (84).

This deliberate, excessive calculation is the mark of an obsessed soul. Year after year Helene has added to the pile, carefully contributing just the required sum so that on the tenth anniversary of Alving's death she can obliterate him forever. She will have paid him back for buying her. Echoes of scene one sound in our ears as she compares herself to Engstrand, who got a paltry sum for marrying Regine's mother, "a fallen woman," while she got an "entire fortune" for marrying "a fallen man." She tells the dismayed Manders how her mother and aunts "did my arithmetic for me," adding ruefully, "If only Mother could see me now" (88–89).

Misused as a daughter, abused as a wife, Helene cannot bear to be told that she was "unfair" to Alving. Such a judgment is so wide of the mark that it inspires heated anger in this most patient of women. To hear the man she loved upbraid her for not being dutiful to a man she loathed, a man he himself sent her home to, tips the scales and forces the truth. For she had found the courage to leave her husband a year after her marriage, but Manders sent her back. She accuses him: "You made me submit to what you called duty and obligation," and "You praised as right and good what my whole soul revolted against as something vile." Manders' renouncement of his love for her, what he calls a "victory over myself," she corrects to his "most cowardly defeat" and "a crime against us both" (92–93).[7]

Helene went back home, endured Alving's intimacy, and bore a child. And yet the degrading falsity of the next nineteen years had one redeeming virtue, for which she is grateful to the pastor. His praising as right what she felt to be wrong made her begin to think, and as she lived through her unhappiness, his credo, like badly stiched material, unravelled seam by seam until she saw it was "machine-sewn" (92). The remembrance of her suffering leads to her finest perception, the theory of the unrelenting ghosts:

It's not just what we actually inherit from our fathers and mothers that lives on in us. It's all kinds of things – old, dead ideas, dead beliefs. They seem to come back from the dead, somehow, and we can't get rid of them. All I have to do is pick up a newspaper, and I seem to see ghosts creeping between the lines. There must be ghosts all over the whole country, as thick as sand. And here we are, all of us, so miserably afraid of the light. (92)

Mrs. Alving can see her celebrated ghosts because she has tragically suffered. Here is no vacillating protagonist searching for the truth, but a woman who berates herself over and over for not telling the truth she already knows, condemning herself for having obeyed other people's rules instead of her own mind and heart. Drumming on the windowpane, she insists on her surest conviction: "What a coward I was" (for covering up the truth); "That's what a coward I am!" (for not telling the truth now); "If only I weren't such a miserable coward!" (I'd tell Oswald the truth about his father); and, once more: "Ah – what a coward – what a coward I have been" (89–90).

Besides wanting to protect her child, Helene had another reason for remaining silent: she knew that she herself would be blamed. "If I did what I ought to do, I would confide in Oswald, I would tell him" (89). But Alving, as she says with characteristic wit and some bitterness, "was one of those people whose lives never interfere with their reputations" (82), a judgment both accurate and prophetic. Strindberg's doctor in *The Father* speaks for Mrs. Alving's detractors when he remarks: "When I saw *Ghosts* and heard Mrs. Alving giving us a postmortem on her husband, I said to myself: 'Damn shame the dead can't speak.' "[8]

The "summation of the play"

The culminating event of *Ghosts* is the ill son's collapse into mindlessness. From his entrance smoking his father's pipe until his onstage exit as he is claimed by his father's disease, Oswald captivates. We listen spellbound as he tries to tell his mother the story of the illness that has robbed him of his power to paint and reduced him to anguish. He must finally lock her in the parlor to force her to hear the hideous truth, which he describes with his own special irony, "smiling sadly" as he remarks that softening of the brain reminds him of "cherry-red velvet curtains – something soft to caress" (128), a mot he delivers shortly before lapsing into stupor on center stage. For Stanislavski, who directed *Ghosts* at the Moscow Art Theatre, the greatest dramatic interest in the play was "Oswald's inner drama: the fact that he knows about his illness," this "condemned man bound to a pillory."[9]

The fatally diseased ghost-son is the fleshly sign of his mother's tragic submission. This powerful proof of the tenacity of the ghosts answers the rhetorical question Ibsen put to himself in his working notes: "These women of the modern age, mistreated as daughters, as sisters, as wives, not educated in accordance with their talents . . . these are the ones who supply the mothers for the new generation. What will be the consequence?" (*OI* 5:468). Oswald is also his dead father's replica; the identification of father and son comes in the startled pastor's shock of recognition: "Ah – that's incredible – ! . . . When Oswald came in through the door with that pipe in his mouth, it was like seeing the father" (72). The sickness Oswald inherited from his mother and father is the central subject of the long conversation between mother and son that composes the second half of act two and, once the Engstrand sub-plot has been completed, concludes act three, as the cast of characters shrinks to the fatal two and the tormented son vainly tries to explain his illness, whose origin he is ignorant of, to the resisting mother.[10]

The tension between what Oswald is – his father's and mother's true heir – and what his mother would make him into – a successful version and justification of her own failed life – informs the two long scenes between them and is resolved only when, in spite of Helene's monumental resistance, the truth manifests itself literally before her eyes. From the beginning, in a series of innocent double entendres, she steadfastly denies the son's identity: she "could almost bless" the sickness that brought him home (125); "Oswald looks like me" (72), she insists when the pastor remarks on the striking resemblance between father and son; all the captain's money has been put into the orphanage so that Oswald can "inherit everything from me" (84). If she is too cowardly to discuss the radical new books she reads, "my son can speak for me" (77). Helen's innocent, free child will live as she never could. All his complaints of headaches, fatigue, and even attacks and near collapses only strengthen her powers of denial. This consistent refusal to listen to her desperate son shows the force of her determination to succeed in her thirty-year-old campaign to think one life and live another. Her resistance remains unshaken even by Oswald's report of the French doctor's diagnosis: "'It's as though you've been worm-eaten from birth.' He actually used the word *vermoulu* . . . And then the old cynic said, 'The sins of the fathers are visited upon the children'" (105).

Undaunted, Helene insists that her son's condition results from overwork and from his return to the dreary Norway he hates. She offers as proof – and as solace – the exemplum of the father. In a total contradiction of everything she has confided to the pastor, the story of young Lieutenant Alving now becomes a sad tale with a simple, determinist moral.[11] Loving life, yet doomed to the boring, provincial town, Oswald's father had no work he loved, no friends except drunkards and bums. And so "what had to happen happened" (122). Helene is even willing, in what Northam terms an "excess of charity" (*Ibsen's Dramatic Method* 71), to take part of the blame herself: "I'm afraid I made your poor father's home unbearable to him, Oswald" (122). Her desperate desire to help her son in his anguish and to soften what she thinks will be a terrible blow – the truth about his sainted father – makes her present her husband to his son as a victim like himself. If misery loves company, what more comforting companion than one's own father?

Helene is deeply shocked by Oswald's response. He is not much affected, he says, by this news about a man of whom he remembers nothing except "he once made me throw up" (125). His mother grasps at a straw: "But surely a child should love his father in spite of everything!". The son responds, "in words so simple and so true," wrote George Moore, "that listening, the heart turns to ice."[12] "When that child has nothing to thank him for? Has never known him? Are you still holding on to that old superstition, you, who are so enlightened" (125).

"Ghosts," Helene replies with a shudder, and thus the son has retaught the mother her own spiritual lesson. What do people "owe" each other? Unless heartfelt and freely given, commitment is false to the soul, a life-denying burden. It is in this sense that disastrous consequences, the legacies of the mothers' and fathers' sins, fall on the children. Ibsen was clear about the play's tragic retribution in one of his working notes: "Nemesis is invited upon the offspring by marrying for extrinsic reasons, even when they are religious or moral" (*OI* 5:467).

For Mrs. Alving's explanation of the father's appetite for life and her ill-placed humility in declaring herself unequal to it are beside the point. She was wrong in thinking that Alving's reputation could matter to his son, or, in the supreme irony of her brave little assumption of responsibility, that it could matter at all. Had she told Oswald the truth years ago, the result would have been precisely the same. For the *fatum* was already there. And so it is that her revelation of the father's ruin, like the news brought by a Greek messenger, has an effect opposite to that intended. The final movement of the tragedy begins as the information offered to ease the son's mind only confirms his worst fears: "Oswald (*with a choked cry*). 'Ah!'" (122). The peripeteia of the ruined father is the son's sure knowledge of his inheritance.

Helene Alving's desperate attempt to bolster the image of a dead reprobate father to a terrified son contradicts her deepest convictions about her marriage and herself. Her willingness to shoulder part of the blame is the response of her unemancipated self, yet another proof of her failure to free herself from notions she claims in the privacy of her parlor to condemn, another faltering in her pseudo-rebellion against the Pastor Manders Way of Life. It is a leaving, a *reste* she cannot throw off, part of the dead cargo she drags around with her, like the twenty-eight years of lies crowned by the building of the absurd orphanage. It belongs in the same ghostly category as her sad remedy for the problem of the illegitimate daughter: "Don't you think the best thing would be to get her settled? . . . I mean – suitably married?" (93). Helene's confusion is documented in Ibsen's own insistence on it: "One main point. She has been believing and romantic – this is not wholly obliterated by the standpoint afterwards attained – 'It is all ghosts'" (A 7:195).

Ibsen brings his action to completion at the end of the last scene between mother and son. Shaw, usually so sure and hard-minded when it came to discussing Ibsen, thought the last scene of *Ghosts* "so appallingly tragic that the emotions it excites prevent the meaning of the play from being seized and discussed" (*Quintessence* 90). And perhaps words do fail here; perhaps only Edvard Munch's evocative drawings can adequately interpret Ibsen's spectacle of a mother being implored by her child to kill him out of

kindness.[13] Yet nothing but this awful request could have completed the play's action after the son's revelation to the mother
that the "real illness" is "the one I got as my inheritance, the illness
(*points to his forehead and speaks very low*) sitting here inside" (127).
The truth that her son will sink into a mindless dependency is a
revolting horror Mrs. Alving refuses to face. And who can blame
her? For with his usual directness, Oswald spares her only the
worst words – "to have to be fed, to have to be – . . ." (128). True
to his perfect construction, Ibsen gives us the summation of the
play in the brilliantly simple declarative-interrogative-imperative
from son to mother: "I never asked you for life. And what kind of
life did you give me? I don't want it. Take it back again!" (129).

The most horrible irony of this merciless drama, which Ibsen
termed one inclement August in Berchtesgaden "a family story as
sad and grey as this rainy day" (P 2:89), is that the mother can
fulfill her obsession to obliterate her hated marriage only by
destroying her cherished child. The son is the scapegoat for the
ideal of "the family" she stayed to preserve; offending and innocent, he would receive his own death like a gift from the woman
who gave him life: "Who else but you?" are his terrible, clear words
(129).

Helene Alving bears a share in the tragedy's catastrophe, but it
is not because of her inadequacy as a wife. She should never have
been Alving's wife at all, of course, but her marriage only serves as
a necessary first condition in the play's tragic schema. For Ibsen
gave her a second chance. Like all such choices, it was exceedingly
difficult, even "impossible." The man she loved, pitiably weak and
terrified of scandal, refused her and sent her home. In her deso-
lation, where would she have gone? In her poverty, how would she
have lived? But it was a choice, nevertheless, to reject or accept
what her soul despised, and she bungled it. And this is what Ibsen
meant when he said that *Ghosts* was a sequel to *A Doll House*: the
wife, aware of her sham marriage and not loving her husband,
chooses to stay with him and live the lie. "I never really listened to
myself" (88), confesses Helene to the pastor, echoing her famous
predecessor. But this time, the admission comes too late.

Helene stayed to preserve the proprieties of the family and the
home. It is easy to understand the epithets Ibsen's contemporaries poured on *Ghosts* when we consider the play's unrelenting
attack on the sacrosanctity of the family. The curtain goes up on

proper bourgeois living to show the unpalatable truth. The wife stays with the husband she does not love and then lives "for the sake of the child." The father transmits syphilis to the son and has his way with the maid, who bears his daughter. The wife buys the maid a suitable husband, similar to her own (although naturally of a lower order), and later guiltily takes the daughter in. The husband finally dies a broken-down *débauché*. The play approaches parody as Ibsen includes the supreme family taboo, incest; the syphilitic son returns home and sees his "salvation" in the body of his half-sister, and the mother, now desperate and ready to give him anything, is willing to let him have her. But it is too much; the Götterdämmerung of The Family comes at the end of act two as the orphanage, consummate symbol of sexual and social hypocrisy, burns to the ground. "Everything will burn," says the diseased son, "And I will burn up, too" (120). And it is Mrs. Alving herself, creator of this monumental deception designed to cover the last traces of the family history, who pronounces the benediction over its ashes, in hammering, repetitive monosyllables of a fatalism no translation can muster: "Det var bedst at det gik som det gik" (117); "It's best that it happened as it happened."

As for the sister–daughter, she plans to do something more exciting than stay home and nurse an invalid. Nowhere does the œuvre offer a better example of the architecture of Ibsenian irony, the cross-referencing that results in double and triple entendres, than the last act of *Ghosts*: Mrs. Alving's old love is blackmailed by the man she bought to shield her husband's reputation, and the money left over after the destruction of the proper family goes to support the infamous projects of the bad family, to launch the bastard daughter in her search for a rich protector and her false father in his purchase of the establishment he plans appropriately to call, in one of Ibsen's most justly famous witticisms, "Captain Alving's Home." Not only would the captain be perfectly at home there, fully appreciating the amenities provided, and not only is the brothel a worthy mirror image of the Alving household, Mrs. Alving having sold herself to its owner, but Alving's own unacknowledged "orphan" daughter will seek her fortune there. The future of the House of Alving is announced when things come full circle as Regine chases after the remnants of the Alving heritage to begin a career inescapably linked to her father's disease. As much Alving's true heir as her half-brother, she will perpetuate the line in a succeeding generation and perhaps, like her father before her, "blight with plagues the marriage hearse."

Present and past unite in the scene of suffering. The shape of the tragedy is Sophoclean only in a general way; the crisis of the drama is the revelation of a dreadful truth about the past. But the famous expository method common to both playwrights, the gradual "leaking out" of the information that culminates in the whole truth, serves differently in *Ghosts*, whose plot structure is a double development in the ironic mode. In Aristotelian terms, the plot of *Œdipus the King* is a straightforward imitation of the action; for both, the end is to discover the polluter, and the protagonist, although he struggles against his own culpability, searches actively for the truth. But the arrangement of the incidents in *Ghosts* would deny that the pollution exists. And it is not merely that Mrs. Alving's dedication of the orphanage and her plans for a new life for herself and her son attempt to annihilate the past, but that they would deprive it from meaning and would thus ignore the tragic reality of life itself by claiming the possibility of beginning it again. And thus the all powerful past, in the retrospective exposition that persistently intrudes *à rebours* on the genteel parlor conversation, must gradually defeat the vain, superficial present until its triumph is announced in the babbling words of the ruined son, who has sought the father without knowing it. His mother insists on the false plot up to the end, desperately, pathetically chattering on:

What horrible things you've been imagining, Oswald. Nothing but your imagination. All this excitement has been bad for you; but now you'll have a good rest, darling, at home with your mother. You can have anything you want, just like when you were a little boy. There, now, the attack is over; you see how short it was? – I knew it. And look, Oswald, what a lovely day we're going to have. Bright sunlight. Now you can really see your home. (130)

But as she turns off the lamp, Apollo, god of disease and light, ushers in the ghost of the father, returning to claim his own in the white glare of a western Norwegian dawn. The illusionist stage widens to the space before the *skene* as it offers up its center spectacle, the broken young man in the dark armchair. "Mother, give me the sun" (131).

Ibsen's poetry of the theatre is eloquent in this unholy alliance of intrigue drama, fourth-wall realism, and Norwegian scenery. "There was the tinkle of glass in the next room, a fire outside the window; there was the sun" wrote the awed Rilke.[14] Now in the parlor the intrigue is over, the secret revealed, the diseased fruit of Helene Alving's cowardice shining in relief against a Bergen fjord. Aristotle's notion that to inspire fear and pity the tragedy should affect those near and dear is carried out with a vengeance as the curtain comes down on a perverse pietà brilliantly lighted, a mother shrieking over her son's slumped body. What she will do with her knowledge we do not know, for either way it is a denouement so terrible that it must never be reported. "Yes! No!" are her last words as she fumbles for the morphine tablets, uttering a fitting summary of her deadly compromises.

CHAPTER 7

A new woman and three housewives

THE DOCTOR'S DISCIPLES: *AN ENEMY OF THE PEOPLE*

DR. STOCKMANN: Balderdash, Katherine! Go home and take care of your house and let me take care of society. *An Enemy of the People* (341)

Ghosts had an initial Scandinavian reception very different from the long shockwaves that followed *A Doll House*; after the press' initial, violent rejection, the play suffered a general but silent censorship. In an unprecedented action, book dealers sent back their copies to the publisher; *Ghosts* was too dirty to sell.[1]

Furious and embittered, Ibsen fought back as he had against the critics of *A Doll House. An Enemy of the People* directly attacks *Ghosts*' detractors in its ebullient protagonist Dr. Stockmann's fulminations against the stupidity of majority opinion and in its portraits of "liberal" journalists. Nor did Ibsen let up on the "woman question"; while Helene Alving, the woman who stayed home, was Ibsen's negative rebuttal of Nora Helmer's critics, "New Woman" Petra Stockmann, her father's chief ally in his fight against corruption, is another kind of answer. Earning her own living, the capable, independent Petra is what Dina Dorf of *Pillars of Society* vowed to become. We meet Petra as she comes home after teaching night school, "delectably tired" (295) and looking forward to a drink. Schoolteacher Petra contrasts with her younger brothers' schoolteacher Rørland, whom Ibsen resurrected from *Pillars of Society* to act as an offstage reminder of the continued institutional transmission of intellectual and moral "ghosts." Ten-year-old Morten says that his sister "must be horribly wicked" since "Mr. Rørlund says that work is a punishment for our sins"; Eilif, two years older and wiser, has heard enough from his father and sister to reject "that stuff." Katherine Stockmann worries

about her sons' exposure to radical thinking, a fear Petra qualifies
as "silly": "At home we have to keep quiet, and in school we
have to stand there and lie to the children . . . If I only had
the means, then I'd start a school myself" (296). When Dr.
Stockmann announces his intention to make public his discovery
that the town's spa, its chief source of revenue, is a health hazard,
his chip-off-the-old-block daughter raises her glass of grog: "Skoal,
Father!" (301).

Petra's name signals her function as foil to her conservative
uncle Peter, leader of the money-minded authorities' attack on
the doctor. Petra eavesdrops as Peter Stockmann tries to browbeat
his brother into denying his discovery; unable to remain silent,
she opens the door to spur her father on. Peter Stockmann, who
regards his namesake with condescension and distaste, calls on
Katherine to bring her husband to his senses.

Mother and daughter face off in the family crisis that follows
Peter's departure. Katherine tries to dissuade her husband from
his campaign with the classic "realist" argument: "Ah, what does it
help to be in the right if you don't have any power?" (321). Petra
is as dismayed as her father by what she regards as capitulation:
"Oh, stop always thinking of us first of all, Mother" (321–22).
Housewife Katherine's reply to her daughter says worlds about the
relation between women's silence and their economic depend-
ence on men: "Yes, it's easy for *you* to talk. If need be, you can
stand on your own two feet" (322). Katherine has no way to
provide for her two young sons except through her husband; it is
because Petra earns her living that she can "afford" to speak her
mind. The Stockmann sons arrive home to hear their resolute
father declare: "I want the chance to look my boys straight in the
eyes when they've grown up to be free men." His wife bursts into
passive tears and his intrepid daughter has the act-two curtain
line: "Father – he's wonderful! He's not giving in" (323).

Ibsen satirizes the hypocrisy of the liberal press through Petra's
experience as a translator for the town's progressive newspaper.
Refusing to translate a sentimental story, Petra tells editor Hovstad
that the piece is "totally opposed to everything you stand for . . .
It shows how a supernatural power . . . arranges everything for
the best" (331–32). Hovstad explains that a liberal newspaper
must print such nonsense because when readers "find a moral
story like this in the back pages, they're more willing to accept

what we print up front" (332). Petra's belief in Hovstad's calling as a journalist – "to pioneer the way for embattled truths" (333) – is shattered when he reveals that his principle motivation for championing Dr. Stockmann is the doctor's daughter.

Dr. Stockmann learns the truth about his collaborators in the battle for justice in the play's most successful comic episode. When Katherine comes to Hovstad's office in a huff of motherly feeling – "I'm here to fetch Stockmann…because I'm the mother of three children, I want you to know" – her husband upbraids her petty allegiance: "Does a man with a wife and children have no right to proclaim the truth?" (340). Less gullible than her husband, Katherine declares: "I know you're the smartest man in town, but you're so very easy to fool, Thomas" (341). Absent-minded, "muddle-headed" Stockmann, as Ibsen called him (*LS* 210), thinking the best of everybody, spends his time in his laboratory while his wife, who runs the house, must deal with the everyday world of tradespeople and ordinary citizens. She understands the significance of his claim "I've got the solid majority behind me": "Yes, that's the trouble, exactly. An ugly lot like that" (341). Her husband then insults his wife's intelligence in one of Ibsen's funnier comic ironics: "Go home and take care of your house and let me take care of society. How can you be so scared, when I'm so secure and happy? (*Walks up and down, rubbing his hands.*) Truth and the people will win the battle, you can count on that." Stockmann is forced to moderate his poor opinion of his spouse's extra-mural capacities when Hovstad and his associates, afraid of their readership, turn against him; printer Aslaksen explains: "It's public opinion, the informed citizens, the home owners, and all the rest – they're the ones that run the press" (343).

Witnessing the power clique betray her husband, Katherine Stockmann catches up with her daughter's and her own buried integrity. Her responsibilities as a mother fade in her response to Hovstad's self-serving declaration that his refusal to publish the doctor's report stemmed partly out of regard for her family: "Oh, never mind about this family" (344). Katherine's indignation gets the better of her when Aslaksen refuses to print the report even at the doctor's expense. Reversing her loyalties, Mrs. Stockmann will enlist her sons to proclaim the truth on the street corner.

The act-four town meeting proves the accuracy of Katherine

Stockmann's opinion of the majority when the people side with the authorities and become a howling, stone-throwing mob. In the next day's stocktaking, Petra's dream of starting a school in which she will not have to lie to the pupils comes true when her father announces his plan to found an institution in which his sons will no longer be taught the majority opinion. Dr. Stockmann's curtain line announcing his "great discovery" that "the strongest man in the world is the one who stands most alone" (386) is not without irony, for on one side of the lone hero stands the wife who takes care of him and on the other the daughter with whom he will found his new enterprise.

SENSE AND SENSIBILITY: WOMEN AND MEN IN *THE WILD DUCK*

GINA: Men are really so funny; they always need something to divide themselves with. *The Wild Duck* (*H* 10:100)[2]

The relation between *An Enemy of the People* and *The Wild Duck* is like that between *A Doll House* and its successor *Ghosts*. While neither *A Doll House* nor *An Enemy of the People* ends happily, both denouements point to new efforts and new lives; Nora and the Stockmanns will start over. But *Ghosts* and *The Wild Duck* end in disintegration. Unlike Nora, Mrs. Alving cannot, as she thought, begin again, for she can never undo the dire consequence of her choices, and Gregers Werle, unlike Dr. Stockmann, does not save life through his revelations, but rather destroys it. *The Wild Duck* looks at the subject of truth telling through a darker lens than its predecessor.

The Wild Duck contains, in Fjelde's phrase, an "abundance of thematic antitheses" (F 389), and it is commonly agreed, both by those who take sides and by those who argue the play's essential ambiguity, that its central conflict is dramatized through the three principal male characters: on one side, Gregers Werle, a self-declared champion of truth; and on the other Hjalmar Ekdal, an evader of truth, and his personal theoretician, the cynical Dr. Relling. But Hjalmar, Gregers, and Relling are more alike than has been supposed. Each regards himself as a man with a mission, and, theorizers all, each in his own way and for his own purpose has convinced himself that life is best lived by applying rules or taking stances. Each would reduce life to a simple system: Gregers insists on the necessity of truth, Relling, of lies, and Hjalmar greedily assimilates every experience to the life-lie of his virtuous toil. And although both Gregers and Relling consider themselves models of rational wisdom, both are men of feeling whose reactions and judgments are highly emotive. They seem, in fact, all sentiment, and the disparity between the two men's rhetoric, which would pass for disinterested, and the self-serving reality it masks, provides a good part of the play's dark comedy.

In opposition to the men's theorizing and sentimentality Ibsen places the women of *The Wild Duck* – Berta Sørby and Gina Hansen Ekdal – who, like Katherine Stockmann, make up a solid minority of sense. And the women's plain thinking, willing efficiency, and unpretentious meeting of life's demands do more than deflate the men's highflown sentiments; they constitute a measure of judgment. For Hedvig, caught between her mother's sense and her father's sensibility, dies a victim of Gregers' clichéd moralism and Hjalmar's self-pitying ego, carefully nourished by Relling's flattery.

Two missionaries

John Northam has noted that Gregers' language exhibits "the grandiose vagueness and generality" of Hjalmar's, and that both men's speech shares an important rhetorical characteristic; "from time to time Gregers' close cross-questioning burgeons forth into the same sort of emotional cliché as Hjalmar uses: 'my best and only friend', 'we two old schoolfriends', 'this certainly shows a kind heart'" (N 117;115).[3] That the reformer and the object of his ministrations speak the same language signals the kinship that permits an instant intimacy after seventeen years of separation. The main common characteristic is a skin-deep high-mindedness. Gregers believes that he lives for disinterested idealism, summoning first the people at Hoidal, and now Hjalmar, to lead lives based on the whole truth about themselves. But Gregers has a personal motive for his mission at the Ekdals: in revealing Gina's past to Hjalmar he can rake up his hated father's supposed sexual offenses and gain vengeance for his dead mother. Gregers' mission – his "claim of the ideal" (108) – nicely complements Hjalmar's – the restoration of his father's honor through an invention that will make the Ekdals rich and famous. Hjalmar's self-deception is of a simpler sort than Gregers'; he denies his father at Werle's dinner party, and the glorious instrument of his rescue mission is, of course, pure fantasy, for the inventing takes place on the sofa as he sleeps off his lunch. Ibsen links the missing invention, fruit of the mind, with the ever present food for the body on Hjalmar's table: "But I'm an inventor, you see – and I'm also the family provider. *That's* what helps me to overcome these lowly circumstances. – Ah, here they come with the lunch!" (106). The real mission of Hjalmar Ekdal is eating.[4]

When Hjalmar is not eating or sleeping, he plays in the attic, an adult-scale playpen with live toys. His childish exuberance is indistinguishable from that of Hedvig as they proudly show Gregers their menagerie. Hjalmar pretends that the contraptions he builds with his father represent real work; the truth is that "It's really so much fun to have things like this around to take care of and fix when they get broken" (102). Hjalmar, who plays at working on photography, plays for real in the attic.

This naive and self-deceived man is a perfect subject for Gregers' "the claim of the ideal" (108). The news that his wife is a fallen woman neatly fits Hjalmar's conception of himself as the family martyr, and Gregers' bathetic "swamp of deception" (122) possesses vast appeal as the locus of Hjalmar's unappreciated sacrifices. Gregers, too, as he explains in his description of himself as messiah, has his cross to bear. His playing retriever to Hjalmar's duck is a natural teaming up; inviting him to see what he has hidden in himself, Gregers is Hjalmar's insidiously attractive double. "My best and only friend" (48), says Gregers, seductively drawing him in. The man from the high valley ("Hoidal") and the man in the attic are made for each other, living high above the baseness of the world, two peas in a sentimental pod.

Two housekeepers

It could be said that Werle's housekeeper Berta Sørby, who was beaten up by her first husband, the late horse doctor, has a real cross to bear. And yet, comments John Chamberlain, there "seems to be genuine generosity of spirit – as well as an unusual degree of objectivity – in the abused Fru Sørby's claim that her first husband was not as base as his worst conduct would indicate."[5] Unlike Hjalmar and Gregers, Berta has put her family past behind her and fended for herself, blaming no one. Rather like Mrs. Linde and Krogstad of *A Doll House*, Mrs. Sørby and Werle have no secrets from each other; she knows about the bad marriage and the old affair with Gina, her friend and confidante. The two women hide nothing, either: "Oh, No, Berta! It's finally happened!" (127), Gina joyfully exclaims at the news of her friend's impending marriage to her old lover.

Mrs. Sørby, who lives and lets live, is a foil of the inquisitive, judgmental Gregers. It is she who calls into question his version of his parents' marriage, in which his mother was a martyr to her husband's philandering, and confronts him with how his father, "a healthy, vigorous man, had to listen during his entire youth and all his best years to nothing but lectures" (128). While Gregers merely conceives of being kind, Fru Sørby truly is; she changes the subject at the dinner party after Hjalmar's *gaffe* about the wine, she makes sure Old Ekdal gets his bottle, and she pays visits to Hedvig, of whom she is very fond, giving her little presents. She also helps the Ekdals' finances by arranging for Old Ekdal to be overpaid for his copywork, a kindness she and Gina hide from Hjalmar to keep intact his self-image as the sole family provider. Berta Sørby has no mission to help the needy, but she manages to get a great deal done all the same. Her appreciative husband-to-be comments on her practicality and independent spirit: "Mrs. Sorby always finds a way out – when she wants to" (55).

Gina Ekdal, another good housekeeper, the virtue for which she is customarily praised,[6] is also experienced in finding a way out. Like Berta, she takes life as it is, which Ibsen underscores by making her a photographer. And Gina shares Berta's efficiency, for it is she who is the family provider, earning the money to buy the food she prepares for her husband to gobble up. Besides taking pictures, Gina is good at retouching when the camera likeness falls short; it is retouching that governs the operation of the Ekdal household, the pretense that Hjalmar, and not Gina, is the breadwinner, and that his great invention will one day transform their modest life. Gina's complicity in the fantasy of Hjalmar's genius is not hypocrisy. When Hjalmar explains to Gregers that his uneducated wife is "not completely without culture" because of her daily contact with him (51), he is, as usual, avoiding the truth to flatter himself. For Gina is entirely free of learning, as her malapropisms and ungrammatical constructions prove, and it is this that constitutes her husband's material and emotional well-being.[7] She is content to do most of the work because her ignorance allows her to believe in her husband's genius; as she explains to Gregers, somewhat better than she knows: "Mr. Werle can well understand that Ekdal is not one of your ordinary photographers" (100).

But Gina's patience with her lazy husband has its limits. She tries, with not much success, to get Hjalmar to do some of the retouching himself. And sometimes his corrections of her speech inspire her to rebellion. When she mispronounces "pistol" as "pigstol," her annoyed husband reminds her, "I believe I've explained that this type of firearm is called a pistol," and receives in return: "Oh, that doesn't make it much better, I warrant" (100). However faulty her vocabulary, Gina knows the difference between things and names, and is thus a better semiotician than her husband.

Ibsen uses Gina's practicality and simplicity to deflate the posturing of Hjalmar and Gregers. Of the four acts that take place in the Ekdal studio, Gina has three of the curtain lines. At the end of act two, Hjalmar pontificates on his rescue mission over the prone body of his drunken father and asks his wife for reassurance: "But maybe you don't believe that?" Gina's reply substitutes the important task for the imaginary one: "Yes, of course I do; but let's first see about getting him to bed" (89). At the end of act three, Gina's remark cuts the idealist missionary down to size: "Ugh – that Gregers Werle – he was always a disgusting thing" (115). And at the end of act four, after Gregers' mischief has done its ugly work, in one of Ibsen's greatest curtain lines – "That's what happens when crazy people come around with their claim of the complication" (139) – Gina's substitution of "the claim of the complication" for Gregers' "the claim of the ideal" constitutes a magisterial deflation; the messiah who preaches the claim of the ideal is a madman who disastrously complicates other people's lives.

Gina is as much Gregers' foil as Relling is: "Ugh, that confounded creature who gave himself the run of our house!" (122). The literal-minded woman and the metaphor-obsessed man confront each other in two passages of brilliant comedy, the "swamp air" and "lampshade" conversations, in which Ibsen uses Gina to subvert what Northam has aptly called Gregers' "chronic symbolism" (N 133):

GREGERS: I, for my part, don't thrive in swamp air . . .
GINA: There's no swamp odors here, Mr. Werle; I air out for sure every
   single day . . . But I've got *this* to say to you, Mr. Werle, that you, who
   made all that filthy mess in your stove, you're not going to come to
   me and talk about stink. (110–11)

After revealing Gina's past to Hjalmar, Gregers returns to bask in
what he thinks will be "a transfiguring light in man and wife"
(123). Gina interrupts his string of adjectives characterizing the
Ekdal household – "dreary, heavy, bleak" – by taking off the
lampshade. Her illumination of the effects of Gregers' meddling
punctures his naive expectations.

   But Gina is more than the debunker of Hjalmar's and Gregers'
sentimental excesses, a "feminine Sancho Panza," in James
Huneker's phrase (A 13:287). In addition to being the traditional
foil character who serves the author of comedy as unmasker of
faults and foibles, Gina *has* character, a solid self-respect that
allows her to make a strong counter-attack against Hjalmar's accusations of duplicity. In the confrontation between them, Hjalmar,
sounding "more like Gregers than ever," as Thomas Van Laan has
commented, having adopted his vocabulary, "his inquisitorial,
accusational manner, and his obsession with guilt and punishment" ("Language" 60), declaims his plight as the innocent victim
of the bad woman who is "the mother of my child!" (120). Gina
opposes the puritanical melodrama of the Gregers/Hjalmar version of her sullied past with the plain truth. When Hjalmar exclaims that he would not have married her if he had known "what
kind you were" (121), she explains to her whining husband that
silence, after all, was the best policy. Hjalmar's clichés rise to new
heights as he kicks the furniture, speaking of the "favored predecessor" and "my Hedvig's mother"; "Haven't you been spending
all your days in repentence and remorse?". The common sense
and unwitting wit of Gina's down-to-earth reply make nonsense of
Hjalmar's sentimental tirade: "Oh, dear Ekdal, I've had so much
to do with the housework and everything else every day . . . God
knows I'd almost forgotten that old affair."[8] Gina knows what she
has been for her helpless husband, asking rhetorically, "But tell
me now, Ekdal – what would have happened to you if you hadn't
found a wife like me?," tactfully adding, "because I've always been
a little more businesslike and able to do things than you. Of
course that's understandable, since I'm a couple of years older"

(122). When Hjalmar hears Berta Sørby declare, "I've always been frank. That's the best policy for us women," he tries to use this against his wife: "What do you say to that, Gina?" But Gina retorts with a less simple philosophy of female behavior: "Oh, we women are really so different. Some have one way and others have another" (128).

Encouraged and supported by Gregers, Hjalmar persists, demanding to know whether "your child has the right to live under my roof" (135). This injustice, too much even for Gina's even temper, leads her to her finest hour as she defies the two men and derides their absurd judgmentalizing:

GINA: (*standing very straight, her eyes shining*). And *you* can ask that?
HJALMAR: You will answer me on this: Is Hedvig mine – or – Well!
GINA (*looking at him with cold defiance*): I don't know.
HJALMAR (*trembling slightly*): You don't know!
GINA: How could *I* know that? A woman like *me*? (136)

Scornfully repeating Hjalmar's definition of her, Gina insists on her selfhood and her dignity. Impenitently, she says to her departing husband: "God forgive you for believing I'm so bad" (148). Gina knows that facts do not constitute truth, that although she was Werle's woman fifteen years ago, Hjalmar is wrong to believe that this matters. She, Hjalmar, and Hedvig are a unit, a truth that cannot be dispelled by some fact from the past. For all his grand ideals, Gregers is a Gradgrind, for what he presents to Hjalmar as "the truth" is nothing but a fact, and an irrelevant fact at that.

Gina's refusal of Gregers' and Hjalmar's ideology that her sexual innocence constitutes her worth is related to her disapproval of the attic. The "depths of the sea" is a dirty nuisance, and it keeps her husband from his work. The attention paid to the wild duck annoys her, and in the long run, she is afraid, the attic will be dangerous. In the complaints of the prosaic housewife Ibsen foretells the dire truth: "Yes, one of these days you and Grandfather'll have an accident with that pigstol . . . Oh, that sacred wild duck – there's been enough blessed mess made for her already" (101).

Ibsen's housewives are related to comedy's self-deprecating *eiron* – in Roman comedy a slave, in Renaissance comedy a valet (whose apotheosis comes in Beaumarchais' Figaro) – figures of the underclass who are smarter, more enterprising, or in some other way superior to their superiors.[9] Like the slave and the valet, Gina keeps to her role of inferior, yet permits herself comments on her betters. Her contest with Gregers resembles that of the *eiron* against the *alazon*, the intruder who disturbs the previously established order. If *The Wild Duck* were a comedy, Gina would oust Gregers.

Daddy's girl

Hedvig feels toward Hjalmar the mixture of physical and emotional longing characteristic of the pubescent girl whose father is the only man in her life. She has a habit of putting her arms around his neck and whispering in his ear. She has learned to make him happy by tempting him with culinary delights and by flattering his vanity; his flowing necktie, she tells him, "looks so well with your long, curly hair" (73). Hjalmar encourages his daughter's attachment, sweeping her up in his arms and petting her. Hedvig is pathetically grateful for these signs of affection. Clasped in her father's arms, she forgets her disappointment at his failure to bring her the promised culinary surprise from Werle's party: "Oh, you dear Daddy!" (76). His declamation that "the poor inventor's only reward" will be that she shall live her life in comfort makes her throw her arms around his neck in love and gratitude: "Oh, you dear, dear Daddy!" (110).[10]

Hjalmar believes, and makes Hedvig believe, that they share a mutual love in a special relationship, a father-and-daughter couple: "You and I, Hedvig – we two!" (119). But the truth is that for Hjalmar, Hedvig is principally a subject for self-serving sentimentalizing. He has made her growing blindness his burden, not hers; he explains to Gregers: "She's happy and carefree and chirping like a little bird, fluttering into life's eternal night. (*Overcome.*) Oh, it's a crushing blow for me" (78). Hjalmar's real attitude toward Hedvig's growing blindness is revealed in the damning unmasking that occurs in act three after Gina has managed to make him do a little work; when Hedvig enters the studio, he accuses her of being her mother's spy, and then, when he has hurt her feelings, he hands over the retouching to her so that he can play in the attic, giving her the warning: "But don't ruin your eyes! Do you

14. Gina (Blanche Yurka) and Hedvig (Helen Chandler) agonizing over Hjalmar in the Actors' Theatre's production of *The Wild Duck*, New York, 1925.

hear that? You're not going to blame *me*; I'm telling you that you must take the blame yourself" (94).

It is sometimes remarked that Hedvig's childish behavior makes her an unconvincing fourteen-year-old, but Hedvig's mental age is below her physical one because she has been encouraged to remain a little girl. Hjalmar has even taken her out of school; as he plays in the attic and Hedvig completes his retouching, she explains to Gregers that her father would not allow her to continue her studies for fear that she would damage her eyes. He has promised to tutor her himself, but "he hasn't had time for that yet" (96).

Hjalmar's complicity in his daughter's growing blindness foreshadows the repudiation that results in her death. Having encouraged her violent, adolescent love, when Gina cannot or will not tell him whether he fathered her, Hjalmar turns on his vulnerable daughter and denies her: "Don't come near me, Hedvig! Go away. I can't stand to look at you" (136). But Hjalmar does have a child, one who comes to belong to him in a horrifyingly final way. Ibsen leaves open the identity of Hedvig's biological father because it should not matter; but whether Hjalmar bears a responsiblity in Hedvig's birth, he, as much as Gregers, bears a responsibility in her death. When he denies her, she becomes frantic, clinging to him and screaming: "Daddy! Daddy! . . . No, No! Don't leave me!" (147). Gina pleads, "Look out for the child, Ekdal! Look out for the child!", but Hjalmar tears himself loose from his desperate daughter to abandon her. When he returns home, it is to deny her a second time, answering her cries of delight by turning his back on her and waving her away: "Go away, go away, go away! (*to Gina.*) Get her away from me, I tell you!" (149). Babbling absurdly about his unfinished memoirs, he catches sight of his daughter again: "In my last moments in my former home, I would like to be spared of intruders." "Is that me?" the bewildered girl asks herself. Sick with despair, she remembers Gregers' suggestion – "The wild duck!" – and taking the gun, goes into the attic. Wailing to Gregers, Hjalmar delivers a paranoical and perverse narrative in which his innocent and loving daughter is transformed into a deceitful and money-hungry hypocrite; she never loved the poor photographer, he bitterly charges, but learning of her parentage, she has been smart enough to bide her time; now she is only waiting for the Werles' invitation to live in luxury to abandon him; "If I asked her then: Hedvig, are you willing to give up that life for me? (*Laughs scornfully.*) Yes, thanks – you can be sure what answer I'd get!" (156). Hedvig's answer comes in the brief stage direction: "*A pistol shot is heard from within the loft.*" It is the sound of the Ekdal family weapon with which Hjalmar claims he and his father once contemplated suicide. But what remained talk for the Ekdal men Hedvig puts into practice. Daddy's girl with a vengeance, Hedvig alone performs the "little celebration out in the loft" (110) that "dear, dear Daddy" promised for her birthday. Hedvig's death, her gift of love, is her birthday present from her father.[11]

"Physician, heal thyself!"

Relling, traditionally considered the raisonneur of *The Wild Duck*,[12] blames Hedvig's death on the meddling moralist Gregers. But it is Relling who has fed Hjalmar's ego and invented the invention; in creating Hjalmar Ekdal the genius of modern photography, Relling, no matter how well intentioned, has made Hjalmar vulnerable to Gregers' ferreting. Bolstered by Relling's lies, Hjalmar lives in a glass bubble of self-importance, conceiving of himself as a great man. Faced with unsavory facts about his life, he has no self to meet the crisis, and the bubble shatters; falling back on his fantasy identity as victim, he makes his daughter the scapegoat for his bewildered frustration. Relling claims to hate missionaries, but he as much as Gregers has a mission in life – encouraging the self-aggrandizement of failures through giving them "life-lies" – and in this sense Hjalmar – and thus Hedvig – are his victims. Relling must blame Gregers and Gregers alone for Hedvig's death because to implicate Hjalmar would be to implicate himself.

Relling's mission is as impure as Gregers', for like the people he claims to save, he, too, has a life-lie to maintain: "Good Lord; I'm supposed to be some kind of doctor, I'm ashamed to say; and so I have to take care of the poor sick people in this house . . . People are nearly all sick, unfortunately" (144). This self-designated doctor of people he considers ill is not precisely healthy. Relling loves Berta Sørby, who says they might have had a life together, but "A woman can't just throw herself away" (128). Perhaps Relling loved the bottle better than Berta; when he makes a jealous remark about Werle's money, she retorts that Werle "at least hasn't wasted the best that's in him. The man who does *that* takes the consequences" (127). Berta's revelation of her impending marriage sends Relling out on another binge with his drinking partner Molvik, whose "demoniac" disease, as Torbjørn Støverud notes, is "an excuse for Dr. Relling's own weakness for alcohol"; Støverud points out that "Molvik's attacks are timed, at least part of the time, by the doctor's need of a companion when he wants to go boozing."[13] The perpetually drunk or hungover sidekick functions as Relling's double. The necessity of the life-lie is a congenial philosophy for the alcoholic doctor; ministering to less intelligent failures, transforming their vices into virtues, he implicitly establishes his superiority and avoids facing himself. Relling's theory of the life-lie is his own particular life-lie, his "invention," and like Gregers' theory of the necessary truth, it is self-serving sensibility masquerading as objective sense.

Rhetoric and reality

Hedvig's private game with matches – "playing burning up" (126) – indicates her susceptibility to the extreme gesture, and in this her misfortune is that she is more her father's than her mother's child. While Hjalmar never performs the great deeds he speaks of, his adoring daughter, who cannot tell the difference between empty talk and action, takes her father at his word. Schooled on Hjalmar's discourse of sacrifice, she is understandably responsive to Gregers'.

Hedvig is enough her mother's daughter to resist Gregers' phrasemongering. She corrects his clichéd poeticism "the depths of the sea" with the literal "the bottom of the sea" and "the sea bottom"; she admits that she herself sometimes thinks the whole attic should be called "the depths of the sea," but dismisses this as "so stupid" (99). Intent on his symbologizing, Gregers is offended by this rejection of the portentous and characteristically over-reacts: "You mustn't say that." Hedvig insists: "Oh yes, because it's only an attic." Later, made miserable by her father's rejection, she agrees to Gregers' suggestion that she "sacrifice" her pet to prove her love. But in the morning light, that part of Hedvig that most resembles her mother tells her that the grand idea is worthless: "Last night, at the time, I thought there was something so beautiful about it, but after I'd slept and thought about it again, I didn't think it was anything much" (146). She counters Gregers' nasty reply – "You couldn't grow up here without something going to waste in you" – with Gina-like realism: "I don't care about that; if only Daddy would come back." Later, her father's repeated rejection and denial make her clutch at Gregers' perverse solution; distracted in her grief and desperate, she fulfills her attic iconography, the frontispiece illustration of an old book she found there: "Death with an hourglass and a girl" (98).

It is customary to remark that in *The Wild Duck*, in Gregers and Hjalmar, Ibsen put Brand and Peer Gynt in the same world,[14] but the more important point, perhaps, is that he put them on the same side. The absolutist and the egoist are soul-brothers and equally deadly, both of them "thirteenth at table." To characterize the attic of *The Wild Duck*, the place of Hedvig's appalling death, as "the refuge of the maimed, the solitary and the defeated," as Muriel Bradbrook does (*Ibsen* 99), is to speak like Hjalmar Ekdal, who surely would have used the phrase if he had known it. Hedvig is not "swept away" by the dreams of the Ekdals, as Bradbrook would have it (100), but she is killed by them. Dead, she is dragged out of the attic on center stage; there are powder burns and blood on her blouse. Nor is she the victim who redeems, a source of enlightenment.[15] Errol Durbach has eloquently described Ibsen's art of dramatizing the futility of Hedvig's death in "the farcical tone of her obsequies, presided over by a drunken priest and his congregants – all seeking refuge from the implications of this grotesque mistake in the clichés of maudlin religiosity: 'Oh, God on high . . . if Thou *art* there! Why hast Thou done this to me?' 'The child is not dead; it sleeps.' 'Praised be the Lord. Earth to earth'" ("Sacrifice and Absurdity" 107).

To claim that Hedvig's death is expiatory is to pluck out the heart of Ibsen's great tragi-comedy, for it is to side with Gregers and speak like him; "Hedvig did not die in vain" is Gregers Werle talk (160). Knowing Hjalmar, we know that "Before the year is out, little Hedvig will be nothing more to him than a pretty subject for declamations . . . spewing out how 'the child was torn prematurely from her father's heart.'" Gregers is sufficiently chastened to reply to Relling's accusation that if he is right, life is not worth living; to maintain that Hedvig's death is redemptive is to go one step better than the purveyor of cheap uplift, to outdo Gregers in insisting on a significance that even he is no longer sure of.

In the play's denouement, Gregers once more drives Hjalmar "to a sickening display of facile emotion," comments Northam, while "Gina, thank God, he has not been able to change. She stands as a rebuke to his idealistic inhumanity, thinking all the time, as he has never thought, of the dignity of the dead child" (N 140). Breaking into the men's gratuitous rhetoric, Gina admonishes her husband, who in an outburst of self-pity is blaming his daughter's death on God, tells Relling not to break Hedvig's fingers, clutched around the pistol, and takes charge of her daughter's body: "But the child isn't going to lie out here like a display. She's going into her own room, she is" (159). In a play that lacks protagonist and raisonneur, whose exposition and crisis remain ambiguous, in which language is suspect and theory kills, there can be only one discourse that is privileged: the simplest plain-speaking, the "non-discourse," down to the badly spoken and the ungrammatical, the "wrong" language mocking the "right" one, and finally, no speech at all.

The women of *The Wild Duck* are anti-rhetoricians; Berta Sørby and Gina Ekdal see – and bear – life as it is. Their "realism" is related to their paradigmatic women's experiences. Left a widow (by a husband who abused her), Berta Sørby supported herself by becoming another man's housekeeper, Werle's paid servant, and Gina Hansen, a "fallen woman" discarded by Werle, married Hjalmar Ekdal. Neither woman cares that the same man who "ruined" one of them years ago will shortly make an "honest woman" of the other. Berta and Gina, who have had to live as they could, are survivors and accommodators. Distrusting absolute demands of moral conduct, they look back to Agnes in *Brand*; all three women resemble the women in Carol Gilligan's *In A Different Voice*. Uncomfortable with abstract notions of right and wrong, the women whom educational psychologist Gilligan studied tended to "define their identity through relationships of intimacy and care."[16] When making moral choices, they were motivated less by what should be than what is. This kind of decision is not the result of a passive internalization of "woman's role" as self-sacrificing nurturer, but rather constitutes an active difference with masculine absolutism: "an ethic of care and response" as opposed to "an ethic of justice and rights."[17]

Implicit in what Berta Sørby and Gina Ekdal do, which is more important than what they say, is the conviction that life is difficult, that people need privacy and mercy, and that there can be no formula for living. If the one truth established in this play about diseased sensibility is, in Van Laan's words, that "reality is prior to the limiting and distorting formulations we make of it" ("Novelty"

31), then Gina's simple imperatives – "Look out for the child, Ekdal! Look out for the child!" (136) – and when the child is dead – "The one must help the other" (159) – are the only ones that make sense.

CHAPTER 8

Taming wild women

THE BEATIFICATION OF REBECCA WEST: *ROSMERSHOLM*

And our conversation had brought us to this point, that any pleasure whatsoever of the bodily senses, in any brightness whatsoever of corporeal light, seemed to us not worthy of comparison with the pleasure of that eternal Light . . . (St. Augustine, *Confessions*)

When *Rosmersholm* appeared, feminists hailed Rebecca West as the portrait of an emancipated woman who embodied, in the words of Gina Krog, one of Norway's most vocal feminists, "the gospel of the future" (Hanson, "Ibsen's Women Characters" 88). The English writer Cicely Fairchild even took "Rebecca West" as her pen name. This response reflects contemporary feminists' eagerness for a role model at the expense of Ibsen's character, for while Rebecca West's independent spirit and liberal thinking are qualities typical of the New Woman, she destroys herself to prove her love for a man and thus embodies with a vengeance the old ideal of feminine self-sacrifice.[1]

Ibsen's model for Rebecca West was indeed a "New Woman," Countess Ebba Piper, a literary, liberal-minded member of Stockholm society who caused a scandal when she fled Sweden with the husband of one of her own relatives. The husband was the great Swedish poet Carl Snoilsky, whom Ibsen had met in 1864 when both of them were living in Rome. When Snoilsky returned to Sweden, he married a rich woman whose family disapproved of a Snoilsky who wrote poetry, an activity they believed tarnished the memory of the male Snoilskys who had served Sweden as soldiers and statesmen for over two hundred years. After publishing a highly praised volume in 1871, Snoilsky stopped writing, a capitulation that made him profoundly unhappy. In 1879, all correct-thinking Scandinavia was scandalized when Snoilsky filed for

divorce and left for Italy with Ebba Piper. They had a long pre-
nuptial honeymoon, during which Snoilsky returned to his poetry
and Piper wrote a travel book. After Snoilsky's divorce the following year, they married.

Snoilsky's defiant liaison with Ebba Piper temporarily transformed him into a revolutionary. In 1881, he defended Ibsen
against the barrage of attacks on *Ghosts*, and a year later he announced his commitment to an aesthetics of social change. But he
found it difficult to put his new conviction into practice; his
aristocratic heritage, his whole upbringing, he came to believe,
made him ill fitted to be a fighter for progress. He recognized "a
gulf between what I will and what I can," and defined himself as
belonging to the race of "troubadour" (*H* 10:326).

In the summer of 1885, during a summer holiday in Norway,
the Ibsens received the Snoilskys for a four-day visit. The creator
of Catiline, Earl Skule, and Brand was deeply interested in
Snoilsky's conflict between what he "willed" and what he "could."
And the creator of Hjørdis, Lona Hessel, and Nora Helmer was
much impressed by the courageous, free-spirited Ebba Piper who
had been instrumental in Snoilsky's decision to abandon a life he
despised. When Ibsen later wrote to thank Snoilsky for a book of
poems, he mentioned "your splendid, great-minded wife" (*H*
18:88). Ibsen could not have given Ebba Piper worthier praise, for
"great-minded" was the term he gave to the quality he admired
most in Suzannah.

On the publication of *Rosmersholm*, in 1886, it was clear that
Ibsen had drawn on the Snoilskys for his two main characters. Bull
notes that in creating Rosmer, "Ibsen rarely based one of his
protagonists so closely on a single living model," and that there
can be little doubt that one of Ibsen's earliest notes for Rebecca
West is a description of Ebba Piper: "emancipated, passionate,
somewhat ruthless, but under a refined exterior" (*H* 10:327).[2] In
John Rosmer, Ibsen made Carl Snoilsky's unsuitability for the
committed life into a governing character trait, an overriding
incapacity for struggle. But in Rebecca West, Ibsen did not
deepen, but rather transformed, the experience of his model.
Like Ebba Piper, Rebecca West helps the man she loves to liberate
himself from conventional morality and an unwanted wife, but
afterwards, she is enshackled by the very chains she sought to
break. The dramatic action of *Rosmersholm*, like that of *Ghosts*,

consists in the gradual annihilation of a wishful plot by a real one, as Rebecca's and Rosmer's plans for ennobling the people are crushed by the revelation of a past that dooms the grand project and its architects.

Rivalling *Ghosts* in the grim harmony of its construction, *Rosmersholm* opens with a vision of its ending. The unofficial, inappropriate mistress of the old Rosmersholm estate, sitting in twilight, is unwittingly crocheting her shroud/wedding veil; the "large, white, woolen shawl which is almost finished" (497) will be ready in time to cover Rebecca West's head for the double suicide in the mill-race. Rosmersholm's household gods – long generations of soldiers, statesmen, and clergymen – silently oversee, from their portraits lining the walls, the interloper's work. Rebecca rises to watch through the window as Rosmer, coming home, takes as always the "long way round" to avoid the mill-race bridge from which his wife Beata jumped to her death. "At Rosmersholm, they cling to their dead," Rebecca remarks, gathering up her grave clothes; "To my mind, miss, it's the dead that cling to Rosmersholm" (498), responds Mrs. Helseth, the superstitious housekeeper who serves Ibsen as chorus.

The life Rebecca gives Rosmer at the play's end neatly completes the drama's unremitting circle, for Rebecca has played to perfection the role of "sacrificial woman." In their first scene together, dead Beata Rosmer's brother Kroll compliments Rebecca: "You know, there's something awe-inspiring about a woman who can sacrifice the whole of her youth to other people" (501). Kroll describes Rebecca's devotion to the dying Dr. West as "an endless ordeal with your foster father, caring for him after he was paralyzed and so irrational."[3] "Yes, there were a couple of hard years before he passed on," answers the modest Rebecca, who then goes on to mouth sisterly platitudes about her fondness for the woman she supplanted; to Kroll's "Weren't they harder still for you, the years that followed?", she demurs, "Oh, you mustn't say that! When I was so very fond of Beata – and she, poor dear, was so pitifully in need of care and a little tenderness"; and, more piously, "I was only a kind of agent acting in her name" (502).

For Kroll, Rebecca's flattering appreciation – "You *are* the soul of kindness" – contrasts with the complaints of a rebellious wife who does not understand him: "That's a lot more than I ever hear at home" (503). Mrs. Kroll has upset the patriarchal order of the family by incomprehensibly acquiring a mind of her own: "All her born days, she's shared my opinions and backed my views in everything, large and small – and now she actually favors the children's side in point after point" (506). The revolution in paterfamilias Kroll's home serves as a comic micro-battle of the national one between conservatives and liberals. Kroll's son leads the dissenting students at headmaster Kroll's own school, and his daughter has embroidered an ominously colored red slipcase in which to hide copies of the liberal newspaper. Crusading Kroll, railing against the "insidious, corrupting, destructive spirit of the age" that has "infiltrated" his home, "where until now we've known only a perfect unity of will" (505–6) – his own – is Ibsen's consummate portrait of the patriarchal mind.

Having concluded that the self-effacing, womanly Rebecca will be a most suitable second wife for the noble Rosmer, Kroll tries to enlist her aid in persuading Rosmer to lend his name to the conservative cause, delivering a pæan to Rosmer – "Your noble, forbearing nature, your scrupulous mind, your unassailable integrity" – and the "Rosmers of Rosmersholm – churchmen and officers. Trusted public servants. All of them, men of unfailing dedication" (509). Unable to bear this rhetoric with a straight face, Rebecca responds to Kroll's exhortation with "*a small, rippling laugh*). Dr. Kroll – all this strikes me as ridiculous beyond words." But before she can enlighten the shocked Kroll on the change at Rosmersholm, the arrival of Ulrik Brendel gives Rosmer the impetus to explain his apostasy himself.

Rosmer's preposterous old tutor Brendel, whom Rosmer's martinet father drove out of Rosmersholm with a horsewhip, serves both as the conservative Kroll's foil and as the delicate revolutionary Rosmer's parodic *alter ego* (as the mad Einar had served as Brand's). "You recall, *mein Johannes*, that I'm something of a sybarite. *Ein Feinschmecker*. And have been, all my days. I love to savor things in solitude" (514). The on-the-skids visionary is stopping off at Rosmersholm on his way to town to liberate the masses: "Yes, the time has come to put on the new man – to cast off that delicate reticence I've displayed till now . . . I shall take hold of life with a fiery hand. Forge on. Thrust upward" (513).

Rebecca, who has tried to take up Rosmer's liberal education where Brendel left off, compliments the tutor as an object lesson for Rosmer: "You're giving the best you have. (*Looks meaningfully at Rosmer*). How many of us would do that?" (514). Encouraged by Rebecca to announce to Kroll his conversion to freethinking, Rosmer uses language that directly echoes Brendel's "Our spirits are breathing at long last the age of the tempestuous solstice. And now I want to lay my wisp of dust on the altar of liberation" (513): "It's a new summer that's entered my spirit . . . It's the forces of liberation I want to give myself to" (517–18).

Kroll's opinion of his brother-in-law's capacity to free his fellow citizens from outworn moral systems reinforces the judgment implicit in the Brendel caricature: "You're a dreamer, Rosmer. Will *you* liberate them?" (518). Unperturbed by Kroll's stormy departure, Rosmer, whose naivete resembles that of Dr. Stockmann, declares, "I feel so relieved, now that it's over" (521), and follows his normal habit of retiring early. Refusing to admit the truth of Kroll's judgment of the man she loves, and making light of Kroll's determination to regain Rosmer, Rebecca ironizes to Mrs. Helseth about the "white horses" that are said to haunt Rosmersholm when an inhabitant dies: "I'm afraid we may hear soon now from one of those ghostly beings" (522). Literal-minded Mrs. Helseth replies: "You really believe, miss, that there's somebody here who's marked to go?" Scoffing at the housekeeper – "Oh, of course not. But there are so many different kinds of white horses in this world, Mrs. Helseth" – the sophisticated, doomed Rebecca exits carrying her white shawl. The first act closes, as it begins, with a conversation about the tenacity of the Rosmersholm dead.[4]

The play's buried exposition emerges in act two when Kroll, now convinced of Rebecca's pernicious influence on Rosmer, exhumes his sister's explanation of her suicide. Kroll reminds his brother-in-law that Rosmer's diagnosis of his wife's mental derangement was not shared by her doctors, who agreed "that her case was open to interpretation" (528). He then reveals what Beata told him: she would destroy herself "so you could be happy – and free to live – as you wished" (529). Two days before she jumped to her death, she told her brother: "I don't have much time. John has to marry Rebecca at once" (530). Kroll's suspicion that his sister was sane is shared by his arch enemy Mortensgaard, editor of the liberal newspaper, who visits Rosmer to seek his political support and tells him of receiving a letter from Beata that gave "no sign" of any mental illness (538); if Mortensgaard heard rumors about "anything disreputable going on at Rosmersholm," Beata wrote, he must not put any stock in them (539). Rosmer insists that had Mortensgaard bothered to inform himself, he would have learned that his "poor, unhappy wife wasn't exactly of sound mind," but Mortensgaard explains: "I did make inquiries, Pastor. But I must say, I didn't get quite *that* impression." Mrs. Helseth, who delivered Beata's letter, later comments to Rebecca: "I don't think she was that far gone" (551).

Rosmer's insistence on Beata's madness goes hand in hand with his insistence on her excessive sexual appetite. He has already complained to his brother-in-law: "I've told you about that wild sensual passion she couldn't control – and expected me to respond to. Oh, she could be terrifying!" (528). But Rosmer, who Ibsen insisted to the director of the Christiana Theatre should be played by "the most delicate and sensitive personality that your theatre can lay its hands on" (*Letters 1845–1905* 301), betrays an overwhelming sexual naivete that thoroughly discredits his notions about what constitutes "wild sensual passion" and suggests that his wife's childlessness had a cause other than sterility.[5] Speaking to Rebecca about their own relation, Rosmer complains: "Of course I knew sooner or later our pure and beautiful friendship might be twisted and distorted. Not by Kroll. I never would have thought that of him. But by all the others with their dirty minds" (541). But Kroll has seen Rebecca, in a dressing gown, in Rosmer's bedroom in the morning; even a clean mind might suppose that Rosmer and his attractive companion, with whom he has been living for well over a year after the death of a wife he disliked, are lovers. Rebecca later confesses to the incredulous Rosmer the "wild, uncontrollable desire" (573) she felt for him, and however much he may be exaggerating, out of inexperience or revulsion, when he describes Beata as "sick with her passion" (542), it is clear that Rosmer was living with two women desperately in love with him and that he was sexually oblivious of one and sexually terrified of the other. Preferring a woman whom morality ruled out as a sexual partner to a woman whom morality dictated he should get with child, he withheld himself from his "over-sexed" wife and gave himself unreservedly – and platonically – to her companion: "I was always thinking of you," he serenely confesses to Rebecca, "and longing only for you. It was with you that I had this tranquil, buoyant happiness, above and beyond all desire" (555). It is easy to understand Rebecca's lingering frustration when Rosmer naively asks her: "How can I account for Beata's horrible accusation?": "Oh, stop talking about Beata! Don't think of Beata any more! Here you've finally been freeing yourself from her. Because she's dead!" (541).

Rosmer's sexual innocence is related to an overriding need to consider himself unfallen. His belief in his ability to ennoble his fellow citizens rests on the certainty of his unblemished goodness, and thus the news of Beata's accusation constitutes an "overwhelming burden" that crushes his notion of himself as a moral leader. Rebecca coaxes him – "You were just starting to live, John. You *had* started already" (543) – and tries to revive their great scheme: "You wanted to go like a liberator from house to house, winning minds and wills to your vision." But Rosmer, sadly shaking his head, tells her: "I'll never again be able to relish the one thing that makes it so marvelously sweet to be alive" (544). Softly, leaning over the back of Rosmer's chair, Rebecca asks, "And what's that, John?", and receives an answer very different from the one she expected: not "the joy of love" but "The calm joy of innocence." Thunderstruck, she steps back, able only to repeat the word: "Yes. Innocence" (544).

Intent on retrieving his guiltlessness, Rosmer decides on marriage to the woman with whom he believes he shares a deep conviction in the value of sexless intimacy: "The thing that drew us together from the start – that binds us so closely to each other – the belief that we share that a man and a woman can live together simply as friends" (545). While the dead Beata was safely hysterical, Rosmer spoke of her with tender affection: "poor afflicted soul" (504). Now, in his marriage proposal, his normally grandiloquent language becomes ruthlessly plain: "Then [Beata's] out of the picture. Completely out . . . It has to be so! It has to! I can't – I won't go through life with a corpse on my back" (546). That Rosmer wants to marry Rebecca in the vain hope of erasing disturbing memories of his relation with his first wife is made plain by his marriage proposal, which is not, as Janet Garton has pointed out, "Will you be my wife?", but "Will you be my second wife" ("The Middle Plays" 112). "What kind of proposal is this?" Garton asks rhetorically; "It is tactless to say the least; surely not even a man who has had several wives would choose that moment to remind his intended of her place in the list. With a playwright so conscious of every word, this insertion must be a pointer; and when one considers the rest of the conversation closely, it becomes apparent that a great deal more is said about the first wife than the second" (112). It is to "drown all these memories" of Beata that Rosmer desperately goes on to offer Rebecca "joy and passion" (546). Marrying her, Rosmer can erase both his former wife and his uneasy conscience about her death: "For me, you'll be the only wife I ever had." Thus saved from himself, with his innocence intact, he can live, in the words of Mrs. Alving, "as though the dead had never lived in this house" (232).

Forced to admit that Rosmer can never free himself from his first wife, Rebecca nevertheless clings to her deluded belief that he has "something great and glorious to live for" (553).[6] But looking out through the window at the mill-race, Rosmer sorrowfully renounces his plans – "Happiness, Rebecca dear – more than anything, happiness is a calm, sure sense of being guiltless" (554) – and continues to torture himself with Beata's inability to understand his and Rebecca's "spiritual marriage": "She saw our relationship through the eyes of *her* love – and judged it by the same measure" (555). Rebecca keeps to her position – "Oh, all these doubts, scruples, anxieties – they're the ancestral curse of the family!" (556) – but she is visibly shaken by Rosmer's torment. A private visit from Kroll, affecting her as Brendel's earlier visit had affected Rosmer, pushes her over the edge of her hesitancy and drives her to confession.

Having reversed his characterization of Rebecca from that of the nurturing to the fatal woman, Kroll accuses her of being "behind all this" (557). Rebecca reminds Kroll of his former affection for her, and although Kroll admits that he was smitten – "Who couldn't you bewitch – if you tried?" – he quickly recovers: "You simply wanted to work your way in at Rosmersholm. Embed yourself here. And I could help you along." Needing to crush his own lingering attraction to Rebecca, resentful at being used, and determined to break Rebecca's hold on Rosmer, Kroll mercilessly announces his discovery of Rebecca's low moral background as the natural daughter of midwife Gamvik and the unsavory Dr. West. Rebecca protests vigorously that Dr. West appeared in the district after her birth, and when Kroll reminds her of her age – twenty-nine, almost thirty – she makes an admission that disproves Kroll's contention: "I'm a year older than I claim to be . . . When

I passed twenty-five – and I was still unmarried – I felt I was simply getting too old" (560). Allowing himself a little joke about a "liberated woman" harboring prejudice about the correct age for marriage, Kroll then plays a last card: "But my computations may be right, after all. Because Dr. West was in the district for a short stay a year before he took the practice." Crying out, *"clenching and wringing her hands"*, the overwrought Rebecca denies Kroll's claim with such vehemence that he demands that she explain her reaction: "What do you expect me to think – ?" (561). Frightened by the insinuation in Kroll's question, but cleverer than her adversary, Rebecca regains her self-possession and throws him off the track: "It's simple enough, Dr. Kroll. I have no desire that people think of me as illegitimate." The red herring is too attractive for Kroll not to grasp; so delighted is he by this evidence of the emancipated woman's "prejudice on that score, too" that he abandons his interrogation and delivers a chiding lecture on Rebecca's superficial liberation. And thus the adroit Rebecca has kept Kroll from guessing the reason for her horror at his contention that she was Dr. West's daughter: she was his mistress.[7]

Blindly intent on saving Rosmer for his mission, Rebecca decides to confess to him her responsibility in Beata's death. To give him "the joy of innocence again" (563), she explains how she acted on his behalf; knowing how frightened he would have been if she had spoken of his "stifling and withering away" in a "desolate marriage" (564), she did nothing to discourage the childless, unhappy Beata from believing that it was her duty to step aside for somebody else. Anticipating the "Rat Wife" of *Little Eyolf,* who lures the crippled boy into the water, Rebecca rid Rosmersholm of its troubling presence and absolved its master of responsibility: "You're innocent. I was the one who lured – who managed to lure Beata into the maze" that "led to the mill-race" (565). Rosmer can continue to live in Eden, while Rebecca takes the blame for the fall. Hinting at the transformation she will later explain, the anguished woman who speaks *"in a broken voice"* insists: "I was a different woman then than I am now, standing here telling about it" (566–67). Rebecca now espouses the philosophy of self-effacement she encouraged in Beata: "What happens to me doesn't matter. It isn't very important" (567).

Rebecca's confession fails to achieve its object, for it is Rosmer's weakness, not his destroyed "innocence," that prevents him from carrying out his mission. This "milk-and-water Superman," as James Huneker termed him,[8] is thoroughly deceived about his capacity for leadership, and Rebecca's grandiose view of him as a moral pathfinder is an excellent example of love's power to blind the judgment. Cutting the pages of periodicals, the armchair revolutionary plans his future as the people's secular apostle, but the first time he quits Rosmersholm to confront the world, he crumbles. The accuracy of Kroll's judgment of Rosmer's incapacity for leadership is quickly proven when in one meeting Kroll and Rosmer's "old circle of friends" make Rosmer recognize that the work of ennobling people's minds is "quite beyond me" (572).

Faced with the failure of her dream, Rebecca can now unburden herself of her great secret. Since the object of her confession was to give Rosmer back his innocence, she omitted what she knew would appall him: "the crux of everything" (572). Having come to Rosmersholm because she had a sense that she "could make out well enough" there, she lost her "fearless free will," she declares to the astonished Rosmer, when she became the prey to a "wild, uncontrollable desire" for him (573). It was this that "swept poor Beata into the mill-race." But once Rebecca had dispatched her sister in passion, she began to undergo a strange transformation: "Rosmersholm has stolen my strength. It's crippled my courage and smothered my will. The time is over for me when I could dare anything" (574). Rebecca answers Rosmer's question – "Tell me, how did that happen?" – with the simplest but fullest of answers: "Through living with you." While Beata lived, Rosmer was "never fully himself"; once his sexually demanding wife was dead, the ethereal pastor was free to lead the wholly spiritual existence he longed for. Sharing this life "in peace – in solitude," Rebecca explains, "when you gave me all your thoughts unreservedly – and all your feelings, so delicate, so fine" brought "the great change . . . overwhelming me, to the depths of my soul." Having helped to remove her rival, Rebecca was desexualized by the object of her passion: "All that other – that unbearable sensual desire – ebbed out of me, far, far away" (575). Rebecca would make one last confession to Rosmer, what she calls "something in my past" that makes her morally unfit for Rosmersholm. But Rosmer, whose horror of sexuality recalls that of Pastor Manders in *Ghosts*, "*recoiling*" from the fallen woman's words, stops her: "No, no! Don't say a word. Whatever it is, let me forget about it" (576).

Lacking strength to bear his failure, Rosmer demands of Rebecca that she give him a reason to live by proving the selfless love she claims. Ulrik Brendel's second timely interruption at Rosmersholm provides Rosmer with the answer to Rebecca's perplexed question: "How can I give you proof?" (577).

Dressed in Rosmer's clothes, his double Brendel continues to parody his former pupil. On his way "downhill," he has come to Rosmersholm for another "loan": "Could you spare me an ideal or two?" (578). Exhorting Rosmer to follow his example, Brendel gives his "beloved disciple" a vivid lesson on the "one immutable condition" for victory in his life's work (579). Like a priest officiating at a rite, Brendel, *"taking her gently by the wrist,"* instructs Rebecca in the precise procedures of her necessary self-immolation: "That the woman who loves [Rosmer] will gladly go out in the kitchen and lop off her delicate, pink-and-white little finger – *here* – right at the middle joint. Moreover, that the aforesaid loving lady, just as gladly, cuts off her incomparably formed left ear" (579–80).

As Brendel, on his way to oblivion, functions as Rosmer's anticipatory double, the dead Beata functions as Rebecca's. The image of Rebecca hacking off parts of her body for Rosmer's sake violently recapitulates Beata's oblation of her intrusive self. The mutilation of the phallic finger and vaginal ear hints at Rosmer's and Rebecca's double suicide and signals the annihilation of sexuality implicit in Rosmer's "victory."

Overcome with sorrow at Rosmer's failure to fulfill the task she encouraged, Rebecca despairs of being able to convince him of his ennoblement of at least one person, herself. He gives her a solution that stirs him to the quick, imitating his ballad namesake Rosmer Merman as he lures the woman who loves him into his watery kingdom:[9] "Have you the courage – and the will – gladly, as Ulrik Brendel said – for my sake, now, tonight – gladly – to go the same way Beata went?" (582). Rosmer claims that Rebecca's voluntary death will enable him to regain his faith in his power "to ennoble the human spirit," but the self-deception and egotism in this justification seem less damning than the pleasure Rosmer receives from the image of a second swaying woman following a

first one into the mill-race: "Oh, I have an image of you, so clear
in my mind's eye – standing out on the bridge – there, at the
center. Now you're leaning out over the railing! Swaying, spellbound, out – and down toward the swirling water, the mill-race!"
Gripping his head in his hands, he blurts out: "There's a hideous
fascination about this – !" He seems momentarily horrified by his
own suggestion – "But this is – it's insanity! Either leave – or stay
here! I take you on your word this one time more." But when
Rebecca insists – "No more quaking and running away. How can
you ever believe me on my word of honor after today?" – Rosmer's
response – "But I don't want to see you defeated" – makes it clear
that it was not to save her life that he retreated (583). His allega-
tion – "You'll never be able to follow Beata" – proceeds from a
conviction that damns his demand as nothing else does: "You're
not like Beata. You're not driven by a warped view of life." That
Beata's suicide followed from a distorted vision of reality does not
alter Rosmer's wish that Rebecca imitate her; abnormal or normal, the woman who loves him proves it by dying.

Rosmer need not have worried about Rebecca's resolve: "But
my outlook is shaped by Rosmersholm – *now*. For the stain of my
sin I have to atone" (583). Rebecca will pay in kind for Beata's
death and at the same time duplicate Beata's sacrifice: "My going
will save all that's best in you." But Rosmer has finally parted with
his self-deluded dream; the truth is, as he himself declares with
frank simplicity, "There's nothing left in me to save." "No, there
is," answers Rebecca, denying the avowal that destroys the *raison
d'être* for her death. She reaffirms her decision in words that
demonstrate her transformation into Beata: "But as for me – from
now on, I'd be no better than a sea-troll, hanging like a dead
weight on the ship that's carrying you forward. I have to go
overboard."[10] Rosmer's decision to accompany Rebecca into the
mill-race proves indeed that in him there is "nothing left to save"
and thus underscores the futility of Rebecca's "sacrifice." Solicitous to the end, Rebecca asks him of his choice to die: "And what
if you're deceiving yourself? If it's only a delusion? One of those
white horses of Rosmersholm?" (584). Rosmer's answer – "It's
always possible" – betrays the ultimate nonchalance about life that
lies at the heart of his character.

Taking Beata's place, Rebecca is blessed by the ex-pastor in
preparation for her sacrifice: "I lay my hand, now, upon your

head. And take you in marriage as my own true wife" (584). The
couple then pledges the love death that will constitute their brief
union:

ROSMER: The husband must go with his wife, as the wife with the
   husband.
REBECCA: But tell me this first: is it you who go with me, or I who go
   with you?
ROSMER: We'll never sift to the bottom of that.
REBECCA: Still, I would like to know.
ROSMER: We follow each other, Rebecca. I, you – and you, me. (584)

This love duet, with its coupling of "you/me" "I/you," recalls
Wagner's liebestod litany "Du Isolde, Tristan ich, / nicht mehr
Tristan, / nicht Isolde." But while liebestod lovers die for a fatal but
triumphant passion, eros has been banished from Rosmersholm.
The couple's embrace on the bridge is the first their bodies have
shared.

   "The Rosmer way of life ennobles," the converted Rebecca has
pronounced, but "it kills happiness" (575). She might have said
simply that it kills. Rollo May writes of the interrelation of will and
eros that "both terms describe a person in the process of reaching
out, moving toward the world, seeking to affect others or the
inanimate world."[11] De-eroticized, deadened into inertia, Rebecca
has lost "the power to act" (574). "The Rosmer way of life – or *your*
way of life*," she explains to Rosmer, has "infected my will . . . And
left it an invalid. A slave to laws that never had mattered to me
before" (575). Moving down from Norway's savage Finmark into
the "regions of Galilean gloom,"[12] Rebecca was tamed by Rosmer
and converted to the "white god" of suffering and renunciation
whose coming Hjørdis felt with horror at the end of *The Vikings
at Helgeland.* Just before Brendel arrives to give his lesson on
Rebecca's mutilation, the despairing Rosmer tells Rebecca that he
has nothing to live for, and with some of her remaining vigor, she
replies: "Oh, but – life renews itself. Let's hold it close, John.
We're out of it soon enough" (577). But Rosmer, as "homesick for
the great void" as his stand-in, is already "homeward bound"
(578) for the mill-race. Simple Mrs. Helseth's curtain line – "No
help now – the dead wife – she's taken them" (585) – interprets
the dual suicide as the vengeance of a wronged wife. But Rosmer
demands that Rebecca destroy herself not to atone for Beata's
death, but to prove her love for him. As Beata destroyed herself

for love of the master of Rosmersholm, Rebecca does likewise, becoming a second dead wife as she takes Beata's place.

Citadel of stagnation, whose children never cry and whose grown-ups never laugh, Rosmersholm, spreading its dark influence over the district "like some sort of plague" (551), is the enemy both of joy and of eros, and thus of life. The play's ending suggests an odd, consoling finality, for Rosmer is the last of his race, and thus the swirling waters into which he and the beatified Rebecca have hurled themselves have also closed over Rosmersholm.

THE ACCLIMATIZATION OF ELLIDA AND BOLETTE WANGEL: *THE LADY FROM THE SEA*

> Love is a thing as any spirit free:
> Women of kind desiren libertee,
> And not to been constrained as a thrall –
> And so doon men, if I sooth sayen shall.
> (Chaucer, "The Franklin's Tale," 59–62.)

Bull suggests that it was Ibsen's absorption in Rebecca's Rosmer-induced transformation that led him to dramatize in his next play, in the relation between Ellida Wangel and the seaman, another story of a man's powerful hold on a woman (*H* 11:25). The two plays also share a second, complementary operating action. Rebecca West and *The Lady from the Sea*'s protagonist resemble each other in their origins – both come from Norway's savage Northland – and in their association with the sea. Rebecca grew up by the sea, and Ellida, on an island within it; Brendel refers to Rebecca as "my seductive mermaid" (579), the creature with which Ellida Wangel is identified. The move by the two women from the wild into tamer terrain provokes a conflict that ends in their domestication. But while Rebecca's acclimatization is fatal, Ellida's is life-renewing, and in this sense *The Lady from the Sea* is a happy pendant to its predecessor.

The Ibsens spent the summer of 1887 on Denmark's Jutland coast, mostly in the seaside resort of Sæby, where Suzannah could take long walks in the neighboring forests and Ibsen could indulge in his habit of sea gazing as he thought out his next play. In Sæby, Ibsen encountered the story of a local author, Adda Ravnkilde, who had committed suicide at the age of twenty-one.

He visited Ravnkilde's home and grave, and read her works with interest. The short story "Pyrrhic Victory" describes a marriage in which the wife, who wishes to become a writer, challenges a husband who demands that she devote her life to him, a conflict Ibsen would dramatize in *The Lady from the Sea* in Lyngstrand's and Bolette's argument about a wife's role in marriage. A repeated leitmotiv in Ravnkilde's autobiographical work is a longing to escape the provincial town for the great world, a dream Ibsen gave to Bolette. Another overriding subject is a young woman's losing battle to overcome her obsessional, self-destructive love for a man, the kind of disastrous attachment Ibsen would dramatize in his protagonist Ellida Wangel's relation with the seaman.

The subject of a woman's unhappy thralldom to a man bears an obvious resemblance to the youthful experience of Magdalene Thoresen, who is generally recognized as having influenced Ibsen's portrait of Ellida Wangel (whom Ibsen first called "Thora"). Ellida's love affair with the mysterious Finn who exercises a mesmerizing effect on her recalls Magdalene Kragh's similar experience with an Icelander in her student days. After these early liaisons, both women made financially secure marriages with men old enough to be their fathers. Her past aside, Madgalene Thoresen influenced Ibsen's protagonist principally in the kinship she felt with the sea. She regarded herself as both a sea and land animal; as an old woman, living on the Danish coast, she once told a visitor, gesturing toward the ocean, "Isn't it superb here? Oh, I belong to the sea. It draws me, it draws me" (*H* 11:26). Ellida Wangel's daily swims beyond the fjord directly recall the habit of Magdalene Thoresen, who continued her vigorous sea-baths into her seventies. Ibsen also has his protagonist voice his mother-in-law's complaint that the fjord waters, too close to land, were stale and unhealthy.[13]

The Lady from the Sea draws on the merfolk of Nordic folklore. The male water-spirit the "nøkk," usually associated with rivers and streams, but sometimes with the sea, charms with his seductive songs and can cast dangerous spells. Through the mere fact of being Norwegian, Ibsen was familiar with this creature, who appears in his poems. He encountered the "havmand," the merman proper, in the Danish and Norwegian ballad collections he read early in his career. Like the "nøkk," the "havmand" can lure, but he is normally more benign that his female counterpart the "havfrue," the mermaid, known for her power to seduce. Another important tradition in Nordic mermaid lore from the Christian era onwards is that of the "good" mermaid who desires to become human so that she may possess a soul. The most well-known version is Hans Christian Andersen's *The Little Mermaid,* which Ibsen knew. The folk tradition also contains many accounts of stranded or captured mermaids who lived unhappily, some of them dying, in their foreign environment. In shaping his drama, Ibsen typically drew on the different traditions as it pleased him. His "merman" possesses the power to seduce, while his "mermaid" feels trapped in the human world, yet longs to be integrated within it.[14]

Ibsen originally called his play *Havfruen* (*The Mermaid*); the transformational pun *Fruen fra Havet* (*The Lady from the Sea*) may have resulted from a recognition that the text's insistence on Ellida as "mermaid" called for a more nuanced title. Early in the first scene, the choral figure Ballested speaks of his projected painting "The Dying Mermaid," in which a stranded mermaid lies "expiring in the tide pools" (594); it is the lady of the house, he explains, who has given him the idea. Ellida herself comes out of the sea to enter the play, her wet hair streaming over her shoulders; "Well, there's our mermaid," greets her husband (603).

Ibsen returns to the plot structure of *The Feast at Solhoug, Love's Comedy, The Vikings at Helgeland,* and *Ghosts,* as he places his female protagonist between two opposing men. Ellida has come to love the man she married out of duty, but she is haunted by memories of a Finnish seaman whom she "wed" years before when he tossed their joined rings into the sea. The return of the seaman, who comes to claim his bride, precipitates the crisis of a drama that is both "marriage play" and fable.

The daughter of a lighthouse keeper, Ellida bears a Viking name, a feminine version of "Ellidi," Fridtjof the Bold's brave ship, which seemed to take on life as it plunged through the waves. Widower Dr. Wangel removed his sea-woman bride from her solitary island and placed her in his house in a city on the mainland. He isolated her within his household, allowing her no responsibilities and separating her from his two daughters. Believing "these matters" to be "beyond her competence" (656), he "wanted her just as she was" (657). He built her a private space, an arbor on the lawn, fitter for a woman from the wild than the verandah frequented by his daughters.

Ellida suffers from a mysterious depression that began when her baby died. She no longer has sexual relations with her husband, and is experiencing an emotional and mental anguish he is unable to cure with medications. He has decided on the extreme remedy of moving with her to the sea, where "the poor sick child will be going home again" (623). His wife belongs not to a human home, but to the wild, not to culture, but to nature, and the paternalistic doctor–husband will cure his ailing mermaid by replunging her into her element.

This solution frightens Ellida, who tells her husband the story of her relation with the sailor to convince him that a return to the sea will expose her to the source of her misery. The tale she tells is a Wagner-like scenario of suprahuman identities and powers. The mysterious sailor, who roamed the seas of the world, wooed the lighthouse keeper's daughter with wondrous descriptions of "the sea in the sparkling sunlight," of "whales and dolphins, and of the seals that would lie out on the skerries in the warm noon sun" (626). He was the sea god – "all these creatures belonged to him" – and she his nereid – "I almost felt that I belonged among them, too." One day at dawn, Ellida received a message to meet her merman lover on a headland, where he told her he had killed his captain in self-defense and was forced to flee. Announcing that they would marry themselves to the sea, he flung their joined rings far beyond land, then left her. Reflecting on her experience, Ellida soon saw how "mad and meaningless it had all been" (627), but although she wrote to the sailor to end it, and then forgot him, he "returned," horribly, during her pregnancy of three years ago; she can still see him before her, wearing his stickpin, a great blue-white pearl "like the eye of a dead fish" (631). And her baby son, who lived only a few months, had eyes that changed with the color of the sea, like those of the sailor.

Ellida's sexual alienation from her husband results from an irrational terror that the seaman "possessed" Wangel's body to father her sickly child. If she obsessively confuses the two men, it is because her marriage is a bourgeois version of the high Romantic idyll on the island. In the confrontation between the Stranger and Wangel, each man stakes his claim on the woman he believes is his. The Stranger declares that Ellida "belongs to" him because of the binding force of their prior "marriage" (644), and Wangel, repeatedly referring to the present Ellida in the third person as "my wife," insists that "the lighthouse keeper's daughter" is his alone (643–44). The object of the men's dispute, who has internalized her husband's view of her as a helpless and ill dependant, clings to his arm in terror, begging him to "save" her.

Ellida's notion of herself is transformed by the Stranger's retort to his rival: "If Ellida goes off with me, she'll have to come of her own free will" (644). While Wangel regards this as madness, for Ellida, "Everything came together in those words – like a beam of light – and I can see things now, as they are" (663). Her epiphany makes her understand that her unhappiness as Wangel's wife comes from the "plain, simple truth," she tells him, that he "bought" her; "out after a new wife," he proposed marriage, and she accepted his "offer." He knew her no better than the Stranger did; having seen her "a couple of times," he simply "wanted" her (662). In marrying, Ellida "sold" herself: the "meanest work – the poorest conditions would have been better – if I'd chosen them myself, by my own free will" (663). Because Ellida did not come to Wangel freely, theirs is "really no marriage" at all and she thus begs him to "dissolve the contract" (663–64). She refuses to take shelter in the dependent identity of a powerless wife: "I must have freedom of choice" (665). Wangel is horrified that Ellida can contemplate leaving him for a stranger, but his wife reminds him that she knew him no better than the sailor, and yet "went off" with him; following a doctor who offers maintenance for life is no more defensible than following a sailor over the sea. And once Wangel took his mermaid home, she felt as rootless there as on the sea. She remarks that if she left, she would not even have a key to give up. Except for their intimate relation, Ellida remained "totally outside" Wangel's life because he "alone" wanted it that way (672). Wangel's segregation of his exotic treasure sealed her off from life on land: "Now I have nothing to hold me here – no foundation – no support – no impulse toward everything that should have been our deepest common bonds" (672).

When the Stranger returns to hear Ellida's decision, Wangel remains fixed in his paternalism: "My wife has no choice in this. I'll both decide – and defend – where she's concerned" (684). Ellida adamantly resists her husband, reminding him that he can

lock her up, but he cannot control her "dreams and desires –
those you can never constrain!" (685). Fearing that keeping
Ellida by force will drive her into madness, Wangel abruptly releases her from their contract. She has become so dear to him that
she may "choose in freedom" on her "own responsibility." It is a
miracle cure; Ellida cries out: "How this – transforms everything!".
Wangel's love has exorcised his wife's demon; the Stranger is no
more to her than "a dead man who came up out of the sea – and
who's drifting back down again" (686). She will now return to her
husband "because I come to you freely – and on my own" (687).
At the play's end, Ballested completes Ellida's iconography as he
comments that mermaids die when left on land, but "people,
human beings – they can acclam – acclimatize themselves" (688).
The great steamer glides out over the fjord, carrying the Stranger
back to sea. It is the last ship before the arrival of winter. The sea-
lanes will soon be locked in ice and Ellida's sea-baths ended, but
she will not miss them, for the mermaid has metamorphosed:
"Once you've really become a land animal, then there's no going
back again" (688).

The resolution of the Wangel marriage plot constitutes an obvious opposition to the ending of *A Doll House*; the "miracle" of the
"true marriage" Nora speaks of comes true when Wangel no
longer treats his wife as a possession but as a free human being.
Accommodation born of love overcomes the past and enables the
couple to begin again, as Ellida says, "with the shared memories of
our lives" (687).

If *The Lady from the Sea* is the happiest of Ibsen's mature plays, it
is only so without its sinister sub-plot. For juxtaposed with the
"celebratory comedy"[15] of the "re-marriage" of the Wangels is the
dark drama of Wangel's daughter Bolette.

The Norwegian parliament's opening Christiania University
(now the University of Oslo) to women in 1882, six years before
the publication of *The Lady from the Sea*, is crucial to Ibsen's sub-
plot.[16] Dr. Wangel had promised Bolette that she could attend,
but his enlightened liberalism vanished when his wife died.
Bolette Wangel became her father's housekeeper, and continues
to perform this function several years after his remarriage. A
dutiful daughter, she is a surrogate wife, taking care of her
younger sister Hilda, running the household, and worrying about
her father's drinking. She accepts his affectionate pats on the

head and understands his absorption in her step-mother's illness. In the little time she has left from housekeeping, she reads books about the subjects she longs to study and dreams about escaping from the "fish pond," as she calls the isolated town, to the great world (635).

The arrival of Arnholm, Bolette's former tutor, provides her with an understanding ear. Voicing her frustration, she wavers between guilt and resentment; although she dreads leaving the father she loves, she believes it unfair that she should have to sacrifice her life for his; "I have obligations to myself, too" (637), she says, echoing Nora Helmer. Encouraged by Arnholm's sympathy, Bolette asks him to remind her father of his promise. But Dr. Wangel, who has declared to Arnholm that he would make any sacrifices for his wife and daughters, now tells him that Bolette's university education is "totally out of the realm of possibility" (674). When Arnholm reports her father's decision, Bolette's disappointment is short-lived, for the well-off Arnholm insists on providing what her father refuses. Bolette is overjoyed by her old tutor's generosity, but her joy lasts no longer than her prior disappointment, for once she has accepted Arnholm's offer, she is asked to do so as Mrs. Arnholm. Recoiling, she regards this as "unthinkable": "You were my teacher. I can't imagine being in any other kind of relationship to you" (677). Arnholm stands by his offer, but Bolette, repeating Nora's refusal to accept Rank's help once she knows he loves her, will not help herself at Arnholm's expense: "There's absolutely nothing I can take from you – nothing after this!" (678). But like his predecessor Guldstad in *Love's Comedy*, Arnholm has determined to have the young woman whether she wants him or not; her feelings do not matter to him, only her person. He coolly asks whether she would "rather stay here at home and watch life slipping away" than marry him and acquire the education she longs for, and then notes the Hobson's choice that will confront her after her father dies: she will either have to "stand alone and helpless in the world" or marry another man for whom she "quite possibly – might also feel no affection" (678). Trapped, Bolette makes the bargain; if she can "live in the world" and "study anything" she wants, Arnholm can have her (679).

Bolette's marriage of convenience differs sharply from those of earlier, more conventional Ibsen women. Penniless Margit,

Svanhild, Helene Alving, and Bolette's own step-mother make marriages of convenience out of womanly duty. Bolette Wangel marries to educate herself. That Bolette's predecessors were expected to marry for financial security for themselves or for their families is unjust enough, but that Bolette, in order to achieve her dream of learning, must also marry a man she does not love seems even more heinous. Bolette resembles Dina Dorf of *Pillars of Society* in her rejection of women's servitude, her desire to escape a provincial environment, and her longing for education. But while Dina gets love along with freedom and learning – she will travel to America and educate herself with a man she loves at her side – Bolette will have to share the bed of a man she views as a "decrepit specimen" (600). One cannot believe that the delights of the intellectual life will compensate for being Mrs. Arnholm. Like the reluctant Svanhild in *Love's Comedy*, who puts off her wedding date, Bolette asks her intended not to announce their engagement. Bolette's novel marriage of convenience – trading herself for self-development – is a contradictory bargain that seems as doomed to failure as those of her more conventional predecessors.

The Lady from the Sea looks back directly to *Pillars of Society* and *A Doll House* in its direct discussions of marriage. More naive than Torvald Helmer, more fatuous than Bernick or Rørlund, the young sculptor Lyngstrand is Ibsen's parodic representative of received ideas on male/female relationships. Rørlund reads aloud to women from a book that preaches their servitude, and Lyngstrand guarantees Bolette that his expertise on marriage comes from "quite a few books" whose happiest notion is the transformation of the wife, who "little by little makes herself over until she becomes like her husband" (650). To Bolette's irreverent question – "Has it ever occurred to you that perhaps a man could also be absorbed that way, over into his wife?" – Lyngstrand answers that this process would be impossible, for unlike a woman, "a man has his vocation to live for" (651). Lyngstrand has to admit that there is something in Bolette's cavil – "All men? Every last one?" – but goes on to pontificate about the calling of the artist, who lives for his art alone. To Bolette's question, "Yes, but what about her?" – the same question Johan put to Bernick about Martha – Lyngstrand makes Bernick's reply: "Her? Who?" The ensuing dialogue, which looks back to *Love's*

Comedy and forward to *When We Dead Awaken,* satirically exposes the egotism inherent in the notion of woman as the artist's helpmate:

BOLETTE: The one he marries. What's she going to live for?
LYNGSTRAND: She'll live for his art, also. I think a woman must feel a
    profound happiness in that.
BOLETTE: Hm – I wonder really –
LYNGSTRAND: Oh, yes, that you can believe. Not only from all the
    honor and esteem that she'll win through him – because I think that
    ought to be reckoned about the least of it. But that she can help him
    to create – that she can ease his work for him by being there and
    making him comfortable and taking care of him and seeing that his
    life is really enjoyable. I think that must be thoroughly satisfying for
    a woman. (651)

This bald sanctimoniousness is more than Bolette can bear: "Why, you have no idea how self-centered you are!" (652). Uncomprehending, Lyngstrand continues imperturbably, paying Bolette what he thinks is a great compliment; about to go south for his health, he asks her to think of him in his absence, for it will make his work "as an artist go easier and faster," and as for her, "I should think it would be quite exhilarating for you, too – out here so remote from everything – to know secretly that you were helping me create" (653). Later, Lyngstrand pretentiously confides to Hilda, who wonders if he will marry her sister when he returns, that by that time Bolette will be too old. For now, Bolette's thinking of him is necessary for his art, and "it's easy enough for her to do, when she hasn't any real vocation in life, anyhow" (681). When he is ready to marry, he will perhaps choose the suitably younger Hilda, and meanwhile, Bolette will have served her purpose, "living quietly in her dreams of me" (581). The similarity to Peer and Solveig is unmistakeable. Man lives, woman lives for him.

One of the most common commonplaces about Ibsen is that *The Wild Duck,* the first of the eight "late plays," marks the beginning of the non-polemical playwright, the point at which "social criticism had faded into the background, where it was to remain for the rest of [Ibsen's] life" (M 512).[17] It is frequently pointed out that Ibsen's last treatment of political issues is in *The Wild Duck*'s successor *Rosmersholm,* and that with *The Lady from the Sea,* Ibsen began the dramas of the individual that would characterize the rest of his plays. "What seemed to matter to him now," writes McFarlane, "were particulars rather than generalities; his attention was addressed to private dilemma rather than public abuse, to what was individual and personal rather than typical or representative" (*OI* 6:17). This distinction does not hold with Ibsen's investigations of women. *The Lady from the Sea* continues to dramatize individual women refusing or reinscribing the narrow identities society assigns them in a main and sub-plot that directly oppose each other. Ellida insists that her husband cancel their marriage when she realizes that she has sold herself to him; Bolette lets herself be purchased, convinced that her fate as a woman is to be forever unfree. And the marriage of convenience she agrees to with her former tutor looks forward to another hellish bargain, the one Hedda Gabler makes with another learned man. *The Lady from the Sea* continues Ibsen's earlier analyses of received ideas about women in Lyngstrand's mouthings on woman as man's servant and helpmeet, notions as sentimental and sexist as the similar ones by Brand, by Rørlund and Bernick in *Pillars of Society*, and by Torvald in *A Doll House*. The ideology that vocationless woman's essential life is her relation to a man who lives for his work will be devastatingly examined in *Little Eyolf* and *John Gabriel Borkman*. The image of woman's absorption into her superior, sponge-like mate will be grotesquely realized in Thea and Tesman in *Hedda Gabler*. The theory of woman as the male artist's serene inspirational aid will be powerfully subverted in *When We Dead Awaken*. The miraculous rebirth of the Wangels' marriage through the husband's recognition of his wife's autonomy is the calm before the storm.

CHAPTER 9

The deviant woman as hero: Hedda Gabler

THE UNREAL WOMAN IN THE REALISTIC PLAY:
HEDDA AS ANOMALY

Sooner or later, they will realize what the play is intended to convey. My husband figures on about ten years for the public to arrive at an understanding of his dramas.

Suzannah Thoresen Ibsen (Z 234)

When *Hedda Gabler* appeared in the Oslo bookshops in December, 1890, it received the worst notices of any of Ibsen's plays since *Ghosts*, nine years earlier. But while the outraged critics of *Ghosts* confidently identified what was wrong with that abhorrent work, the word that appears most often in the early reviews of *Hedda Gabler* is "incomprehensible" (*H* 11:261). One reason for the bewilderment was the play's resolute realism; the work now valued as the high point of Ibsen's realist method confounded its first audience with the insistent mimeticism of a natural, broken dialogue.

But if the language was too realistic, the protagonist was too unreal. Reviewers in Scandinavia, England, and the United States accused Ibsen of wilful obscurity on the grounds that a Hedda Gabler could not exist. For the literary critic of Oslo's *Morgenbladet*, Hedda was a "monster created by the author in the form of a woman who has no counterpart in the real world."[1] The *Aftenposten* reviewer declared highhandedly: "We neither understand nor believe in Hedda Gabler. She is not related to any one we know."[2] The less composed author of "The Ibsen Question" for England's *Fortnightly Review* found Hedda to be such an "impossible" woman that the "real" women of Norway and Germany should be angry at Ibsen for inventing her (Hedda was evidently so far removed from Englishwomen that they had no need to bother).[3] For the *New York Times* reviewer of the first American production, Ibsen must have intended Hedda as a pathological case like those "in the pages of the *Journal of Mental Science.*"[4]

The play's early commentators generally depended for logic on begging the question; they refused Hedda the status of woman because they found her unwomanly. Like the early critics of *A Doll House* who rejected the play on the grounds that no real woman would leave her children, *Hedda Gabler*'s detractors dismissed it as mere anecdote because its protagonist was an "inhuman woman – a savage . . . atrocious and intolerable" ("The Ibsen Question" 737–38).

Recognizing the brilliance of *Hedda Gabler*, later commentators have nevertheless echoed the critical position that Ibsen's protagonist is so outrageous that the play cannot be "about" anything. In the most thorough consideration of *Hedda Gabler* as a masterpiece of realism, Jens Arup notes that when Hedda "moves through a career of crime so wanton and so sordid, above all so wilfully unreasonable," we "are forced into reaction against her" ("On *Hedda Gabler*" 14); but while "every utterance and every action [of the play] is packed with meaning in its application to the situation of the play itself," Ibsen did not provide a "set of categories" with which to judge Hedda. The drama is thus wholly self-referential, "too realistic to have any meaning whatever" (7). Muriel Bradbrook makes a similar point: Ibsen's protagonist is "a study in a vacuum," and yet the spectator is given "no frame, no comment" by which to judge her (*Ibsen* 117). This "coldest, most impersonal" of Ibsen's dramas, Weigand comments, inspires in us only "cold curiosity and contempt," and in the end, is "simply a spectacle of life from which we retire with shock" (*The Modern Ibsen*; 242, 244). Ibsen's protagonist remains an enigma and his drama a work about nothing but its strange self.

One of the most frequent comments about Hedda Gabler is her paucity of motive. Many of the play's early denigrators deemed this a flaw in Ibsen's dramaturgy; the *Fortnightly* writer's complaint is typical: Hedda is "malignant to the point of murder with no sufficient cause" (738). Other commentators have taken Hedda's lack of motive as part of Ibsen's purpose. Edward Dowden, that barometer of correct Victorian opinion, noted that Hedda "comes from the void, and into the void she goes"; had her "luck been better" than to be the wife of a husband she scorned, "her existence would not have been been essentially changed" (A 13:254). Lou Andreas-Salomé, whose volatile, fifteen-page indictment of Ibsen's "monster" makes her the fiercest of all Hedda's detractors, speaks of Hedda's "complete lack of motive power," her "poverty-stricken soul," her "lifeless iciness," and asks rhetorically, "What could have surfaced from the nature of a Hedda, except bored and therefore irritable mischief that stems from petty motives?"[5] Elizabeth Hardwick analyzes: "Hedda Gabler is unusual, I believe, in having no motivation whatsoever . . . [She] is a temptation, very special, like the Serpent, chosen by nature, by some casual stroke of fate, to represent threatening, willful, beguiling coldness."[6] Hardwick, like Dowden, is confident that if Hedda's life had been different, she would have been the same: "She is not the flower of environment, but rather of inner essence" (63–64). Harold Bloom agrees; "even if the Norwegian society of her day had allowed her to rise to Chief Executive Officer of the firearms industry, Hedda would still have been sadomasochistic, manipulative, murderous, and suicidal."[7] Like Coleridge's motiveless Iago, Hedda acts as she acts because she is as she is, a vicious, evil nature. Hedda, in other words, was born bad.

THE DEFECTIVE WOMAN: HEDDA AS TYPE

That [Hedda] is dramatically worth the while is beside the question. Her ending by a pistol shot is justice itself; alive she fascinates as does some exotic reptile. She is representative of her species, the loveless woman. James Huneker (A 13:288)

Henry James, one of the contemporary commentators who admired *Hedda Gabler*, praised Ibsen for taking up "one of the last subjects that an expert might have been expected to choose," namely "the study of an exasperated woman" ("On the Occasion of *Hedda Gabler*" 251). But James found the subject herself strangely particularized. He noted that Ibsen, who is "dealing, essentially, with the individual caught in the fact," occasionally, as in *Hedda Gabler*, "leans too far on that side," and thus we cannot be sure of Hedda's "type-quality" (255).

Most of Hedda's commentators do not share James' uncertainty about her "type-quality." In fact, much of the criticism of *Hedda Gabler* can be described as a determined effort to classify its protagonist as a defective form of Woman. For the author of an early monograph on Ibsen, Hedda Gabler represented "a complete perversion of womanhood."[8] Brandes, who as usual defended Ibsen's play, called Hedda "a true type of degeneration" who does not "even" meet the bottom line of womanhood, "the ability to yield herself, body and soul, to the man she loves" (B 106). More recently, Harold Beyer called *Hedda Gabler* "another study [after *Rosmersholm* and *The Lady from the Sea*] of female distempers."[9]

Relatedly, Hedda has been characterized as an example of the "New Woman," but as aimless bourgeoise, "a grimmer counterpart" of Nora Helmer, "a doll turned monster . . . She is the idle, emancipated woman – and what she is to do with her emancipation, the devil only knows."[10] Sigrid Undset was so annoyed by Ibsen's taking this type of woman seriously that she devoted an essay to belittling the play. Undset structures her bitingly condescending argument on a comparison between Ibsen's drama and Jane Austen's novel *Emma*. Like Austen's protagonist, Hedda has nothing to do and so spends her time meddling in other people's lives. However, "a hundred years ago," Undset claims in 1917, the woman "whose only special ability is the one of doing mischief" could not do so much harm that a Mr. Knightly "could not come in the end, stroke the pussycat a little and then carry her away"; later, "each and every little common cat was told that her highest attribute was . . . that she was a distant relative of lions and tigers." Ibsen took his protagonist seriously, but Austen and Undset know what women like Hedda Gabler really amount to, all those "many silly little Heddas [who] played with dangerous toys, and [for whom] it went as wrong with them as it does with Hedda Gabler."[11]

Freudian interpreters have classified Hedda as a study in sexual neurosis. Ingjald Nissen, one of Norway's most distinguished psychoanalysts, argued in 1931 that Ibsen's protagonist has internalized her puritan culture's notion of sexual intercourse as debasing, and married the passionless Tesman because he did not threaten her sexually. Once married, she is physically revolted by her husband, but will not admit that she has sexual needs, or that some other man could satisfy them.[12] Gail Finney has recently argued that Hedda is "the personification of the hysterization of the female body, or the reduction of the woman to her status as female," yet uses Freud's criteria to diagnose Hedda as a true hysteric: Hedda's "antipathy to sex – evident in her outraged reaction to Løvborg's sexual overtures years before, in her coldness toward Tesman, and in her assurances to Brack and Løvborg that she intends to remain faithful . . . is akin to the disgust with the genitals of the opposite sex which Freud views as 'one of the characteristics of all hysterics, and especially of hysterical women' " (160).[13] Unlike Nora, who "moves from hysteria and the consideration of suicide to feminism, Hedda remains caught in hysteria" (164).

Psychiatrist Karl Stern is grateful to Ibsen for providing in Hedda a textbook case of the "phallic woman" who refuses the normal female "desire to receive, to hold and to nourish."[14] This is why Hedda cannot give herself to Løvborg. She burns his manuscript because as a woman she cannot produce manuscripts and is jealous of his male capacity to do so. While Ibsen refrains "from an explicit moral, to us, the spectators, the moral is implicit" (146): the phallic woman in *The Taming of the Shrew* was merely "good for a laugh," but by the end of the nineteenth century, "the thing had become deadly serious" (160), and Ibsen's play is a timely warning against a deplorable phenomenon in modern life.

The men Hedda should have loved

Like the critical tradition that claims that the heart of *Ghosts* is Mrs. Alving's failure to be sexually warm to her husband, the argument that *Hedda Gabler* is the study of a loveless or frigid woman puts at the center of the play the protagonist's failure to love a man. But while Captain Alving exists only by reputation, the protagonist's husband in *Hedda Gabler* is not only alive and present, but one of Ibsen's most successful comic creations – George Tesman the medieval historian, a solid, if plodding, scholar, but an infantile adult. This has somewhat widened the critical terrain. Only an occasional critic admonishes Hedda outright for not loving Tesman,[15] but critics who maintain that Hedda's physical antipathy to him substantiates her coldness, repression, or hysteria, implicitly mean that Hedda should have liked, or at least not minded, sleeping with him. Hedda's refusal of Brack is also sometimes named as proof of her sexual abnormality.[16] The favorite victim of Hedda's erotic failure, however, is neither Brack nor Tesman, but Tesman's foil, the maverick historian Eilert Løvborg. Weigand speaks for many critics when he notes that "Hedda would have loved Løvborg had she been capable of either sympathy or genuine passion" (*The Modern Ibsen* 250). Other commentators take Hedda's rejection of Løvborg as the determining factor in the play's action. For Martin Esslin, "Hedda's inability to give herself to Løvborg" elicits "tragic results."[17] Similarly, Else Høst claims that Hedda's erotic cowardice is the center of the drama, whose principal conflict is between engaging in life and living vicariously. Hedda's taste for hearing about forbidden pleasures underscores her inability to love, and together with her victim Løvborg, and Brack, Hedda makes up a "triumvirate of sin" (*Hedda Gabler* 124).

Analyzers of the play's action often accord primary importance to Løvborg. For Jens Arup, the center of the play is Hedda's "attempt, and her failure, to gain control over Løvborg" ("On *Hedda Gabler*" 28); Harley Olton considers the play's principal action to be Hedda's destruction of Løvborg and a "second principal action" the struggle between the loveless and the loving woman over Løvborg's soul;[18] Maurice Valency even names Løvborg as the play's protagonist (*The Flower and the Castle* 181).[19]

The woman Hedda should have been

Commentators who treat Hedda as a destructive or inadequate woman frequently hold up her foil Thea Elvsted as a model of the true, i.e., maternal woman. For Stern, Thea represents normal, receptive femininity against Hedda's perverse phallicism. For Høst, Thea's unswerving devotion to Løvborg serves to point up Hedda's cold selfishness. Making similar points, Stein Olsen reads Ibsen's hair symbolism as embodying a lesson on true femininity; unlike Hedda, the thicker-haired Thea has the courage to challenge society's conventions by leaving her husband to follow the man she loves, and her "hair is a manifestation of her femininity and a symbol of those female instincts which Hedda either does not possess or refuses to acknowledge."[20] Both Høst and Olsen echo Lou Salomé: "[Thea] tears the bonds that fasten her . . . because she knows that Løvborg needs her. As timid and modest as she is, she has courage at the center of her love" (*Ibsen's Heroines* 136). Valency summarizes: "The difference between the two aspects of womanhood could not be more emphatically demonstrated. Hedda cannot help a man create, either biologically or intellectually, because . . . she desires to arrogate the masculine role to herself. Thea is willing to take the passive role. She is able, accordingly, simply by being a woman, to make men behave like men" (*The Flower and the Castle* 201). Hedda should have been like Thea and wanted what Thea did.

THE AUTHOR'S RIGHT TO A SUBJECT: HEDDA'S REALITY

HEDDA: Oh yes, Judge – I was going to say, you make your bed and then you lie in it (729).

Hedda's detractors base their arguments against her on the unstated premise that she should have been other than what she was. James' comment remains the best starting point for a response to this critical position: "That Mrs. Tesman is a perfectly ill-regulated person is a matter of course, and there are doubtless spectators who would fain ask whether it would not have been better to represent in her stead a person totally different. The answer to this sagacious question seems to me to be simply that no one can possibly tell" ("On the Occasion of *Hedda Gabler*" 251). The playwright begins, moreover, where his protagonist's critics end; what interests him is the dramatic "use" of "a wicked, diseased, disagreeable woman" (252). And after one has experienced Ibsen's "use" of Hedda, James notes, "one isn't so sure" that she is wicked and "by no means sure" that she is disagreeable (252).

Any discussion of the "reality" of Hedda should take note of the fact that Ibsen said that he had based her on a woman he knew in Munich. She was called "Alberg" and "Gabler" may be an anagram of her name. Nothing else is known about her except that she killed herself by taking poison (K 398). More importantly, to argue that Hedda is an evil or motiveless anomaly is to ignore Ibsen's finely drawn, ample presentation of the reality his protagonist lives and has every reason to hate. To claim that Hedda is a defective or neurotic woman because she loves none of the men in the play is to assume that simply because they are there, she ought to love one of them; it is to ignore her own feelings about them, as though she had no rights in the matter. The popular stance that if she had sexually yielded to Løvborg, her life would have been happy, assumes that for Hedda, her love life is her whole life, when nothing suggests that this is so, or if not, then it ought to have been. The notion that Løvborg's death is the heart of the play is unconvincing as dramatic theory alone because it privileges the fate of a secondary character over the protagonist's; it is akin to claiming that Duncan's destruction is the center of *Macbeth*. Like *Ghosts* and *Rosmersholm*, *Hedda Gabler* is a drama of ripe condition that plays out the final phase of an old, relentless, plot. Its dramatic action is the final development of the life indicated by the play's title, the last two days of a cornered woman's increasingly futile effort to live a life she despises and her consequent decision to end it.

In the first two scenes of the play, which take place, respectively, between Miss Tesman and the maid Berta, and between Miss Tesman and George Tesman, Ibsen characterizes the enemy world into which Hedda has married, which he described as follows: "George Tesman, his old aunts, and the faithful servant Berta together form a picture of complete unity. They think alike, they share the same memories and have the same outlook on life. To Hedda they appear like a strange and hostile power, aimed at her very being" (*LS* 299). The *mater familias* of this group, George Tesman's maiden aunt Juliana Tesman, has come to pay the returned honeymoon couple a morning visit. The play begins with a conversation between Miss Tesman and Berta on Berta's sad transfer from the aunts' house. Miss Tesman makes the first of many references to her life of self-sacrifice: "Lord knows it was misery for me to give you up" (696). Berta, who also lives for others, i.e., the Tesmans, is "*on the verge of tears*" at the end of "all those many blessed years" and worries that she will not be able to please her new mistress. Miss Tesman reminds her of Hedda's extenuating social position: "Well, of course. General Gabler's daughter." Ibsen gives us a glimpse of Hedda's pre-Tesman existence in Miss Tesman's admiring description: "What a life she had in the general's day! Remember seeing her out with her father – how she'd go galloping past in that long black riding outfit, with a feather in her hat?" Both women agree that they "never would have dreamed then that she and George Tesman would make a match of it" (696).

Miss Tesman repeats her surprise shortly after she greets her nephew: "And that it was *you* who carried off Hedda Gabler" (699). And indeed, only his adoring aunt could imagine George

Tesman, so oblivious to his wife's body that he is unaware of her pregnancy, as a masterful suitor. What George immediately and exuberantly announces to the woman he still calls by his chilhood appellation "Aunt Julie" is a book pregnancy, the "whole suitcase stuffed full of notes" he made from the archival discoveries of his honeymoon (298). Having noticed Hedda's condition the pre-ceding evening, Miss Tesman is eager for George to confide his "expectations," but he can only reply: "I have every expectation in the world of becoming a professor" (699). The domestic indus-tries to which George Tesman gives his attention – those of his book on Brabant handicrafts – are the dead ones of the middle ages.

The conversation of Juliana and George Tesman is heavily marked by the moralistic cliché, the language of Gregers and Hjalmar in *The Wild Duck.* Tesman has learned how to speak it – "You, who've been father and mother to me both" (698) – from his adoptive parent, whose true language it is: "Ah, dear God – if only my poor brother could look up from his grave and see what his little boy has become!" (697); "What other joy do I have in this world than smoothing the path for you, my dear boy?" (701). The Tesman language is the natural expression of the Tesman view of life, a morality play in which the virtuous prosper and the wicked fail. And the Tesmans, of course, belong to the former category; with sanctimonious satisfaction, Miss Tesman assures her good boy: "Yes, and those who stood against you – who wanted to bar your way – they've gone down. They've fallen, George. The one most dangerous to you [Eilert Løvborg] – he fell farthest" (701).

Maiden aunt and nephew constitute an affectionate couple of worshipful, adoptive mother and attentive, surrogate son. Follow-ing family tradition, George takes off his aunt's hat, then fondly pats her cheek. She takes his hands, gazing at him in rapture: "How wonderful it is having you here, right before my eyes again, George!" (698). When his aunt, who treats the thirty-three-year-old doctor of philosophy as though he were still the orphaned child she took in years ago, reveals the news of her latest parental gift – the mortaging of her own and her sister's pension as security for George's carpets and furniture – he objects at first, but accepts the inevitable: "Oh, Auntie Julie – you never get tired of making sacrifices for me!" (701).

Juliana Tesman emerges from these two scenes a paragon, approaching parody, of a familiar nineteenth-century type of self-sacrificing womanhood, the good spinster who devotes her life to a male relation, like Martha in *Pillars of Society*. But unlike Martha, who comes to realize that she has thrown her life away, Miss Tesman clings to the object of her sacrifice. She has already welcomed her nephew home the evening before, yet she hurries to visit him early the next morning: "I simply had to look in on you a moment" (697). The grotesque mortage of two elderly sisters' only income assures George's continuing grateful dependance.

The object of Miss Tesman's adoration is a *tantegutt*, an "aunts' boy," doted on from childhood and protected from adult life. With his aunt's encouragement he complacently continues to be the subsidized dependent. But while he seems more boy than man, he speaks with the kind of tick normally associated with age, punctuating his sentences with a superfluous "uh?".[21] Overjoyed to see his aunt on the morning after he returns from his honeymoon, he is as attached to his protector as she is to him: "Dear Aunt Julie! . . . Way out here – so early in the day – uh?" (697).

Hedda's first scene is composed of a series of confrontations with the Tesmans, the first a small skirmish with her aunt by marriage. Coming on, in Janet Suzman's phrase, "in a high old state of panic,"[22] Hedda forces down her desperation to act the part of the coolly correct bourgeoise, responding to the aunt's greeting with "Calling so early? This *is* kind of you" (702). Miss Tesman is "*slightly embarrassed*" by this reminder of her assiduity, as well she might be. Hedda politely assumes that it is the maid, not the arriving Miss Tesman, who left the door open, but objects to its being closed; the too numerous bouquets of flowers make the room stifling.[23] Miss Tesman introduces a more important *contretemps* when she announces a surprise for George, whose reaction to the sight of his old slippers is perhaps the most successful of Ibsen's touches in characterizing him: "Oh, my – you kept them for me, Auntie Julie! Hedda! That's really touching! Uh!" (703). Hedda remains polite, but when her husband continues to insist on his love for these important objects and approaches her with them, she moves away. Tesman obtusely follows her to insist: "Imagine – Auntie Rina lay and embroidered them, sick as she was. Oh, you couldn't believe how many memories are bound up in them." Moving away again, Hedda holds on to her composure as she answers "But not for me," but the Recovery of the Slippers so irritates her that she strikes back at aunt and nephew in the now famous complaint about the "old hat" lying on a chair: "We're never going to manage with this maid, Tesman." In something of a small huff, Miss Tesman acknowledges her ownership of the hat, along with a parasol. Hedda must then listen as her husband points out how "plump and buxom" she has grown on their honeymoon, how "much she's filled out," a comment that stops his aunt, on her way out, in her tracks: "Filled out?" Tesman's explanation of his marital privileges – "Of course, you can't see it so well when she has that dressing gown on. But, I, who have the opportunity to" is interrupted by his repulsed wife: "Oh, you have no opportunity for anything!" Miss Tesman, "*gazing at [Hedda] with folded hands*" as if her nephew's wife had been made pregnant by the holy spirit, "*goes up to her, takes her head in both hands, bends it down and kisses her hair.*" Captive Hedda is then forcibly baptized with her new name and the Tesman blessing: "God bless and keep Hedda Tesman – for George's sake" (704–5). Hedda hears her fate sealed as the Tesmans have the last word: "I won't let a day go by without looking in on you two." "Yes, please do that, Aunt Julie! Uh?" (705).

Hedda's physical restlessness and her annoyance with her dolt-ish husband and his clinging aunt are the tip of an iceberg of aversion. We see with what self-control Hedda "*gently*" loosened herself from the old aunt's unwanted embrace with a mere "Oh – ! Let me go" (705) when she is free to show her feelings. As Tesman repeats offstage to his departing aunt his gratitude for the prized slippers, Hedda, like a prisoner behind bars, "*moves about the room, raising her arms and clenching her fists as if in a frenzy.*" Flinging back the curtains, she stares through the glass doors of her prisonhouse and collects herself. Once more "*calm and controlled,*" she replies to her returning husband with a veiled declaration of misery: "I'm just looking at the leaves – they're so yellow – and so withered . . . Yes, to think – that already we're in – in September." The pregnant Hedda's hesitation at pronouncing the month betrays her dread; she's counting the ones that remain. Now "part of the family" (703), Hedda is trapped for life in the stultifying world of the Tesmans, pregnant by a boy/man entranced by his slippers.

15. Hedda (Eva Le Gallienne) in the Civic Repertory's production of *Hedda Gabler*, New York, 1934.

The pathos in Hedda's entrapment lies in her effort to impose her adopted, "public" view of her marriage on her private feelings. She makes unsuccessful efforts at being an affectionate wife; trying to conquer her loathing, she occasionally calls her husband "dear," and she promises to make up with the aunt for the hat incident. She lies as she explains her wounding remark as a natural reaction to bad manners: "throwing her hat about in a drawing room! It's just not proper." This remark is normally taken as evidence of Hedda's "hatred of impropriety" (Finney 164), but Hedda was angry not because the hat was there, but because the aunt was, and most of all, because she herself was. When Tesman learns that he will have to compete for his expected professorship with rival historian Løvborg, Hedda is unable to feign concern at the prospect of their reduced circumstances. Speaking of their marriage deal, she exhibits a deep, emotional fatigue at the whole charade: "(*rising slowly and wearily*). It was part of our bargain that we'd live in society – that we'd keep a great house – ." Hedda's energy returns as she remembers the "one thing left" to her; she looks at her frightened husband "*with veiled scorn*" as she explains: "General Gabler's pistols" (721). The pistols belong to the pre-Tesman time when Hedda was free, and her vague threat looks forward to the precise use she makes of one of them the following evening, as Ibsen ends his first act by pointing to the end of his last.

The question of every first-time reader or spectator of Ibsen's first act – how Hedda's marriage came about – is answered in the first scene of act two as the protagonist unburdens herself to the confidant. Hedda's complaints about her honeymoon – "the most unbearable thing of all" was being "everlastingly together with – with one and the same person" (724) – give Judge Brack the opening to ask why she married Tesman. "Good Lord, does it seem so remarkable?" she replies (725). At age twenty-nine, finding a husband was imperative: "I really had danced myself out, Judge. My time was up." Everyone believed that rising scholar Tesman would become famous, so when he "kept pressing and pleading to be allowed to take care of me – I didn't see why I ought to resist." Hedda makes an important addendum: "It was certainly more than my other admirers were willing to do for me" (725); nobody else, in other words, asked.[24]

Grasping at straws to make her marrriage bearable, Hedda has foolish hopes of pushing her husband into politics, and tests her plan on Brack, seeking reassurance that other people do not find Tesman as absurd as she does: "And I don't find anything especially ridiculous about him. Do you?" (725). The wily judge complies: "Ridiculous? No-o-o, I wouldn't say that." Brack is counting on the Tesman misalliance to help make Hedda his mistress, and as she tests him on Tesman, he tests her on herself. Guilty about the hat incident, Hedda relates it to Brack as an example of "these things [that] come over me, just like that, suddenly. And I can't hold back" (728). Brack names the source of Hedda's cruelty – "You're not really happy – that's the heart of it" – and Hedda acquiesces: "And I don't know why I ought to be – happy. Or maybe you can tell me why?" She punctures Brack's response – "because you've gotten just the home you've always wanted" – with the real story, telling of the occasion on which Tesman was walking her home, "writhing in torment" because he could think of nothing to say, and she pitied him, coming out "with some rash remark about this lovely house being where I'd always wanted to live." Brack's suggestion that Hedda needs "some goal in life to work toward" prompts her to reveal her plan of a political career for Tesman, and although she agrees with Brack that this would hardly suit him, she even wonders whether he could rise to the post of cabinet minister. This fantasy is quickly squelched when the judge explains that to attain such a position, one has to be wealthy. Hedda's frustration explodes as she bitterly berates the moneyless family of nobodies she has married into: "Yes, there it is! It's this tight little world I've stumbled into – (*Crossing the room.*) That's what makes life so miserable! So utterly ludicrous! Because that's what it *is*!" (730).

Hedda's notion that she would be less unhappy if Tesman were a cabinet minister is akin to the self-deceived reasoning of what she terms the "bargain" of her marriage, her giving her self in return for financial security and social standing.[25] What Hedda reckons with in neither case are her feelings. Too integral to separate her pregnancy from its ludicrous inception, she rejects it as heatedly as Tesman's allusions to their physical intimacy. And the bumbling man whose timidity she pitied turns out to have a great deal to say about two topics – his specialty and his slippers – and what Hedda thought would be a satisfactory marriage of convenience has turned out to be a nightmare of boredom and odious conjugal duty: "Oh yes, Judge – I was going to say, you make your bed and then you lie in it" (729).

That Hedda seeks to save herself from her entrapment through the career of the husband with whom she is trapped displays a pathetic conventionality. But Hedda also displays an equally strong unconventionality in her refusal of motherhood as her natural woman's vocation. When Brack pretends to offer a woman's "most solemn responsibility" as a last solution to Hedda's unhappiness, she angrily and absolutely refuses it: "Be quiet! You'll never see me like that!" (730). Brack's disingenuous objection that Hedda, after all, must "have a talent for what almost every woman finds the most meaningful –" is interrupted: "Oh, I told you, be quiet!" (730). Brack's parroting the conventional wisdom that women's fulfillment lies in childbearing and his sly suggestion that motherhood can make up for marriage can only anger a woman who denies her pregnancy because it is the dire sign of her entrapment and who knows that she has no "talent for such things" (730). Tesman is bad enough, and a real baby would be worse.

THE *AGENTS PROVOCATEURS*

HEDDA: Yes, what a bargain *that* was! Oh, if you only could understand how poor I am. And you're allowed to be so rich! (745)

The appearance of Thea Elvsted and Eilert Løvborg, who function as foils, respectively, to Hedda and Tesman, drives the development of *Hedda Gabler.* Løvborg's qualities gallingly show up Tesman's deficiences, and Thea's happiness cruelly contrasts with Hedda's misery. Goaded by the example of the happy couple, the envious Hedda vents her rage and frustration on them. Løvborg is also Hedda's *alter ego* as well as Tesman's foil. He tells her the truth she tries to suppress – that in marrying Tesman, she threw herself away – and his scorn for what the world thinks makes him seem to her a liberated and courageous being. Her attempt to help him make a triumphant end represents a desperate, vicarious attempt to flee her prisonhouse.

Besides her pistols, the only other subject that arouses Hedda's interest in act one is Eilert Løvborg. When she receives Thea's note, Hedda disparagingly identifies her old schoolmate as "the one with the irritating hair that she was always showing off" (706), but then "*bursts out*": "But wait – isn't it somewhere up in those parts that he – that Eilert Løvborg lives?" (707). The slip of the pronoun suggests that Løvborg is often in Hedda's thoughts. When Thea arrives, Hedda listens avidly to her pleas to Tesman to look after Løvborg, who, although reformed, might be lured back by town life into his old reprobate ways. Eager to know about Thea's and Løvborg's relation, Hedda gets Tesman out of the room by suggesting that he write an invitation to Løvborg, then "*forces Mrs. Elvsted down into the armchair*" (711). Using comically obvious ruses – kissing "my own dear Thora," making her call her by her first name – Hedda persuades the guileless Thea to confide in her.

Part of Thea's function as Hedda's foil is to serve as her counterpart in entrapment; like Hedda, Thea made a marriage of reason with the only man who asked. While the clock ran out on penniless, upperclass Hedda, working woman Thea made the practical and paradigmatic governess' marriage: when the wife died, she replaced her. The results were much the same. Thea, who loathes her husband as much as Hedda loathes hers, speaks for both of them: "I just can't stand him! We haven't a single thought in common. Nothing at all – he and I" (713). The resemblance stops here, however. Hedda despises Thea's thoroughgoing serviability, her humbleness before her husband, who married her because she was useful to him and inexpensive to keep: "That's stupid of you." At the same time, Hedda is shocked that Thea has left her husband and followed Løvborg: "But what do you think people will say about you, Thea?" Thea's reply – "God knows they'll say what they please" (714) – establishes her as Hedda's unconventional foil. But Thea's unconventionality is the approved sort for women; she risked her reputation for a man: "I only know I have to live here, where Eilert Løvborg is – if I'm going to live at all." Thea follows this declaration with an account of her storybook relation with Eilert. Because she disapproved of his vices, he gave them up and was able to write a book. Hedda now shows her own unconventionality – the unacceptable sort – as she comments on how a good woman's love turns an alcoholic frequenter of brothels into a new man: hiding "*an involuntary, scornful smile,*" she replies: "My dear little Thea – just as they say – you rehabilitated him." A corresponding cliché of female/male reciprocity follows as grateful Thea explains how Løvborg made "a real human being" out of a blank slate: "Taught me to think – and understand so many things" (714–15). Hedda cannot resist asking whether Løvborg tutored Thea along with her step-children. Thea's account ends with the inevitable, hackneyed culmination: the worshipful woman became her master's helpmate: "And then came the wonderful, happy time when I could share in his work! When I could help him!" (715). "Like two true companions," Hedda remembers, and then she has to hear that Løvborg also used the word with Thea: "Companions! You know, Hedda – that's what he said too!" Hedda has one small satisfaction; a troubling presence mars Thea's happiness, a woman in Løvborg's past, "someone he's really never forgotten," who once threatened to shoot him. The proper Hedda acquires a disreputable double as Thea confides that the woman in question is probably "that redheaded singer" Løvborg used to frequent, for it was known that "she carried loaded weapons" (715).

Thea Elvsted is a sterling example of the nineteenth-century womanly ideal Lyngstrand holds forth on in *The Lady from the Sea*, the devoted companion who serves a man in his work.[26] That Thea is fulfilled by grateful servitude to Løvborg, who used her as a crutch to keep himself on the straight and narrow, seems to Hedda a self-effacing sentimentality. But while she is contemptuous of Thea for the relation, she is jealous of her because of the man.

Sensual Eilert Løvborg is asexual George Tesman's foil with caricatural vengeance; lean and gaunt in his black suit, he suggests the very devil. In this version of the Ibsenian pattern of a female protagonist placed between two opposing men, the physical contrast underscores the psychological one: Løvborg's hair and beard are dark brown, while Tesman's are blond; Løvborg's long, pale face with "*reddish patches over the cheekbones*" (732) contrasts with Tesman's "*open, round cheerful face*" (697). Løvborg is established as Tesman's more successful rival just before he enters when Tesman excitedly reports to Brack and Hedda that "Aunt Julie said she couldn't for the world believe that [Løvborg] would stand in my way again" (731). Having just had her plans for Tesman crushed by the judge, Hedda listens to the two historians' shop talk, in which Løvborg emerges as original and creative, and Tesman ordinary and unimaginative. Hedda has already heard Tesman speak of Løvborg's "remarkable talents" (718) and praise the work that Løvborg now dismisses as "a book that everyone could agree with" (732). He has now completed the "real book – the one that speaks for my true self" (733). Like comedy's straight man, Tesman feeds to his superior counterpart lines that inspire belittling responses: "Yes, but my dear Eilert – [the old book] comes right down to our own time!" When Løvborg explains that his new book treats the future, Tesman naively replies, "But good lord, there's nothing we know about that!", and the perspicacious Løvborg produces his coup: "True. But there are one or two things worth saying about it all the same." For Tesman, safely ensconced in the details of medieval handicraft, Løvborg's prophetical analyses seem "extraordinary! It never would have occurred to me to write about anything like that." At her post by the glass door, Hedda, "*drumming on the pane*," remarks: "Hm – no of course not." She then hears the superior man graciously remove himself from competition for the professorship and the inferior man break into expressions of gratitude and joy, referring, as usual, to his aunt's wisdom: "But, my Lord – then Aunt Julie was right after all!" (735). Her husband's spine-lessness is disdainful to Hedda; "*regarding Tesman with a cold smile*," she remarks: "You look as if you'd been struck by lightning" (735).

Løvborg's function as Tesman's superior foil is to rub in Hedda's mistake. He also confronts Hedda directly; at the beginning of their tête-à-tête, his repetition of her maiden name – "Hedda – Gabler! . . . Hedda Gabler!" (736) – is a reproach to Hedda Tesman before the reproach is made: "Oh, Hedda, Hedda – how could you throw yourself away like that!" Løvborg pretends to misunderstand the objection Hedda makes to his calling her by her first name – "It offends your – love for George Tesman" – so that Hedda will confirm what he knows to be true: "Love? You *are* absurd!" (737). But this is not enough; "Was there no love with respect to me, either?". Hedda equivocates as she slyly repeats the term that Løvborg used with her and Thea: "To me it was as if we were two true companions" (738). Løvborg and Hedda remember the "secret closeness" of the long afternoons when Løvborg made his "confessions" of "the drinking, the madness" (738–39). When Løvborg blames Hedda for having ended their relation, she plays the offended maiden: "Shame on you, Eilert Løvborg! How could you violate my trust when I'd been so – so bold with my friendship!" (739). But Løvborg's obvious continuing passion for her, his assurance that he has never told Thea about their relation because "She's too stupid for that sort of thing" (740), revive Hedda's feeling of intimacy with Løvborg and make her want to confide the truth. Perhaps the strongest expression of Hedda's sexual misery with Tesman occurs in her declaration to his foil that she desired him: leaning closer and speaking softly, she confesses that not carrying out her threat to shoot him was not her "worst cowardice – that night." Hedda wants Løvborg to know that she wanted him; it is a declaration, however secret, of the desire she concealed, an escape, however fleeting, from her wretched marriage.

It is this conversation that has given rise to the popular argument that had Hedda yielded to her desire for Løvborg, it would have resulted in their mutual happiness. But no one has explained how, and nothing in either Løvborg's or Hedda's character suggests that passion would have conquered all. The weak, alcoholic Løvborg is unpromising both as a lover and a husband. That he is self-destructive, even suicidal, is clear: "Oh, why didn't you do what you said! Why didn't you shoot me down!" (739). And as David Jones has pointed out, Løvborg is a victim of the notion of "good" and "bad" women; his taste for liquor and prostitutes is not merely a weakness but a compulsive corruption: his "vices – hard drink and soft women – are never indulged without the ravages of guilt, confession, and absolution" ("The Virtues of *Hedda Gabler*" 465). Hedda listened to Løvborg's "confessions" because she wanted to hear about a world that as a young woman, she was "forbidden to know anything about" (739). Why Hedda did not pass from forbidden thoughts to forbidden acts is understandable. While the violence with which she ended their relation suggests the force of her desire, Hedda has too much self-respect to become Løvborg's woman. If those who chastise her for not yielding to him mean that she should have married him with a view to reforming him, what sort of satisfaction could Hedda Gabler Løvborg have felt in keeping her husband off the bottle and taking dictation for his books? And in what way would being a man's nurse/secretary constitute a more fulfilling life than being a society hostess? Of course Hedda married the "wrong man," but Løvborg can hardly be Mr. Right. The marriageable man is sexless, the sexual man unmarriageable.

Løvborg rewards Hedda for her precious admission with a resentful and egotistical attack. He cannot forgive her for not giving in to him, and taunts her with cruel comparisons to the newly arrived Thea, making sure to use his and Hedda's private vocabulary: ". . . we two – she and I – we really *are* true companions . . . And then the courage she has, Mrs. Tesman . . . Enormous courage – where I'm concerned" (741). That Løvborg considers Thea's pursuit of him courageous is irritating enough; that he uses it to lecture Hedda for her cowardice adds insult to injury. Hedda gets her own back as she taunts Løvborg with his fear of taking a drink, and exposes his "true companion" who trusts him completely as "distraught" with fear that he will backslide (742). Løvborg now has a reason, however bad, to do what he wants; accusing Thea of duplicity, he drains the glass and announces his decision to go to Brack's drinking party.

Hedda wants to remove Thea's influence on Løvborg both because she is profoundly jealous of it and because she despises it as demeaning. Løvborg should be drinking punch with the men and not tea with teetotaler Thea. Løvborg's attachment to Thea is a betrayal of Hedda's idea of him as a Bacchanalian free spirit; like a valkyrie, Hedda will send her man off to conquer his enemy, flushed with spirit as he reads aloud his book "with vine-leaves in his hair – fiery and bold" (745). And the powerless Hedda has another reason for wanting Løvborg's victory: "For once in my life, I want to have power over a human being," she confesses to her rival. Thea's innocent supposition that Hedda already has power over someone – her husband – breaks the crust of a simmering volcano of jealous rage: "Yes, what a bargain *that* was! Oh, if you only could understand how poor I am. And you're allowed to be so rich!" (*Passionately throws her arms about her.*) I think I'll burn your hair off, after all!" (745). A ninny like Thea has influenced the exciting Løvborg while Hedda must bear the ignoble Tesman. But now Hedda has replaced Thea's baneful influence, for at "ten o'clock – Eilert Løvborg comes – with vine leaves in his hair" (746).

Løvborg as Bacchant is as implausible as Tesman as Minister of Education, and the ease with which Løvborg returns to his vice and the violence with which he does so expose Hedda's view of him as a desperate idealization of his addictions. She refuses to admit the truth in Tesman's remark that Løvborg "is still quite irreclaimable" (751). "Don't you mean that he has more courage to live than the others?" Hedda persists; "Good Lord, no – I mean, he simply can't take his pleasures in moderation." Even Brack's supplementary report – that the drunk Løvborg left his party to attend another, given by the infamous "singer" Diana, which ended in a brawl with the police – fails to shake Hedda's insistence on Løvborg's capacity for grand action. She ruefully remarks that "he had no vine leaves in his hair" (756), but when Løvborg announces his decision to "put an end to it all," Hedda rushes to ready him for romantic self-immolation, making him promise to do it "beautifully" (761).

There is no tenderness in Hedda's feeling for Løvborg, only passion, and in the end, made utterly selfish by her misery, she does not care whether he – or anybody else – lives or dies. She does not understand that for Løvborg (as for Oswald in *Ghosts*), his work is his life, the expression of the best that is in him; she says of the manuscript she has hidden in the desk behind her: "Well – but when all's said and done – it was only a book" (761). When she tells Løvborg, "I want you to have a souvenir from me" (762), and opens the desk drawer to retrieve not the manuscript but rather the pistol, it is only the spectator who feels the lead weight of a terrible choice. For Hedda, walking resolutely toward the desk, in one of Ibsen's most ferocious dramatic ironies, the manuscript is not present as an alternative to the weapon; it was slated for destruction the second she saw it in Tesman's hands: "No, don't give it back!" she had cried (752). She remained silent as Løvborg and Thea agonized over the loss of their "child"; hiding the manuscript upon Brack's arrival, upon Løvborg's return, she locked it in the drawer; she is only waiting to be left alone in order to destroy it. She will obliterate this rankling fruit of Thea's and Løvborg's intimacy, and Løvborg's decision to kill himself changes nothing; after all, if Hedda has to bear Tesman's child, Thea cannot have the consolation of being the widowed mother of Løvborg's. For Hedda, destroying Thea's and Løvborg's offspring is nothing less than pure poetic justice: "Now I'm burning your child, Thea! You, with your curly hair! (*Throwing another sheaf in the stove.*) Your child and Eilert Løvborg's. (*Throwing in the rest.*) Now I'm burning – I'm burning the child" (762).

THE CLOSING AND THE SPRINGING OF THE TRAP

HEDDA: Not free. Not free, then! (*Rises impetuously.*)
   No – I can't bear the thought of it. Never! (776)

Ibsen opens his last act with a dark, silent prologue, intermittently broken by Hedda's fitful piano playing. Our third, telling glimpse of Hedda alone, the pantomime recapitulates the frenzy of the earlier two occasions: the immediately preceding act-three curtain and the earlier "silent soliloquy" (Suzman, "The Play in Performance" 92) of act one, whose stage business it imitates.[27] The curtain rises on the silhouette of black-garbed Hedda pacing back and forth, like a caged panther, in the unlit drawing room. She goes into the inner room, strikes chords on the piano, returns to the drawing room, then moves to her post at the glass door, lifts the curtains, and stares out, this time not on autumn daylight but on darkness. Dressed for death, Hedda officially mourns Tesman's Aunt Rina, but like Chekhov's black-garbed Masha in *The Sea Gull*, she seems in mourning for her life.

   Hedda is forced deeper into her misery by Miss Tesman, who arrives on a mission. The aunt knows very well that her nephew has informed Hedda of Rina's death: "But all the same I thought that, to Hedda – here in the house of life – I ought to bear the news of death myself" (763). The gratuitous contrast betrays the aunt's real reason for the unnecessary visit, which is to make Hedda confirm her impending motherhood: "Ah, Rina ought not to have passed on just now. This is no time for grief in Hedda's house." Hedda, "*changing the subject*," tries to make civil small talk, but cannot turn the aunt from her dogged purpose: "At my house now we'll be sewing a shroud for Rina. And here, too, there'll be sewing soon, I imagine. But a far different kind, praise God!" When Tesman arrives, his aunt lectures him on the proper reaction to Rina's death with the Panglossian "You should rejoice in your grief," and when she follows this advice with a statement of her plan to fill Rina's empty bed with "some poor invalid in need of care and attention," her do-gooding begins to appear sinister; Jens Arup notes that "she suddenly seems like a witch out of Grimm, waiting for an innocent and small child to knock at her door" ("On *Hedda Gabler*" 32). Miss Tesman has plans to impose her avid selflessness – "And I do so much need someone to live for" – on her nephew and his wife: "Well, thank God, in this house as well, there soon ought to be work that an old aunt can turn her hand to" (765). The broad hint at Hedda's pregnancy is lost on Tesman, who seizes his aunt's offer to express his wish that she could move in: "Yes, think how pleasant it could be for the three of us if –." Squelched by Hedda's "If –?", he finishes *"uneasily"*: "Oh, nothing. It'll all take care of itself. Let's hope so. Uh?" Miss Tesman, who has understood Hedda's "If –?" very well – "Ah, yes" – decides that it is time to go, but she is determined to have her way: "And perhaps Hedda has something to tell you, George" (765).

Hedda knows she must break the news, but she cannot bring herself to say the words: "I'm going to – (*Impatiently breaking off.*) No, no – you ask your Aunt Julie. She's the one who can tell you" (767). Tesman's joyful hand clapping, his "Uh?", his intention to share his joy with the maid, only deepen Hedda's disgust: "Oh, I'll die – I'll die of all this! . . . Of all these – absurdities – George." Tesman quickly adds another absurdity: "And then, that you've started to call me George, too! Imagine! Oh, Aunt Julie will be so glad – so glad!" Tesman had quickly abandoned his scruples when Hedda told him that she had burned Løvborg's manuscript for his sake, proving himself to be as dishonest as he is gullible, and Hedda cuttingly confronts her husband with his hypocrisy: "When she hears that I burned Eilert Løvborg's book – for your sake?" Eager to report to his aunt his wife's passion for him, George misses the irony: "Well, as far as that goes – this thing with the book – of course, no one's to know about that. But that you have a love that burns for me, Hedda – Aunt Julie can certainly share in that!" (767).[28]

Hedda grasps at one slender means to continue living with "all these absurdities." Her vision of Løvborg's triumphant self-obliteration will help her bear her sordid life. When Brack reports the news of Løvborg's fatal wound, she grandly announces *"in a clear bold voice.* "At last, something truly done! . . . Eilert Løvborg's settled accounts with himself. He's had the courage to do what – what had to be done" (770). The hesitation signals her unspoken "what I want to do." But through her pistol she has privately participated in Løvborg's great deed, and he has freed her, symbolically, along with himself: "Ah, Judge – what a liberation it is, this act of Eilert Løvborg's . . . I mean for me" (772).[29]

University of Winchester
Tel: 01962 827306
E-Mail: libenquiries@winchester.ac.uk

Borrowed Items 05/11/2013 15:38
XXXX0952

Item Title	Due Date
Ibsen's women	08/11/2013

Indicates items borrowed today
Thankyou for using this unit

Beside Løvborg's triumph, Thea's defeat of Hedda hardly matters. The hyper-motherly secretary miraculously gives birth to a new child out of her pockets as she produces Løvborg's notes. As she did with Løvborg, Thea will perform the twin feminine functions of inspirer and recorder, and the protobook of Løvborg's notes will be parented by her and Tesman to full development.[30] Hedda bears Thea's new birthing with equanimity; "that pretty little fool" (760) has, after all, been deprived of Løvborg, and that she has transferred her services to Tesman is of no consequence. As Tesman and Thea pore over the dead man's notes, Hedda declares to Brack: "I simply know that Eilert Løvborg's had the courage to live life after his own mind. And now – this last great act, filled with beauty!" (772). But then Brack reveals that he did "a little editing" for "poor Mrs. Elvsted's sake" (773); Løvborg was found not in his own rooms but in Miss Diana's, where he had gone in desperation to demand his manuscript. In spite of the low site of the high action, Hedda clings to a saving fact. Brack had reported that Løvborg's wound was in the chest, and although Hedda was disappointed that it was "not the temple," still, "the chest is just as good" (770); now she repeats "In the chest – yes" (773). But Brack reveals a last, damning truth: Løvborg's fatal wound was in the groin. The reduction of Hedda's serenely triumphant hero to a desperate man shot in the bowels mockingly annihilates her grand illusion. Løvborg's shining deed, Hedda's survival strategy, has become, like the rest of her life, degraded beyond measure: "What is it, this – this curse – that everything I touch turns ridiculous and vile?" (773).

Hedda follows this ultimate deprecation with quick resolve. She insists on clearing the desk in order to gain access to her weapon, and hiding the pistol under piles of sheet music, she carries it into the small room beyond the parlor, where, when she has heard the last of Brack's story, she will return to shoot herself.

But she must suffer a last indignity. In a strikingly original use of stage convention, Brack is the confidant turned blackmailer, the protagonist's false ally and would-be seducer. The sleek, middle-aged judge, "*thickset, yet well-built, with supple movements*" (716), exudes the phallus. With a pronounced preference for "sneaking in the back way" (722), he resembles a large tom cat in the prime of his career. Even his physiognomy is feline: "*His face is roundish, with a distinguished profile. His hair is short, still mostly black, and carefully groomed. His eyes are bright and lively"* (716). The town roué's seduction plan for Hedda is cliché itself; after a time, the bored, unsatisfied wife will fall into his knowing arms. In making the "triangular arrangement" with Brack, Hedda made it clear that her sexual favors were not included, but acknowledged that the *bon vivant* judge, "not in the least a specialist," who "can talk about all kinds of lively things," would be "a great relief" (726). Hedda is aware of the crassness underneath the suave judge's manner – "that digusting judge" (743) she calls him – but has no doubts about being able to manage an affable *ménage à trois*. But when Brack senses Hedda's interest in Løvborg, he gives her a proprietary warning that shakes her confidence: "If he came like an intruder, an irrelevancy, forcing his way into – [the triangle]," it "would almost be like turning me out of my home" (756). It occurs to Hedda that this man who wants to be "the one cock of the walk" can be "a dangerous person," and she comments: "And I'm thoroughly grateful – that you have no kind of hold over me." Later, Hedda recognizes that the man she thought would relieve her from Tesman's small-mindedness is in fact "a kind of special-ist, too" (772), and in the end, the connoisseur of adultery tries to use his expertise on her, following his blackmail regarding the pistol found in Løvborg's pocket – "Well luckily there's no dan-ger, as long as I keep quiet" – with a gallant reassurance: "My dearest Hedda – believe me, I won't abuse my position" (776). The vain judge is foolishly sure of his ground, for he has no "position." His offer is too odious to contemplate: "Not free. Not free, then! (*Rises impetuously.*) No – I can't bear the thought of it. Never!" (776).

Hedda kills herself on an inner stage, a micro-parlor that houses the inheritances of her Gabler life – the portrait of her father and her old piano. She closes the curtains as she enters, then plays an overture to the action, a wild dance melody. Tesman protests: "But Hedda dearest – don't go playing dance music tonight! Think of Auntie Rina! And Eilert, too!" (777). Putting her head out between the curtains like a grand guignol, Hedda announces her offensive little drama – "And Auntie Julie. And all the rest of them. From now on I'll be quiet" – then closes the curtains again. Hearing Tesman and Thea plan their evenings at his aunt's house, Hedda asks gratuitously: "But what will I do evenings over here?". Like a man-who-would-be-cuckolded,

Tesman blithely notes that the good judge will be happy to keep Hedda company; crowing his triumph, Brack calls out: "We'll have great times here together, the two of us!" But he knows her as little as Tesman does. "Yes, you can hope so, Judge, can't you?" Hedda calls out *"in a clear, ringing voice"*; then come her last words, a sarcasm – "You, the one cock of the walk –" – which she punctuates with the exclamation point of the pistol shot. Tesman runs to open the curtains on a dead *tableau vivant*, Hedda lying full-length on the sofa.

HEDDA'S DIFFERENCE

BRACK: (*in the armchair, prostrated*). But good God! People don't *do* such things! (778).

Hedda is the zenith of two Ibsen patterns, the strongminded, "unwomanly" woman, whose prototype is Furia of *Catiline*, and the frustrated wife in a marriage of convenience, whose prototype is Margit of *The Feast at Solhoug*. The two patterns merge in *The Vikings at Helgeland*'s protagonist Hjørdis, with whom Hedda is often compared. Ibsen's first Norwegian biographer Henrik Jæger was the first to note the resemblance in his pithy remark that Hedda was "a Hjørdis in corsets" (*H* 11:267). And the arms-bearing, horse-riding Hedda, married to a passive man she despises, indeed resembles the "eagle in a cage" that Hjørdis terms herself, a Brynhild shut up in a parlor. Like Furia, Hjørdis, and Rebecca West, Hedda attempts to spur her hero to heroic deeds, and like the other ambitious men – Catiline, Sigurd, and Rosmer (and later Solness of *The Master Builder*) – Løvborg is ill-matched with the "womanly" woman, whose passivity stands in the way of his mission; echoing Catiline and Sigurd, Løvborg complains: "It's the courage and daring for life – that's what she's [Thea's] broken in me" (760). But Hedda is unlike her predecessors in an essential way. Married to the wrong man, Margit and Hjørdis view flight with the right one as the solution to their unhappiness. Tamed by Rosmersholm, Rebecca West dies to prove her love for its master. Even the indomitable Furia loves her enemy Catiline. But Hedda not only loves no one, but is a cynic about love, "that syrupy word" (724).

When *Hedda Gabler* appeared, Danish author Herman Bang commented that it was greeted with such consternation because "here was a play about an egotistical *woman.*"[31] The non-nurturing Hedda is a misfit in a bevy of servers. Thea lives to serve men; "Then what will I do with my life?" (759) she frantically asks when Løvborg announces their separation, but she quickly attaches herself to his old rival. Miss Tesman also lives only to serve, as does Berta, a servant by occupation. The selfless paragons Miss Tesman and Thea Elvsted have no self; sentimentalists who have absorbed their culture's ideal of woman as servant, they are domestic angels to Hedda's devil. The service of the two offstage women, representing the two female polar identities saint and whore – pure Aunt Rina, uncomplaining invalid and embroiderer of slippers, and debauched Diana, entertainer and prostitute – frames that of the women in the play. Only Hedda will not serve. She does not want to live for a man, but like one, i.e., for herself. "She really wants," Ibsen wrote in a working note, "to live the whole life of a *man*" (*OI* 7:487).

Ibsen masculinizes Hedda by giving her Amazon tastes for horses and weapons, a penchant for irony, and a disdain for feminine occupations. His explanation that he called his protagonist Hedda Gabler to indicate that she "is to be regarded rather as her father's daughter than as her husband's wife" (*LS* 297) is well known. Ibsen reverses traditional masculine and feminine qualities in Mr. and Mrs. Tesman more strongly than in any other of his couples; Tesman loves to wait on Hedda, fears her pistols, cannot understand her irony, and adores slippered domesticity. Ibsen separates female biology from psychology as relentlessly as in the third act of *A Doll House*; Hedda is pregnant, but not motherly, while the childless Thea is maternal. Characteristically, Ibsen takes his conception to its extreme: Hedda refuses motherhood both as her natural vocation in life and as a compensatory identity for her marriage, and in rejecting woman's *raison d'être*, she rejects womanhood.

Like Hedda's life, her death does not respect the norms of proper feminine behavior. Myths of female suicide have traditionally focused on two themes – defeated love and ruined chastity – in keeping with the normative assumption that women live for love, men for themselves.[32] The two most famous female suicides of nineteenth-century fiction – Anna Karenina and Emma Bovary – reinscribe this tradition, as do the suicides of the numerous "ruined maidens" and "fallen women" of the nineteenth-century stage, from Hebbel's *Maria Magdalena* (1844) to Strindberg's *Miss Julie* (1888).[33] But Hedda does not destroy herself because she has failed to satisfy a patriarchal norm, but because she refuses to. Being Mrs. Tesman, living with the "eternal aunts" (727), bearing and then living for a child – all this sickens her. The men she knows treat her as a sexual possession as blatantly as Torvald Helmer treats Nora: Tesman thinks she burns with love for him, Brack believes she will become his ardent mistress, and Løvborg cannot forgive her for not sleeping with him. Both the assumption and the presumption are enormous, as intolerable as those of the aunt's view of her as the Tesman matrice. Hedda frees herself from them all, thumbing her nose at "Auntie Julie. And all the rest of them" (777).

The most striking thing about Hedda, remarked Brandes, is that her "evil side is represented with so much force" (B 107). Hedda exhibits to the end the abrasive irony that has made her so odious or enigmatic to her commentators. Relishing what Ibsen termed the "burlesque touch" of Thea and Tesman devoting themselves to Løvborg's manuscript (*OI* 7:484), Hedda bids a condescending farewell to the new couple, bitingly imitating Tesman – "Well? Getting on with it, George? Uh?" – and commenting on Thea's easy transfer of her services: "Here you are, sitting now beside Tesman – just as you used to sit with Eilert Løvborg" (776). As oblivious to irony as her new master, and with Løvborg scarcely cold, Thea yearns to serve another man: "Oh, if I could only inspire your husband in the same way." Hedda's derisive retort – "Oh, that will surely come – in time" – underestimates Tesman's readiness for flattery: "Yes, you know what, Hedda – I really think I'm beginning to feel something of the kind." It is not really surprising that Hedda prefers death to life with such a man.

Elizabeth Robins, the American actress who produced the first English *Hedda Gabler* and played the title role, relates in her fine book *Ibsen and the Actress* how she was determined not to make Hedda "what is conventionally known as sympathetic" because her "corrosive qualities" are what make her a great character: "the revolt against her commonplace surroundings that the bookworm she had married thought so elegant; her unashamed selfishness; her scorn of so-called 'womanly' qualities; above all, her strong need to put some meaning into her life, even at the cost of borrowing it, or stealing the meaning out of someone else's" (20–22).[34] Hedda refuses life on terms that two kinds of women would find acceptable: "the simple sort would have made a comfortable humdrum life with Tesman. Behind Tesman's back the slavish-minded would have led an accidenté existence with Judge Brack and his successors" (28).

Hedda's death and Ibsen's play challenge what Elizabeth Ermarth has called "the literary convention of consensus," the old critical assumption that "we live in a world of common agreements."[35] It is this world that Brack speaks for in the famous last line of the play: "People don't *do* such things!" (778). In *doing* what "people don't *do*," deviant Hedda dies acclaiming her difference, the pistol shot her final "Non Serviam."

CHAPTER 10

The glories and dangers of the rejuvenating feminine

SOLNESS: . . . there's more in you of the bird of prey . . . No. You're like a dawning day. When I look at you – then it's as if I looked into the sunrise. *The Master Builder* (833)

MAY LOVES OF A SEPTEMBER LIFE

In 1889, the Ibsens vacationed in their perennial summer haunt, the little town of Gossensass in the Austrian (now Italian) Tyrol. It was here, in what Ibsen would later write to her was "a necessity of nature" (*LS* 282), that the sixty-one-year-old playwright met eighteen-year-old Emilie Bardach, the first of the "princesses" of his later years.

Emilie Bardach was the only daughter of wealthy Viennese Jews. Her photograph shows a face of regular traits (Ibsen wrote to her of "your lovely, serene features" [*LS* 286]) and a corseted, hour-glass figure. She lived the restricted, aimless life of a young woman of her class and epoch, making social calls and attending concerts, balls, the opera, and picture exhibitions. She was an accomplished amateur singer. In 1889, she was summering with her mother in Gossensass, whose market square had been baptized the "Ibsenplatz" in honor of its most famous summer resident, and where each summer an Ibsen Festival was held. Fräulein Bardach and Ibsen met in early August, and spent much time together before she returned to Vienna at the end of September. They never saw each other again. The publication of Ibsen's letters to Bardach and of extracts from what she claimed was a diary of the Gossensass summer has led to much speculation about the nature of their relation and its influence on Ibsen's work. It is probably fair to say that of the women in Ibsen's life, Emilie Bardach has inspired the most commentary.

In 1923, seventeen years after Ibsen's death, Bardach collaborated with her friend American writer Basil King on two essays, "Ibsen and Emilie Bardach," which claimed to feature portions of Bardach's diary.[1] According to the King/Bardach narrative, Ibsen and Emilie Bardach met after the Ibsen Day festivities; Ibsen went for a walk "in the Pflerschthal, a valley on the outskirts of the town, with a stream flowing through it, and a view of mountains and glaciers. Here he saw a girl with a book seated on a bench" (King 1:808). On earlier occasions, they had "examined each other with that mutual gaze which breaks down barriers" (809). This time, Bardach answered Ibsen's look "with a little smile" and they had their first conversation: "He learned her name, her parentage, her home residence, and the fact that in Gossensass they lived so near together that his windows looked into hers" (810). Later, the narrative records that when Bardach caught a cold, Ibsen visited her, climbing over the garden gate. A diary entry reads: "We talk a great deal together. His ardor ought to make me proud." As time passed, Ibsen's interest became increasingly serious, and five weeks after they met, things had so developed that Bardach wrote rhapsodically:

Passion has come when it cannot lead to anything, when both of us are bound by so many ties. Eternal obstacles! . . . Yesterday afternoon we were alone together at last. Oh, the words! – if they could only have stamped themselves on my heart more deeply and distinctly! All that has been offered me before was only the pretense at love. This is the true love, the ideal, he says, to which without knowing it he gave himself in his art. (811)

A week before Bardach's departure, Ibsen wrote in her album a line from *Faust*: "Hohes, schmerzliches Glück – um das Unerreichbare zu ringen!" (812); "High, painful happiness – to strive for the unattainable!" On the morning of their last day together, he gave her a photograph of himself with the now well-known inscription on the back: "An die Maisonne eines Septemberlebens [To the May sun of a September life] – in Tyrol. 27.9.89. Henrik Ibsen" (*OI* 7:546).[2] Her diary entry reads: "He says that to-morrow he will stand on the ruins of his happiness. These last two months are more important than everything that has gone before. Am I not reasonable to be so terribly quiet and normal?" (King 1:813).

The diary extracts indicate that Bardach was both deeply touched by Ibsen's ardor and at the same time felt confused and inadequate: "How small I seem to myself that I cannot spring to him!" (King 1:811); "What am I to think? He says it is to be my life's aim to work with him. We are to write to each other often; but what I am to write?" (812). On the day of her departure, the diary entry records: "He means to possess me. This is his absolute will. He intends to overcome all obstacles. I do what I can to keep him from feeling this, and yet I listen as he describes what is to lie before us – going from one country to another – I with him – enjoying his triumphs together" (814).

The train from Verona to Vienna passed through Gossensass at three in the morning. At half past two, when Bardach and her mother emerged from the hotel, they found Ibsen waiting to accompany them to the station. "It was all over quickly, the lamps of the engine alone lighting their good-bye" (815).

In 1928, five years after the King/Bardach article appeared, the French writer and artist André Rouveyre published an essay in *Mercure de France* that contained a memoir Bardach had written in answer to Rouveyre's request.[3] The memoir is a disjointed, sentimental narrative of three printed pages that moves from the "furies of destiny that have faded my memory" (262), to the nature of the Tyrolean peasant, to the charm of old Gossensass, and finally to Bardach's relation with Ibsen. Before she met him, Bardach claims, every client of the hotel dining room witnessed how he stared at her as he routinely sat over his glass of beer (a habit he later renounced when she told him she found it distasteful), and after they met, he confessed that he had fallen in love with her at first sight. Bardach describes their têtes-à-têtes during which she had the honor of opening his telegrams, for which effort he called her his "collaborator" (263), and summarizes: "How can I describe the greatness of this great man? There are some things that seem too precious to profane by describing them" (263). The main interest of Bardach's memoir is that it contains an account of her meeting with Ibsen that is completely different from that in the *Century Magazine*. The romantic account of the meeting in the mountain valley has been replaced by a mere mention that Bardach was introduced to Ibsen by a mutual acquaintance after a concert at the Ibsen Festival. Since Bardach had also given this version of the meeting in a brief, uninformative article she wrote a year after Ibsen's death,[4] it seems probable that this account is the accurate one, and that she either invented the version in the *Century Magazine*, or, perhaps more probably, that thirty-four years after the fact, she confused her initial meeting with Ibsen with a later encounter.[5]

The authenticity of Bardach's reminiscences is made more problematic by a typescript Bardach sent Rouveyre which she claimed was a copy of her diary, and from which he quotes three passages translated into French.[6] Bardach assures Rouveyre in a letter that she changed "not a word" in her original diary, and at the same time notes that the typescript is a document she dictated to a stenographer "a few years ago."[7] She notes that the typescript contains "everything I thought important" in the diary, and that she eliminated passages that concerned people other than Ibsen. She adds: "But yesterday I found the original of my diary – and in comparing [the original and the typescript] – I found that I had eliminated too much – and that it's interesting to know the whole atmosphere of Gossensass – it's like a prelude, then the beginning – how I was absolutely indifferent to him and how he inspired me with his passion." It was presumably to communicate the "whole atmosphere of Gossensass" that Bardach added on the typescript's margins several pages of handwritten notes that describe her social relations with the town's other summer residents. The German typescript contains passages that are identical, or nearly identical, to the English extracts in the article in *The Century Magazine*, as well as passages that are not in the article, for example, Bardach notes that she sent Ibsen a card during her journey between Gossensass and Vienna, and that she received a telegram from him at one of the stations along the route.[8] That there are passages in the typescript that are not in the *Century Magazine* article proves nothing, of course, since the article features only extracts. That there are dissimilarities in similar passages in the two texts, however, as well as a few passages in the *Century Magazine* diary that are not in the typescript casts serious doubt on the authenticity of both documents. It seems likely that the typescript, which Bardach notes in 1928 that she dictated "a few years ago," was written in 1923 for use in the article in *Century Magazine*. In any case, one wonders why, if there was an original diary, Bardach needed to produce a typescript.

In 1977, Hans Lampl claimed to be giving the world the "original manuscript" of Bardach's diary in the preface to his edition of the photocopy of the typescript in the University Library, Oslo. He gleefully noted that Meyer had been wrong when he claimed that the diary had been lost.[9] In 1996, Robert Ferguson, having read Lampl's edition of the typescript, noted that the diary "recently turned up in Paris."[10] Given that Lampl's edition was published in 1977, Ferguson's "recently" is strange. Apparently, neither Lampl nor Ferguson had read Bardach's letters to Rouveyre, copies of which are available in the same University Library file that contains the typescript, for if they had, they would have seen that Bardach repeatedly distinguishes between what Lampl and Ferguson call the "diary," i.e., the typescript, and its original, what Bardach calls "my diary." Even if the original typescript should turn up, it is not a diary of the summer at Gossensass but a document Bardach produced many years later.[11]

Whatever the differences among the *Century Magazine* extracts, the memoir in Rouveyre's article, and the typescript Bardach sent Rouveyre, and whether or not Bardach wrote a diary in Gossensass, Ibsen's own letters to Bardach, whose authenticity is not in question, bear out the clear impression of the three accounts that Ibsen felt a strong romantic attachment to her.[12]

The tone of Ibsen's first two letters, written from his home in Munich, is that of sadness mixed with romantic nostalgia: "No more sunshine. Everything gone – lost. The few guests still left could, of course, not offer me any compensation – for the brief and beautiful Indian summer of life" (*LS* 280). Ibsen ends his first letter by reminding Bardach that he writes letters "only in telegraphic style" (281). His second letter, like the first, begins by thanking Bardach for her "dear letter" he has read "over and over again" and continues: "I cannot repress my memories of summer. Nor do I want to. What I experienced then, I experience over and over – and over again . . . I constantly brood over this: was our meeting stupidity or was it craziness? Or was it stupidity as well as craziness? Or was it neither?" (281–82).

Ibsen had been home a month when he wrote the next letter. The tone of romantic nostalgia has disappeared in what is little more than a note to inform Bardach that the new photograph he promised her is not ready. Three weeks later, she received it accompanied by a note in which Ibsen apologizes for not having answered a letter from her and assures her that she is "always and will always be" in his thoughts. He reminds her of his dislike of letter writing, and ends with a teasing hint: "To create is beautiful;

but to live in reality can now and then be much more beautiful"
(*LS* 285).

Ibsen's next two letters are an interesting mixture. The romantic tone qualifies them as "love letters," and yet their author seems, if not satisfied, at least resigned, to imagine the beloved in his mind. In the first, he writes of the "enigmatical princess" hiding behind her "lovely, serene features" and describes how he ponders on the "enigma itself": "It is, after all, a small substitute for the unattainable and – unfathomable reality. In my imagination I see you always adorned with pearls. You love pearls so much. There is something deeper – something hidden in your love of pearls" (*LS* 286). Ibsen's next letter repeats the familiar "writing letters is not my line" (*LS* 288), and continues in the equally familiar tone of romantic nostalgia: "I got to know you as a lovely summer apparition, dear princess. As part of the season of butterflies and wild flowers." And then the poet transforms the "summer apparition" into a winter one: "I see you in the Ringstrasse, light, quick, gliding along, gracefully wrapped up in velvet and furs. I see you also at soirées and parties – and particularly at the theater, leaning back, with a somewhat tired expression in your enigmatical eyes." He would also like to see her at home. "But I cannot quite succeed in doing that since I do not have the necessary facts to go by." Then comes a dash of cold water: "Frankly speaking, dear princess – in many definite respects we are strangers to each other. In one of your earlier letters you have said almost the same thing in regard to my writings since they are not accessible to you in the original language. Let us not think about it" (*LS* 288).

On the same day, December 22, Bardach wrote to Ibsen the first of the three (not two, as Meyer has it [M 622]) extant letters from her to him. She enclosed a photograph and described "a little thing" she has painted for him, a landscape on some deerbells, "something which would be entirely meaningless if it did not refer to Gossensass." And then comes the pitiful request: "How much longer will you let me wait [?] – This detailed letter which is to answer so many things for me – yet, no – please do not think of this as a reproach – I do not say it in this sense. I want to send Christmas greetings to your wife . . . From my heart, Emilie" (*OI* 7:554).

Ibsen wrote a brief letter of thanks for the "beautiful, charming" photograph that gave him "an indescribable joy" (*LS* 289). He also noted: "My wife received your kind Christmas card with great pleasure." Two weeks later, he wrote briefly to thank her for two unanswered letters; he had been ill with influenza, and was sorry to hear that she had been stricken as well, about which he had had a presentiment: "In my imagination I have seen you lying in bed, pale, feverish – but irresistibly beautiful and lovely as always" (*LS* 289).

He sent her the blow on February 7:

I feel it is a matter of conscience to break off my correspondence with you, or at least limit it. You must, for the present, have as little to do with me as possible. You have other tasks to pursue in your young life, other aims to devote yourself to. And I – as I have already told you personally – I can never be satisfied with a relationship through letters. To me that seems like doing things by halves; there is something untrue in it (*LS* 290).

He is not quite ready, however, to give her up: "And when we meet again, I shall explain it to you more fully. Until then you will always remain in my thoughts. And even more so when we are rid of this disturbing, tiresome, halfway measure of corresponding with each other" (290).

Bardach responded with a rather pathetic, yet dignified letter. After asking Ibsen's pardon for writing to him again so soon, she agrees to "remain silent," but has enough pride to tell him: "the tasks and the feelings to which, as you put it, I 'in my young life' am to give myself – I cannot have dictated to me" (*OI* 7:558). She then speaks of her misery, reminds him of his promise of abiding friendship, and gently demolishes his argument: "And does it go with friendship not to know whether the other is ill, well – happy or miserable? And then – must not the thought present itself to me that *you* will avoid a future meeting; how, if you don't write, am I to know where we can meet each other again?" (558).

Bardach's effort to change Ibsen's mind met with failure. He did not even reply to her letter. Six months later, she wrote him of her father's death; he replied warmly, although, as usual, late. Three months later, at Christmas, she found the courage to write again and to send him the gift she had made for him a year earlier: "And what do you think of my painting for you of that ruin in Gossensass on one of those so-called deer-bells, which I bought there? You saw me coming from there so often" (*OI* 7:561). She reminds him of her pain; she is sorry to have heard about *Hedda*

Gabler "so indirectly" in the newspapers; she leads "a gloomy and barren life" (561).

She received a six-line reply acknowledging receipt of her "dear letter" and the "bell with the beautiful picture." Suzannah Ibsen also found the picture very pretty. "But I beg you: for the time being, please do not write me. When circumstances have changed, I will let you know. I shall soon send you my new play [*Hedda Gabler*]. Receive it in kindness – but in silence! I should like to see you again and talk to you! Happy New Year to you and to your mother" (*LS* 298). This time, Bardach "remained silent." And Ibsen never let her know that circumstances had changed.

Meyer claims that Ibsen's letters to Bardach are "no more than those of an affectionate old man to a charming schoolgirl (though we must bear in mind that he was writing in a foreign language . . . that he was always an extremely inhibited letter-writer, and that he must have been very careful not to commit himself on paper)" (615). But surely Ibsen's nostalgic recollections of joyful hours with an attractive younger woman whom he considers a beautiful "enigma," and whom he imagines adorned with pearls, swathed in velvet and furs, and lying in bed "irresistibly beautiful and lovely as always" (*LS* 289), represent something more than the thoughts of "an affectionate old man." The author of these letters is romantically involved with the woman he is writing to. It is worth noting that in both versions of the "diary" Bardach writes of Ibsen as a "volcano" who made her younger suitor, a certain baron, seem tame: "But how much calmer he was! – how inarticulate! – beside this volcano, so terribly beautiful!" (King 1:811; typescript 9).

It is true that Ibsen avoids salutations, signs himself "Yours devotedly," and refers occasionally to Bardach as "dear child." Zucker, like Meyer, notes "the cautious manner of the writer in expressing himself always in phrases and pauses that might mean much or might mean nothing at all" (Z 228). But if Ibsen was being careful, there was something to be careful about. Ibsen had declared his love for Bardach and at the same time had glorified the impossibility of a life together, citing the great Romantic poet: "Hohes, schmerzliches Glück um das Unerreichbare zu ringen!" Either way – consummated or renounced – Ibsen had insisted to Bardach that their love had great significance for him. Now, back home, things took on a different light; in front of his writing desk, the fantasy of "going from one country to another" with Emilie Bardach gave way to the reality of thinking out a new play in Munich, and living out a "hohes, schmerzliches Glück" through an exchange of letters must have seemed a difficult, even ludicrous undertaking. And there was, of course, Suzannah Ibsen, to whom he was deeply bound. Ibsen's letters are those of a divided man, still drawn to the woman who had inspired his passion, but at the same time afraid of encouraging her feelings. After four months, her too frequent letters, her little presents, her assurances that their relation helped her bear the monotony of her existence, let him know that he was the most important person in her life. He did not want the responsibility, and so he dropped her. Trying to spare her, he explains his decision as a "matter of conscience"; she has other things to think of in her "young life" (*LS* 290). His second reason – that he could not bear "doing things by halves" (*LS* 290) – rings truer, recalling what he had written to Bjørnson years earlier about having separated from his family because "being only half understood was unendurable" (*LS* 68). If he could not have a complete relation, he preferred no relation. Whatever suffering this brought to Emilie Bardach, or to Marichen and Hedvig Ibsen, went by the boards. As for his own pain, he preferred to wrench Bardach out of his heart rather than continue a lingering relation that brought him disturbing memories. He even asked his wife to burn a photograph Bardach had given him.

Eight years after Ibsen broke off with her, Bardach ended her enforced silence by sending him a telegram of congratulations on his seventieth birthday. He replied, using, for him, the exceptionally warm salutation "Herzlich liebes Fräulein!": "Accept my deepest thanks for your letter. The summer in Gossensass was the happiest, the most beautiful of my whole life. I scarcely dare to think about it. And yet I *must*, always. Always!" (*LS* 330).

Ibsen's thank-you note was the last communication between himself and Bardach. In 1906, a few weeks before Ibsen's death, Bardach contacted Brandes and gave him Ibsen's letters to her for publication.[13] When their appearance caused a scandal, she proclaimed her innocence: "I can only say that this went completely against my feelings and intentions. In Gossensass, Frau Ibsen went out of her way to be especially kind to me. But was it necessary to wait until her death, so to speak, to reveal this beautiful, grand,

and, at the same time, innocent relation to *those* who are deeply interested in such things?" ("My Friendship with Ibsen").

This explanation is at least partly disingenuous. Perhaps Bardach naively believed that because of Brandes' sponsorship, the letters would be received as part of respectable literary posterity, but even so, the phrase "innocent relations" totally contradicts the romantic attachment chronicled by the letters themselves. What is clear is that Bardach wanted very much to make public her relation with Ibsen.

Bardach's later collaboration on the two essays featuring her diary reflects the same desire. It was Bardach who initiated the publication of the diary extracts in both *The Century Magazine* and *Mercure de France*, two highly respected publications with wide readerships. She repeatedly writes in her letters to Rouveyre of her great desire to have her diary published in French along with the French translations of Ibsen's letters to her.[14] There was also the question of money, which, given her reduced circumstances, was natural enough. Her family had lost its fortune in the Great War, which had caught Bardach in Berne, and when the money arriving from Vienna became virtually worthless, she was forced, in King's words, to "earn her bread" (1:806). It was after she had failed to sell Ibsen's letters that she suggested to King the publication of her diary extracts. Scholar Sigmund Skard was told by acquaintances of Bardach that King sent her the full *Century Magazine* honorarium of a thousand American dollars.[15] Bardach's correspondence with Rouveyre also contains a strong monetary component. In her first letter, she lies when she writes that even in her worst financial crisis she never thought of selling Ibsen's letters, and makes it clear in a genteel manner that she is open to selling them now: "I wonder sometimes if I wouldn't have done better to sell these autographed letters to a collector capable of appreciating them" (March 15, 1928). In her third letter she makes it clear that "my own interests in the form of money, alas," enter into the question of a French publication of her diary (April 27, 1928). Promising to send the diary typescript in each succeeding letter, she finally sends it only when it is clear that Rouveyre will make no financial arrangement with her.[16] That she sent it at all, however, is proof that she wanted to see it published even if she got no money for it. At fifty-two, with no aim in life, no profession, no family (her only brother had died young and she never married), Emilie Bardach may have wanted to make some mark on life through revealing that she had been loved by a great man. In any case, the relation seems to have been so important to her that she wanted the world to know everything about it.

And what, finally, did it mean to Ibsen? During the months that followed his letter breaking off with Bardach, he planned and wrote *Hedda Gabler*. Because the play's composition followed the Gossensass summer, and because Bardach shared with Ibsen's protagonist an aristocratic beauty and a high social position, she has often been said to have influenced Ibsen's portrait of Hedda, or even to have been Hedda's model.[17] But when one considers the real and the fictional woman, what strikes one are the enormous differences between them. As Arild Haaland has argued in an incisive essay, nothing in Bardach's letters connects her – "a warm and direct being, completely ready to adapt herself to the famous and overwhelming poet" – with Hedda Gabler. Haaland then asks pointedly: "Is it likely that Ibsen, after having met with this very young woman's whole trust and openness, and after having been in love with her, as the letters clearly give the impression, afterwards sat down to immortalize the impression of the original through a portrait of Hedda Gabler? Such an act would be very difficult to imagine" ("Ibsen og [and] Hedda Gabler" 567–68).

Zucker argues that Ibsen saw in Bardach an example of the type of woman he had noted in early plans for *Rosmersholm* (she was to have been Rosmer's daughter), but abandoned: "highly gifted, without any application for her talents" (Z 224). It seems "beyond question," Zucker writes, that the "Viennese society girl" influenced in this respect the protagonist of *Hedda Gabler* (Z 231). Although Emilie Bardach can hardly have been the first intelligent and bored female socialite with whom Ibsen was acquainted, she was the first with whom he had a close relation, and perhaps knowing her led him to think more deeply, as Zucker puts it, about "the parasitical position of young women in genteel circles" (Z 231).

Else Høst believes that Ibsen's relation with Bardach was the impetus for *Hedda Gabler*. The young woman had awakened Ibsen's passion, and to combat "the grip of sensual life" that threatened his settled existence, Ibsen incarnated his struggle in his protagonist (*Hedda Gabler* 137). Høst asks rhetorically whether Hedda, "with her fascination for forbidden pleasure, her cautious tasting of it, her cowardice and envy of those who risk giving

themselves up to life – is she not precisely an image of her creator's conflict between living and his artist's calling" (137). It has
been noted that Hedda embodies certain traits of Ibsen: for Koht,
"the fear of risks and responsibilites" (397), and for Meyer, similarly, "the fear of scandal and the fear of ridicule" (648).[18] One
could also point out that Hedda shares with her creator a scathing
intelligence, a sardonic humor, and an impatience with fools. But
whichever personal characteristics Ibsen gave to Hedda, his protagonist's futile struggle to live a life she despises seems to bear no
resemblance to a conflict between living and the artist's calling.
To take Hedda's refusal to sleep with Løvborg as signifying her
failure to "live" is, as I have argued, greatly to simplify her predicament; and to maintain that this refusal represents Ibsen's conflict
between loving Emilie Bardach and keeping to his calling ignores
the fact that Hedda has, notoriously, no vocation – except, perhaps, as she notes, that of boring herself to death. And in this, she
is Ibsen's opposite. There is no doubt that during the Gossensass
summer, Ibsen wanted "to live fully" with Emilie Bardach; he was
as serious in his passions as he was in everything else. And certainly he must have experienced a difficult time afterwards. But
Hedda's struggle seems an unlikely portrait of his own.

What Weigand found to be the irrelevance of *Hedda Gabler* to
Emilie Bardach led him to conclude that writing the play was
Ibsen's way of clearing his mind of her. The "upheaval" of the
Gossensass summer so threatened Ibsen that he wrote *Hedda
Gabler* "as an exercise in self-discipline, with a grim determination
to focus his mind upon a situation as remote as possible from
anything tinged with the warmth of personal experience. In doing
so, he resorted, for an artist, to an unprecedented method for
regaining his self-control" (242–43).

The only analysis Ibsen ever gave of his relation with Bardach
suggests that Weigand may have been right. In February, 1891,
Ibsen attended the Berlin premiere of *Hedda Gabler* and had lunch
with the scholar Julius Elias.[19] Elias later reported that Ibsen confided to him, "chortling over his glass of champagne," that a
female character in his next play would be based on a woman he
had met in the Tyrol.

What fascinated and delighted her was to steal other women's husbands.
She was a demonic little wrecker; she often seemed like a little beast of
prey who would have liked to include him in her booty. He had studied

her up close. But she had no luck with him. "She did not get me, but I got her – for a play. I imagine (here, he chortled again) that afterwards she consoled herself with another man." In matters of love, she could only experience morbid fantasies.[20]

As Meyer notes, Ibsen's description is "impossible to reconcile, either with Emilie's diary extracts and letters to him, or with his letters to her" (M 626). How does one explain Ibsen's false account of his ascendancy over a scheming woman? As Elias presents it, it does not seem to have been an instantaneous invention to entertain him, but an analysis Ibsen had thought out. A year had passed since he had asked Bardach to stop writing to him, a request he reiterated in response to her Christmas letter of 1890, less than two months before the lunch in Berlin. If Ibsen immersed himself in *Hedda Gabler* to clear his mind of Bardach, then he succeeded admirably. He was now able to "bury" her by transforming her into a seductress – a fictitious model for Hilda Wangel – and rationalize his own unkept promise by casting himself as her near victim.

Unfortunately for Bardach, so authoritative was Ibsen's voice that his account of her was widely accepted: she was called a "temperamental Viennese flapper" (Lavrin, *Ibsen* 114); she "charmed Ibsen and scared him by saying that she wanted to steal men from their wives" (Lamm, *Modern Drama* 126); "Perhaps some reflection of Emilie Bardach's merely cerebral erotic occupations and her professed unscrupulousness in stealing men is to be seen in Hedda Gabler and the later trait, too, in Hilda Wangel" (Downs, *Six Plays* 183). Even Ibsen's biographers Zucker and Koht, who had studied both Ibsen's letters and King's articles, were perfectly credulous. Koht writes that Bardach "was fascinated by the idea of taking a man from his wife. Ibsen understood both the naivete and the demonic impulse revealed by this statement and was wary" (K 392). Like Koht, Zucker paraphrases the passage from Elias; he then adds that Ibsen found "a great deal of heart and womanly understanding" in Bardach, whom Zucker had interviewed for his biography (Z 226). It apparently did not occur to Zucker to compare the woman he met with the woman Ibsen described. Bardach, who died at the age of eighty-three, on November 1, 1955, saw herself reinscribed in both biographies as a preying femme fatale and foiled marriage wrecker.

It is sometimes claimed that Ibsen's experience with Bardach

brought home to him his stunted personal life and left an irrevocable stamp on his work. He had experienced, Gosse wrote, "that
dangerous susceptibility" of an elderly man who "sees the sands
running out of the hour-glass, and realizes that in analyzing and
dissecting emotion he has never had time to enjoy it . . . From this
time onward, every dramatic work of his bears the stamp of the
hours spent among the roses at Gossensass" (A 13:167–68).
Ibsen's latest English biographer follows his first; Meyer claims
that Ibsen's relation with Bardach brought "an immediate and
drastic change" in his life (M 626), and that the mood of *Hedda
Gabler* and Ibsen's four subsequent plays – *The Master Builder, Little
Eyolf, John Gabriel Borkman,* and *When We Dead Awaken* – derives
from Ibsen's failed erotic relation with Bardach. Having "suppressed his longings for so long, he now had the opportunity to
fulfill them but was unable to do so. As a result of his meeting with
Emilie Bardach a new glory, but also a new darkness, entered his
work" (M 627).

Meyer claims that Ibsen's relation with Bardach "arose solely
from the needs of his imagination" (M 620), and at the same time
that Ibsen's unfulfilled longing for her was so great that it resulted
in a decisive turning point in his work. Clearly, both of these
propositions cannot be true, and I believe that neither is. Ibsen's
letters show overwhelmingly that his feelings for Emilie Bardach
were those of a man as well as a writer; his insistence on her
physical loveliness and his nostalgia for the happiness they had
shared are not the expressions of a man who was interested in a
woman primarily as poetic inspiration. Ibsen had fallen in love. As
for the "new darkness" in the Ibsen canon, it would be difficult to
find in Ibsen's last five plays a drama sadder than *The Wild Duck*,
bleaker than *Rosmersholm*, or grimmer than *Ghosts*. Of the five
plays from *Hedda Gabler* on, two – *Little Eyolf* and *When We Dead
Awaken* – end in reconciliation. Taken as a group, Ibsen's last five
plays seem no "darker" than those that preceded them.

The fact that Ibsen continued to seek out the company of young
women after his break with Emilie Bardach argues against the
notion that she represented for him a last, wasted chance at love.
The Gossensass summer marked a beginning rather than an end,
for the young woman from Vienna had unlocked Ibsen's heart,
and although he soon closed the door to her, it remained open

for the concert pianist Hildur Andersen, whom he would meet upon his return to Norway.

Meanwhile, in Munich, Ibsen saw much of his second "princess," Helene Raff, a twenty-four-year-old German woman who would later enjoy a successful career as a novelist and painter. He had met her in Gossensass, where she observed his attentions to Bardach. Raff's sarcastic way of referring to Bardach in her diary suggests that she was jealous: "Die B. mit I. ganz toll" [The B. completely mad about I.]; "Die B. geknickt" [The B. heartbroken] (*OI* 7:563). Upon her return to Munich, Raff patrolled the Maximilianstrasse, the street where Ibsen lived, for several days without success; "finally," she records, on October 19, she met him (563). She notes on the following day that she saw him, on the following, that she read an essay on him, and on the following, that she waited on the Maximilianstrasse until he appeared. The brief diary entries continue for a year and a half until the spring of 1891, when the Ibsens left for Norway. Repeatedly, Raff walked the Maximilianstrasse, recording her meetings with Ibsen in a special "Ibsen Diary," and learned Norwegian in order to read Ibsen's plays in the original.[21]

Raff, who had been Bardach's confidante, did not want Ibsen to regard her as her replacement. She wrote in the Ibsen Diary: "The fact that [Ibsen] used certain expressions which reminded me of what Fräulein Bardach had repeated to me gave me an uncomfortable feeling. I asked him please not to talk to me as he had to her ... To which he gave the naive answer: 'Ah, that was in the country. In the town one is much more serious'" (*OI* 7:565). Ibsen's answer was not only not naive, but disingenuous; he was still writing nostalgic letters to Bardach, affirming her continued presence in his life. But Raff need not have worried about becoming a substitute for Bardach. Ten days after this conversation, Ibsen wrote her a letter in which he noted: "My wife is so truly, cordially fond of you. And I too. As you sat there in the twilight and told us various things so thoughtfully and understandingly, do you know what I thought then, what I wished? No, you do not know. I wished – alas, if I only had such a dear and lovely daughter" (*LS* 280). Raff's interest in Ibsen does not seem to have been daughterly; she noted in her diary two weeks later that she felt "shocked and hurt" when she located Ibsen on the Maximilianstrasse and he took her home "to his wife" (*OI* 7:566).

Ibsen was extremely fond of Helene Raff. He liked her for her strong spirit, and he praised "das Gesunde" in her. "How healthy you are, and yet at the same time delicate" (*OI* 7:566). He admired her for her devotion to her painting, and encouraged her to work hard. She recorded in the Ibsen Diary that he "would wish me to realize myself. Because, you know, 'this is man's highest task and greatest good fortune'" (*OI* 7:564). When she gave him a portrait she called "Little Solveig," he was delighted; later, after he moved to Norway, she sent him a seascape. He thanked her for it in a tender letter: "Now little Solveig shall be hung beside the sea picture. Then I will have you wholly and altogether before me – and within me." He would like to see her, "dearest Miss Raff"; perhaps she could take a "fleeting" summer holiday in Norway (*LS* 306). When he sent her *The Master Builder*, he wrote on the flyleaf: "Helene Raff! A voice within me cries for you" (*OI* 7:571). The inscription is an allusion to Ibsen's aging protagonist Solness and the young Hilda Wangel. Raff had once asked Ibsen why he was fond of her, and he replied: "You are youth, child, youth personified – and that is something I need – that hangs together with my production, with my writing" (*OI* 7:565).

Because Ibsen never let their relation develop beyond a warm friendship, Raff decided that all his relations with young women were the same as theirs. In 1927, thirty-six years after she last saw Ibsen, Raff, aged sixty-two, wrote the following statement in a letter to Zucker, an analysis which both he and Meyer quote as definitive: "Ibsen's relations with young girls had in them nothing whatever of infidelity in the usual sense of the term, but arose solely out of the needs of his imagination; as he himself said, he sought out youth because he needed it for his poetic production" (Z 226–27; M 620). Raff added a prim cavil – "I must admit, however, that because of this need of the aging man who yearns for youth, he at times struck a too-devoted tone face to face with young women" – and pointed out Suzannah Ibsen's deficiency in understanding her husband's need for young women, "which of course had nothing in common with infidelity in the current sense of that term" (Z 246).

Suzannah Ibsen was too intelligent to mistake sexual abstinence for proof of romantic indifference. She had good reason to be annoyed by Ibsen's attentions to Emilie Bardach, and much better reason to be disturbed by his attachment to Hildur Andersen, even if, in both cases, there was no "infidelity in the current sense of that term."

Ibsen first met Hildur Andersen when she was ten years old. During the summer of 1874, during a visit to Norway, he visited her parents to renew his acquaintance with the Andersen and Sontum familes. Hildur Andersen's father was a childhood acquaintance, and her mother was the daughter of Mrs. Helene Sontum, Ibsen's kind landlady in Bergen. At ten, pianist Hildur was a musical prodigy. Later, at twenty-three, when she went to Vienna to perfect her talent, she contacted Sigurd Ibsen, an attaché at the Norwegian legation, who wrote to his father of "this quick and intelligent young artist" and her fervent admiration for Ibsen's work.[22] In 1891, when Ibsen returned to Norway for good, one of the first visits he made was to the Andersens, where he met Hildur, now twenty-seven, for the second time. The relation between the playwright and the pianist would last nine years, until Ibsen's failing health confined him to his home, and he marked its importance for him and his gratitude to her by giving her a diamond ring engraved with the date of September 19. It is normally supposed that something of marked importance happened on that day, but since they met in August, it is possible that September 19 marked their first month of friendship.

When Ibsen met Hildur Andersen in 1891, she was already an exceptional woman. On her way to a distinguished career as one of Norway's first professional women pianists, she had followed her studies in Oslo with long periods in Leipzig at the music conservatory (1882–86) and in Vienna with the master Leschetizky (1887–90). She had made her debut in 1886, in Oslo, where she played Schumann's Piano Concerto in A-Minor, and had had her first solo concert three years later, where she played Beethoven's Piano Concert in G-Major and a Liszt fantasy. Her supple technique and her intelligent reading of the music caused a sensation.

Hildur Andersen would make a considerable contribution to Norwegian cultural life. For many years, she gave an annual series of chamber-music concerts, and she lectured widely on Romantic music, becoming famous for her analyses of Wagner. She was a much sought-after teacher; she examined works from historical as well as musical points of view, a novel method that had great importance for the young musicians she trained. She earned many awards, including the King's Gold Medal of Honor. She died in 1956, at the age of 92.[23]

Since Ibsen met Hildur Andersen after her return to Oslo from a hiking trip, and since Hilda Wangel appears in hiking clothes in act one of *The Master Builder*, tradition has it that Ibsen met Andersen dressed this way on the very day she came home. Whether this is true or not, the athletic pianist was extremely fond of hiking. Forthright of speech and character, she had a reputation for possessing an "ardent and courageous artistic temperament" (K 432). She was passionately interested in literature, art, and the theatre. In the fall of 1891, Suzannah Ibsen, who suffered from a severe case of crippling rheumatoid arthritis, went to Italy to take a cure, and Hildur Andersen became Ibsen's constant companion in Oslo. In spite of his relative indifference to music, Ibsen accompanied Andersen to a concert. They also visited art galleries, attended lectures, and went to the theatre; she was at his side in the stage box at gala performances of *Hedda Gabler* and *The League of Youth*. They were also present at Knut Hamsun's notorious series of lectures on modern literature. Sitting in the first seat in the front row, with Andersen beside him, Ibsen listened quietly on the first night as Hamsun pointed to Ibsen's stunted emotional life as the reason for his inadequacy as a psychologist. A particularly foolish part of Hamsun's talk dealt with *Rosmersholm*; showing his own bias, and mistaking a purpose for a blunder, Hamsun claimed that Rosmer's weakness made him an unconvincing aristocrat. As Hamsum grew more and more nervous, Ibsen remained immobile. Two days later, he told Andersen that they were going to attend the second lecture. She asked, "You don't mean that you want to hear that arrogant person again?" and Ibsen replied: "Don't you understand that we have to go to learn how we are supposed to write?" (Bull, "Hildur Andersen" 49–50).

Independent and high-spirited, Hildur Andersen was a young Ibsen woman come to life, a Petra Stockmann, an older Dina Dorf. Because their relation was not the only significant thing in her life, as it had been for Bardach, Andersen did not make Ibsen feel responsible for her well-being. Nor did she pursue him, like Raff, but rather left Oslo for Vienna six months after they met to pursue her music. Fellow artists who shared the same exacting tastes and the same commitment to their work, Ibsen and Andersen were kindred spirits who took great pleasure in each other's company. She was honored by the attentions of the great author whose work she admired passionately, and he by the attentions of an exceptional young woman who was doing what Ibsen told Helene Raff that she should aim for: she was realizing herself.

When Andersen was invited to play for the first time in Copenhagen, Ibsen wrote to Edvard Brandes "as a petitioner," as he put it, on her behalf. He noted that while she "enjoys a very good reputation as a performer in this country, she has a certain not unnatural dread of Copenhagen." He asked Brandes to make sure that she was received kindly. "She is an intimate friend of mine – a good, wise, and faithful friend" (*LS* 340).

Ibsen left a revelatory record of his feelings for his "intimate friend" in a letter to the other Brandes brother:

Dear George Brandes, I cannot resist sending you my special thanks for your "Goethe and Marianne von Willemer" [an article in *Tilskueren*, January, 1895]. I was not acquainted with this episode from Goethe's life. Perhaps I read about it long, long ago in G.W. Lewes' *Goethe*, but I must have forgotten about it because it had no personal interest for me at that time. Now the case is quite different. When I think of the character of Goethe's works during those years, the rebirth of his youth, it seems to me I should have known that he must have been blessed with something as wonderful for him as meeting this Marianne von Willemer. Now and then fate, chance, providence can indeed be rather kind and well disposed toward one. (*LS* 311–12).

Ibsen had, in fact, forgotten that he knew about Goethe's liaison with Marianne von Willemer. He had expressed his opinion of it years earlier to John Paulsen: "That damned billy goat!" (P 1:72–73). Now, indeed, the case was "quite different."

During Andersen's absences from Christiania, Ibsen kept much more to himself, attending no lectures or concerts. Upon her return, they took up their old habits. Inevitably, there was gossip. In 1894, while Suzannah Ibsen was again in Italy, it was rumored that Ibsen planned to divorce her. Magdalene Thoresen wrote to her about the rumor, and Suzannah wrote to her husband to ask him if it were true; how seriously she took it is perhaps indicated by the fact that in the same letter, she insisted that Ibsen find them a less damp apartment. Ibsen sent her a bristling reply in which he blamed his mother-in-law for repeating stupid gossip and assured his wife: "I can solemnly declare to you that I have never seriously thought or intended anything of the sort and that I never shall think or intend it" (*LS* 315). He went on to say that he would find a more suitable apartment and reiterated his wife's demands: "You won't live on the ground floor because of the cold floors, and you won't live on the upper floors because of the steps. But, as I said, your wishes shall be satisfied" (*LS* 316). Six weeks later, he wrote to describe in detail a new, handsome apartment he had leased that met all her requirements (and that would turn out to be their last). He did not mention that Hildur Andersen was helping him to furnish it.

When Suzannah Ibsen returned to Oslo, she refused to receive Andersen in her home, but this did not deter Ibsen from continuing the relation. Only his ill health would finally stop him from seeing Andersen. Toward the end of 1899, he consulted a doctor, Andersen's cousin Christian Sontum. He had his first stroke a few months later and the following year he suffered attacks of paralysis and a second stroke that made it almost impossible for him to walk. Virtually confined to his apartment, he was cut off from contact with Andersen. They last saw each other on a winter's day. She was out walking, and came across Ibsen being driven in a carriage. When he caught sight of her, he asked the coachman to stop, threw off the carriage rugs, stretched out his arms towards her, and called out: "Bless you! Bless you!" (Bull, "Hildur Andersen" 54).

In 1910, four years after Ibsen's death, Hildur Andersen was interviewed by a journalist in the newspaper *Verdens Gang*.[24] Ostensibly, the subject was Andersen's forthcoming concert, but the interviewer was clearly more interested in Andersen's relation with Ibsen. She obliged by showing him some dedications in the margins of her Ibsen books, and the fair copy of *The Master Builder* that Ibsen had given her. When the interviewer then asked her, "Aren't you Hilda, Miss Hildur?", she laughed and replied with characteristic bluntness: "Let's not talk about that. Don't you think we have enough of these Hilda's, who keep cropping up, in the North, in Denmark, and God knows where?" (Anker 2:121). The journalist persisted, asking Andersen if she planned to publish Ibsen's letters to her. She replied tartly that she had been asked that question by masses of people from all over the world. She then revealed something that may attest more powerfully than anything else to the importance Ibsen placed on their relation: "And it *was* Ibsen's intention that [the letters] be published. He talked about it. And he also expressed it in his letters" (121). Andersen then quoted from a letter – "Hildur! Take good care of your letters, as I do" – and said: "I have our whole correspondence, both his letters to me and my replies, which he gave back to me. 'Take good care of them,' he said, 'they are destined for a higher purpose.' He wanted them all to be published together" (121–22). Andersen then added her own opinion of this enterprise: "But – No! Not yet, anyway. Don't you think we have enough reminiscences for now?" (122).[25] Andersen then spoke of Ibsen's deep affection for her family, characterizing it by recalling a wish Ibsen had made to her mother. He had asked her to tell him beforehand when he could come to see the family; that way, he said, "I can enjoy my happiness in advance." Andersen added: "How people misjudged him. They thought he was cold" (122).

After the deaths of Ibsen, Suzannah Ibsen, and Sigurd Ibsen, Andersen promised Francis Bull that after Bergliot Ibsen's death, she would grant him permission to read Ibsen's letters to her and the dedications he had written in her copies of the plays. Clearly, she did not want to vex or hurt any member of the Ibsen family. In *The Three Ibsens*, Bergliot Ibsen dismisses her beloved father-in-law's inconsequential "little flutters, his 'Schwärmerein'," and mentions only one of them by name, noting that anyone who reads Dr. Elias' account understands "with what detachment [Ibsen] analyzes and sees straight through someone like Fräulein Bardach, who regarded herself as Ibsen's destiny" (BI 174). Bergliot Ibsen omits the name of the woman Ibsen kept company with for nine years, dismissing her by quoting from Ibsen's letter to Suzannah denying the divorce rumor.

Bergliot Ibsen's book was published in 1951, and she died two years later. But Hildur Andersen changed her mind about giving Bull access to her Ibsen papers. And she also made another, related decision; sometime before her death in 1956, she cut out Ibsen's dedications in her copies of the plays and burned them along with his letters and telegrams.

The only words from Ibsen to her that Hildur Andersen ever allowed to be printed were a few lines from a letter he wrote in the summer of 1895, when she was hiking in Telemark: "You should have seen more of Skien and heard more of it, also. For Skien is the town of the storming, rushing, seething waters. At least, that's how I remember it. Over the whole city are songs in the air from the waterfalls. It was not for nothing that I was born in the city of the waterfalls" (Bull, "Hildur Andersen" 49). Ibsen gave Andersen a signet seal made from a lump of ore discovered in the ruins of the fire that destroyed Skien; it was the last remains of the church bell of his childhood.

Ibsen addressed Hildur Andersen by the informal "du" (whose German equivalent he used neither with Bardach nor Raff), and by her first name, which Koht notes was "quite extraordinary for him to do with a woman" (K 432). The closeness of Ibsen's tie to Andersen, and, relatedly, his great respect for her taste and intelligence are illustrated by the extraordinary exception he made to one of the abiding rules of his life. He wrote *The Master Builder* in 1892 while Andersen was studying in Vienna; notoriously secretive about his work, especially his work in progress, which he kept fiercely to himself, not speaking of it to anyone, Ibsen now sent a constant stream of letters and telegrams to Andersen about the progress of the play he was writing. And she replied with letters and telegrams of her own. All through the spring and summer of 1892, as *The Master Builder* took shape, Ibsen and Andersen exchanged ideas on Ibsen's work in progress. It is the only time in his career that he collaborated with anyone.

Ibsen's relation with Andersen resulted in another surprising departure from his usual *modus vivendi*. Normally careful to preserve his working papers, he destroyed his notes and drafts for *The Master Builder*, along with Andersen's letters and telegrams. If Andersen did publish the epistolary record of their relation, Ibsen was making sure that her correspondence on *The Master Builder* would be excluded. Were the notes and the correspondence so intimate that protecting his and Andersen's privacy was more important to Ibsen than giving posterity another example of his working methods? Or was his decision another example of his characteristic refusal to admit that his work could be influenced by another person? Perhaps it was both.

After Andersen's death, Bull interviewed her maid of forty years, who told him that she could remember well two inscriptions and one note that Ibsen had sent her mistress. The first inscription, dated September 19, 1900, was a dedication to a set of Ibsen's collected works: "Hildur, These twenty-five twins belong to both of us. Before I found you, I sought and searched as I wrote.

I knew that you were somewhere in this big, wide world; and after I found you, I wrote only about princesses in one form or another. H.I." The second inscription was a quotation from *Peer Gynt* that Ibsen had written in an edition of *Ghosts*: "Oh, life – ! No second chance to play! / Oh, dread – ! Here's where my empire lay!" And the note, which accompanied a bouquet of nine red roses, read: "Nine red roses for you, nine rose-red years for me. Take the roses as thanks for the years" ("Hildur Andersen" 48–49). One can call the dedication a pretty piece of gallantry and point out that Ibsen had called Bardach and Raff his "princesses" before he met Andersen. But the lines from *Peer Gynt* are words of avowal: they had met too late. The red roses, consummate symbols of passion, and the romantic expression of gratitude, refute the claim that Hildur Andersen was only important to Ibsen for his "poetic production." Ibsen is thanking her not only for meeting the needs of his imagination, but the needs of his heart; she had immeasurably brightened his last good years, and he loved her for it. It is this he was commemorating when he gave her the diamond ring engraved with the date of their private anniversary.

The accuracy of Andersen's maid's recollections was proven in 1979 when Øyvind Anker, having been shown the dedications by their private owners, published them in his *New Collection* of Ibsen's letters. Equally important, Anker verified the discovery announced by a provincial newspaper, *Halden Arbeiderblad*, in 1962, of two letters and two visiting cards from Ibsen to Andersen. The newspaper had published only the salutation and signature of one letter – "To my wild bird of the woods" and "Your, your master builder" (Anker 1:393;394) – and the salutation of another – "My own dearest, loveliest princess" (Anker 1:401) – and the texts of the two cards. The first reads "To the princess" (Anker 1:388), and the other bears a date – "19 September 1891–1895" – and a message: "Thanks for everything, everything, in these four, full, rich years! A thousand greetings!" (Anker 1:424). Most importantly, the full text of the letters that Anker published with the permission of the Ibsen family and Andersen's surviving relatives indisputably confirms all the earlier evidence of Ibsen's love for Andersen. "Where are you flying off to now?" he asks his wild bird of the woods, who had returned to Europe to study. "Are you circling over Leipzig? . . . Are you ever coming home again? I'm going to see your mother to get some news of you. Perhaps there

will be a letter for me . . . I'm writing mostly for my own sake because I feel the need to send you something . . . Oh, how I long for the princess . . . how I long to come down from the high world of dreams and do what I said I would – so many, many times! In the meantime, a thousand heartfelt greetings! Your, your master builder" (January 7, 1893; Anker 1:393–94). Nine months later, when Andersen was enjoying a very successful tour in Norway, Ibsen wrote to his "dearest, loveliest princess":

> How terribly long it seems since I last heard from you. But it cannot be otherwise, for you are living in the midst of triumphs and celebrations. I am so deeply happy for you. Only don't forget me in all this . . . I have thought about you so much, my sweet Hildur! You can imagine how sad it is to stand in front of No. 35 [the address on Karl Johans Gate where the Andersens lived; they had recently moved]. The windows stand there so tall and cold and empty. No curtains and no flowers. And no princess comes . . . And no charming head peeks out. No white little hand signals to me from a distance. Yes, it is completely and utterly empty! . . .
>
> Oh, Hildur, let me see you again unchanged, the way you were when you left me. I have a feeling that I have loaned you out to many, many strangers. I want you to stay the same as you were. Are you listening to me, Hildur? Will you promise me that? A thousand greetings go to you from your forever loyal Henrik Ibsen (October 22, 1893; Anker 1:401–2).

Did Hildur Andersen misplace these two surviving letters, or did she purposely save them from the stove, along with the dedicated books and the visiting cards, knowing that they would later be discovered and almost certainly be published? Even if she misplaced two letters and some cards, it seems wholly improbable that she could overlook the volumes on her own shelves. It also seems likely that a woman of her character would have made a good job of obliterating everything if she wanted to. But why, then, did she not keep all the letters, as Ibsen had asked her to, and publish them, or leave them to someone else to publish after her death? And why was she careful to burn her own letters? Apparently, she preferred to keep from the world her own feelings for Ibsen, and most of his feelings for her, with the exception of a few indisputable proofs.

Ibsen's biographers insist that his relation with Hildur Andersen, like that with Emilie Bardach and Helene Raff, was not physical. Koht would have it that Ibsen's feelings for Andersen were purely platonic: "What he valued in their relationship was the joy of opening his heart to a young, richly gifted feminine soul" (K 432). Meyer believes that Ibsen was erotically attracted to Andersen, as he was to Bardach and Raff, but that the reason he did not "develop any of his infatuations into a full sexual relationship" was that he was afraid of the reality of sex when offered it, and may even have been impotent (M 620). He asks rhetorically: "What man not frightened of sex would be shy about exposing his sexual organs to his own doctor?" (M 648). One could answer: "A good many, perhaps." A man's timidity about "exposing his sexual organs" to a physician is not generally accepted as evidence of his fear of sex, much less of his impotence. More importantly, Meyer is assuming that all three women wanted, or would have consented to have, a sexual relation with Ibsen, and that it was Ibsen who refused it. But it is not only the man who decides. It may be true that Ibsen, who had, in Zucker's phrase, "an extremely keen sense of the fitness of things" (Z 228), and who was deeply bound to his wife, did not want "a full sexual relationship." But nothing in the letters or diary versions of the proper bourgeoise Emilie Bardach, or in the "Ibsen Diary" of the less conventional Helene Raff, suggests that either woman would have committed the outrageous act of engaging in a sexual liaison. And Hildur Andersen's upright character more than suggests that she would not have consented to it, either. But passion can be expressed in other ways besides "a full sexual relationship," like gifts of diamond rings and red roses. The real point is that it is unimportant whether Ibsen and Andersen slept together. They found a *modus vivendi* that suited them and that was worthy of the feelings they had for each other. Whatever did not happen between them, many other things did, to their private and mutual joy.

Ibsen's relationships with his three "princesses" is, of course, an example of the familiar pattern of the long married, aging man who seeks rejuvenation through younger women. But even if the thirty-year-old Ibsen marriage had subsided into a deep friendship (which can hardly be considered unusual), it is not true that Ibsen "had turned his back on romantic love for a woman who could enable him to achieve his ambitions, and Emilie Bardach, Helene Raff, and Hildur Andersen were living symbols of what he had rejected" (M 747). Ibsen married Suzannah Thoresen because he was in love with her. It was, in fact, "love at first sight"; after the second time he saw her, Ibsen wrote his bride-to-be an exceed-

16. Emilie Bardach (1871–1955). The "princess" of the Gossensass summer.

17. Hildur Andersen (1864–1956). Accomplished concert pianist and the love of Ibsen's late years.

18. Henrik Ibsen at the age of fifty-nine (1887).

ingly romantic proposal of marriage, waited in trepidation for her reply, and was overjoyed when she accepted. It is true that Suzannah Ibsen believed wholeheartedly in her husband's talent and encouraged him as no one else did, but Ibsen did not choose his "dearest cattttt" as a means to his advancement.

The Master Builder is often considered to be Ibsen's most directly autobiographical work. Ibsen once said that the play's protagonist Solness contained more of himself than any other of his characters (K 433), and the drama of the aging master builder, buried in a dead marriage yet tormented by guilt at having sacrificed his wife's life to his work, terrified of the younger generation and longing for the restorative power of Hilda Wangel's youth, is frequently read as a "personal confession in disguise" (Lavrin, *Ibsen* 114), a dramatization of Ibsen's failed personal life, his "sexual unhappiness."[26] Clearly, Solness' attraction to the youth and vitality of his "princess" Hilda Wangel reflects Ibsen's relations with Bardach, Raff, and Andersen. While Solness' guilt towards his wife may reflect "Ibsen's feeling that he had deprived his own wife of something by having lived so intensely and self-centeredly for his art" (K 433), it may be that if Ibsen felt guilty, it was less because of his dogged devotion to his work, which Suzannah Ibsen overwhelmingly supported, than because of his awareness that his superbly intelligent wife had not developed her own talents, but had devoted her life to his career. But as for the claim that the Solness marriage is "painfully identifiable as Ibsen's own,"[27] the wallowing in silent resentment and self-recrimination that marks the Solness marriage bears little resemblance to the relation between the Ibsens, who, when they were displeased with each other, expressed their feelings with a frankness that was notorious. And one has only to read Ibsen's letters to his wife while she was away from Oslo to see his deep affection. Hating to write letters, Ibsen writes frequently and in detail of everything his wife would want to know about: his own health, news of friends and family, the household affairs, the arrangements for his daily meals and their menus, the state of the Ibsens' financial investments, negotiations for productions and publications of his plays, and the weather. Very solicitous of Suzannah's poor health, he is worried when he does not hear from her and relieved when he does: "How happy and reassured I am to hear that so far everything has gone well!" (*LS* 309). And Ibsen misses his wife's company: "The evenings are lonely, but I sit and read at the dining table." Ibsen's letters are not those of a man chained to a woman whose presence burdens him. Some weeks after the Gossensass summer, in one of his jottings, Ibsen noted: "A huge prejudice, this: that one only loves one person" (*OI* 7:485).

Hilda Wangel is to some extent, and in different ways, a mixture of Bardach, Raff, and Andersen. After Bardach saw the play, she said, "I didn't see myself" (King, "Ibsen and Emilie Bardach" 2:91), and certainly nothing about Bardach resembles Hilda Wangel, whose ruthlessness is that of the invented "demonic little wrecker" Ibsen had chortled about to Julius Elias; Solness' phrase to describe Hilda – "a bird of prey" – directly recalls Ibsen's phrase to Elias – "a beast of prey." But when Bardach said that she did not see herself in *The Master Builder*, she also noted, "but I saw him" (King 2:91). Solness' exhilaration, his ecstatic promises of a new, triumphant life with "a princess that I love" (856) directly recall the glorious plans Ibsen had envisioned with his princess in Gossensass, and the "kingdom of Orangia" (806) is the name Ibsen had given to the kingdom he would create for her. Hilda's unconventionality undoubtedly owes something to Helene Raff, who recorded in her "Ibsen Diary" that Ibsen delightedly called her a "heathen" because she had been educated neither by church nor school; she had "grown up in the forest" (*OI* 7:565). And Solness' declarations of his longing for Hilda's youth recall Ibsen's statement to Raff characterizing his fondness for her. Of the three women's influence on the play, Hildur Andersen's is the most important. On the external level, hiker Hilda, with her robust health and brash way of speaking, directly recalls Andersen. The phrase "wild bird of the woods" in Ibsen's letter to Andersen quotes from Solness describing Hilda (833), and Ibsen's declaration to Andersen that he wanted to do "what I said" with her "many, many times" quotes from Solness' promise to Hilda that he will kiss her "many, many times" (856). Ibsen's closing "your, your master builder" in his letter is an inversion of Hilda's "my, *my* master builder" at the end of the play (860). More importantly, the miraculous affinity between Solness and Hilda reflects that between Ibsen and Andersen, and Solness' adulation of Hilda as his rejuvenation reflects the feelings Ibsen expressed in his letter to Brandes about Goethe and Marianne von Willemer. Ibsen paid Andersen a private and loving compliment by having Solness and Hilda meet on September 19. And he sent Andersen's closest friend a first edition of the play with the following note: "Along with best wishes for a merry Christmas, I give you this copy of Hilda's and the master builder's drama" (Anker 1:393).

But the end of Hilda's and the master builder's drama is the opposite of Hildur's and the master dramatist's. Andersen's major importance for *The Master Builder* lies not in what she shares with Hilda Wangel, but in what she does not. A woman devoted to her own vocation, Andersen did not need to seek fulfillment through the heroic deeds of a great man. Instead of demanding, as Hilda does of Solness, that Ibsen do the "impossible," Andersen, perfecting her professional skills in Vienna, helped Ibsen write a play about a woman who makes this demand of a man who dies in fulfilling it. Ibsen was careful to finish *The Master Builder* on September 19 (1892), and when Andersen came home, he made her a gift of the first fair copy. This fanciful construction of what might have happened if the playwright and his "good, wise, and faithful friend" had not known how to love each other was her play as well as his.

BELOVED NEMESIS: *THE MASTER BUILDER*

The most important model for Hilda Wangel was herself as a young girl. Dr. Wangel's younger daughter in *The Lady from the Sea*, Hilda has a decided taste for the macabre. That the dying Lyngstrand will never become the sculptor he plans to be, she finds "thrilling"; it's her "privilege," she says, to think so (619). Hilda also finds it "thrilling" to catch the tough, old carp in the Wangels' pond (634). What Hilda finds the opposite of thrilling are unheroic men: "Look at him, creeping along!" she says of the fatally ill Lyngstrand (617). The only man who merits Hilda's favorite epithet is the sailor in Lyngstrand's sculpture who takes physical revenge on his unfaithful wife. The excitement Hilda finds in violence and death is also reflected in her "thrilling" fantasy of having a dead husband, of being a "young grieving bride" dressed in "black right up to the neck" (682). Hilda is as obsessed with sex as she is with death. Knowing that Lyngstrand will never return from his European trip, she queries him and Bolette on their marriage plans. She contemptuously dismisses the thirty-seven-year-old Arnholm as an erotic subject, but specu-lates absurdly that her step-mother is flirting with him.

In a striking example of literal, linear intertextuality unique in Ibsen's plays, Hilda Wangel is the only major character to appear twice;[28] it is the Hilda of *The Lady from the Sea* whom master builder Solness met when he came to her town ten years ago. Seeing him place the wreath on the high church tower was far more thrilling than killing carp or musing on widow's weeds. Hilda's excitement lay both in Solness' professional prowess and the titillating possi-bility of his death: "What if he slipped and fell – he, the master builder himself!" (805).

In *The Lady from the Sea*, Hilda's macabre tastes and pubescent interests provide an unusual comic relief to the drama's serious action. But what is oddly amusing in the earlier play has serious consequences in *The Master Builder*, whose twenty-three-year-old Hilda retains, under her disarming honesty, her taste for male heroics tinged with danger. In *The Lady from the Sea*, Hilda's repeti-tion of "thrilling" seems a mere reflection of her immaturity, but in *The Master Builder*, her favorite word resonates suggestively, for her adult charm and sexuality have conferred power upon her. Lyngstrand tells Hilda in *The Lady from the Sea* that when he returns from his journey, he will consider marrying her; by then, she will have matured into a good-natured young woman. If Lyngstrand had returned to Lysanger, he would have found Hilda an exception to his theory of female development.

The early scenes of *The Master Builder* establish the unhappiness that makes Solness take Hilda for an immediate and miraculous remedy for what ails him. The play opens with a tableau of the master's workers, a trio of silent laborers: the dying Brovik, "*a gaunt old man*," his son Ragnar, "*with a slight stoop*," and Ragnar's fiancée Kaja, "*a delicate young girl . . . rather sickly in appearance*" (785). The middle-aged man who enters, "*strong and forceful*," contrasts strongly with his weak subordinates. Stroking the hair of his bookkeeper, growling at Ragnar, exploding at the tastes of his vulgar clientele, Solness seems the epitome of strength and self-assurance. But the conversation with Old Brovik that follows re-veals a man so eaten up with fear of the "younger generation" that he has transformed the insecure Ragnar into an enemy. Learning that the clients he so disparaged have asked Ragnar to design their home, he bursts into bitter defensiveness: "So, that's it!

Halvard Solness – he ought to start giving up now! Make room for youth. For even the youngest. Just make room! Room! Room!" (789–90). Brovik, who badly wants to see his son succeed before he dies, appeals to reason: "Good Lord, there's room enough here for more than one man –" (790). Solness gives a lame, almost comic response – "There's not that much room here anymore" – followed by a near tirade violently in excess of what the situation warrants: "I'm not giving up! I never give ground. Not voluntarily. Never in this world, never!" Helpless against his persecutory panic, Solness will not relent even when the old man reminds him: "Shall I go into death so poor?" (790).

Solness so fears Ragnar's leaving to start his own firm that he resorts to the grotesque ploy of pretending to love Ragnar's fiancée Kaja; if she stays, so will Ragnar. Solness manipulates Kaja, petting and kissing her, accusing her of wanting to desert him. She shivers with excitement, "*sinks down before him*" in a pathetic display of slavish love: "Oh, how good you are to me! How incredibly good you are!" (792).

As the swooning Kaja falters back to her desk, another of the sickly people who surround Solness enters. His wife Aline "*looks thin and careworn*" (792). Dressed in black, with her blonde hair in ringlets, she seems both ghost-woman and child. She speaks "*rather slowly in a plaintive voice*," expressing her disapproval of her husband through a double entendre of accusatory politeness: "I'm afraid I'm intruding." Even the rather obtuse Doctor Herdal understands her innuendos, for example, "You've certainly been in luck, Halvard, to have gotten hold of that girl" (794).

Aline Solness' little barbs against her husband fulfill his own wish to be punished by her. Solness confides in the doctor that when Aline's family home burned down twelve years ago, she never recovered, while he "rose from those ashes" to become the "top man" in his field (799). The guilt he feels for his success is linked to the fear of being displaced that "racks" him morning and night"; because he had such extraordinary luck earlier, now things will "have to change." The doctor's commonsensical rejection of Solness' fear – "Oh, rot! Where's this change coming from?" – calls forth an explosion that recalls the earlier one to Brovik: "Someone or other will set up the cry: Step back for *me*! And all the others will storm in after, shaking their fists and shouting: Make room – make room – make room! Yes, Doctor, you better look out. Someday youth will come here, knocking at the door –" (800).

In the *coup de théâtre* that follows, Solness' personification takes on literal life in Hilda's famous knock. After her arrival, the doctor attempts a witticism: "Youth *did* come along, knocking at your door." "Yes, but that was something else completely," Solness "*buoyantly*" replies (802). But he has mistakenly identified his adversary, who is not a young, male rival but a young, female admirer. Not since *Ghosts* has there been such a sense of fatality in an Ibsen play. Hilda enters bringing Solness' death with her as though she were carrying it in her knapsack. Her name, as is often noted, connects her to the valkyrie Hild; as surely as Hild chooses the warriors for Valhalla, Hilda marks out Solness for heroic death.

Arriving with only the hiking clothes on her back and a change of underwear, Hilda seems a fine, free spirit. Dr. Herdal remembers meeting her the preceding summer at a mountain lodge, where, he teases her, she was something of a flirt. Sounding like Lona Hessel, Hilda responds: "I'd a lot rather do that than sit knitting knee socks with all the old hens" (801). Hilda invites herself to spend the night, then gives herself the run of Solness' work room, making an inspection tour of its contents. Sizing up the competition, she wants to know the sex of the bookkeeper who writes in the ledger, and upon learning it, her marital status. Solness playfully suggests that if his bookkeeper leaves, perhaps Hilda would like to take her place. Hilda adamantly declines, for she has different plans for herself and the master builder: "Because there are plenty of other things to be done around here. (*Looks up at him, smiling.*) Don't you think so too?" (804).

Hilda startles, then charms Solness with her marvelous recollection of his heroic construction of ten years ago and his even more heroic deed: "I'd never dreamt that anywhere in the world there was a builder who could build a tower so high. And then, that you could stand there right at the top, large as life!" (805). Solness remembers a group of schoolgirls, especially "one of those little devils in white – how she carried on, screaming up at me" until she almost made him lose his balance. "That little devil," of course, "was *me*," replies Hilda. But the master builder could never have fallen, she insists; the very source of her excitement was his total self-control: "It was so wonderfully thrilling to stand below, looking up at you . . . And that you weren't the least bit dizzy!" Solness questions Hilda's certainty of his perfect equilibrium, but she refuses to listen: "How else could you stand up there singing?" The master builder again protests: "I've never sung a note in my life." "Yes," she insists, "you were singing then. It sounded like harps in the air" (805).

The tone of child-like worship that characterizes Hilda's account of her hero's climb thinly disguises an erotic sub-text; her description of her mounting excitement as she watched the master builder's progress to the top of the tower, at which point she felt his power within her and heard vibrating music, is a narrative of lovemaking in which Solness functions as a masterful, experienced male who brings an aroused, inexperienced young woman to orgasm. Hilda follows the tale of her voyeuristic sexual experience with an account of what she calls "the *real* thing" (806). In the best tradition of nineteenth-century "women's fiction" (the kind Emma Bovary read in the convent), her hero came to her house after his climb, encountered her alone in a room, and was immediately struck by her beauty. He paid her fulsome compliments, calling her his "princess" and promising to come back in ten years and carry her off to his "kingdom." He then took her in his arms and kissed her "many times" (807). Although Solness admits that in an expansive state of mind, he might have paid a young girl a few banal compliments – "Well, after a good meal one's not in a mood to count pennies" (806) – he refuses the rest: "Yes, I most emphatically do deny it!" (807). But Solness is flattered and fascinated by Hilda's account of his extraordinary effect on her, and her pouting and sulking when he refuses her story make him relent. Within seconds, "These things you've been saying – you must have dreamed them" becomes "Oh, all right, for God's sake – so I *did* the thing too!" Solness even allows Hilda to take him through a litany of his lovemaking: "That you threw your arms around me?" "All right!" "And bent me back?" "Way over back." "And kissed me." "Yes, I did it." "Many times?" "As many as you ever could want" (807–8).

Solness humors Hilda because she brings him relief from his wretchedness. Her growing physical health contrasts sharply with Aline's sickliness. Her taste for dramatic domestic architecture, her vision of homes with towers – "something pointing – free, sort of, into the sky" (810) – marks her as Solness' soulmate: "How odd

that you should say that. It's exactly what, most of all, I've wanted."
Hilda's faith in Solness' genius, coupled with her youth and determination, make her a perfect ally for a man who fears the loss of
his powers: "I've been so alone here – and felt so helpless watch-
ing it all. (*Dropping his voice.*) I should tell you – I've begun to grow
afraid – so awfully afraid of the young" (811).

In his self-absorption, Solness sees Hilda, as he sees Kaja and the
Broviks, in terms of the use he can make of her, and Hilda
promises a willing servitude: "Can you find a use for *me*, Mr.
Solness?" (812). Envisioning his competitive powers reborn, the
jubilant builder replies: "Oh, of course I can! Because I feel that
you've come, too, almost – under some new flag. And then it's
youth against youth –!" But Hilda's question is deceptive, for
although her lips tremble as softly as Kaja's as she repeats her
obeisant plea – "*Can* you find a use for me?" – she herself has a use
for the master builder. Solness' reassuring reply – "You're the one
person I've needed the most" – is not wholly satisfactory. For
although she gazes at Solness in rapture, declaring, "Then I have
my kingdom!," she quickly alters her response in her act-one
curtain line: "*Almost* – that's what I meant" (813).

Hilda insists on her maturity at twelve – "Oh, maybe I wasn't so
much of a child, either. Not quite the little kitten you thought"
(809) – but she confuses sexuality with adulthood. She has left her
father to attach herself to another older man. Nourishing for ten
years the memory of the "thrilling" time when "Mr. Solness," her
hero, "acted up" (810), she demands to feel now what she felt
then. Her explanation to Solness of how "in all seriousness" she
could continue to believe for ten years in her hero's return to give
her a "kingdom" reveals the girlish eroticism of her obsession: "If
you could build the highest church tower in the world, it seemed
to me you certainly should be able to come up with some kind of
kingdom, too" (809). It is a short step from believing that a
provincial Norwegian church tower is the world's highest to sup-
posing that its builder can provide one with a magic life. Hilda
stops time, as in a fairy tale; the ten years are up, and she has come
to claim her ageless prince, who is still the man hanging the
wreath on the high church tower. That Hilda suffers from ar-
rested development is obvious;[29] in the Solness home, she sleeps,
appropriately, in a nursery. What is remarkable is Ibsen's use of
her abnormality, whose "case history" aspect he makes widely

symbolic. Hilda is Youth with a vengeance, for she has never grown up.

The relation of Solness and Hilda is characterized by an interlocking, one-sided view each has of the other: the aging man's vision of the vibrant younger woman – a courageous free-spirited helpmate who will restore his failing powers – complements the young woman's vision of the successful older man – a heroic father figure whose achievements will give meaning to her own life. But the inspirational muse who empowers Solness against the youth he fears is also an obsessed young woman bent on reliving at any cost an ecstatic erotic encounter; Hilda's great architectural pioneer is also an acrophobic, frightened man at the height of the "male climacteric" (F 781). From beginning to end, Solness and Hilda cling to the half-truth of their complementary identities, and much of the originality of *The Master Builder* lies in its partial privileging of this shared illusion. In contrast to its predecessors *Pillars of Society, A Doll House, Ghosts, An Enemy of the People, The Lady from the Sea,* and *Hedda Gabler,* whose action expresses the movement traditional to Western drama since Greek tragedy – that of illusion to reality – *The Master Builder* does not strip away its characters' deceptions, but rather intensifies them. The crisis of the action is not reversal followed by revelation, but the climax of a crescendo of illusion that remains unchallenged even in the play's denouement.[30]

Princess Hilda seems the answer to the aging man's prayers, the understanding woman *par excellence*; the misunderstood man exclaims: "Oh, Hilda, how amazingly lucky for me that you've come! Now at last I've got someone I can talk to" (822). Hilda talks as well as she listens; she tells the insecure builder exactly what he wants to hear: "Nobody but you should have a right to build. You should be all alone in that" (821). Hilda also allows Solness to throw off the guilt he feels toward his wife. Listening raptly as he tells her about finding the crack in the chimney in Aline's family home and keeping it a secret, she belittles his self-laceration when she learns that the fire started elsewhere: "Then what's the point in all this sitting and mooning around about a cracked chimney?" (830). Solness needs a "robust conscience," like her own, that would free him of his scruples and allow him to "dare" what he "most wanted" (831–32). She responds *"with great vehemence"* to his comparison of her to "a bird of prey": "And why not a bird of prey? Why shouldn't I go hunting as well? Take the spoil I'm after?" (833). Solness quickly retracts his comment: "No. You're like a dawning day. When I look at you – then it's as if I looked into the sunrise." He must deny her ruthlessness because it conflicts with his notice of her as his deliverer, a feeling so strong that it seems to him as though he must have "called" her to him (833).[31]

What follows produces the same ironic jolt as Hilda's knock on the door in act one: "What did you want with me?" "You, Hilda, are youth." "Youth that you're so afraid of?" "And that, deep within me, I'm so much hungering for." "(*Hilda rises, goes over to the small table, and takes up Ragnar Brovik's portfolio.*)" (833–34). The woman who will save Solness from his rival is his rival's unwitting agent. Hilda denounces Solness' fear – "If Ragnar Brovik gets his chance, he'll hammer me to the ground" (834) – as unworthy in its pettiness: "For shame, Mr. Solness! . . . Don't say those things!" (835). Like the great man that he is, Solness must release Ragnar, a deed Hilda equates with Solness' heroic climb: "I want to see you great. See you with a wreath in your hand – high, high up on a church tower! . . . So – out with your pencil!" (835).

By forcing Solness to recommend Ragnar's drawings, Hilda frees him from his humiliating dependency on his subordinate and heals his sick fear. He can now let Kaja and Ragnar go. He follows his decision – "Now Ragnar can do some building" – with a broad hint that he himself will inaugurate the new house: "We'll be hanging the wreath up this evening – (*Turning to Hilda*) way up high at the top of the tower" (837). Hilda frees Solness, but dooms him at the same time, for after Solness hangs the wreath, Ragnar will be able to do all the building he wants.

Solness believes that he must have "called" Hilda to him because she speaks for the part of him that longs to throw off his self-doubt and pursue his vocation. Aline is Hilda's foil in a triangle that replicates that of *Catiline*: a male protagonist, bound by guilt and habit to a protective wife who begs him to abandon his ambition, is drawn to a fatal woman who urges him to heroic deeds. In language whose forthright banality brashly expresses the dichotomous psycho-sexual argument, Aline and Hilda duel over Solness: "For heaven's sake, Miss Wangel, what are you thinking of! My husband – who gets so dizzy!" "He dizzy? Impossible!" (838). Like Catiline's wife Aurelia, Aline cares only for her husband's physical safety; jolted out of her hostile lethargy by the prospect of Solness' climbing the tower, "*terrified*" she leaves to find the doctor. Hilda then uses Furia's dual method of denigration and flattery to coax her hero on: "*Is* it true or isn't it? . . . That my master builder dares not – and *can* not – climb as high as he builds? . . . *You* could never be dizzy!" (838–39). Like Catiline, who characterizes his life with Aurelia as "part death, part lethargy" (67), and welcomes Furia because he recognizes in her "the genius and image" of his own psyche (69), Solness accepts the challenge of the female *alter ego* whose demands represent his inmost wish; Hilda's kingdom is nothing less than the extraordinary structures the master builder longs to create, and in inaugurating the new house, he is marking out the future she is inspiring him to achieve: "In the topmost room of the tower – that's where you could live, Hilda – live like a princess . . . So we'll hang the wreath this evening – Princess Hilda" (838–39).[32]

Hilda will inhabit the house Aline refused. Solness built it to help his wife forget her loss and thus make "things go better" between them (815). But Aline does not want to stop mourning: "(*breaking out in lamentation*). You can build as much as you ever want, Halvard – but for *me* you can never build up a real home again." Solness despairs of his dead marriage: "Not the least glimmer of light in this home!" (817). Aline implacably corrects him: "This is no home, Halvard."

Aline's grim joylessness is linked to her religion of duty. She prepares Hilda's room because "It's no more than my duty" (802), and shops for Hilda because "It's simply my duty" (819). She blames the collapse of her marriage and the death of her sons on her lapse from her obligations as wife and mother after the fire; she tells her husband, "I had my duties on both sides – both to you and to the babies. I should have made myself strong" (817). This self-analysis of moral failing is overwhelmingly ironic in its erroneousness, for it was Aline's devotion to duty that caused the children's deaths. Solness confides to Hilda: "Aline came down with fever – and it affected her milk. Nurse them herself, she had to do that. It was her duty, she said" (824). Like Mrs. Alving, in performing her woman's duty, Mrs. Solness unwittingly destroyed her offspring. The twin sons drank the poisoned drink of duty, and died.

A similarly perverse irony lies in Solness' mistaken assumption

19. Aline (Margaret Barker) confiding in Hilda (Joan Tetzel) in the APA
Repertory Theatre's production of *The Master Builder*, New York, 1955.

that Aline's unhappiness results from their children's deaths.
Unburdening himself to Hilda, Solness guiltily explains that the
fire that allowed him to pursue his calling destroyed his wife's; "*her*
lifework had to be cut down, crushed, broken to bits, so that mine
could win through" (826). Aline herself had a gift for "building,"
Solness lyrically laments, "building up the souls of children"
(827). This vision of Aline's calling is a ludicrous glorification of

the sorry motherhood she regrets. In the tête-à-tête between Hilda and Aline that begins act three, Hilda, who has no scruples about bonding with her rival, sympathetically speaks of Aline's sad life: "Poor Mrs. Solness. First you had the fire" (842). Referring to the death of the babies, Hilda adds: "And then what was worse followed." Aline's uncomprehending reply – "Worse?" – hints at the revelation to come. Hilda strengthens her euphemism – "The worst of all" – but Aline's still uncomprehending "What do you mean?" forces her to name the terrible event: "You lost your two little boys." Aline is surprised: "Oh, *them.*" A member of Pastor Manders' moral universe, she explains that "that's something quite different, that. That was an act of Providence, you know." The babies' deaths were a "just punishment" for her own lack of strength, and as for the babies themselves, "We can only be happy for them. Because they're well off – so well off now." It is not the children she mourns; "No, it's the small losses in life that strike at your heart." She names the family portraits, the old silk dresses, "all Mother's and Grandmother's lace – that burned too. And just think – their jewels!" (842–43). The last item of the fire losses are the children Aline mourns: "(*Heavily.*) And then, all the dolls" (843). "*Choking with tears,*" she tells Hilda the story of the "nine beautiful dolls" who were destroyed; "Oh, that was hard – so hard for me." She had mothered them since her childhood, even after her marriage, hiding them from her husband. "But then, poor things, they were all burned up. No one ever thought about saving *them.*" It is not the real babies she mourns – "Oh, *them*" (842) – but the fakes – "*them*" (843). Mother of dolls, not children, Aline justifies her sorrow in a chilling image: "Because, you see, in a way there was life in them too. I used to carry them under my heart. Just like little unborn children." Mourning the trappings of decorative femininity – laces, silk dresses, jewels – and play motherhood – a bevy of dolls – Aline was not, as her husband sentimentally pronounces, deprived by her children's deaths of becoming "the woman she could have been" (831). Solness, obsessed with his own psychic life, knows nothing of his wife's.

Stunned by Aline's confidences, Hilda remarks to Solness, "I've just come out of a tomb" (844), and although she spares Solness the real cause of his wife's suffering, her conversation with Aline makes her falter momentarily in her campaign to advance her kingdom. She will leave to save Aline's feelings, for if she stays, she says to Solness, "you know so well what would happen" (845). "So much the better," he wildly replies, and accuses her of abandoning him: "And what'll become of me when you're gone?" Hilda replies: "You have your duties to her. Live for those duties." But living for others is an ethic that violates Hilda's fierce allegiance to the self. Annoyed by Aline's repeated explanations of her kindness as no more than a hostess' duty, Hilda bursts out: "I can't stand that mean, ugly word! . . . Duty, duty, duty! . . . As if it's made to cut" (820).[33] Hilda is Aline's foil in the oppositional pattern of *Brand* and *Ghosts* – Agnes' and Oswald's joy of life – expressed in images of sun and light, versus Brand and Pastor Manders' duty. Solness says of his marriage, "Never a touch of sun!" (817), and when Hilda enters: "Ah! But it's brightening up" (818). Sun-loving Hilda basks in Solness' garden: "Ah – you can sit and really sun yourself here, like a cat" (841). Solness' plea that Hilda stay with him – "I'm alive, chained to the dead. (*In anguish.*) I – *I*, who can't go on living without joy in life!" (842) – appeals to her innermost conviction. She muses on the foolishness of self-sacrifice: "Not daring to take hold of one's own happiness . . . Just because someone you know is there, standing in the way" (846). Coaxingly, Solness reminds Hilda of her love of the "Viking spirit." Wanting to cede to him, she asks: "And the other? Say what that was!" Solness' citation of Hilda's theory of the right guide to life – "A robust conscience" – settles the matter. "*Vivacious once more,*" she jettisons the obstacle of the suffering wife and presents Solness with a design for living based on Oswald's twin components of happiness, the joy of life and the joy of work: "We two, we'll work together. And that way we'll build the loveliest – the most beautiful thing anywhere in the world" (848).[34]

Recalling Hjørdis' dream of life with Sigurd, Rebecca's with Rosmer, Hilda's vision of the harmonious life is the joining of eros and vocation. But while Rebecca and Hjørdis wish for joy and work within and of the world, the site of Hilda's projected happiness is another realm. The "loveliest – the most beautiful thing" that she and Solness will construct is not only "a castle," for "who ever heard of a kingdom without a castle!" (847), but a "castle in the air" (848). Isolated from the world, "very high up – and free on every side," the lovers' castle will have a high tower from whose balcony its two, superior denizens will look down on "the others"

(847). Like a saga woman taunting her man with his cowardice, Hilda blurs Solness' physical and moral weaknesses as she speaks "*contemptuously*" of the "dizzy conscience" that will keep him from realizing the castle (848). His reply is to commit himself irrevocably to her: "From this day on we'll build together, Hilda." To her skeptical question – "A real castle in the air?" – he answers, "Yes. One with solid foundations." But Solness, the "idea man" who never became an architect, has never understood foundations; that is why he needed the Broviks, for "calculating stresses" and "all that damned detail work" (796). Solness' impatience with the rudiments of construction makes him a perfect builder for Hilda's "castle in the air," where passion will last even as it is domesticated, and where corporeal and incorporeal will merge in a private and perfect land of two.

In the last scene between Hilda and Solness, the master builder elevates their romantic vision to metaphysical status. Now wholly bound to Hilda, sure of her power to renew his life, Solness reveals to her the most important meaning of the fire. It was God who had the house burn down and the children die so that Solness could "enhance His glory" by building churches (854). Solness rebelled against Him on the top of the Lysanger church tower, the only time in his life that he had been able to conquer his vertigo: "Hear me, Thou Almighty! From this day on, I'll be a free creator – free in my own realm, as you are in yours." That Solness regards himself as co-equal with God entrances Hilda, who now understands the significance of what she heard: "That was the singing I heard in the air!" (855). Promethean Solness thought he had won the battle, and from then on built no churches, only "homes for human beings." But "His mill went right on grinding," for Solness discovered that the secular dwellings he built were worthless: "Human beings don't know how to use these homes of theirs. Not for being happy in." Now, through Hilda, Solness understands "the one thing human beings can be happy in," Hilda's castle. But God's mill continues to grind, for Hilda demands a test: "Then let me see you high and free, up there!" She refuses the truth in Solness' sad reply – "Oh, Hilda – I'm not up to that every day" – by "*passionately*" insisting: "I want you to! I want that! (*Imploring.*) Just once more, master builder! Do the impossible again!" (855–56). In their final dialogue, re-

CHAPTER 11

Women who live for love

RITA: I only care about you! Only you in this whole world!
You – you – only you! *Little Eyolf,* act 1 (887)
RITA: But can you guess what I'll be doing – after you're
gone? *Little Eyolf,* act 3 (933)

Ibsen followed *The Master Builder* with another drama of a man
driven by his vocation and divided between two opposing women.
But in *Little Eyolf,* the centrality of the man fades to give place to
one of the women, and the love triangle is subordinated to the
action of her transformation. The argumentative discourse in the
third act of *A Doll House* underlies the non-polemical mode of
Little Eyolf as protagonist Rita Allmers breaks the pattern of her
husband-centered life. In the end, it is Rita who teaches her
husband, a moral philosopher, the meaning of his own vocation.

Little Eyolf opens with a scene of unacknowledged rivalry between two women whose reason for living is the same man. Rita
Allmers is performing the wifely task of unpacking her husband's
suitcase when she is surprised by a visit from her husband's half-
sister Asta. The affable dialogue's slip is showing. Rita asks if Asta
has met a "special friend" (868), road builder Borgheim, on the
steamer, and Asta's irritated response shows that her heart does
not belong to Borgheim. That Rita is anxious for Asta to find a
man is understandable in view of her sister-in-law's reaction to the
news of her brother's homecoming: "(*Joyously, coming closer*).
What! Alfred's home?" So close does Asta feel to her brother that
she accounts for her visit by their telepathic correspondence:
"*That's* what drew me out here!" Rita quickly establishes her own
connection; hearing of her husband's coming just an hour before
he arrived, "it was all the more delectable, getting him back that

way." Asta exhibits excessive solicitude – "He's not depressed? . . . Not the least bit tired, even? . . . And then the mountain air may have been too raw for him" – while Rita displays excessive attachment: "Ah, but how lost I've felt without Alfred! How empty – like a desert! Oh, it was as if this house were an open grave –!" (869). Asta considers Rita's feelings unreasonable – "Now, really! What's it been – six, seven weeks –?" – and comments that it was "high time [Alfred] got away"; in fact, he "should have a hiking trip in the mountains every summer." Asta knows what Alfred needs: an annual reprieve from Rita. She also knows what is best for Eyolf, Rita and Alfred's nine-year-old son: he reads too much, she tells his mother, and admonishes her to do something about it.

That Rita has good reason to resent her sister-in-law is established when the object of their shared adoration appears. The warmth in Alfred Allmers' greeting – "Asta! Dearest Asta! Here, already! How wonderful to see you so soon!" (870) – matches that of Asta's own response to the news of his homecoming. Asta is Alfred's ally in the writing of his *magnum opus, Human Responsibility*, which she was sure "would practically write itself" if Alfred "could only get away." Rita considers *Human Responsibility* her enemy because Alfred spends his days and nights writing it.

When Alfred makes his grand announcement that he has abandoned his book for "higher duties," the relieved Rita "*radiantly*" grasps his hand (882). But it was not Rita, but rather "thoughts of Eyolf," Alfred explains, that led him to his decision. He will sacrifice the book to devote himself to the education of his crippled son, who under his tutelage will develop into the whole moral and mental man: "All the tentative nobility in him I want to help to grow – and blossom and bear fruit. (*With more and more fervor, getting up.*) And I'll do more than that! I'll help him bring his dreams in harmony with what he's capable of." Alfred's grandiose language and his portrayal of himself as his son's deliverer suggest self-indulgence; Northam comments, "as we watch Alfred pace the room under the eyes of his adoring womenfolk, it looks like a piece of private self-display, the cock among the hens" (N 192).

Hearing the exaggeration in her husband's rhetoric, Rita sensibly asks him, "Can't you work for yourself and for Eyolf both?" (882), while Asta's unconditional admiration for Alfred makes her empathize completely: "What a fearfully hard struggle this must have cost you" (883). Alfred grandiloquently summarizes: "I can't split myself between two callings. But I'll follow human responsibility through – in my own life." Taking his wife's and sister's hands, he announces their roles as twin helpmates in his project, but Rita bitterly refuses a partnership with Asta: "With both of us. Then you *can* divide yourself" (883).

While Alfred would be shocked at the notion that Asta is Rita's rival, Rita knows that she is. Alfred's reluctance to have his half-sister marry Borgheim goads Rita into crying out why she herself wants it: "Because then she'd have to go off with him, far away!" (887). Alfred's naive surprise – "You want to be rid of Asta!" – provokes Rita to express her real fear: "Yes, because at last then I'd have you for myself alone! Except – not even *then*!" Already suffering from the rejection whose approach she suspects, she "*bursts into racking sobs.*) Oh, Alfred, Alfred – I *can't* let you go." Alfred rejects his wife's emotionalism with the same argument Asta used earlier – "But, Rita darling – be reasonable!" – a judgment that calls forth Rita's desperate declaration: "I only care about you! Only you in this whole world! (*Throwing her arms again around his neck.*) You – you – only you!" (887).

Rita's panicked possessiveness results from her understanding that Alfred's choice to live for Eyolf signals his final sexual repudiation of her. Looking at her husband "*with flashing eyes,*" she tells him: "Oh, if you knew how I've hated you – ! . . . Yes – when you sat in there by yourself and pored over your work – till late, late into the night" (887). She fights for her sexual identity: "I can't go on here, just being Eyolf's mother. Just that, and nothing more, I tell you, I won't! I can't!" (889). Expressing the theory of normal female sexuality that would later be argued by Freud, Alfred claims that motherhood ought to satisfy Rita, dodging the issue of their sexual relation in his reply to her declaration that she wants to be "everything" to him: "But you *are* that, Rita. Through our child –." Rita, who has reminded Alfred that she bore Eyolf for his sake, rejoins: "Oh – sentimental gush! That's all it is. No, don't try to hand me that." Alfred irrelevantly remarks, "And you were so fond of Eyolf before," as though a woman's affection for her child were a substitute for sexual love. Rita answers that she pitied Eyolf because Alfred "hardly gave him a second glance"; Alfred's new "mission" will be worse for Eyolf than his former neglect because Alfred's all-consuming attention will now be focused on something that's "more than a book; he's a live human being" (888). When Alfred gravely reiterates that his "highest mission" is "to be a true father to Eyolf" (889), Rita refuses both her husband's and her own role in the new household trinity: "And *to me?* What will you be *to me?*" Alfred's response – "I'll go on loving you. From the depths of my soul" – is beside the point: "I don't care about the depths of your soul. I want you – every part of you – the way I had you in those first, sweet, ravenous weeks." Rita's bitter description of the preceding evening, a doomed effort to recreate the passionate early days of her marriage, explains her resentment. With her fragrant hair down, she welcomed her husband home with champagne after long weeks of missing him, but when she began to undress, he talked only of Eyolf. He was especially interested in the child's digestion. Lying full-length on the sofa, Rita quotes, "'The champagne was there, but you touched it not.'" His voice turning hard, Alfred replies: "No, I didn't touch it" (890).[1]

Alfred tries to justify his sexual indifference by normalizing it: "But, my dearest Rita – human beings change over the years – and we have to as well – just like everyone else" (891). But Rita excludes herself from Alfred's standard; thoroughly humiliated, "*with smoldering eyes,*" she threatens her husband: "Oh, you don't know what things could be roused in me if – ... If I discovered one day you no longer cared for me." In her anger, like the wronged wife of an errant husband, Rita blames not the man but rather the person who has ousted her in his affections: "See! The moment you mention Eyolf's name, you get weak and your voice trembles" (892). Clenching her fists, she is "almost tempted to wish – ah!" She refuses to finish her phrase, but it is clear that she means "that Eyolf did not exist." She knows that her remark is mean and terrible, and has some notion of her displacement of blame: "If I'm vile and evil, Alfred, it's *your* doing" (893). But cries from the shore make the Allmers' quarrel gratuitous; the child has drowned while his parents were arguing over him.

Got up in the colors of hell, with her "black, hooded cape" and "red umbrella" (874), the sinister "Rat Wife," the Pied Piper who lures Eyolf into the water, is a fantastic amalgam of devil and death. She is also a real woman by the name of Wolf. Her dual identity is underscored in Eyolf's wondering if Miss Wolf becomes a werewolf at night. Former *femme fatale* turned exterminator, the Rat Wife once lured men, but now vermin. The "lure-game" drains your strength, the old woman comments (876); once she worked alone, but now enfeebled in her powers, she is aided by a black, canine assistant, "Mopsemand," i.e., "Pug Man", who rests in a black bag when he is not working. The Rat Wife's account of how she and Mopsemand lure "the rats and all the little rat babies" into the water fascinates and frightens Eyolf. "I'll never go out there, Auntie" (875), he says to Asta, but he will, and farther, when the current takes him far past the islands into the sea.

The Rat Wife, as Barry Jacobs has shrewdly demonstrated, is a "cruel distortion of Rita," who shares her "savage desire to be the sole object of her beloved's devotion" ("Ibsen's *Little Eyolf*" 606). Crooning over the "sweet little creatures" she lures, the Rat Wife explains "*with glistening eyes*" how she and Mopsemand work (875). The *tour de force* of her narrative comes at its end, in the acccount of the principal target of her early career, her unfaithful "own true love" whom she lured "down under, with all the rats" (877–78). Her rage against the betrayer of her youth parodies Rita's all-consuming love/hate for Alfred, and in removing Eyolf, in pitilessly making Rita's undeclared wish come true, the Wife becomes a monstrous portrait of a woman who lives for love: "You – you – only you!" (887).[2]

As the Rat Wife parodies Rita, Eyolf parodies Alfred. Father and son enter the play together, with Alfred leading the crippled boy by the hand. Eyolf, who is "*underweight and appears sickly*," is a caricatural reduction of the "*lean, slightly built*" progenitor at his side (870). Eyolf's insistence that he dress in a uniform and his pathetic plan to become a soldier parody his father's grand scheme to forbid his reading and make him into a "real outdoor boy" (886). Stroking his son's hair, Alfred remarks sententiously of his abandoned life's work: "there'll be someone coming in time who'll do it better" (871). Eyolf's lameness functions symbolically like that of the Ugly Brat in *Peer Gynt*; as the Woman in Green explains to the Brat's father, Peer, ". . . he's lame / In his leg as you're lame in your mind" (78). Alfred's son's disability is a sign of his own, the essential weakness that makes him rationalize his repudiation of his wife and the abandonment of his book as necessary measures in his new "humanly responsible" life.

As he would subordinate Rita to Eyolf while the boy lived, after his death Alfred avoids Rita to seek solace in Asta, the first "Eyolf" of his creation. Since Alfred was disappointed because Asta was not born a boy, his little sister dressed up in Alfred's old clothes and became "Eyolf." Alfred and Asta recreate their pre-Rita existence, "really a beautiful time," Asta characterizes it, when the two of them were "alone" (899). Although she qualifies their old game as "childish," Asta eagerly joins Alfred in recalling the details of her costume: "the blue blouse and the knee pants" (900). That Asta was made to wear boys' clothes because Alfred was ashamed of not having a brother cannot be true, both because it "seems absurdly inadequate to the situation," as Northam has pointed out (N 197), and because the Eyolf game was played, as Asta remarks, "only when we were at home alone" (900) and thus saved Alfred no embarrassment. Alfred's wish that Asta disguise her sex has been interpreted as his refusal to admit his sexual desire for her; the incest taboo had to be reinforced by protective clothing.[3] But perhaps Alfred asked Asta to don his clothes because he liked regarding a young boy who "dressed up and walked around." Did the isolation of their life together coupled with Asta's young age and unquestioning admiration make a homoerotic fantasy possible? In any case, if some latent sexuality was represented by the cross-dressing, it was disguised by the "nice Sunday clothes" Asta wore. And whatever else she was for Alfred, Asta-Eyolf was worshipful younger brother, Alfred's perfect little clone. "Little Eyolf," as Alfred called his little boy-sister, is an early version of what the newly dead little Eyolf would have become if he had lived: Alfred's creation, "the fulfillment of our family line" (882–83).

Commentators on *Little Eyolf* have noted the marked difference between Alfred's and Rita's initial reaction to their son's death. Alfred wavers between philosophical musings on the order of the world and what Northam calls "affronted egotism," a kind of resentment against his spoiled plans (N 196), while Rita, feeling the death on her pulses, grieves for the boy, for Alfred, and for herself.[4] The drowned Eyolf lay under the water with his eyes open, and Rita is haunted by the "big open eyes" (906) that signal both perennial accusation and utter irretrievability. "Day and night I'll see him the way he was lying down there." Like Gina in *The Wild Duck*, Rita "looks at the child"; like Hjalmar, Alfred thinks of what the child's life means to him.

Burdened by grief and guilt, Rita seeks out her husband to share the sorrow. He accuses her of wishing the child dead; as she

Asta's response – "It alters everything" – is, of course, a declaration of love. Choosing to misunderstand, Alfred maintains that their relation remains "just as sacred. And it always will be." The great attraction for Alfred of life with his "sister" is that he is not required to make love to her.

Asta, like Rita, has lived for Alfred, but unlike Rita, she has also lived through him. Rita demands to be happy for herself, Asta finds her joy in Alfred's. Her account to Borgheim of her life with her "brother" describes her perfectly vicarious existence. Borgheim "cannot imagine" how beautiful it was, Asta says, and names Alfred's achievements: "Such as the time when Alfred took his exams – and he ranked so high. Or when he began to work his way up, post by post, in one school or another. Or when he'd be writing on an article" (921). Alfred and Asta lived like the exemplary married couple of Lyngstrand's paradigm in *The Lady from the Sea*; the man lives for his vocation, and the woman, who has none, identifies wholly with his aspirations and makes herself over in his image; "I'm the one who's been shaped by you," Asta tells Alfred (902).

Asta has to face a last trial before she leaves. Alfred begs her to stay, but his clear terms – "With Rita. With me. Me – your brother" – make her "*now resolved*" to go (925). She understands that if she stayed, Alfred would expect her to continue her role in the Eyolf game, the sister/brother couple.[8]

Asta's decision to marry the vigorous Borgheim, builder of roads and foil to the bookish Alfred, is an attempt to bury her love for Alfred through a relation with another man. Although Asta has told Borgheim that if she married him, he would only have "half" of her (923), still, a man she is fond of but does not love is better than no man at all. Dependent Asta exchanges ethics for engineering, one man for another through which to live.[9]

As Asta remains the same, Rita changes. Eyolf's death has revealed to her the exclusionary love for Alfred that made her neglect her son. The same honest intelligence and sense of self that allow Rita to refuse her husband's reification of her, first into "mother," then into "fatal temptress," allow her to confront her moral failing and try to redeem it. She begs the woman she considered her rival to join her and Alfred in terms that show that her demand for Alfred's whole affection has vanished along with her jealousy: "Oh, Asta, I implore you, please – stay here and help

us!" (925). She senses that she is undergoing some strange transformation, and searches for the meaning of what she can only call
"something changing in me now" (928). She suggests that Alfred
resume work on the project she formerly considered her enemy –
"I'm willing to share you with the book" – and offers to help him
find a way to live (929).

Alfred is thinking of another course, which he explains by the
philosophical parable he has fashioned out of his hiking trip. This
account, which is sometimes considered an irrelevant blot on the
play, contrasts Alfred's wish to escape Eyolf's death with Rita's
attempt to confront it. Unable to cross a great, desolate lake,
Alfred tried to go around it through the mountains. When he
convinced himself that he was irretrievably lost, he experienced a
strange elation; it seemed as though he and death were "walking
together, like two good traveling companions" (930–31). Alfred
(who like Rosmer seems homesick for the great void) now ponders rejoining his companion in the place where everything
"seemed so natural – so very simple." Alfred's solution is the third
of his life-denying strategies for coping with his son's death: self-
laceration and penance, a life with his sister that is not subject to
the "law of change," and now death itself, the cul-de-sac that ends
all difficulties.

Although Rita is saddened by Alfred's decision to leave, her
response to it strikingly opposes her earlier uncontrolled panic at
the thought of losing him. Alfred gives her a project to fulfill after
his departure, directing her to destroy the shanty town that
houses the boys who saw Eyolf drown: "Let them go under – as
they let him go under!" (932). But Rita has decided on an opposite plan:

RITA. As soon as you've left me, I'm going down to the shore and bring
    all those poor, mistreated children back up with me into this house.
    All those rowdy boys –
ALLMERS. What will you do with them here?
RITA. Learn to love them. (933)

In place of Alfred's vengeance, Rita would substitute love. As Jacobs
notes, "the elaborate parallel Ibsen had established between Rita
and the Rat Wife has been neatly reversed" as Rita lures the
children "not to death, but to the possibility for a better life"
("Ibsen's *Little Eyolf*" 613). The "Rat Wife" in Rita, living for passion
and revenge, has given way to the moral self she buried under her

20. Rita (Katya Medbøe) unburdening herself to Alfred in the National
Theatre's production of *Little Eyolf*, Oslo, 1978.

obsession for Alfred. And whereas Rita gave birth to Eyolf to please her husband, her transformation, which she experiences as "like something giving birth" (928), makes her choose her new motherhood, loving the boys "as if they were my own" (933).

Alfred's immediate response to his wife's decision – "I don't know a single person in this world less equipped for something like this than you" (933) – recalls Torvald Helmer's to Nora's announcement that she is leaving. Because Nora knows nothing of the world, she will fail; because Rita has lived for Alfred's love, she cannot learn to love children. And Rita's reply – "Then I'll have to educate myself for it. Train and develop myself" – recalls Nora's: "No, I don't [know anything of the world]. But now I'll begin to learn for myself" (193). Like Nora, Rita has lived for a man, and like her also, she acknowledges her error. When Alfred comments that Rita must have "undergone a change," she replies: "It's true, Alfred. You took care of that. You've made an empty place inside me. I'll have to try to fill it with something. Something in the shape of love" (933). No sentimentalist, Rita agrees with Alfred's cautionary remark that "it isn't love that's behind this": "No, it isn't. At least, not yet" (934). But Rita has discovered that she has a self other than that of Alfred's sensual mate; "*somewhat diffidently*," she tells him that she used to listen when he and Asta talked about "human responsibility"; "And now I want to try myself to carry it on – in my own way" (934).

Rita's way is to do good rather than to write about it. In the dichotomous categories of *Brand*, the man is the idealist, the woman the realist; Alfred's terrain is mountains, Rita's the lower realms. Rita is associated with temporal love, Allmers with "higher" duties. Finding an essentialist contrast here, Weigand writes that the play "offers a fine basis for generalization. Man, being encased in the strait-jacket of ideology, never able to get away, in his judgment of conduct, from general standards, is at a disadvantage over against woman, who dispenses with abstract reasoning, with ideology, content to base her conduct on the bidding of specific impulses" (*The Modern Ibsen* 350). This analysis reflects the old ideological chestnut: Woman equals Nature, Man Intellect, Woman is Feeling, Man Reason. But Ibsen blasts these gendered categorizations as strongly in *Little Eyolf* as in *The Wild Duck*. Rita's critical mind, which from the beginning of the play to the end makes her puncture her husband's posturings, also allows her to analyze her moral failing. She acts not from impulsiveness, but from considered reason. It is the woman of the house who puts into practice the "general standard" of human responsibility. As Rita tries to win her "pardon from those great, open eyes" (935), Eyolf's eyes become those of all children, including the boys who watched him drown, for human responsibility means caring about other people's children as well as one's own.

In *Little Eyolf*, as in *Catiline, The Vikings at Helgeland, Rosmersholm*, and *The Master Builder*, the passionate woman points the man toward his vocation. But *Little Eyolf* parts with its predecessors, for it is the woman who chooses the vocation as her own, and the man who follows. Formerly seduced by Rita's beauty, the ethical philosopher is now tempted by her goodness. He asks: "Maybe I could join you? And help you, Rita?" (935). Rita will keep her husband, after all, but on terms wholly different from the ones she formerly insisted on.

The ending of *Little Eyolf* has been frequently viewed as problematic because "the happy ending is not sufficiently grounded in the character portrayal."[10] Commentators have found it difficult to accept both the moral seriousness of a frankly sexual woman and to grant the weak Alfred the will to achieve Rita's project. But to maintain that Ibsen conceived of the play's ending as "happy" is to ignore the dramatic situation – two people's shattered lives – and the tentative, carefully shaded text. "Let's see if it can't work," Alfred says *"in a low voice."* Rita answers "(*almost inaudibly*). Let's try, Alfred" (935). Alfred goes to raise the flag from the half-mast of mourning to the top of the pole, over the fjord where Eyolf drowned, then returns to the side of his wife. "There's a hard day's work ahead of us, Rita" (935).[11]

Little Eyolf is named after the little boy who briefly appears only to disappear because in the end, it is the understanding of their dead child that his mother and father achieve. Eyolf knew why the boys taunted him for his lameness: "They're probably jealous of me. You know, Papa, they're so poor they have to go barefoot" (874). Struck by Rita's decision to help the boys, Alfred admits: "Actually, we've never done much for those poor people down there . . . So it's hardly surprising, perhaps, that they wouldn't risk their lives to save Eyolf" (934). Rita adds: "If you consider, Alfred – are you so sure that – that we would have risked our own?" Husband and wife admit their indifference to the people to whom, as Rita says, they closed their hands and hearts. "There is no happiness in these lines," writes Arnold Weinstein, "but it is as close to a rendering of grace as any Ibsen play ever came" ("Metamorphosis" 315).

Rita's and Alfred's project embodies Rita's, not Alfred's, "law of change." Like all energy, which does not die but rather conserves itself in a changed form, Rita's vitality and strength, formerly concentrated on her passion, now express themselves as a capacity to confront moral failing and a willingness to find a way to live with it. The change in Alfred's law was mere ending, reflecting the cynical old adage that nothing lasts forever. Rita's law is life-affirming, not change as the death of something, but as its transmutation. Rita leads Alfred toward a vision of life as struggle and process, evolutionary and earthly. The play opens on Rita, *"brimming with vitality,"* wearing a brightly colored dress, bathed in *"warm sunlight"* (867). It closes with Rita in mourning black, cloaked in twilight, but waiting for the morning.

DOWN AMONG THE DEAD WOMEN: *JOHN GABRIEL BORKMAN*

BORKMAN: . . . You're a woman. And so it seems, to your mind, that nothing else in the world exists or matters.
ELLA: Yes, nothing else.
BORKMAN: Only what touches your own heart.
ELLA: Only that! Only that! Yes. *John Gabriel Borkman* (986)

Of Ibsen's last four ambitious men – Solness, Allmers, Borkman, and Rubek – Borkman seems the most ruthless. He coolly trades Ella Rentheim, whom he loves, for a position in a bank, then marries her sister Gunhild. The betrayed Ella is generally taken to be the play's raisonneur; in a comment typical of the play's criticism, Kenneth Muir writes that Borkman, "guilty of a betrayal of both women through his egotism," is condemned both by Ella and "by the audience" for his misdeed.[12] Borkman's mistaken choice is said to be the heart of the play, whose focus is the revelation of three failed lives – his own and those of the two sisters. David Grene notes that Ibsen is insisting, characteristically, that "there can be no success built on the surrender of a man's deepest sexual attachment. The kingdom and the power and the glory are not only a poor bargain for the loss. They do not come into your possession – only their mirage."[13]

Borkman is often compared to two earlier betrayers of women, Bernick of *Pillars of Society* and Sigurd of *The Vikings at Helgeland*. Like Borkman, Bernick "is an unscrupulous financier who has renounced the woman he loved and married her sister, for the sake of making a career" (Weigand, *The Modern Ibsen* 356). Sigurd gives the woman he loves to his blood-brother and marries her foster-sister. Like Bernick and Sigurd, Borkman "sacrifices love for 'higher' considerations" (K 444).

While it is true that in Borkman, one of drama's great obsessional characters, Ibsen creates an astonishing portrait of an egotist, Borkman only takes part peripherally in the play's dramatic action, the conflict between Ella and Gunhild over the possession of Gunhild's and Borkman's son Erhart. And the development of this action does not characterize its antagonists as simply, or even principally, as Borkman's victims. Ibsen is less interested in Borkman's abuse of Ella and Gunhild, cruel though it was, than in the women's continuing absorption in their victimization. Consumed by Borkman's transgressions against them, they have spent years nursing their injuries. It is often noted that Gunhild and Ella embody Ibsen's familiar pattern of the strong and the gentle woman; Gunhild of the "*iron-gray*" hair (943), with her Valkyrie name, her harshness and bitterness, is the "masculine" woman, while Ella, with her "*silvery white*" hair (944), her softer, Latinate name, her warm sympathy for Erhart, is the "feminine" woman. But as the play develops, these dissimilarities become insignificant as Ella is revealed to be as bent on her vengeance as Gunhild. After finishing a draft of the play, Ibsen made a change in the act-one stage directions that better reflects the relation between Gunhild and Ella; in the draft, Ella is "older than her sister and resembles her" (*OI* 8:7), and in the final version, the sisters are twins.

Ibsen frames the first act of his drama with characteristic symmetry. It begins with Gunhild's involuntary whispering of her son's name – "Erhart! (943)" – and ends with her anguished whispers: "Erhart! Erhart – be true to me!" (966). Within the parameters of Gunhild's expectation and desperation, act one develops first as a dramatization of her dual obsession with her husband and son, and secondly, as a veiled, then open and ferocious combat between the sisters.

Like *Little Eyolf, John Gabriel Borkman* opens with a scene between

21. Ella (Wenche Foss) and Gunhild (Ingerid Vardund) battling over Erhart in the National Theatre's production of *John Gabriel Borkman*, Oslo, 1991.

two women who are rivals for the same man. But before their competition for Erhart begins, Gunhild and Ella quarrel over the object of their former rivalry, Borkman. Upon her twin's arrival, Gunhild begins to speak almost immediately of Borkman's embezzlement of sixteen years ago, the great grievance she can "never stop brooding on" (945): "I can't comprehend how anything like this – anything so appalling could overwhelm one family!" (945). Gunhild has no sense of herself as anyone except Borkman's wife, and thus when he was sent to prison, the shame fell equally upon her. So deep is her hatred for her husband that she has refused to see him in the eight years since his release from prison. The magnitude she ascribes to Borkman's sin against her is revealed by the exalted language she uses to describe her reason for living: "restitution for my name and honor and fortune! For the whole of my desolated life" (947).

Ella seems the voice of sweet reason when she chides: "You have a hard heart, Gunhild" (946). Ella's bias against Gunhild soon asserts itself, however, when she blames her for Borkman's ruin. When Gunhild bitterly points out that Borkman, too, blamed his crime on her, when it was he who insisted that they live in luxury, Ella remonstrates: "It's exactly why you should have held back." It was Gunhild's task to protect her husband from his own irresponsibility. Because Gunhild took Borkman away from Ella, Ella has to consider her a bad wife; Ella would have done better by him.

Gunhild's obsession with her husband's crime against her is matched by an equally powerful obsession with her son as her deliverer. She has cast Erhart long ago in the role he is now almost old enough to play: "There's an avenger living!" (948). The son will achieve a brilliant career and thus redress his father's injustice to his unfortunate mother and redeem "the family, the house, our name" (948).

Although Ella's disapproval of her sister's plans for Erhart is genuine – "Tell me, Gunhild – is that the aim Erhart himself has for his own life –?" (949) – it also reveals her self-deception, for she, too, has her own personal mission for him. While Gunhild's demand of Erhart represents a straightforward expression of her feelings, Ella's does not. She has convinced herself that she has "a certain kind of right to Erhart" (955) because, she tells his mother, she loves him disinterestedly and wants to "free him" from Gunhild's "domination" (956). But the truth comes out when Gunhild's triumphant crowing – "You had him in your net – right up to his fifteenth year. But now, you see, I've won him back!" – destroys Ella's demeanor of objective concern: "Then I'll win him again from you!" Ella's declaration of what she wants from the young man shows that her own demands are as onerous as Gunhild's: "I want his affections – his soul – his whole heart –!" (957). Ella takes advantage of her power as provider to the ruined Borkmans to try to bribe her sister; when Gunhild swears that she will "take to the roads" if Ella moves into the Borkman house, she counters with: "All right. Then let me have Erhart" (959).

The object of the sisters' struggle has other plans for his life than to carry out his mother's mission or give his soul to his aunt. The twenty-three-year-old Erhart, showing *"early signs of a moustache"* (959), seems uncommonly unfitted for causes. He is preceded into his mother's living room by his lover, the *"singularly handsome"* and thoroughly unrespectable Fanny Wilton, a divorced woman in her thirties who possesses a full figure, red lips, and *"rich, dark hair."* Erhart and Fanny have come to deliver Frida Foldal, a young pianist who comes to play for Borkman, and Erhart is almost comically desperate to make his visit as short as possible. Although he clearly feels affection for Ella, he invents an excuse to escape by insisting that she go to bed to rest from her journey. When Gunhild and Ella break out openly into their combat – "You want to tear him from me!" "Yes, Gunhild, if I only could!" – Erhart, *"writhing as if in pain,"* bursts out: "Oh, I can't take this anymore!" (965).

After Erhart's departure, the sisters' resumption of their battle reveals the force of their mutual jealousy. Although they have recognized Fanny Wilton as their natural enemy, in one sense she is welcome: "Better her than you," says Ella, and Gunhild understands: "I say the same. Better her than you" (966). Erhart's happiness is insignificant compared to the importance of their possessing him: "Whatever the end result for him –" says Ella. When Ella leaves, Gunhild performs a private dance to the strains of the "Danse Macabre" wafting down from Borkman's room. Throwing herself on the floor, twisting and moaning, she gives voice to her ruling passion: "Erhart! Erhart! – be true to me! Oh, come home and help your mother! I can't bear this life any longer!" (966).[14]

Ella's visit to Borkman in act two shows her to be as obsessed with Borkman's abandonment of her as Gunhild is with his crime. Upon entering his sanctuary, she immediately reminds him of their old love, answering his hesitant question – "Is that – is it Ella?" – with "Yes – it's 'your' Ella – as you used to call me" (980). She insists on his past erotic attachment to her – "I don't have the dark curls tumbling down my back anymore. Those curls you once liked to wind around your fingers" – and declares the result of his betrayal: "A lifetime wasted" (981). The shocked Borkman protests that if Ella had married the man who gave him control of the bank in exchange for her, "You could just as well have been happy

with him. And *I* would have been saved, then" (982). Borkman's
egotism and emotional obtuseness are overwhelming, but his obsession with his blighted career is not more powerful than Ella's
with her lost love. Borkman's admission that he still loved Ella
when he married Gunhild makes Ella revile him as if his betrayal
of her took place the day before. He committed "a great, intolerable" crime against her, "the crime that's beyond all forgiveness"
(985). Backing away, Borkman accuses her of "raving," but she
continues: "The great unforgivable sin is – to murder the love in
a human being . . . You abandoned the woman you *loved*! Me, me,
me! The dearest that you had in this world you were ready to sign
away for profit. It's a double murder you're guilty of! Murder of
your soul, and of mine!" (985–86).

Borkman analyzes Ella's judgment and its violence as normal
for a person of her sex: "How well I recognize that overbearing
passion in you, Ella. I suppose it's very natural for you to see this
the way you do. You're a woman. And so it seems, to your mind,
that nothing else in the world exists or matters . . . Only what
touches your own heart" (986). Ella's response – "Only that! Only
That! Yes!" – demonstrates her full agreement with her antagonist, who completes his theory of sexually determined value systems by supplying the other half: "But you have to remember that
I'm a man. As a woman, to me you were the dearest in the world.
But in the last analysis, any woman can be replaced by another."
Ella cleverly counters this bald contention on male uses of
women: "Was that your experience when you took Gunhild to
marry?" And although Borkman has to admit that it was not,
nevertheless his "life's work" helped him to bear his marriage, and
it was this that mattered: "The earth, the mountains, the forests,
the sea – I wanted to subjugate all the riches they held, and carve
out a kingdom for myself, and use it to further the well-being of so
many thousands of others." Since no other condition would satisfy
the man who gave Borkman the means for his advancement,
Borkman gave up Ella: "And he helped me halfway up toward the
enticing heights I longed for" (987). Ella's response reinforces
Borkman's notion of the normal female *weltanschauung*: "You put
to death all the natural joy in me . . . All the joy a woman should
know" (987).

Having charged Borkman with the responsibility for her failed
life, Ella now blames him for her hard heart. Borkman has as-

sumed that her interest in Erhart, whom she took in at the height of the scandal, developed "out of compassion" (988). She corrects him: "I've never known any compassion – since you left me! I'm wholly incapable of that. If a poor, starving child came into my kitchen, freezing and weeping, and begged for a little food, then I left it up to my cook." If Erhart Borkman was the one person she could love, it was because he was a compensation for the motherhood Borkman had deprived her of: "You've cheated me of a mother's joy and happiness in life." Ella's mammoth grievance is now complete: Borkman deprived her of love, marriage, and of motherhood – "all the joy a woman should know" – and in doing so, destroyed her.

Borkman's absorption in his uncompleted mission and Ella's in Borkman's desertion of her make the man and the woman sterling representatives of the reductive masculine and feminine systems of a dichotomously gendered world. The foiled male striver and the loveless woman express their failed lives in images whose extremism approaches parody: "I feel like a Napoleon, maimed in his first battle" (974); "Through all those years it's grown harder and harder – and finally impossible – for me to love any living creature. Not people, nor animals, nor plants" (987).

Borkman's contention that his embezzlement of his own stockholders was a mere detail, that if he had been given a little more time, he could have covered his losses and become a hero of industrial progress, is dubious on practical grounds and unacceptable on ethical ones. And Ella Rentheim's claim that Borkman is to blame for her wasted life rests equally on very doubtful hypotheses. Even if we accept her implicit argument that John Gabriel Borkman was the only man she could ever have loved, her contention that he is to blame for her indifference to all other creatures in the world, including vegetable life, is so excessive as to be ludicrous. As for the attendant claim that Borkman deprived her of motherhood, there were any number of orphans available in Norway (in establishments similar to the Captain Alving Memorial Home), from which Ella could have had her pick of children. The fact is that she did not want to be "a mother," but rather the mother of Borkman's children. She took Erhart Borkman away from Gunhild and kept him for eight years because he was flesh of the flesh she loved. Just as Borkman was the only man she could love, his child was the only child she could mother, and since he cheated her of conceiving it, she would take it away from the woman who did.

The goal of Ella's visit to Borkman makes Gunhild's emotional need for Erhart seem, in comparison, almost normal. Ella first deals the *coup de grâce* that she will shortly die from an illness that her doctors concluded was "perhaps" the result of "a severe emotional upheaval" (990), an implicit accusation that Borkman is responsible for her impending death. She then asks Borkman's permission to take Erhart: "I *must* have the child of my heart, my one and only again, before I go!" But she wants Erhart less to ease her dying than to miss her afterwards: he will be the "one single person who'll think of me and remember me warmly and tenderly – the way a son thinks, remembering the mother he's lost" (991). And then she comes to her most important request. She claims to be tortured by the thought that after her death, the Rentheim name will die. She begs Borkman, in the name of "a mother who's about to die": "Don't let it happen! Let Erhart carry on the name!" (991–92). The Borkman name will be obliterated, and thus Ella can both supplant the man who wronged her and triumph over Gunhild. Like his mother, Ella would make Erhart her avenger.

Both Ella and Gunhild should have asked Erhart's opinion before battling over his future. His departure with Fanny Wilton, the crisis of the play's action, does not resolve the conflict but rather stops it by making it moot, thus underscoring the futility of Ella's and Gunhild's struggle. The act-three scene is a painful recapitulation and development of the act-one scene between the sisters and Erhart. Having received a desperate summons from his mother, who has eavesdropped on Ella's and Borkman's conversation and is terrified of Ella's plans, Erhart bursts in: "What do you want me for, Mother?" (1000). Stretching out her arms toward him, Gunhild gives voice to her overwhelming emotional investment in her son: "I want to see you, Erhart! I want to have you with me – always!". She screams out to him Ella's scheme to assume his "mother's place" and the two women present their claims:

ELLA (*looks imploringly at him*). Erhart, I can't afford to lose you. You must be aware that I'm a lonely – dying woman . . . Will you stay with me to the end? Commit yourself wholly to me – as if you were my own child –?

MRS. BORKMAN (*breaking in*). And abandon your mother and perhaps your mission in life as well? Do you want that, Erhart? (1001)

The dramatic irony reaches an almost intolerable pitch as we witness the furious energy of the sisters' futile competition. Gunhild thinks that she has won after Erhart refuses to return to his aunt: "You won't get him! You won't get him, Ella!". And Ella replies: "I see. You *have* won him back" (1002). Erhart is forced to tell both of them the truth in plain, ugly words: "My God, Mother – I'm young! The air here in this room – I feel it's going to smother me completely . . . Oh, Aunt Ella, it's not one shade better with you . . . All this morbid concern about me, this – this idolatry, or whatever it is. I can't take it any longer!" When Borkman, seeing in his son a last chance for himself, asks Erhart to join him in a father/son venture to build a new life, Ella urges Erhart to accept, and Gunhild recognizes her motive: "Just so *I'm* not the one who takes him from you" (1004). "Precisely," Ella answers. Erhart, cornered and furious, "*in a blaze of emotion,*" screams his refusal: "I want my chance to live, for once! I want to live my own life!" After his departure, Gunhild, "*her folded hands dropping,*" utters one word: "Childless"; it is as if she had said "Lifeless." The play's third act ends, like its first, with the anguished Gunhild calling out her son's name.

As the play's crisis, at the end of act three, recapitulates the confrontation between the sisters and Erhart at the end of act one, the denouement, the scene between Borkman and Ella at the end of act four, recapitulates the scene between them at the end of act two. Ella accompanies Borkman in his feverish dash out of the house and stages a second confrontation with the man who wronged her. On the top of the hill, she sorrowfully reminisces about the "dreamland" they once envisioned together (1020). But Borkman does not hear her. Bent on another dream, that of the empire that eluded him, he envisions his steamships joining the globe and hears his factories whirring, the "outworks enclosing the kingdom" (1021). Ella returns to her old accusation: "Yes, but John, the wind blows ice-cold from that kingdom!" Borkman replies by uttering a passionate declaration of love, not to Ella, but to the gleaming minerals of his mines: "I feel the veins of metal, reaching their curving, branching, beckoning arms out to me . . . I love you, lying there unconscious in the depths and the darkness! I love you, you riches straining to be born – with all your shining aura of power and glory! I love you, love you, love you!" And thus the failed venture capitalist declares his undying attachment to the "one real, enduring romance he has known" (F 940).

Ella, *"with constrained but mounting agitation* (1021), cannot let this pass without damning it: "But up here in the daylight – here there was a warm, living human heart that beat for you. And this heart you crushed" (1022). Although Ella had promised, when Borkman gave his consent to Erhart's taking her name, that everything was "made up" between them (992), she cannot part with her victimization. She accuses him again: "I said it once before to you this evening; you've murdered the capacity to love in the woman that loved you" (1022). Because of this crime, she prophecies, he will never win the prize he "murdered" for. As the angina grips his heart, Borkman remarks: "I'm almost afraid your prophecy is right, Ella." Believing that she has at last succeeded in making Borkman acknowledge his great error, Ella replies: "It would be exactly the best that could ever happen to you." Then seeing him clutch his chest, she asks: "What was it, John?" The dying Borkman, slumped against the bench, replies: "A hand of ice – that choked my heart." Intent on her accusation, Ella insists: "John! Now you feel it, the ice hand!" But unredeemingly in love with his glittering, lost treasure, Borkman has the last word: "No – no ice hand. It was a hand of metal" (1022).

And thus Borkman goes to his grave with his conscience intact, his last words a rejection of Ella's condemnation. Borkman reverses Sigurd's confession at the end of *The Vikings at Helgeland* as he remains stubbornly unrepentant of his crime against the woman he loved, insisting to the end on the importance of "higher considerations." Unlike Hjørdis, Ella is not accorded even the small compensation of the man's remorse. And unlike Sigurd, Borkman refuses the notion that his life's work is linked to his personal life by making vocation in stalwart and superior opposition to love. In the end, it is a man's work that counts, and "any woman can be replaced by another" (986).

Having no work, no place within the world, Ella and Gunhild live for the private life, for the rewards of "all the joy a woman should know" (987). When Erhart, and then Borkman withdraw from their lives, their consuming rivalry dies a natural death. Gunhild suggests, "And so, at last, we two might reach our hands out to each other," and Ella agrees: "Now I think we can" (1023–24). As the two women join hands over Borkman's corpse, mirror images of each other, Ella pronounces, in the play's last line, a eulogy for the three of them: "We two shadows – over the dead man" (1024).

When Edvard Munch paid Ibsen the compliment that *John Gabriel Borkman* was "the most powerful winter landscape in Scandinavian art" (M 747), he was acknowledging Ibsen's genuis in portraying the frozen soul. The man and two women are mere automata of their obsessions. *John Gabriel Borkman* implicitly refuses the notion that it is in the nature of things that man should live for achievement, and woman, the personal life, by dramatizing the grotesque lives of three people who live by it.

Like *Brand* and *Peer Gynt, A Doll House* and *Ghosts, Enemy of the People* and *The Wild Duck, Rosmersholm* and *The Lady from the Sea, Little Eyolf* and *John Gabriel Borkman* are a diptych. "Only you, Alfred! Only you!" cries Rita; "I must have my one and only!" cries Ella; "Erhart! Erhart!" cries Gunhild. But while Rita learns to live for other reasons besides "all the joy a woman should know," Ella and Gunhild waste their lives lamenting its loss.

CHAPTER 12

The revolt of the muse: When We Dead Awaken

> As servant, woman has the right to the most splendid
> apotheoses.   Simone de Beauvoir, *The Second Sex*

Responding to a comment by his French translator on the meaning of *When We Dead Awaken*'s sub-title, "A Dramatic Epilogue," Ibsen wrote: "You are quite right when you say that the series which ends with the epilogue really began with *The Master Builder*" (*LS* 342–43). Ibsen's last four plays form a quartet with variations on the theme of male achievement, four portraits of ambition-ridden men whose overriding aim is to achieve greatness. All four use women to serve their aspirations: master builder Solness broods guiltily on how he profited from his wife's property to begin his career even as he plans greater work to come with his newfound female inspiration; moral philosopher Allmers, having married for money in order to write a great book, invents a rationalization that allows him to reject both his wife and the book he has failed to write, and seeks self-approbation in another woman's admiration; businessman Borkman, having traded his fiancée for a promising position and having married her sister, justifies his choice until his unrepentant death; following his three predecessors, sculptor Rubek of *When We Dead Awaken* uses first one woman, then another: he exploits his model for his art, then purchases another woman for his wife, and when she fails to understand his artist's soul, wishes to replace her with his former model. In what Francis Bull aptly terms "arbeidsegoism" ("Henrik Ibsen" 451), for the artist, like the builder, the philosopher, and the financier, women are instruments in his quest for achievement.

In all four plays, the instrumentality has unexpected consequences, and the pattern of male doer/female instrument ironically alters. In *The Master Builder*, Hilda Wangel, the eager helpmate of the aspiring male – "Can you find a use for *me*, Mr. Solness" (812) – succeeds so well in restoring the builder's faith in his powers that he attempts the impossible feat she demands of him and dies. The transformation of Rita Allmers in *Little Eyolf* dramatizes a powerful reversal in which the woman whose money was to have given her philosopher husband the leisure to write *Human Responsibility* becomes the agent of the failed writer's becoming humanly responsible. John Gabriel Borkman's use of Ella and Gunhild to achieve his financial empire both proves gratuitous and makes of the women his implacable enemies who at the play's end shake hands over their exploiter's corpse. In *When We Dead Awaken*, Rubek's model returns from the dead to haunt him in a dramatic action that recalls that of the three preceding plays; like Ella and Gunhild, Irene confronts the ambitious man who wronged her with his crimes against her; like Rita, former instrument Irene morally educates her exploiter; like Hilda, Irene is both the deliverer and the nemesis of the man she serves. But while *When We Dead Awaken* recapitulates the patterns of the male/female relationships in the first three plays of the quartet, it also adds a coda, for what is implicit in the earlier three dramas the epilogue makes explicit. Irene's revolt against Rubek constitutes a direct challenge to the notion of female instrumentality in the service of male achievement.

Art's handmaiden

The notion that artistic creation is a male domain has been central to Western patriarchy, an aesthetic corollary to the religious dogma that God the Father fathered the world. In their tracing of this aesthetic, Sandra Gilbert and Susan Gubar quote Gerard Manley Hopkins' pronouncement as representative: the artist's "most essential quality" is "masterly execution, which is a kind of male gift, and especially marks off men from women . . . The male quality is the creative gift" (*Madwoman* 3). It is man who creates woman. From Eve, Minerva, Sophia, and Galatea, patriarchal mythology has defined women "as created by, from, and for men, the children of male brains, ribs, and ingenuity" (12). For Gilbert and Gubar, Norman O. Brown "perfectly summarizes" the gendered basis of this aesthetics: "The lady is our creation or

Pygmalion's statue. The lady is the poem; [Petrach's] Laura is, really, poetry" (13).

Brown blurs Petrarch's inspiration with his creation, for if woman is made by man, she also functions in the creative process as the male maker's inspirer. The muse is the most euphemistic, because most ethereal, of the servicing identities bestowed upon women by men. Daughters of the father god Zeus, the muses of antiquity were good female powers who inspired the male artist to productive creativity: "Happy is he whom the Muses love, and sweet flows his voice from his lips."[1] When the Sirens, bad female powers who tempted men to wasteful sexuality, tried to compete with the popular muses, they lost their wings and fell into the sea. The muse continued to prosper in medieval and Renaissance times; Dante invoked her, and the European and English Renaissance poets paid homage to her powers, Christianizing her to make her a proper inspiration for their song.[2] The muses outlasted the Romantics' theory of individual inspiration. Blake, Byron, and Whitman call upon her aid. The muse is the aesthetic sister of man's spiritual servant, the "eternal feminine"; as the latter helps him to find truth, the former inspires him to create.

For Robert Graves, the muse's most ardent modern disciple, all true poetry is "necessarily an invocation of the White Goddess, or Muse."[3] Recalling his Victorian predecessors' predeliction for the fatal woman, British poet Graves worships a chthonic goddess in terms that recall Pater's celebration of the Mona Lisa; the muse is "the Mother of All Living, the ancient power of fright and lust – the female spider or the queen-bee whose embrace is death" (*The White Goddess* 10). The true poet is "in love with the White Goddess, with Truth; his heart breaks with longing and love for her. She is the flower-goddess Olwen . . . but she is also Blodeuwedd the Owl, lamp-eyed . . . or Lamia with her flickering tongue" (373). But however powerful the muse, creativity remains a male province: "woman is not a poet. She is either a Muse or she is nothing" (371).[4]

In *The Second Sex*, Simone de Beauvoir argues that competitive man has always conceived of the muse as female because he "wants to achieve without the help of other men the goals he has set for himself" (1: 290). And because man envisions woman as more profoundly related to Nature than he is, the poet imagines that through her he can "sound the depths of silence and the fecond Night." Woman possesses, man likes to think, "a wisdom which he cannot claim, more instinctive than his own, more immediately in touch with the real; these are the 'intuitions' which Egeria delivers to the man who consults her; his ego left unbruised by contact with her, he can question her as he would the stars."[5] Like other servicing identities men have assigned women – care giver, guide, mediator – the muse is a role of the Other, who allows the subject man to "go beyond himself without limiting himself" (295). But women exist without men's intervention, and thus while "woman" incarnates men's fantasies, women prove the falsity of the fantasies, and so the whore must be created to flank the virgin. Applying de Beauvoir's analysis to Graves' theory, we see why his Lamia joins the flower-goddess. Graves' insistence on the muse's inaccessibility – her mysterious, secret power – and on the danger inherent in the poet's attempting to possess her is refigured in de Beauvoir's analysis of man's need for woman to remain always the Other.

De Beauvoir cites Kierkegaard in her documentation of patriarchal culture's distancing, or idealization, of woman as muse, quoting from *In Vino Veritas*: "Through woman the ideal becomes a part of life, and without her, what would man become? Many a man has become a genius thanks to a young woman . . . but no man has become a genius thanks to the young woman he married . . . It is through a negative relation that woman makes man creative" (*The Second Sex* 295). De Beauvoir analyzes: "Woman is necessary to the extent that she remains an Idea into which the man can project his own transcendence; but she is dangerous as an objective reality, existing for herself and limited to herself." She adds the famous anecdote: "It is in refusing to marry his fiancée that Kierkegaard believed that he had established the only worthwhile relation with womankind" (295–96).

The Freudian theory of the creative process as a sublimation of sexuality bears a strong similarity to Kierkegaard's account of the necessary "negative relation" between the male creator and the woman who inspires him. Freud summarizes: "The very incapacity of the sexual instinct to yield complete satisfaction as soon as it submits to the first demands of civilization becomes the source, however, of the noblest cultural achievements which are brought into being by ever more extensive sublimation of its instinctual components" ("The Tendency to Universal Debasement" 160). The artist desires woman, Otto Rank explains, but regards her with fear since she represents the demands of life over art. So he represses his desire, camouflaging his hostility by idealizing the woman and turning her into the muse. Ceasing to threaten his purposes, the woman now aids him to achieve them. The artist thus subordinates life to art as the woman provides him with poetic progeny.[6]

In Kierkegaard's theory, sexuality is a hindrance to creativity, while in Freud's, it is the source, but only because its incapacity to satisfy the "demands of civilization" results in its sublimation into art. Sexuality conflicts with culture; the threatening sirens must be stilled in favor of the productive muses.

Woman into marble: the killing of Irene

The relation between Rubek and Irene in *When We Dead Awaken* constitutes a savage caricature of the gendered aesthetic of man/inventor, woman/invented, man/maker, woman/muse. Meeting his former model Irene after years of separation, Rubek believes that he is complimenting her when he remarks on her importance in his Pygmalion enterprise, the sculpting of "the noblest, the purest, most ideal of women" (1051): "I could use you for everything I needed . . . To me you weren't a model. You were the soul of my inspiration" (1052). Kierkegaardian idealist and Freudian sublimator, Rubek theorizes to the woman who loved him that there had to be distance between them because of his conviction that if he touched her, "then my spirit would be profaned so that I couldn't have created what I was striving for." An erotic relation with a woman would distract and weaken the ambitious man, "sick with wanting to create the greatest work of my life" (1051), and while Rubek was greatly aroused – "nearly driven out of my senses" – by Irene's physical beauty, he was "first and foremost an artist," and thus the naked woman before him "became a sacred creature, to be touched only by worshipful thoughts" (1051–52).[7]

Irene embraced her servicing role with a mystical devotion that seemed absolute and boundless: "I raised three fingers in the air and swore I'd go with you to the world's end and the end of life.

And that I'd serve you in all things" (1050). The luxuriousness of
Irene's language as she recalls the past to Rubek underscores the
completeness of her servitude: in "full, free nakedness – . . . Yes,
with all the throbbing blood of my youth, I served you! . . . I fell
down at your feet then and served you" (1051–52).

What Rubek believed to be Irene's continuing joyful display of
her body in the service of his high art – "that work that we two
came together in every morning like a sacrament" (1070) – was a
painful, humiliating collaboration. Irene describes to him how
day after day, she watched him, "not a man," but "only an artist,"
staring at her body as he sculpted it, "infuriatingly self-controlled."
While she was longing for his love, he was forcing her into the
mold of the pure woman for which she was model, a rejection that
inspired her rage: "Whenever I undressed myself and stood there
naked for you, I hated you" (1070).

Containing her anger and resentment, Irene stripped herself
naked during the week in silent acquiescence to Rubek's use of
her and clothed herself on weekends to share celibate rest days
with her "lord and master" (1069). On the shores of Lake
Taunitz, Irene participated in another kind of game, a private
pastime she and Rubek called "Lohengrin's boat." Making swans
of water lilies and boats of dock leaves, they dreamily sent their
vessels afloat. Irene recalls that Rubek flattered his muse even on
holiday: "You said I was the swan that drew your boat" (1076).
Rubek's sexual rejection of Irene in the name of his art is reinforced by the allusion to the Lohengrin tale, with its virgin
knight's rejection of his bride for a "higher" goal, the search for
the grail.

Having struggled against her resentment and longing, having
forced herself to imitate the woman of Rubek's invention, on the
completion of the statue Irene stood "breathlessly waiting"
(1074), hoping that the artist would turn into the man. But
instead of love for the woman, Rubek expressed gratitude to the
muse: "Thank you from the bottom of my heart, Irene. This has
been an extraordinary episode for me" (1075).

Devastated by Rubek's repudiation, Irene left the man "who
didn't need my love – *or* my life anymore" (1047). Her grievous
disappointment turned to despair and mental derangement:
"They came and bound me. Strapped my arms together behind

my back – Then they lowered me down into a tomb, with iron bars for a trapdoor. And the walls were padded – so no one up above on the earth could hear the shrieks from the grave" (1050).

The former muse's account of her post-Rubek life parodies her relation with the sculptor. The half-fantastic quality of the story underscores its caricatural function. She killed two husbands – what she wanted to do to Rubek – and destroyed her children before they were born – what she should have done to the statue: "If I'd exercised my rights then . . . I would have killed that child . . . Afterward, I killed it innumerable times. In daylight and darkness . . . in hate – and revenge – and agony" (1047). Her cabaret role as "a naked statue in a living tableau" is a vulgar version of her posing for the artist (1048). But at least, she taunts Rubek, she got paid for this work, while her service to him was free; moreover, the men who looked at her became her lovers, unlike Rubek, who "held out better" (1048).

Irene began to search for Rubek when she realized that she had given him "something quite irreplaceable. Something one never ought to part with" (1054). He comments, "three-four years of your youth," but she corrects him: "Little prodigal that I was – I gave you far, far more than that." He has forgotten the "rarest gift" she offered him: "I gave you my young, living soul. And that left me empty inside. Soulless . . . That's why I died" (1055).[8]

Rubek's refusal of Irene's love is the last example in Ibsen's work of a reoccuring male sensibility that objectifies female desire to be used, or not used, as the man needs. When one is an object, not a subject, writes Jean Baker Miller, one's "sexual impulses and interests are presumed not to exist independently. They are to be brought into existence only by and for others – controlled, defined, and used" (*Toward A New Psychology of Women* 63). In *The Vikings at Helgeland,* in spite of their mutual passion, Sigurd gives Hjørdis to Gunnar in the name of their male bond; Peer Gynt refuses Solveig sexually and makes her into a self-serving ideal of female chastity; in *Emperor and Galilean,* Julian forces the sexual Helena into the mold of the pure woman he deems necessary for his empire; in *Pillars of Society,* Bernick rebukes his wife's passion for him and lectures her on the quiet companionship necessary to married love; in *A Doll House,* Torvald habitually fantasizes when he makes love to his wife of eight years that she is still the virgin bride he married; in *Ghosts,* Pastor Manders forces Helene Alving to return to her husband and perform her conjugal duty; in *The Wild Duck*, Hjalmar chastises Gina for the sexual life she had before they met; in *Rosmersholm*, Rosmer classifies Beata's desire for him as abnormal and is oblivious to Rebecca's; in *Hedda Gabler*, Tesman and Brack take Hedda's sexual compliance for granted, and Løvborg berates her for not sleeping with him; in *Little Eyolf*, Alfred refuses Rita's sexuality and would reduce her to the role of their child's mother; in *John Gabriel Borkman*, Borkman betrays his and Ella's passion in the name of his ambition. In *When We Dead Awaken*, Rubek refuses Irene's sexuality in the name of his art, and in so doing, like all his predecessors, he is both refusing the woman's full humanity and denying her autonomy.

The transmogrification of Rubek's statue

When the aspiring Rubek first conceived of his monumental "Resurrection Day," he made a very conventional choice for his allegorical figure: a virgin woman. Resurrection would be expressed by the old notion of the redemptive power of female chastity embodied in the sculptor's "pure young woman – untouched by worldly experience – awakening to the light and the glory, with nothing ugly or unclean to cast off" (1072). But after Rubek completed his marble woman, what was to have been his masterpiece failed to satisfy him. He confesses to Irene that after her departure, the conception for which she had served as model began to seem both naive and false, a product of a time when he as yet had no knowledge of life and "how this world works." Since his notion of resurrection had now become "something larger" and "more complex," he "enlarged the composition" of the statue to represent "a piece of the curving, bursting earth" through whose cracks "human beings swarm up now, with disguised animal faces. Women and men – exactly as I knew them from life." The completed statue was not inspired by Irene, but by what Rubek himself, as he explains to her, "saw through my own eyes in the world around me" (1072).

Rubek's evolution made him considerably diminish both the ideality and the importance of the ideal woman; he made her face less luminous, "toned down," and moved her off her pedestal into the sculpture's background (1073). The central allegorical figure is now a man who "dips his fingers in the flowing water – to rinse them clean . . . In all eternity he'll never be free to experience resurrection." "Resurrection Day" is no longer represented by a joyous "pure young woman" (1072), but by despairing, imperfect women and men foregrounded by a male figure symbolizing "remorse for a lapsed life" (1073). Resurrection is no longer expressed as certain, but as impossible. Anxiety has replaced ecstasy. Rubek is no longer an idealizer of reality but a visionary commentator on earthbound humanity's suffering. The sentimental figure of the pure woman rising to heaven, an example of academic salon art, has given way to expressionistic human–animal figures. Rubek, in other words, has become a modern artist.

Irene's own resurrection undermines the ideology embodied in the statue for which she posed; she has risen from the dead not to ascend to heaven as a serenely triumphant virgin, but to stay on earth long enough to confront the man who refused her sexually. But at the same time, she also clings to a saving illusion. Unaware of the statue's transformation, she believes that her suffering served the cause of art and thus had a sacrificial meaning. Although she hates the statue because it represents Rubek's rejection of her, she also loves it because it achieved "glory and honor" (1046). The celebrated sculpture she calls "*our* creation, *our* child" was a compensation for the real children Rubek denied her (1070). When Rubek reveals that what she remembers "later became something else" (1071) and describes the new group, she protests "(*as if choked with misery*). My whole soul – you and I – we, we, we and our child were in that one figure alone" (1073). With unconscious egotism, Rubek tries to justify his transformation: "Yes, but listen now, how I've introduced myself in the composition. In front, by a spring . . . a man sits bowed down by guilt, as if he can't quite detach himself from the earth's crust." In place of Irene, Rubek was the model for the central allegorical figure; the artist has replaced the muse with himself.

Irene bitterly analyzes Rubek's substitution of himself for her: "You killed my soul – and then you model yourself in remorse and penance and contrition – (*Smiles.*) – and you think that settles the score" (1073). The fittest appellation Irene can find for the man who wronged her is the accusatory "Poet!" She explains to the uncomprehending sculptor: "Because, my friend, there's something extenuating in that word. Something self-justifying – that throws a cloak over every sin and human frailty" (1074).

22. Irene (Lise Fjeldstad) reclaiming her autonomy in the National Theatre's production of *When We Dead Awaken*, Oslo, 1994.

Rubek's defiant self-defense only reinforces the truth of Irene's accusation: "I'm an artist, Irene. And I'm not ashamed of the human frailties I might carry around with me. Because, you see, I was *born* to be an artist. And no matter what, I'll never be anything else" (1074). Rubek's identity as artist justifies his whole conduct, for genius knows no law.

Rubek's revelations force Irene to acknowledge a devastating truth about herself. Her belief that her participation in the statue's creation constituted the one achievement of her failed life is a delusion. Her devotion to the cause of art was irrelevant, her humiliation and suffering useless. Irene's recognition of the futility of her service leads her to realize the enormity of her instrumentality: "But *I* – was a human being – once! And *I* – also had a life to live – and a human destiny to fulfill. See, I let that go – gave it all up to make myself your instrument – Oh, that was suicide" (1074). Irene describes her error in the terms of a central Christian allegory of good and evil, Christ's temptation by Satan. In language that explicitly recalls that of the account in *Matthew* 4:9–10, she relates how arch-tempter Rubek "inveigled" her to a mountain top and promised to show her "all the glories of the world" on the condition that she follow him and do what he ordered (1077). "And right there, I fell on my knees – and worshipped you. And served you." Irene let herself be tempted by the devil of feminine self-obliteration in the service of masculine achievement.

Art, life, and the uses of women

Although Rubek's final version of "Resurrection Day" brought him the fame and fortune he desired, his elation was short lived; "all the talk about the artist's high calling and the artist's mission, and so on, began to strike me as basically empty" (1063). Rubek decided to substitute life for art, for after all, as he explains to his wife Maja, "Isn't life in sunshine and beauty altogether more worthwhile than to work on till the end of your days in a damp, dripping hole, slaving yourself dead tired over lumps of clay and blocks of stone?" (1064). As the intelligent, beautiful Irene was the perfect woman with whom to create, the simple, vivacious Maja was the perfect woman with whom to live, and so Rubek purchased her for his wife, promising her, as was his practice, to show her "all the glories of the world." But Rubek's attempt to substitute life for art was unsuccessful, as he explains to his partner in living: "I've come to realize that it's absolutely not in me to find happiness by enjoying a life of leisure . . . I have to stay active – creating work after work – until the day I die. (*With difficulty.*) That's why I can't go on with you any longer, Maja" (1064–65).

The down-to-earth Maja's response to her husband – "In plain terms, does that mean you've grown tired of me?" – releases the truth hidden under Rubek's rhetoric: "Yes, that's what it means! I've grown tired – insufferably tired and bored and worn out by living with you!" (1065). To Rubek's surprise, Maja is relieved by his rejection. She is as dissatified with her unsociable, intellectual husband as he is with his gregarious, simple wife, who readily admits that she neither cares nor knows anything about "art and such" (1061). She is as eager to separate from Rubek as he is from her: "I can always find something new for myself somewhere in the world. Where I'll be free! Free! Free!" (1066). For Maja, being "free" means being at liberty to leave Rubek for another man, her newfound lover Ulfheim, Rubek's foil, a vulgar bear-hunter who, she notes, "hasn't a trace of the artist in him" (1058).

In place of her, Rubek explains to his wife, with characteristic egotism, he needs "companionship with someone who could fulfill me – complete me – be one with me in everything I'm striving for" (1062). To meet this need, he plans to replace Maja with Irene; tapping his chest, he explains to his inadequate wife: "In here, you see – here I carry a little, tiny casket . . . And in that casket all my visions lie stored away. But when [Irene] went off without a trace, the lock on the casket clicked shut. And she had the key – and she took it with her. You, my dear little Maja – you had no key" (1065).

Rubek assumes that Irene will gladly take up her former servicing role, for what he wants must be what the woman wants to give him. He resists the truth of Irene's accusations, refusing to discuss his treatment of her – "Let's stop talking about the past" (1047) – except to justify it on the grounds of his "artistic mission" (1052). Oblivious to her feelings, he denies his summary judgment of their collaboration – "I said 'episode'? I don't generally use that word" (1075) – and rejects her account of her death – "Oh, Irene, give up these wild obsessions –! You're alive! Alive, alive!" (1050).

It is not what Irene has lived through that matters to him, but how she can live for him now. Finally humoring her repeated contention that her suffering has made her a dead woman, prince Rubek metaphorically waves a magic wand to resurrect his sleeping beauty: "Oh, but now you've awakened, Irene!" (1067). But Irene's life is not a function of Rubek's desires, and she cannot be revived so easily: "I still have the heavy, deep sleep in my eyes." Insisting that he and his rediscovered love will experience "the light of a new dawn," Rubek refuses Irene's caution – "Don't ever believe that" – on the grounds of his own desire: "I do believe it! And I know it! Now that I've found you again" (1068).

Rubek's longing for Irene repeats the selfish pattern of their earlier relation; he wants her because of the use he believes he can make of her. Refusing both the reality and the futility of his earlier exploitation of her, he begs her to come to live with him "just like the days when we created together. You could open up everything that's locked away in me" (1077). He rejects her blunt response – "I don't have the key to you any longer" – with a deluded plea whose selfish desperation makes it pathetic: "You have the key! You alone have it! (*Beseeching her.*) Help me – so I can try to live my life over again!" In her unqualified refusal to repeat her service, Irene emphatically transforms Rubek's "my life" to the plural: "Aimless – dead dreams. *Our* life together can never be resurrected" (1077).

Looking at the woman

Rubek's refusal to see Irene as she is, is a wishful, determined resistance to the reality before his eyes: "*Her face is pallid and drawn, like a plaster mask; her eyelids droop and her eyes appear unseeing. Her gown is full-length and clings in long, regular, vertical folds to her body . . . Her carriage is rigid, her pace stiff and measured*"; the "*large, white crepe shawl*" that covers her head and upper body suggests a shroud (1040). A parody of Rubek's statuesque virgin, Irene is both dead woman and sculpture, a grotesque embodiment of Rubek's objectification of her, his refusal of the living woman in favor of a fictive woman of his own creation. In imploring Irene to return to him, Rubek is ignoring what he has made her: "And what of me?" she asks him; "Have you forgotten what I am now?" (1090).

What Joyce called Irene's "inner power of character"[9] allows her to persevere in the repeated assaults on Rubek's self-justifications that finally force him to abandon his defenses and abruptly admit the hard, succinct truth: "I put the dead clay model above the joys of life – and love" (1091). But even as Rubek recognizes his error, he would deny its consequence. For Rubek, like Mrs. Alving, recognition is all: "At last, we're free! And there's still time for us to live, Irene." But as in *Ghosts*, the past inexorably dooms the present: "Too late. Too late . . . The desire to live has died in me" (1091). Woman is not infinitely replenishable.

Rubek at last looks at Irene not as he would like her to be for him, but as she is. Her brutal contrast of herself to Rubek's joyous, resurrected virgin – "Your young woman risen from death can see the whole of life laid out and embalmed" (1091) – breaks his last resistance. His recognition of Irene's deadness is both an admission of the irrevocability and magnitude of his crime and an acceptance of his responsibility to expiate it in kind: "Then let our two dead souls live life to the full for once – before we go down in our graves again!" As Irene died through serving him, he will die for using her.

As the reconciled lovers go up the stormy mountain to their symbolic wedding in death, they meet Maja and her bear-hunter going down to enjoy the life and love that Rubek refused with Irene. Maja's song about her liberation from Rubek – "I am free as a bird, I am free!" (1092) – comments also on the couple walking toward the avalanche, who are experiencing a more exalted liberation. *When We Dead Awaken* ends in an apotheosis of love, a brief, ecstatic *liebestod* in which the lovers celebrate their newfound union in extravagant metaphors of ascension and light: "Up in the light and all its flaming glory. Up to the peak of promise! Up there we'll celebrate our marriage feast . . . Yes, through all, all the mist – and then up to the topmost peak of the tower that gleams in the sunrise" (1091–92).[10]

Hand in hand, Irene and Rubek climb toward their celebratory end, but in the double love death that ends the play, one of the lovers is already dead. It is when the man looks at the woman not as a function of himself, but as a person apart from himself, that he recognizes this. He then makes the supreme gesture, and joins the woman in the state to which he damned her.

A dramatist's epilogue

If Ibsen considered *When We Dead Awaken* a conclusion to the three plays that preceded it, he also thought of it as an epilogue in a larger sense. Replying to a newspaper reporter who asked him if he had sub-titled *When We Dead Awaken* "A Dramatic Epilogue" to signal that it was his last play, Ibsen said: "Whether I write any more is another question, but what I meant by 'Epilogue' in this context was only that the play forms an epilogue to the series of plays that began with *A Doll House* and now ends with *When We Dead Awaken.* This last work deals with experiences I treated in the series as a whole, and makes of it a totality, an entity, and now I am finished with it. If I write anything else, it will be in another context and perhaps also in another form" (*H* 19:226). The usual interpretation of Ibsen's remarks is that he was referring to the adoption of a new style; he meant, writes Meyer, "that he was finished with orthodox realism and was intending to move . . . back towards poetry and symbolism" (785). But Ibsen pointedly designates the subject of whether he would continue writing as "another question," a matter quite apart from his explanation that *When We Dead Awaken* was an epilogue to *A Doll House* and the plays that followed it. Ibsen's insistence that he meant no more than he said confirms that he had used *epilogue* not as a synonym for its homologue *prologue,* i.e., an introduction to a new series of plays, but in the word's normal meaning: "a concluding section that rounds out the design of a literary work."[11]

When We Dead Awaken "makes a totality, an entity" of the series of plays that begins with *A Doll House* because only in it does the radical search for truth, Ibsen's great theme, lead to resolution. The finality of its harmonious closure strikingly contrasts with the open-ended conclusions of its ten predecessors. In *A Doll House,* in which the truth arrived at is also that of a demeaning notion of women, Nora ends her inauthentic marriage and slams the door on a bewildered husband. In *Ghosts,* fatally diseased Oswald provides his mother with the terrible significance of her ceding to Pastor Manders' demand that she perform her womanly duty. Nora leaves for the unknown, while Helene Alving's new knowledge makes her scream out her impossible alternatives: "Yes! No!" In the last act of *An Enemy of the People,* the health crusader Doctor Stockmann gathers up the stones thrown at him by the mob that refused the truth he told them; at the end of *The Wild Duck*, the truth crusader who wanted to let the light into the Ekdal home is confronted with the body of the innocent girl his meddling destroyed. Doctor Stockmann will have to renew the battle for truth against the people; Gregers' raking up the past will lead only to Hjalmar's invention of another maudlin sentimentality to justify the death of his daughter. In *Rosmersholm*, the self-designated bringer of truth to his fellow citizens abandons his mission at the first obstacle and demands of the woman who loves him that she imitate his first wife and die to prove her love for him. The play ends with the double leap into the mill race. In *The Lady from the Sea*, the unhappy ending of the sub-plot, Bolette's capitulation to a loveless marriage, sharply contrasts with the happy resolution of the main plot. At play's end, trapped Bolette silently watches the great ship slip out of the fjord into the sea. In *Hedda Gabler*, the protagonist comes to realize the full horror of the entrapment of her bargain marriage and chooses to destroy herself rather than continue a life she abhors. The play ends in a pistol shot. In *The Master Builder*, Solness and Hilda fashion an exalted romantic fantasy in which he plays the role of the heroic man and she the egeria who will inspire him to new achievement. At the end of the play, Solness fulfills what Hilda demands of him, falling to his death as he does so. In *Little Eyolf*, Rita learns to recognize the obsessive passion for her husband that made her neglect her son; she leads Alfred to admitting his own neglect and they join in a plan to redeem their lives. But even here, in the play whose reconciliatory ending most resembles that of *When We Dead Awaken*, the solution remains tentative; as the Allmers acknowledge, they have a "hard day's work ahead" (935). In *John Gabriel Borkman*, the protagonist never admits the wrong of either his criminality or his exploitation of Ella and Gunhild, and dreams to the end of the industrial empire that eluded him; the lives of the bitter, men-obsessed women are as bleak as Borkman's. The play ends with a tableau of a man's corpse and two women dead in life, "two shadows – over the dead man" (1024).

In sharp contrast to its ten predecessors, *When We Dead Awaken* concludes in a sure, rapturous conciliation. The commonly noted vertical movement of the drama's three settings – from a sea-level spa to a mountain resort to a high mountainside – marks a clear, spiritual ascension. Irene's name means peace, a signification underlined by the play's last line, "Pax Vobiscum." Ibsen ends his series of dramas of modern life with words of healing and benediction.

While writing *When We Dead Awaken*, Ibsen felt truly unwell for the first time in his life. He wrote the play at a fever pitch, as though he was afraid that he would fall seriously ill before finishing it,[12] and three months after its publication, he suffered the first of the debilitating strokes that made further writing impossible. It is hard not to speculate that he feared that the play might be his last, and that he wanted to close his life's work on a note of harmony. A year earlier, events had occurred that lent a sense of finality to his achievement – the long series of gala celebrations in Norway, Sweden, and Denmark that marked his seventieth birthday, and the preparation of the Norwegian and German collected editions of his works. His career was crowned.

With an irony characteristic of him, at the same time that Ibsen closed his œuvre with a drama that ends in reconciliation, he cast a critical eye on the artist's nature that made the œuvre possible. Rubek's use of Irene is Ibsen's version of a perennial literary subject, the artist's isolation from and exploitation of life.[13] With the exception of Falk in *Love's Comedy*, Rubek is the only Ibsen protagonist who is an artist, and as in the earlier play, Ibsen mercilessly examines the egotism and self-absorption of a man for whom the world and its people are grist to his mill. And in this, *When We Dead Awaken* is a personal epilogue. As he had drawn on himself for the portraits of Falk, Brand, Peer Gynt, and Solness, he did likewise for his portrait of the artist, whose similarity to himself, Koht remarks, he "seems to be deliberately pointing out" in Rubek's development from a romantic to a realist artist (K 458). And although Rubek is a sculptor, the "bitterest term of abuse which Ibsen can find" for him, notes McFarlane, is "poet"; Irene's accusation that Rubek killed her soul, then modelled himself as a figure of remorse, is not only a judgment on Ibsen's vocation, but a mocking commentary on Ibsen's own definition that to write is to pass judgment upon oneself; in judging this act of judging, *When We Dead Awaken*, McFarlane concludes, "pronounces upon the author a meta-judgement of extreme severity" (*OI* 8:33–34).

It has become a commonplace to narrow the general autobiographical content of *When We Dead Awaken* – the portrayal of the artist as an exploiter of life – to a claim that the play is an allegorical meditation on the conflict between love and art in which Rubek's unwise choice of art is Ibsen's. "Nowhere do we find," writes Meyer, "so complete and merciless a self-portrait as the character of Arnold Rubek. The aging artist, restless in his married life, restless in the homeland to which he has returned after a long sojourn abroad, restless in his art, shocked . . . into the realization that to reject love is to reject life; such is Ibsen's Portrait of the Dramatist as an Old Man, painted at the age of seventy-one" (M 786).[14]

This schematic reading needs correcting on several grounds. While Rubek's dissatisfaction on returning home, a minor theme in the drama, undoubtedly reflects Ibsen's ambiguous feelings about having returned to Norway after twenty-seven years of exile, it is improbable that Rubek's unhappy relation with his wife reflects Ibsen's relation with Suzannah; Rubek's marriage with a woman who has no understanding of his art represents the opposite of Ibsen's marriage. Rubek's failed union with the young, beautiful Maja more likely reflects what Ibsen believed would have been the result if he had taken the young, beautiful Emilie Bardach to show her, as he had promised in a heated moment, "all the glories of the world." It is even less certain that Ibsen was "restless in his art" or that Rubek's rejection of "love" and thus "life" for art represents the choice of his creator. First, as I have pointed out earlier, it is indisputable that in marrying Suzannah Thoresen, Ibsen chose a woman he loved; Ibsen also loved Hildur Andersen, but theirs was a relation between artist and artist, and if he had left his wife for her (a prospect he deemed preposterous), this choice would not have meant choosing "life" over "art." On the contrary, Andersen acted as Ibsen's consultant on the writing of the play partly based on their relation, *The Master Builder.* Most importantly, nothing suggests that Ibsen regarded "life" as synonymous with "love," and it is curious that the biographers and critics who themselves manifestly have not given up work for love claim that Ibsen himself regretted not having done so. In fact, Ibsen famously regarded his writing as nothing less than a calling, so much so that to answer it was, in Koht's words, a "categorical imperative, a moral injunction so binding, it was his religion" (K 160). In one of his first letters to his publisher, Ibsen noted: "I feel that it is my task in life to use the gifts God has given me to awaken my countrymen from their torpor and to force them to see where the great questions are leading us" (*LS* 54–55). About the same time, he wrote in a letter to King Carl in a petition for a writer's grant: "I am not fighting for an existence free from care but for that lifework which I firmly believe God has given me to do" (*LS* 56–57). To have abandoned his lifework for "life" would have made Ibsen despise himself. For Ibsen, the bad life was the aimless life, the vocationless Peer Gynt life of wasted talent, and thus wasted self. It was precisely his own Peer Gynt streak that he struggled against through his famous clock-like routine, made possible in great part by an efficient wife who unconditionally supported his work and whose integrity and freedom of mind were essential influences upon him.

Not only did Ibsen continue to view his work as his reason for living, but as he gained international fame and his influence grew, he "came to look at himself and his career as a part of history" (K 449). Recognition of his achievement had enormous importance for him. When he attended his seventieth-birthday celebrations and received the lavish honors never before (or since) awarded to a Norwegian, he was unabashedly moved at the enormous outpourings of love and respect that capped his great career. He was filled with joy when the kings of Denmark and Sweden awarded him, respectively, the rarely given Grand Cross of the Order of Dannebrog and the Grand Cross of the North Star Order. The two great medals would crown his already extensive collection and mark his importance in the world at large.

Even after a series of strokes that left him virtually unable to walk, Ibsen said that if his health returned, he would write a new play. More and more enfeebled, he continued to watch over his literary affairs. Exhausted and half paralyzed, he was not too weak to try to protect the life's work he had written in the Dano-Norwegian language, lending his voice to Bjørnson's attack on the development of "New Norwegian" as an official language of Norway: "I will not be my own executioner. I will not be that" (K 462). About a year before he died, six and a half years after he wrote *When We Dead Awaken,* by which time he had become almost completely disabled and confined to his bed, he called out in his sleep: "I'm writing! And it's coming along wonderfully" (Bull, "Henrik Ibsen" 464).

Those who claim that Rubek's choice of art over life reflects Ibsen's own deeply regretted choice ignore the result of Rubek's subsequent reverse decision: a regret bordering on despair. His abandoning his lifework to "live" with Maja was a colossal error, for, as he tells her: "I've come to realize that it's absolutely not in me to find happiness by enjoying a life of leisure . . . I have to stay active – creating work after work – until the day I die" (1064).

The perennial reading of *When We Dead Awaken* as the dramatization of a struggle between the irreconcilable aims of life and vocation[15] ignores Irene's anti-Kierkegaardian lesson to the artist, which is not that he should have abandoned art for life, but that he should not have split his life in two and made love the enemy of his work. Unlike Maja, who happily replaces the artist with the man, Rubek with Ulfheim, Irene loves and respects art; Rubek's crime against her and against himself was not that he was an artist, but that he was "only an artist. Not a man" (1070). Answering Julius Elias' question about the meaning of *When We Dead Awaken*, Ibsen wrote: "I cannot undertake a plain and simple explanation of what I meant. Irene's hints must rather be considered as a kind of *Wahrheit und Dichtung*'" (*LS* 341). For Ibsen, the "truth and poetry" of his play lay in Irene's challenge to Rubek's absolutism; that he used the title of his revered Goethe's autobiography to characterize this challenge indicates how strongly he supported it.

When We Dead Awaken does not dramatize an epiphany on the part of its author on the superiority of love to vocation, but, on the contrary, constitutes the final example in the Ibsen canon of one of its overriding subjects: the interrelation between work and love. In *Catiline*, *The Vikings at Helgeland*, and *The Master Builder*, the strivings of the ambitious Catiline, Sigurd, and Solness are inextricably linked to their erotic bond with a woman; in *Little Eyolf*, it is the erotic Rita who discovers a vocation for herself and her husband. *Lady Inger of Østråt* and *Love's Comedy* dramatize warring allegiances to vocation and love that lead to disaster in the former and to stalemate in the latter. In *The Vikings at Helgeland*, *Pillars of Society*, and *John Gabriel Borkman*, a man's betrayal of love for a value deemed superior poisons both lives and work. In *The Pretenders*, Haakon and then Skule temper their harsh absolutism as they allow love to influence vocation, and in *Brand*, the protagonist's refusal to do so undermines the goal of his vocation and destroys the son and wife he loves. In *Peer Gynt*, Peer's rejection of Solveig's love is part of his refusal to find a vocation, to "become himself"; in *A Doll House*, Nora abandons her folly of living only "for love" and leaves to find out who else she might become. In *Hedda Gabler*, Hedda destroys herself because she has nothing to live for besides fulfilling the degrading role of wife to a man she loathes; in *John Gabriel Borkman*, Borkman, the man who lives only for vocation, and Ella, the woman who lives only for love, are sad parodies of the absolutist life. Commenting on Brand's refusal to allow love to mitigate the demands of his vocation, Ibsen wrote that he could just as well have constructed the same conflict "about a sculptor" (*LS* 84), and he later did so in *When We Dead Awaken*. The necessary relation of love to vocation posited in Ibsen's last play and in his work as a whole is not one of conflict but of complementarity, not of "either/or" but of both. From beginning to end in the Ibsen canon, as Oswald tries to teach his mother in *Ghosts*, the joy of life and the joy of work go hand in hand.

Ibsen's women and Ibsen's modernism

> What will be the outcome of this mortal combat between two epochs, I do not know. But anything is better than the existing state of affairs.
>
> Ibsen, letter to Brandes, April 4, 1872 (*LS* 123).

It is a commonplace that Ibsen earned the status of the founder of modern drama by inventing the realistic prose play and making the theatre a forum for debate. In the words of one authoritative study of modernism, the origins of modern European drama lie in "the compulsive attention the eighties and the nineties gave to the problematic and the contemporary" and "the restless exploration of the resources of prose as a dramatic medium. Both things point unwaveringly back to Ibsen."[1]

Historians of modern drama customarily place the status of women among the contemporary problems Ibsen put to debate. Eric Bentley writes: "Calling attention to the rotten bottoms of ships, the subjection of Victorian wives, the ravages of syphilis, and the corruption of municipal politics and journalism, [Ibsen] made himself the father of the reformist drama of the end of the century."[2] Similarly, Robert Brustein puts "women's rights" alongside "divorce, euthanasia, [and] cures for syphilis" in his list of the issues of "social amelioration" and "political reform" normally associated with Ibsen's work.[3] For John Fletcher and James McFarlane, "the role of women in society" is an "Ibsenist problem" along with "the menace of pollution" and "the conflict across the generation gap" (Bradbury and McFarlane 501).

To place "the subjection of Victorian wives," "women's rights," and the "role of women in society" on the list of the problems debated by Ibsen and his contemporaries is to ignore the centrality of the "woman question" in the development of modern drama. As Peter Gay has conclusively shown, from the 1850s to the end of the century, Europe was highly preoccupied with feminism's challenge to patriarchy ("Offensive Women" 169–225). Consistently overlooked in discussions of the origins of modern European drama is the fact that it developed in conjunction with this raucous contemporary debate. The woman question is central to the three plays with which Ibsen introduced the drama of realism: *Pillars of Society* (1877), *A Doll House* (1879), and *Ghosts* (1881). Strindberg, the most important figure in the development of modern drama after Ibsen, "rose in revolt against the feminist movement," as he himself put it,[4] in the famous plays of his naturalistic period: *The Father* (1887), *Miss Julie* (1888), *Comrades* (1888), and *Creditors* (1888). The plays of Hauptmann, who dominated the German stage for twenty years, examined the issues of women's rights (*Before Sunrise*, 1889) and equality in marriage (*Lonely Lives*, 1891), and exposed the viciousness of the double standard (*Rose Bernd*, 1903). In Germany, too, the subject of Wedekind's *Spring's Awakening* (1891), *Earth Spirit* (1894), and *Pandora's Box* (1898) is the corrupt sexual ethos of patriarchy.[5] In France, Brieux wrote polemical plays on the double standard and the commodification of women (*The Three Daughters of Monsieur Dupont*, 1898), on society's victimizing silence on syphilis (*Damaged Goods*, 1902), and on the evils of forced motherhood (*Maternity*, 1903). In England, the debate over the woman question preoccupied Ibsen's champion Shaw, who put varieties of the "New Woman" on the stage in *The Philanderer* (1893), *Mrs. Warren's Profession* (1893), and *Candida* (1894). All of Wilde's comedies – *Lady Windemere's Fan* (1892), *A Woman of No Importance* (1893), *An Ideal Husband* (1895), and *The Importance of Being Ernest* (1895) – expose the unfairness and downright silliness of the double standard. Indisputably, the woman question had prime importance for the originators of modern drama.[6]

If it is important to insist on the pervasiveness of the woman question in the development of modern drama, it is equally important to distinguish between it and other issues of the "problem drama" that can be addressed by public policy or social engineering. For women, unlike rotten ship bottoms, syphilis, pollution, and the generation gap, but, like men, are not problems but human beings. Ibsen did not consider women a problematic population whose function in society needed defining. Nowhere does he debate "women's role in society," for in Ibsen throughout, society is the enemy. In *A Doll House*, Ibsen's most explicit treatment of the woman question, the conflict is between society's demand that Nora embrace the woman's role that it has determined for her – "Before all else, you're a wife and mother" – and her refusal in the name of her own autonomy: "I believe that, before all else, I'm a human being" (193). Nora does not leave the doll house to find some other role in society, but, on the contrary, to try to discover the self she refused in living a role. *A Doll House*, succinctly noted James Huneker, "was the plea for woman as a human being, neither more nor less than man" (A 13:275).

Ibsen's insistence on women as autonomous human beings is the most striking manifestation of the radicalism that makes him a standardbearer of modernism. Whatever particular meanings "modernism" takes on when it is used to categorize different writers or genres, scholars of the diverse movement agree that its chief characteristic was a thoroughgoing revolt against the prevailing order: it was one of the "cataclysmic upheavals of culture" (Bradbury and McFarlane 19); it was "committed to everything in human experience that militates against custom" (Ellmann and Feidelson vi). From the 1870s to the end of the century, "Ibsenism" was synonymous with modernism because Ibsen was the most fearless debunker of the idols of Western culture during a time when "ideas, ideals, relationships unchanged since time out of mind were vulnerable to attack and open to amendent" (Gay, "Offensive Women" 172).

The relation between Ibsen's representation of women and the "Ibsenist problem" can better be understood in relation to Ibsen's affinity with modernism's important theorist Brandes. In the 1871 "Inaugural Lecture" in the series that later became the great comparative study *Main Currents in Nineteenth-Century Literature*, Brandes wrote the now famous passage: "What keeps a literature alive in our days is that it submits problems to debate. Thus, for example, George Sand debates the problem of the relations between the sexes. Byron and Feuerbach religion, John Stuart Mill and Proudhon property, Turgenev, Spielhagen and Emile Augier social conditions. A literature that does not submit problems to debate loses all meaning" (388). Brandes concluded his lecture with a call to arms that makes it clear that "problems" should be debated in the context of nothing less than a general revolution in thinking: "For it is not so much our laws that need changing as it is our whole conception of society. The younger generation must plough it up and replant it before a new literature can bloom and flourish" (397).

Brandes' revolutionary theory rang a resounding bell in Ibsen's thinking. In his letter of congratulations, Ibsen wrote to Brandes that the first volume of his lectures was "continually" in his thoughts and had even kept him from sleeping (*LS* 122). "It is one of those works that place a yawning gulf between yesterday and today . . . It reminds me of the gold fields of California when they were first discovered. They either made millionaires of men or ruined them . . . What will be the outcome of this mortal combat between two epochs, I do not know. But anything is better than the existing state of affairs" (*LS* 122–23).

Exhibiting what Koht has called Ibsen's "characteristic habit of probing to the source of things" (K 33), Ibsen's representation of women reflects the "mortal combat" between the old and the modern because it refuses one of history's "true universals," the centuries-old pan-cultural reality of woman's subordination to man.[7] Woman's secondary status is an example of what sociologists call "permanent inequality," in which a group of people is ascribed as naturally inferior to another because of race, class, sex, religion, nationality, or other characteristics ascribed at birth. Members of the group are said to be unable to perform the tasks that the dominant group prefers and assigned work that the dominant group does not want to perform. The unequal relation is legitimized by making it part of society's "natural laws," for example, woman's place is the home, man's is the world.[8]

Because the psychology of permanently unequal relations demands that the subordinates develop character traits pleasing to the dominant group – submissiveness, passivity, lack of initiative – the subordinates are forced to act in hidden or indirect ways. In *A Doll House*, Nora plays the fool and saves her husband's life without his knowing it, in *Ghosts*, closet businesswoman Mrs. Alving runs her husband's estate, in *Hedda Gabler*, Hedda plays the satisfied bourgeoise and plots secretly to bring some meaning into her life, in *When We Dead Awaken*, Irene pretends to embrace her servicing identity as Rubek's muse. As long as the subordinates adapt or seem to adapt to the dominants' view, they are considered well adjusted; when they do not, and rebel, they are considered abnormal: the judgment of Torvald on Nora's leaving her family in *A Doll House*, of Manders on Mrs. Alving's leaving her husband in *Ghosts*, of Wangel on Ellida's newfound independence from him in *The Lady from the Sea*, of Rubek on Irene's refusal to repeat her service to him in *When We Dead Awaken*. Subordinates often know more about the dominants than vice versa: Nora knows how to manage Torvald by flattering his ego, Mrs. Alving recognizes the insidiousness of Pastor Manders' moral universe, Hedda recognizes and loathes the pettiness of the Tesmans, Irene perceives Rubek's colossal ego; in contrast, Torvald does not know his resourceful wife, Manders is shocked when Mrs. Alving confronts him with her liberal notions, the Tesmans have no inkling of Hedda's despair, Rubek is oblivious to Irene's suffering. The subordinates also know more about the dominants than themselves, for if one's fate depends on pleasing others, there is little reason to know one's self: what Nora has ignored, but wants to discover, what Mrs. Alving has refused to face, what Hedda has tried to repress, what Irene represses and then acknowledges.

Implicit in the notion of woman's permanent inequality is that she is instrumental rather than autonomous, that her purpose is not to be but to serve. From *Catiline* to *When We Dead Awaken*, Ibsen consistently dramatizes what Georg Simmel called the "tragedy of the female" in history – that women have been "treated and valued as mere instruments" (*On Women, Sexuality, and Culture* 115). Ibsen's plays attack the ideology of woman as the servicing sex through direct satire, through disparaging portrayals of men who regard women's servitude as part of the natural relation between the sexes, through the woman's victimization in the plays of the female-centered triangle, and through the valorization of the autonomous woman over the subservient woman in the plays of the male-centered triangle. The patterns often inter-connect, appearing together in the same play.

Direct satire of woman's servicing role informs *Love's Comedy*, in Falk's peevish insistence that Svanhild's task as a woman is to serve him as muse, *Pillars of Society*, in priggish schoolmaster Rørlund's reading to the town ladies from *Woman as the Servant of Society*, *The Wild Duck*, in unproductive Hjalmar's preoccupation with being served hand and foot by his working wife and daughter, *The Lady from the Sea*, in naive Lyngstrand's platitudes on woman's happy lot as helpmate to a superior man, and *Hedda Gabler*, in Thea's avid

confident, sexual, strong, successful, worldly; to be feminine is to be cooperative, expressive, focused on home and family, gentle, helpful, intuitive, naive, nurturing, sensitive, sympathetic, tender weak.[9] The first androgynous character in Ibsen's plays is his first female character, Furia, who is aggressive, adventurous, decisive, self-confident, and sexual. The second is the equally aggressive and equally sexual Margit. The protagonist of *Lady Inger of Østråt*, who participates in the masculine domains of war and politics, is, she says, more of a man than the men who follow her. Hjørdis, the protagonist of *The Vikings at Helgeland*, is a female warrior in the tradition of Ariosto's Bradamant and Spenser's Britomart; she is decisive, self-confident, and possessed of a boundless energy. Hjørdis and Inger's participation in the masculine world underscores the message in Hjørdis' lament for her sex: "A woman! A woman! Ah, nobody knows what a woman is capable of!" (52). *Pillars of Society*'s raisonneur Lona Hessel is adventurous, decisive, knowledgeable, self-confident, strong, and successful. In *A Doll House*, the weak Torvald's notion of himself as a stalwart male rock is exposed as self-deception by his near hysterical reaction to the news of Nora's forgery. In *Ghosts*, it is Mrs. Alving who is the successful administrator; Pastor Manders, who views himself as a strong, shrewd businessman, is easily blackmailed by an obvious fraud. In *An Enemy of the People*, naive Dr. Stockmann believes that when the people are told the truth, right will win the day, while his wife, a woman of sense, knows better; in *The Wild Duck*, Gregers and Hjalmar are weak, hyper-emotional sentimentalists, while Gina and Berta are strong and practical, and it is Gina, not Hjalmar, who is the family provider. In *Little Eyolf*, the strong, analytical Rita exposes her weak husband's self-serving posturings. In *Rosmersholm* and *Little Eyolf*, the effeteness of Rosmer and Allmers contrasts strongly with Rebecca's and Rita's sexuality. In *Hedda Gabler*, domestic Tesman putters about in his beloved slippers, while horsewoman Hedda shoots pistols and paces the floor, longing to escape her woman's prison of home and family.[10]

Ibsen's androgynous characters reflect his challenge to the sexual polarization that has characterized patriarchy since its inception. Gerder Lerner summarizes patriarchy's major assumption about gender:

Men are 'naturally' superior, stronger and more rational, therefore designed to be dominant. From this follows that men are political citizens and responsible for and representing the polity. Women are 'naturally' weaker, inferior in intellect and rational capacities, unstable emotionally and therefore incapable of political participation. They stand outside of the polity. Men, by their rational minds, explain and order the world. Women by their nurturant function sustain daily life and the continuity of the species. While both functions are essential, that of men is superior to that of women. (*The Creation of Feminist Consciousness* 4).

Ibsen's plays dramatize this split personality of the relation between the sexes in all its defectiveness. The sexual polarization of life and the superiority of the masculine sphere are challenged by the portraits of the deluded men of *The Vikings at Helgeland, The Pretenders*, and *Brand*, who denigrate women in the name of their man's world; for Sigurd, his relation with the man with whom he shares Viking polity takes precedence over his love for a woman; in *The Pretenders*, Haakon and Skule reject both the women they love and their own feelings to harden themselves for their battle for power; in *Brand*, the protagonist's sex-based theological system relentlessly separates masculine strength from feminine weakness. All four men come to learn that in refusing their feelings, they have refused the feminine within themselves. *The Vikings at Helgeland, The Pretenders*, and *Brand* implicitly propose a psychological androgyny between the sexes, what Caroline Heilbrun has defined as a "spirit of reconciliation" that suggests "a full range of experience open to individuals who may, as women, be aggressive, as men tender" (*Toward a Recognition of Androgny* x).

A Doll House rejects the notion of polarized male and female natures by its challenge to the nineteenth-century ideology of the "two spheres" – the notion that woman's weakness and emotionality make home her "natural castle," in Peter Gay's term ("Offensive Women" 224), while man's superior strength and sense destine him for the public world outside. Sensitive, naive Torvald owes his life to the hidden resourcefulness of the woman he treats as a human pet.

The Master Builder, Little Eyolf, John Gabriel Borkman, and *When We Dead Awaken* challenge the notion of a dichotomously gendered world through a representation of characters who wholeheartedly embrace it. The couples in these plays are obsessional portraits of men and women consumed by their masculine and feminine identities, the men judging themselves by their achievement and the women by their success as lovers, wives, or mothers. While Solness and Rubek possess the fame and fortune that Borkman and Allmers have failed to achieve, all four men embody the notion that man's purpose in life is to strive for accomplishment within the world. They are perfect representatives of Georg Simmel's analysis of the Western ideal of the masculine self, which "externalizes itself" to fulfill its aims and ambitions; man "signifies something" that is "independent of him" as he creates the ideas and artifacts of culture (*On Women, Sexuality, and Culture* 89). Aline, Rita, Gunhild, Ella, and Irene embody the accompanying notion about women that Karen Horney characterized as "the overvaluation of love," the ideology that women's inherent character makes personal relationships with men and children the only fulfilling aspect of their lives, that their "every thought should center exclusively upon the male or upon motherhood, in much the same manner expressed in Marlene Dietrich's famous song 'I know only love, and nothing else'" ("The Overevaluation of Love" 182).

While Ibsen's male strivers seek to fulfill their masculine role, his female strivers struggle against their feminine one. And in this, the female individual in Ibsen's drama is a modern figure in a way that the male individual is not. In "The Sociology of Modern Drama," Lukács points to the notion of "autonomy" that in the latter half of the nineteenth century challenged established hierarchical patterns by perpetuating conflicts in "the relation of higher to lower rank (master to servant, husband to wife, parents to children)"; modern drama is necessarily "the drama of individualism" (439). The woman as autonomous individual in Ibsen's plays is an individual in Lukács' modernist sense: she rebels against the inferior status assigned her. The Ibsenian male individualist revolts against a prevailing order, but his autonomy is a given.[11] Ibsen's male strivers from Catiline to Solness belong to the Western literary tradition that reaches from the Promethean to the Nietzschean rebel, while his female strivers from Inger to Irene embody the modernist struggle to escape from the prison of gender.[12]

Ibsen's reoccuring paradigm of a woman's conflict between her prescribed, gendered identity and her individual autonomy –

what society tells her she must be and what she is free to become – embodies what Richard Ellmann and Charles Feidelson have called the "two faces, positive and negative, of the modern as the anti-traditional: freedom and deprivation, a living present and a dead past" (*The Modern Tradition* vi). The struggles of the rebellious female protagonists of Ibsen's early plays prefigure those of Ibsen's later, more well-known female rebels. Inger must choose between personal and political allegiances; Margit rages against her dutiful marriage; Hjørdis protests Sigurd's treatment of her as a possession; Svanhild, who has wanted a career, capitulates to the marriage market.

With *Pillars of Society*, Ibsen's women individualists become directly iconoclastic as they openly confront the received ideas that deny their autonomy. In her rejection of the dictates on feminine behavior of a society she condemns as a "bachelors' club" (117), Lona Hessel embodies the "positive" aspect of the modern: "freedom" and "a living present." Her castigation by the good citizens is a splendid example of Brandes' remarks on enforced femininity in the foreword to his translation of Mill's *The Subjection of Women*: "We treat our women's spirits the same way the Chinese treat their women's feet, and like the Chinese, we do it in the name of beauty and femininity. A woman whose feet have grown freely and healthily seems unfeminine and ugly to a Chinese. In our bourgeois little China, a woman who develops freely seems to be an ugly and unfeminine malformation."[13] Aberrant Lona Hessel scorns the reigning pillars of society, whom she would replace by new ones: "the spirit of truth and the spirit of freedom" (118).

The experience of Lona Hessel's successor Nora Helmer also embodies the positive aspect of the modern as anti-traditional. Nora knows that Torvald's contention that she is above all a wife and mother reflects "what the majority says," "what's written in books" and taught by religion (193). In rejecting this ideology – "I don't believe in that anymore" (193) – she rebels against the shared opinion of ordinary people, intellectual opinion, and religious authority – in other words, nothing less than the whole combined weight of her culture – that she was put on earth to serve others.

Ghosts exhibits perhaps better than any other literary work the negative face of modernism: the depiction of deprivation and a dead past. One of the most sinister studies in literature of a woman's submission to authority, Ibsen's play dramatizes the tragedy of Helene Alving's cowardice. Bowing to Pastor Manders' dictate – "Woman, go home to your lawful husband!" (137) – the failed individualist Mrs. Alving conceives the syphilitic son, an embodiment both of the power and the madness of the "old, dead ideas, dead beliefs" that doomed him (92).

The dead past haunts Rosmersholm as it haunts Mrs. Alving's Rosenvold. Rebecca would bring the living present to Rosmersholm as Lona Hessel brings it to the town in *Pillars of Society*, but she succumbs to the ghosts that govern the old bastion of conservatism, becoming a second "dead wife" as she duplicates the futile feminine sacrifice of her predecessor. But the finality dramatized in the play's ending is less the power of the past than its passing, for Rosmer, the embodiment of the dead past, also destroys himself.

In *Rosmersholm*'s pendant *The Lady from the Sea*, a woman also acclimitizes to a man's world, but not to die, but to live. Ellida's newfound autonomy transforms her notion of herself, and both the ailing woman and the ailing marriage are healed. The past recedes before the living present as though it had never been. But if the main plot of *The Lady from the Sea* represents the positive face of modernism, its sub-plot represents the negative; in selling herself for her cherished dream of education, Bolette exchanges one sort of deprivation for another. In the resolutions of main plot and sub-plot, the living present and the dead past coexist.

The Lady from the Sea's successor *Hedda Gabler* dramatizes the two faces of modernism within a single figure. As in *Ghosts*, the negative face is represented by a dead past that condemns the protagonist to a life of deprivation. But while Mrs. Alving, recognizing the inauthenticity of the received ideas that govern her life, continues to live inauthentically, Hedda chooses the quick end. And in this, the deviant woman of *Hedda Gabler* embodies both the positive as well as the negative face of modernism, for if the weight of the past deprives her of any life except a ludicrous marriage and forced motherhood, her freeing herself from this past in the only way she can reflects her triumph over it. The tragedy of Hedda is that in her world, she can achieve autonomy only by dying.

In *Little Eyolf*, as in *A Doll House*, a crisis occurs in the life of a married couple that forces the woman to realize that living her life for the man is a denial of her dignity as a human being. In her determination to redeem her neglect of her child by caring for the poor boys, Rita accepts the accountability that comes with autonomy. The past has given way to a present that looks toward a future.

In *When We Dead Awaken,* Irene returns from her psychic annihilation to repudiate a past that deprived her of life. In refuting Rubek's contention that her function in life is to serve him as muse, she claims her right to a life of her own. She also recognizes her own compliance in her instrumentality. Her recognition that in allowing Rubek to use her, she committed "a mortal sin against myself" (1074) echoes Helene Alving's analysis of her failed life – "I never really listened to myself" (125) – and recalls Nora's answer to Torvald's assertion that her most "sacred duty" is to serve others: "I have other duties equally sacred . . . Duties to myself" (193). Irene's change also complements Rita's; while Rita feels her transformation as a kind of birthing, Irene experiences hers as an awakening from the dead. Her rage against her exploiter and her insistence on her own worth repudiate the gendered world that prescribes her instrumentality.

The struggles of Ibsen's women in a world that deprived them of full human lives dramatize a battle between worn-out doctrines and principles and the rebellious impulses of a new world beginning to be born. Ibsen was the kind of genius commonly called "ahead of his time" because he saw the future in the present. These women of the end of the last century, fighting against assumptions as old as recorded time, are the fullest embodiment of Ibsen's modernism.

Notes

1 I borrow these titles from two fine essays, Jerome Loving's "Whitman's Idea of Women," *Whitman, Sex, and Gender* (*The Mickle Street Review* 11 [1989]) 17–33; and Marlon Ross' "Naturalizing Gender: Woman's Place in Wordsworth's Ideological Landscape," *English Literary History* 53 (1986): 391–410.

2 "Gender: A Useful Category of Historical Analysis," *American Historical Review* 9 (1986): 1066.

3 Ibsen advised author Magdalene Thoresen that as a writer, one has "to be extremely careful in discriminating between what one has observed and what one has lived through because only the latter can be the basis of creative work" (*LS* 96–97). He wrote to Danish critic Peter Hansen, "Everything that I have created as a poet has had its origin in a frame of mind and a situation in my life. I never wrote because I had, as they say, 'found a good subject'" (*LS* 100).

1 ROOTS

1 The source for my discussion of Ibsen's parents and their marriage is Oskar Mosfjeld, *Ibsen og [and] Skien* (Oslo: Gyldendal, 1949). Mosfjeld based his book on printed and oral accounts of relatives and neighbors who knew the Altenburgs and Ibsens.

2 For a detailed account of Knud Ibsen's financial career, based on records in the Skien municipal archives, see Mosfjeld 60–75. It is sometimes claimed in Knud Ibsen's defense that he was a victim of the general recession in the timber business at the end of the 1830s, but Mosfjeld shows conclusively that his financial ruin occurred well before the flush times ended.

3 For Einar Østvedt, author of *Henrik Ibsen og hans Barndomsmiljø* [*Henrik Ibsen and the World of his Childhood*], it is obvious that Ibsen "inherited his powers as an artist" from his mother (Skien: Oluf Rasmussens Boktrykkeri, 1977) 48. Koht notes Marichen Ibsen's talent but declares: "On the whole, however, [Ibsen's] mother's

influence on him was of a nature other than artistic. After her marriage she devoted herself entirely to her children and home, caring for them with a tenderness that all who knew her have commented on" (K 23). Motherhood has been reduced to nurturing; it was in caring for her son, of course, that Marichen Ibsen introduced him to what she herself loved. When he was old, Knud Ibsen made up verses to demonstrate that his famous son had inherited his poetic talent from him. These rhymes, which in Mosfjeld's phrase are "pathetically banal," illustrate rather the contrary. Here is one example: "I bought a calf, but it was half" (Mosfjeld 22).

4 There remain ten extant copies of the book, usually referred to as *Harrison's History of London.* The Venstøp volume has been lost. (Østvedt 52).

5 Knud Ibsen's use of his wife's family's money to advance his ambition is echoed in the behavior of Bernick of *Pillars of Society,* Allmers of *Little Eyolf,* and Solness of *The Master Builder.*

6 Halvdan Koht, "Hedvig," *Ibsen Årbok* 1 (1952) 66.

7 Later, in a letter to Georg Brandes, Ibsen noted: "In writing *Peer Gynt* I had the circumstances and memories of my own childhood before me" (*LS* 212).

8 Knudsen himself, a poet and member of parliament, liked to boast when he was in his cups that he was the famous dramatist's father. Oskar Mosfjeld was the first to dispose of the Skien rumor by demonstrating its utter lack of evidence, and Ibsen's later biographers have followed suit.

9 The facts about Else Jensdatter and her son are taken from Meyer (M 31–32). When Ibsen was an old man, and an almost legendary figure in Oslo, it was gossiped about that Hans Jacob Henriksen visited his father to ask for money. Before slamming the door in his face, Ibsen is said to have given him five crowns with the explanation that since the sum was what he had given his mother, it should be enough for him. Meyer notes that although the story may be nothing but a malicious rumor, Francis Bull, "who is usually right in such matters," believes it to be true (M 689).

10 Koht writes: "Unquestionably [Ibsen] draws on this painful experience [his relation with Else Jensdatter] when he describes how the greenclad troll woman brings Peer Gynt their bastard child" (K 38); Bull notes that Peer's experience with the Woman in Green is the strongest example of Ibsen's deep, continuing revulsion toward his parentage of Hans Jacob Henriksen ("Henrik Ibsen" 276–77).

11 "*Kindermord* and Will in *Little Eyolf,*" *Modern Drama: Essays in Criticism,* ed. Travis Bogard and William I. Oliver (New York: Oxford University Press, 1965) 192.

12 *I Ungdomsbyen med Henrik Ibsen* [*In the Town of Henrik Ibsen's Youth*] (Grimstad: Ibsenhouse and Grimstad City Museum, 1966) 102.

Clara Thue Ebbell, who lived to be ninety, was a well-known author of biographies, novels, and children's books.

13 "Henrik Ibsens [Ibsen's] Stellanea," *Edda* 3 (1915) 88.

14 *Ibsen's Poems*, trans. John Northam (Oslo: Norwegian University Press, 1986) 48.

15 Gisle Johnson converted Clara Bie during the "Johnson Awakening" that swept over Norway in the 1850s.

2 THE SEMINAL WOMEN OF THE EARLY CAREER

1 Ronald G. Popperwell, "Ibsen's Female Characters," *Scandinavica* 19 (1980):5. In an eight-page essay, Popperwell classifies all Ibsen's women into types. The Aurelia/Furia, good/bad pattern remains intact in the early plays; Lona Hessel of *Pillars of Society* represents a new kind of female savior through "moral principles which are articulated in the human sphere"; in Mrs. Linde of *A Doll House* is found the "saving power of the 'eternal feminine'" (7). Ibsen's "Self-Sacrificing Woman" is represented by Agnes of *Brand* and Mrs. Alving of *Ghosts*. The "Demonic/Active Woman," who is "masculine" – Furia, Hjørdis, the Woman in Green of *Peer Gynt*, Rebecca West, Hedda Gabler, Hilda Wangel, and Rita Allmers – victimizes the feminine woman (8). Popperwell suggests that Ibsen has a program for women: "this would mean neither being the eternal woman, nor the active/demonic type, nor entering into the realm of male ideas, not becoming a man [sic], but a *menneske* [person]" (12).

2 The terms are Sherry Ortner's in her groundbreaking essay "Is Female to Male as Nature is to Culture?" (86).

3 Ibsen had much in common with Sallust's Catiline: an exemplary health, including an extraordinary resistance to cold, heat, and hunger, a disdain for the ordinary, a great ambition, and, principally, an essential rebelliousness. It was this that made Catiline the consummate enemy of the status quo, perfectly represented in Ibsen's mind by Cicero, "the indefatigable spokesman of the majority," as he called him (*OI* 1:110), whose orations inspired Ibsen with an instant and life-long aversion.

4 "Introduction," *Catiline* 60. Van Laan's essay is the most thorough discussion of Ibsen's first play, offering a painstaking account of the drama's biographical and intellectual background and of Ibsen's sources.

5 In *Fiesco*, the hero's passive wife Leonoro and her rival the Countess Julia, the "Machtweib," the "Powerful Woman," are, respectively, thoroughly good and thoroughly evil; neither woman represents a side of the hero's psyche. In the sub-plot of *Götz*, Weislingen betrays the saintly Maria for Götz's enemy, the ambitious "Machtweib" Adelaide, who entices Weislingen to change his allegiance and who is hanged for her villainy. Weislingen deserts Maria for Adelaide not

because Adelaide's policies reflect his own desires, but because he is the slave of his passion.

6 "Das leidende Weib in der dramatischen Literatur von Empfindsamkeit und Sturm und Drang," *Monatshefte* 69 (1977): 159–73.

7 For a good discussion of Ibsen's indebtedness to Oehlenschläger, see Van Laan, *Catiline*, 61–68.

8 In *The Vikings at Byzantium*, Zoe, the dark woman, acts out of lust for Harald, the Viking hero, offering to murder her monarch husband and award Harald the throne, while Maria, the light woman, vows to follow Harald wherever fate leads him. Harald loves Maria, but the arrival of another light woman, Elisif, Harald's former bethrothed, complicates the plot. Harald's predicament is resolved when Zoe stabs Maria; he can now marry Elisif. Apparently, one light woman is worth another.

9 Asbjørn Aarseth, "Ibsen's Dramatic Apprenticeship," *The Cambridge Companion to Ibsen* (Cambridge University Press, 1994) 3.

10 In his psychoanalytical version of the conventional view of Ibsen's male-centered triad, *Catiline's Dream* (Urbana: University of Illinois Press, 1972), James Hurt contends that *Catiline* contains a general mythic pattern present in all Ibsen's plays: the "gentle woman" cooperates with the hero toward his "project of the will" while the "fascinating woman" tries to "tempt the hero to some fatal action" (8). Hurt's schema seems confused, for it claims both that the gentle woman is a partner in the project of the will, and that she represents love as opposed to will. It also ignores the text of *Catiline*, in which the gentle woman opposes the hero's project and the fascinating woman promotes it, and in which the hero's project and the fatal action are the same.

11 Brian Johnston, *To the Third Empire: Ibsen's Early Drama* (Minneapolis: University of Minnesota Press, 1980) 35. Johnston claims that Furia is a "classic example of the destructive, antimasculine, matriarchal, and chthonic power that Eric Neumann sees as the agency surrounding and imprisoning the male ego" (38). He adds: "But at the same time Furia alone fully understands Catiline's heroic aspirations" (38). That Furia liberates rather than imprisons Catiline's ego suggests not only that she is not "a classic example" of Neumann's archetype, but a bad example.

12 *Woman as Image in Medieval Literature from the Twelfth Century to Dante* (New York: Columbia University Press, 1975) 17–35.

13 Sixty years later, Rikke Holst Tresselt recalled these souvenirs to Pierre Georget La Chesnais, the editor and translator of the monumental French edition of Ibsen's works, *Œuvres complètes d'Henrik Ibsen* (Paris: Plon, 1930–45) 3:62. 16 vols. Fru Tresselt also recited from memory Ibsen's proposal poem.

14 Thirty years later, when Ibsen went to Bergen on a visit, he saw his old sweetheart; he asked her, "But how was it nothing came of our

affair?" Rikke laughed and replied, "But my dear Ibsen, did you forget that you ran away?" "Yes, yes," he answered, apologetically, "I never was a brave man face to face" (K 83).

15 Northam writes that the poem refers to Ibsen's affair "with a young Bergen girl, Rikke Holst" (*Ibsen's Poems*, trans. Northam [Oslo: Norwegian University Press, 1986] 20).

16 Ibsen's statement that *Lady Inger* was the result of his failed love affair is sometimes taken as a reference to the play's sub-plot, the love affair between Inger's chief enemy Nils Lykke and Inger's daughter Eline. Made a new man by love, Lykke rushes to undo his villainy, but he arrives too late. Other than its hasty beginning and end, Ibsen's love intrigue seems to have no connection with his romance, and Meyer is rightly impatient with the notion that Ibsen's comment refers to his sub-plot: "Surely it is obvious that it is the tragic and nihilistic mood of the play which stemmed from the unhappiness of that summer" (M 117).

17 Koht believes that Lady Inger's affair recalls Ibsen's with Rikke Holst and that Ibsen used "for special effect, a female to portray himself" (K 85). Inger "wanted to avenge her nation's honor, but, weak as any woman, she fell in love, with a man from the enemy's side" (85). But Sten Sture was "well disposed toward [Lady Inger's] party" (329), and Inger feels not guilt but joy at having loved him. Nothing in her story parallels Ibsen's; on the contrary, the situations are opposite, for Inger followed her heart in spite of the difficulties she knew would follow.

18 A similar conflict takes place in plays of the *Goethezeit*, e.g., Goethe's *The Natural Daughter*, Schiller's *The Maid of Orleans* and *Maria Stuart*, and Kleist's *Penthesilea* and *Kate of Heilbronn*. But in the German plays, the female hero who seeks power must be legitimized by the patriarchy. See Julie D. Prandi, *Spirited Women Heroes: Major Female Characters in the Dramas of Goethe, Schiller and Kleist* (New York: Lang, 1983).

19 The pattern also structures the eight-page *Norma, or a Politician's Love*, a parody Ibsen wrote in 1851 after seeing Bellini's opera in Oslo. The hero betrays the strong Norma, the "Government Opposition," for the passive Adalgisa, the conservative "Government," and when the spirited Norma attempts to kill him, he is transformed on the spot by the prime minister into a "demi-god, or – as people express it today – into a Cabinet Minister" (*OI* 1:198).

20 Here sentimental, the curtain sunrise will be put to brilliantly mordant use in the ending of *Ghosts*.

21 The woman-centered triangle also figures in sub-plots of *A Doll House* (Kristine Linde, her husband, and Krogstad), *Hedda Gabler* (Thea Elvsted, her husband, and Løvborg), and *Brand* (Brand's mother, her husband, and the man she rejected).

3 LOVE AND MARRIAGE

1 *Brev fra [Letters of] Magdalene Thoresen, 1855–1901*, ed. Julius Clausen and P. Fr. Rist (Copenhagen: Gyldendal, 1919) 17–18.

2 Magdalene Kragh had another trial to face. Shortly after she arrived in Norway, in the autumn of 1842, she discovered that she was pregnant. In March, Pastor Thoresen took her to Oslo, where in June of 1843 she gave birth to a son whom the pastor placed in an orphanage, his "parents unknown." Naturally, this event was kept quiet. Later, Thomsen took the boy.

3 *My Grandmother's Story* is based on their relation. In 1858, the married, twenty-six-year-old Bjørnson succeeded Ibsen at the Bergen theatre and the widowed, thirty-nine-year-old Magdalene Thoresen fell in love with him. In *My Grandmother's Story*, the widowed, thirty-eight-year-old grandmother falls passionately in love with a younger, married man. Magdalene described her book as "the closest to my heart of everything I have written"; Bjørnson, furious and scandalized, called it "utterly disgusting" (Engelstad, *History* 1:112).

4 Georg Brandes, *Levned [A Life]* (Copenhagen: Gyldendal, 1905) 1:149. 3 vols.

5 John Paulsen, a writer who thought of himself as Ibsen's "Boswell," remarked in *Samliv med Ibsen [Living with Ibsen]*, one of Ibsen's biographers' important sources, that there was something of Magdalene Thoresen in Margit of *The Feast at Solhoug* (P 2:52). McFarlane, maintaining that the "only awkward thing is the chronology" (*OI* 1:23), makes the intriguing speculation that Margit may be based on Magdalene, and Signe on Suzannah, that Ibsen may have been intimately acquainted with his colleague, and that "one cannot be wholly sure that Ibsen and Suzannah had not met before" the day that Ibsen's biographers ascribe (23). But chronology is not the only stumbling block in identifying Magdalene with Margit and Suzannah with Signe; it is true that Magdalene was passionate, but it seems improbable that the intellectual, intrepid Suzannah could have been the model for a "wholly naive" woman. It is also unlikely that Suzannah, who was a formative influence for the strong woman Hjørdis, of *Vikings*, could earlier have been the model for the weak woman Signe of *Feast*. Moreover, Ibsen noted in the preface to *Feast* that when he abandoned *Vikings*, he kept its women characters, and thus the Margit/Signe pairing is something he had in mind some time *before* he conceived of *Feast*. Ibsen's comment that "all sorts of things intervened, mostly of a personal nature" (*OI* 1:373), to make him put aside *Vikings* to write *Feast* would seem to have nothing to do with women; there is no evidence that he had a romantic relation with any woman between the break up with Rikke Holst and the meeting with Suzannah Thoresen.

6   *The Correspondence of Henrik Ibsen*, trans. Mary Morison (1905; New York: Haskell House, 1970) 58.

7   John Paulsen either naively or disingenuously took the Ibsen household's frugality and the couple's arguments as signs of Suzannah's martyrdom, and wrote a *roman à clef*, *The Family Pehrsen*, in which the vain, domineering, husband, burdened by a drunken father, living off his friends and taking to the bottle himself, is helped through his crisis by his martyred wife, a great literary buff. The melodramatic novel helped to cause the widespread belief that the Ibsens' marriage was unhappy. Paulsen, whom the Ibsens received generously and considered a friend, strangely thought he could write such a novel with impunity. Ibsen sent him a postcard with a one-word message – "Scoundrel!" – and his signature. They never saw each other again.

8   *Henrik Ibsen paa [on] Ischia, og [and] "Fra Piazza del Popolo"* (Gyldendal: Christiania, 1907) 243–44.

9   Ibsen encountered many examples of brave, combative women in the sagas. In *The Saga of Gisli*, Gisli's wife Aud attacks her husband's enemy Eyjolf, who tries to bribe her with a purse of silver, by swinging the purse at his nose "so that the blood spurts out all over him" (51); when Gisli makes his last, gallant stand, Aud fights Eyjolf off with a club. "I knew long ago that I was well-wived, but I did not know until now how well," the appreciative Gisli responds (56). In *The Saga of Eric the Red*, "Aud the Deep-Minded" fits out a raiding ship with twenty-three men under her command; in the same saga, the pregnant Freydis taunts Karlsefni and his men, who run away from the redoubtable Skrælings, and faces the Skrælings alone; pulling her breasts out of her dress, she slaps her sword against them and declares: "I could put up a better fight than any of you!" (152), which she then proceeds to prove. (Jones, trans., *Eric the Red and Other Icelandic Sagas*).

10 Hallgerd's character has been the subject of much controversy; in a well-known essay, the great Norwegian critic Hans E. Kinck argued that Hallgerd's trouble-making results not from a capricious "female nature," as the saga writer seems to indicate, but from her disgust with her peace-loving husband, that only a union with a great warrior could fulfill her heart, and that the saga writer failed to understand her. ("Et Par Ting Om Ættesagaen. Skikkelser den Ikke Forsto" ["Notes on the Family Sagas. Misunderstood Characters"], *Sagaenes Ånd og Skikkelser* [*The Spirit and the People of the Sagas*] [1916; Oslo: Aschehoug, 1951] 9–46). Kinck's analysis of Hallgerd is strikingly descriptive of Ibsen's Hjørdis, who was partially inspired by her; Kinck could have bolstered his own reading by referring to Ibsen's.

11 *Ibsen* (New York: Collier, 1977) 46.

12 For the place of erotic love in the Sentimental and Romantic traditions, see Hagstrum, *Sex and Sensibility* 186–246.

13 Two minor, type characters illustrate satirically Falk's thesis that marriage destroys both love and fine ambitions; Lind, who dreamed of serving emigrants as a minister in America, settles for the post of schoolteacher once he becomes engaged, and Styver, formerly a prolific versifier, explains that his "inspiration dried up all at once" (102) when he married. But Ibsen's most severe satire is reserved, characteristically, for the clergy. Pastor Straamann ("Strawman"), a radical poet, married in defiance of poverty and planned to live happily in an artist's garret; now the would-be writer is a country parson and his muse a worn-down mother of twelve.

14 *The Correspondence of Henrik Ibsen,* trans. Mary Morison (1905; New York: Haskell House, 1970) 58.

15 As Brian Downs points out, the source for Svanhild's decision is almost certainly Kierkegaard (*Six Plays* 33). In both "The Seducer's Diary" (1843) and "Repetition, An Essay in Experimental Psychology" (1843), Kierkegaard had argued that when two people decide that they are meant for each other, it is time to separate; to possess the beloved is to destroy both love and creativity. Ibsen protested when this parallel to *Love's Comedy* was pointed out, maintaining that he had read little of Kierkegaard; this may be so, but Ibsen was certainly familiar with Kierkegaard's ideas, which were a burning topic of the day. How much Ibsen was indebted to Kierkegaard remains problematic.

16 Born in Bergen, Holberg became a professor of metaphysics (and later, of history and geography) at the University of Copenhagen.

17 "Watch your mouth, Espen!" says the maid in *Jean de France.* "The time will come when society will consider brains more important than sex and ability greater than name. When our intellects are weighed I shall be elevated to the position of magistrate and you won't be any higher than a pancake!" (*Jeppe of the Hill and Other Comedies* 74).

18 *Seven One-Act Plays by Holberg,* trans. Henry Alexander (Princeton University Press, 1950) 205.

19 The original Latin text, *Nicolai Klimii iter subterraneum,* appeared anonymously in Leipzig because Holberg's Copenhagen publisher wanted to avoid the obligatory Danish censorship. The book was quickly translated into Danish, German, Dutch, English, and French, and, before the end of the century, into Russian and Hungarian. It was one of the most scandalous texts of the European enlightenment.

20 *Ibsen's Poems,* trans. John Northam (Oslo: Norwegian University Press, 1986) 118.

21 For Legouvé and his influence on Camilla Collett, see Gravier, *D'Ibsen à Sigrid Undset* 69–71.

22 *Amtmandens Døtre* has been called in English "*The Sheriff's Daughters*" and, more commonly, "*The Governor's Daughters.*" Both "sheriff" and

"governor" are inexact titles for the Norwegian official in question, for which there is no British or American equivalent. Collett's groundbreaking novel has only recently been translated into English: *The District Governor's Daughters*, trans. Kirsten Seaver (Norwich: Norvik Press, 1992).

23 See Agerholt, *History* 9–15.

24 *The District Governor's Daughters'* moral idealism and outpouring of feeling reflect its affinities with the Sentimental novel. The tone of *Love's Comedy*, although written only eight years later, is light years away from that of Collett's novel; its irony is the voice of modernism.

25 This is Falk's comment in the brief prose draft *Svanhild* (1860) that Ibsen completed and rewrote in verse as *Love's Comedy* two years later.

4 LOVE AND THE KINGDOM

1 Koht, 160–62; Bjørn Hemmer, *Brand; Kongsemnerne [The Pretenders]; Peer Gynt* (Oslo: Universitetsforlaget, 1972); Brian Johnston, *To the Third Empire: Ibsen's Early Drama* (Minneapolis: University of Minnesota Press, 1980).

2 Ibsen's juxtaposition of male and female worlds is similar to Shakespeare's in *The Comedy of Errors, Henry VIII*, and *Othello*; see Carole McKewin, "Counsels of Gall and Grace: Intimate Conversations between Women in Shakespeare's Plays," *The Woman's Part: Feminist Criticism of Shakespeare*, ed. Carolyn Swift Lenz, Gayle Green, Carol Thomas Neely (Urbana: University of Illinois Press, 1980) 117–32.

3 The phrase is Adrienne Rich's in "The Kingdom of the Fathers," *Of Woman Born* 69.

4 Koht quotes Ingebjørg's exit line as the "one theme" which governs the women of *The Pretenders*: "To love, to sacrifice all, and to be forgotten – that is a woman's story" (162). But Skule's discarded mistress is characterizing her own life; when Ibsen revised the play, he changed "a woman's story" to "my story." In his first essay on Ibsen, Brandes had objected to Ibsen's occasional habit of putting in his characters' mouths pronouncements that bordered on sententiousness and used Ingebjørg's line as an example (B 29–30). Ibsen wrote to Brandes that he had been "completely right" (*H* 16:249).

5 *Shakespeare and the Nature of Women* (London: Macmillan, 1975) 294.

6 "*The Pretenders* – Historical Vision or Psychological Tragedy?" Kittang notes the importance of the play's women characters and the necessity of a study analyzing their function in the play's representation of the Christian–romantic myth (86). Since the women represent a value superior to the highest value encoded in the myth – the unification of Norway – they function outside, rather than within, the myth's ideology.

7 Ibsen said that his protagonist was inspired by Skien's pastor Lammers, the fanatical preacher who won Marichen and Hedvig Ibsen's allegiance, but later denied it; this may have been because Lammers confessed his wrongs to receive a state pension and ended his days as a painter of altar pictures. Ibsen also said that his friends Christopher and Thea Bruun, brother and sister, influenced his portraits of Brand and Agnes. Christopher was a devout but free-thinking radical minister who refused a pastorate because of his conviction that the state church was corrupt. Thea Bruun's influence on Agnes probably lay in her selflessness; dying of tuberculosis, she nursed her brother, terminally ill with the same disease. She was engaged to Ibsen's summer roommate, Finnish sculptor Walter Runeburg, and modelled for his statue "Resurrection," which Ibsen may have remembered later in Irene's modelling for Rubek's sculpture "Resurrection Day" in *When We Dead Awaken.*

8 *Brand* may owe even more to Kierkegaard than *Love's Comedy.* Disdain for institutionalized Christianity and the notions of dichotomous moral choice and of the supremacy of the will are such essentials of Kierkegaard's philosophy that Brandes' first response to *Brand* was that Ibsen was attempting to be Kierkegaard's poet (B 21).

9 La Chesnais notes that Ibsen based Gerd on a mentally deficient peasant girl called Ingeborg Hellsylt, whom he had encountered on a folklore gathering expedition. She escaped from her parents' farm to run in the mountains and had the habit of pelting with rocks people who displeased her. La Chesnais comments that of all Ibsen's characters, Gerd is perhaps the one most "copied after nature" (*Œuvres* 7:29).

10 Inga-Stina Ewbank comments that Brand's language here "is nothing so much as an anticipation of the mixture of unctuousness and chauvinism in the speeches of a Rørlund [of *Pillars of Society*]. One more twist, and his rhetoric would be clearly satirical in purpose" ("Ibsen on the English Stage" 44). I find Ibsen's rhetoric as strong here as in any speech he gave to his later male chauvinists; since Brand has a theological basis for his sexism, his theory seems doubly pernicious.

11 Ibsen was familiar with the conventional Christian justification for evil through the sermons of his childhood. And in Grimstad, Voltaire was one of his favorite authors.

12 See the discussion in Ewbank ("Ibsen on the English Stage"), who defends Ibsen by pointing to the power of the original text's hammering compound nouns unavailable to the English translator.

13 I have quoted Ibsen's original Latin phrase and not *The Oxford Ibsen*'s translation "God is Love!", which obscures the meaning.

14 *Sol*, sun, and *vei*, way; Henri Logemann suggests in his fascinating study of the language and sources of *Peer Gynt* that the second

syllable of Solveig's name may also relate to the Old Norse *veig*, woman (*Commentary* 47).

15 The affection between Aase and Peer led Georg Groddeck to claim that their relation is literature's best example of the psychoanalytic theory of damaging mother/son attachment (*"Peer Gynt,"* Fjelde, *Ibsen: A Collection* 64). But to maintain that "for Aase, Peer is always the little boy" (64) is to deny Aase's awareness that her son is sexually attractive and her insistence that he marry. Groddeck's claim that mother and son live in a play-world ignores Aase's attempt to give Peer socially mobile ambitions: "Ah, my Peer, a girl with land / Clear property, an heiress!" (13). And far from being cripplingly attached to his mother, Peer is an inveterate womanizer. Aase and Peer love each other, but they live in frequent conflict, and it is Ibsen's witty rendering of this tension-ridden relation that makes his portrait of a mother and her late adolescent son masterful.

16 This detail and other parallels to *Faust* are the subject of A.L. Andrews' "Ibsen's *Peer Gynt* and Goethe's *Faust,*" *JEGP* 13 (1914): 238–46.

17 Seter girls spent the summer months guarding cattle in isolated mountain meadows, called "seters," and thus constitute a ready-made category of "women without men."

18 This prophecy echoes that of *Macbeth*'s witches. *Peer Gynt* is shot through with Shakespearean echoes. Fjelde remarks that "Ibsen's series of pointed references to Shakespeare, Molière, Holberg, and Goethe may be taken both as an *hommage* to his great predecessors, their influence and inspiration, and as a discreet bid to be considered in their company" (*Peer Gynt* 221).

19 For a fuller discussion of the hulder, see my discussion of *St. John's Night* in chapter 2.

20 *Norske Eventyr* [*Norwegian Fairy Tales*], collected and published by P.C. Ashbjørnsen and Jørgen Moe over a thirty-year span (1841–71), was proof of the greatness of the Norwegian folk imagination during the long years of Danish domination, and powerfully affected both Norwegian national self-respect and Norwegian literature and art. Ibsen was inspired by the brief tale of Peer Gynt to write *Peer Gynt*, and he found in other fairy tales the Great Boyg, The Woman in Green, Soria-Moria Castle, and Gudbrand Glesne's ride.

21 This may be the best of Fjelde's successes in keeping the rhyme, the sense, and the wit of Ibsen's original text.

22 Peer's refusal of Solveig's sexuality anticipates Freud's analysis of a type of male sexual failure in the essay "On the Universal Tendency to Debasement in the Sphere of Love": "Where they love they do not desire and where they desire they cannot love. They seek objects which they do not need to love, in order to keep their sensuality away from the objects they love" (183).

23 Much ink has been spilled over whether the error in Goethe's famous line is Ibsen's or Peer's. In the draft manuscript, Ibsen wrote what seems to be "Das evig weibliche ziet uns herann" with an evident wavering in spelling in *ziet* and with the first syllable of *herann* crossed out (*OI* 3:477). Logemann argues that the wavering in spelling proves that the misquotation was the result of Ibsen's faulty memory (*Commentary* 220). Ibsen's son was sure that his father would not have misquoted Goethe except on purpose, and wrote to Logemann to tell him so. I agree with Sigurd Ibsen. Ibsen's German was good, Goethe was one of his adored authors, and he and Suzannah were rereading *Faust* aloud while he was writing *Peer Gynt*. What may have happened is that when Ibsen checked his draft quotation against the German master's line, he added the missing *h* to the verb and was then inspired to substitute *an* for *hinan*.

24 I have departed from Fjelde's version – "To the boy inside you're mother and nurse" (208) – and have translated the line literally.

25 I have again departed from Fjelde's version – "Oh, hide me, hide me within!" (209) – because the phrase *der inne*, "there inside," carefully repeats the preceding "To the boy inside, you are the mother." *Inne* refers to Solveig's lap as well as to her heart. Fjelde's translation remains the closest to the original text, whose physicality has bothered English translators; Meyer has "O hide me in your love! Hide me! Hide me!" (*Peer Gynt* [Garden City: Doubleday, 1963] 63).

26 Ronald Popperwell, "Ibsen's Female Characters," *Scandinavica* 19 (1980): 6. F.L. Lucas finds the following lesson in Ibsen's portrait of the ideal woman: "Pretty women wither; clever women can grow cold, harsh, odious – crowing hens; but in loving goodness women can sometimes be supreme. That is the kind to marry" (*The Drama of Ibsen and Strindberg* [New York: Macmillan, 1962] 103). Georg Groddeck analyzes: "Woman's morality is a wonderful thing . . . Peer ranges the whole world about, and at home there waits one who is at the same time mother, wife, and woman. That is the essence of life, except that man is not always fortunate in finding a Solveig to be both wife and mother to him" ("Peer Gynt," Fjelde, *Ibsen: A Collection* 65–66). A curious statement for a psychoanalyst, implying, as it does, that the Oedipal relation is the best, the claim that finding a mother/wife/woman is the "essence of life" for the normative "man" not only excludes woman from knowing "the essence of life," but also from knowing that she represents it, for she "can know nothing, being woman" (70). For Horst Bien, Solveig's generosity makes her the exemplary woman in a Marxist society (*"Peer Gynt* – i dag" [*"Peer Gynt* – Today"], *Contemporary Approaches to Ibsen* 3 [1977]:91–98). Åse Lervik comments, "Everything Solveig does, she does for her relation with a man. If this represents the future's type of woman in a new, classless society, it also recalls perfectly what we call in Norwegian

making coffee for the revolution" ("Mellom Furia og Solveig" ["Between Furia and Solveig"] 77).

27 Ibsen said several times that *Emperor and Galilean* was his most important work, a judgment that not even the play's greatest admirers would agree with. Although Part One contains some successful scenes, the play as a whole is long-winded and repetitive, suffering from what McFarlane calls its "cloudy philosophy" (*OI* 4:3). The play also contains a good bit of unsuccessful "mysticism" that led Archer to compare the play to a Victorian melodrama *The Sign of the Cross* and tempts a modern reader to compare it to a Hollywood Biblical epic. For a good discussion of this question, see Brian Johnston, *To the Third Empire: Ibsen's Early Drama* (Minneapolis: University of Minnesota Press, 1980) 264–71.

5 THE POETRY OF FEMINISM

1 "The Fifty-First Anniversary," *Hudson Review* 10 (1957) 416.

2 *Ibsen's Drama: Author to Audience* (Minneapolis: University of Minnesota Press, 1979) vii. In the Modern Language Association's *Approaches to Teaching "A Doll House,"* editor Yvonne Shafer speaks disparagingly of "reductionist views of [*A Doll House*] as a feminist drama" (New York: 1985) 32.

3 (New York: Random, 1979) 179.

4 *The Making of Modern Drama* (New York: Farrar, 1972) 65.

5 *The Theatre of Revolt* (New York: Little, Brown, 1962) 105.

6 Even Errol Durbach, in his sympathetic discussion of Nora in A Doll's House: *Ibsen's Myth of Transformation* (Boston: Twayne, 1991), disparages feminist interpretations of the play as "propaganda by the militant sisterhood" (92), a contention contradicted by Durbach's own feminist reading: "Nora spearheads a cultural revolution in women's sensibility by refusing to accept the traditional view that women hold of themselves, which is absorbed through a process of insidious osmosis from the standard archetypes devised by men" (122). One critic who does not join the backlash is David Thomas in his survey *Henrik Ibsen* (New York: Grove, 1983): *A Doll House* "was intended to be a profoundly revolutionary play, deepening the critique of patriarchal attitudes [Ibsen] had initiated in *Pillars of Society*" (73).

7 (New York: Random, 1915) 117.

8 The changed version was a failure; later, Hedwig Neimann-Raabe, the first German Nora, played the original ending with great success.

9 The two performances of *A Child Wife* were the first Ibsen performances in English in America. The text, by schoolmaster William M. Lawrence, was never published and is now lost. See Einar Haugen, "Ibsen in America: A Forgotten Performance and an Unpublished Letter," *JEGP* 33 (1934): 396–420.

10 "The Coming of Ibsen," in *The 1880's*, ed. Walter de la Mare (Cambridge University Press, 1930) 167–68.

11 William Archer, "The Mausoleum of Ibsen," *Fortnightly Review* 54, n.s. (1893) 78.

12 Toshihiko Sato, "Ibsen's Drama and the Japanese Bluestockings," *Edda* 81 (1981) 292.

13 Frederick and Lisa-Lone Marker, "The First Nora: Notes on the World Premiere of *A Doll House*," *Contemporary Approaches to Ibsen* 2 (1971): 89.

14 For a discussion of the ideologies at work in the reception of *A Doll House* from Ibsen's day to ours, see my "The Uses of Interpretation: the Reception of Ibsen's *A Doll House*," *Reception Studies*, ed. Rien T. Segers (Bern: Peter Lang, 1993): 173–82.

15 See, for example, Marvin Rosenberg, "Ibsen versus Ibsen or: Two Versions of *A Doll House*," *Modern Drama* 12 (1969): 187–96.

16 "Nora," *Edda* 46 (1946): 13–28.

17 "The Ibsen Question," *Fortnightly Review* 55 (1891) 732.

18 "The Will and Testament of Ibsen," *Partisan Review* 23 (1956) 80.

19 "Ibsen and the Actors," *Ibsen and the Theatre*, ed. Durbach, 130. In a later essay, Sprinchorn maintains that the critique of Strindberg, who "saw that Nora was an hysterical type, easily going to extremes," remains "the most penetrating examination of *A Doll House*" ("Ibsen, Strindberg, and the New Woman," *The Play and Its Critics: Essays for Eric Bentley*, ed. Michael Bertin [New York: University Press of America, 1986] 54).

20 "Recasting *A Doll House*: Narcissism As Character Motivation in Ibsen's Play," *Comparative Drama* 20 (1986) 158. Even Nora's sweet tooth is evidence of her unworthiness, as we see her, in June Schlueter's description, "surreptitiously devouring the forbidden [by her husband] macaroons"; she even "brazenly offers Rank some macaroons" and then lies in her denial that the macaroons are hers. Eating macaroons in secret may suggest that "Nora is deceitful and manipulative from the start" and that her exit thus "reflects only a petulant woman's irresponsibility" ("How to Get Into *A Doll House*," *Approaches to Teaching Ibsen's* A Doll House," ed. Shafer, 64–65). Secret macaroon eating seems an unlikely moral issue; more importantly, it is through this household convention that Ibsen dramatizes the *modus vivendi* of the Helmer marriage, in which Nora is expected to practice cookie-jar trickeries in the couple game between the strong, wise husband and his weak, foolish wife.

21 Sprinchorn claims that Torvald has been given short shrift on the stage: "writing at a time when the sympathies of the audience would lie mainly with the husband," Ibsen "had to darken the character of Torvald" to give Nora "a fighting chance" ("Actors" 121). Sprinchorn suggests that our attitude toward the play would change

dramatically "if we saw the latest movie idol" as Torvald so that his qualities of "elegance and charm" could stand up against Nora (120); he makes much of the fact that Ibsen wanted Gustaf Fredricksen, a reigning matinee idol, to play Torvald in the first Swedish production. It is true that Mel Gibson would make a good Torvald, but elegance and charm hardly provide opposition to Nora's argument. While Torvald's personal qualities may explain how Nora could have fallen in love with him, they are irrelevant to her accusation that he has treated her as his plaything. And women do, after all, fall out of love with charming men every day.

22　*Ibsen: The Open Vision* (London: Athlone, 1982) 85.

23　Morris Freedman, *The Moral Impulse: Modern Drama from Ibsen to the Present* (Carbondale: Southern Illinois University Press, 1967) 4.

24　Richard Pearce, "The Limits of Realism," *College English* 31 (1970) 337.

25　"*A Doll House* Revisited," *Modern Drama* 27 (1984) 593. Quigley notes that one of the "major ironies of the play is Nora's somewhat inconsistent choice of staying her first night 'alone' with Mrs. Linde" (593). Where would Quigley have Nora sleep? In the street? Blaming the victim, Quigley writes: "Nora's prime concern is apparently to please rather than to reach agreement and understanding. And that determination to please seems designed, at least in part, to get her what she wants without the need for agreement and understanding . . . It would then be the daughters of Eve who, by their characteristic behavior, mould the sons of Adam" (591–92). Quigley maintains that Nora should learn to see the good things as well as the bad in the doll house and concludes "the play is not advocating as a solution Nora's rejection of what society has to offer" (601). One would like to know what Quigley thinks Nora should have learned to like in her doll house and what society had to offer a woman in 1879.

26　*Selected Plays*, trans. Evert Sprinchorn (Minneapolis: University of Minnesota Press, 1986) 1:208. 2 vols. This is the only English version I have been able to find that does not purge the preface of its most misogynist passage, in which women are declared to be a "stunted form of human being" compared to "man, the lord of creation, the creator of culture" (208).

27　*Norsk Litteraturantologi*, ed. Ronald G. Popperwell and Torbjørn Støverud (London: Modern Humanities Research Association, 1976). 2 vols. I am grateful to Bjørn Hemmer for calling my attention to this recent rewriting of Ibsen's ending.

28　The reason why it is never felt necessary to make the point that women are not excluded from the significance claimed, say, for Peer Gynt in his search for the self is that men, *ipso facto*, are considered suitable universal figures; the best explanation for this phenomenon remains Simone de Beauvoir's groundbreaking analysis of woman as "the other" in *The Second Sex*.

29 *Unpopular Opinions: Twenty-One Essays* (New York: Harcourt, 1947) 142.

30 "Introduction," *Eight Plays by Henrik Ibsen*, trans. Le Gallienne (New York: Modern Library, 1982) xiv.

31 *On Deconstruction: Theory and Criticism After Structuralism* (Ithaca: Cornell University Press, 1982) 86.

32 See, for example, Chamberlain, *The Open Vision* 96–98.

33 Ibsen despised utilitarianism and thus disliked Mill on principle. He once wrote to Brandes that he could not understand why Brandes had taken the time to translate *Utilitarianism* into Danish. Its "sagelike philistinism" (*LS* 137) reminded him of Cicero (Ibsen's "bête noire") and Seneca.

34 During the celebrations in Stockholm, Ibsen received young women in his hotel room, gave them photographs of himself, told them that they reminded him of his Hilda of *The Master Builder*, and kissed them; for these and other details, see M 773–74. Ibsen was especially taken with one of the women in a troupe of folk dancers, twenty-six-year-old Rosa Fitinghof. He wrote her a few brief, nostalgic letters afterwards from Oslo, where he saw her a second and last time the following year (along with her mother), and kept her letters to him in his desk drawer. In 1988, the important Oslo newspaper *Aftenposten* announced with great fanfare the discovery of Rosa's relation with Ibsen in an article called "She Was the Evening Sun of his Life" ["Hun var kveldssolen i hans liv"] (Dec. 24). The article contains nothing not previously available in the Ibsen biographies.

35 Laura Marholm, "Die Frau in der skandinavischen Dichtung: Der Noratypus," *Freie Bühne für modernes Leben* 1 (1890): 168–71; Ricciotto Canudo, "La représentation féministe et sociale d'Ibsen," *La Grande Revue* 38 (1906): 561–72; Louie Bennett, "Ibsen as a Pioneer of the Woman Movement," *Westminster Review* 173 (1910): 278–85.

36 Lou-Andréas Salomé, *Henrik Ibsens Frauengestalten nach seinen sechs Familiendramen* (Jena: Diederichs, 1892); Alla Nazimova, "Ibsen's Women," *Independent* 63 (1907): 909–14; Georg Brandes, *Henrik Ibsen and Bjørnstjerne Bjørnson*, trans. Jesse Muir, rev. William Archer (London: Heinemann, 1899). Strindberg's fulminations against the feminism of *A Doll House* are well known. In the short story "A Doll House," a captain's wife reads *A Doll House*, loaned to her by a feminist friend, and decides to leave her husband. The captain wins her back through flirting with the perfidious feminist. In the play *Comrades*, Axel and Bertha, both painters, break up when Bertha's painting is accepted by the salon and Axel's refused; Strindberg dresses the demasculinized Axel in women's clothes. In *A Madman's*

Defense, an autobiographical novel, Strindberg refers to liberated women as "fools" and "half-women" (trans. Ellie Schleussner, rev. Evert Sprinchorn [Garden City: Doubleday, 1967] 251, 258).

37 *The New Spirit* (New York: Modern Library, [1890]) 9.

38 As Stanley Weintraub has shown, Ibsen was not the first writer to use the woman/doll metaphor. Dickens' Bella Rokesmith of *Our Mutual Friend* complains to her husband: "I want to be something so much worthier than the doll in the doll's house." And here is Shaw's Marian in *The Irrational Knot:* "I want to be a wife and not a fragile ornament kept in a glass case. [My husband] would as soon think of submitting any project of his to the judgment of a doll as to mine." ("Ibsen's 'Doll House' Metaphor Foreshadowed in Victorian Fiction," *Nineteenth-Century Fiction* 13 [1958]: 67–69).

39 Meyer notes that Collett and Ibsen "had many arguments about marriage and other female problems" (M 434).

40 "New Norwegian," one of Norway's two official languages, is the product of the language reformers' efforts to create a written language based on various dialects of the Norwegian "landsmaal" as opposed to the heavily Danish "riksmaal."

41 For the characteristics of the New Woman, see Gail Cunningham, *The New Woman and the Victorian Novel* (New York: Macmillan, 1978).

42 Letter to me, April 23, 1989.

43 Over ten years after *A Doll House* appeared, Brandes repeated in the press Archer's erroneous remark that Nora's original had borrowed the money to decorate her house. Widely circulated, Brandes' comment caused Laura Kieler great distress. She later described to Kinck an emotional, four-hour meeting between herself and Ibsen in which she begged him to deny Brandes' assertion; although Ibsen was moved to tears, he refused. Meyer terms Ibsen's refusal "cowardly and hypocritical"(M 635); at the same time, he suspects that the story of the tearful interview may be "the confused and colored fantasy of an old lady whose life had been a protracted tragedy" (M 680). While it is true that Kieler suffered greatly in her personal life, she enjoyed a long and productive career as an author. Her books went through many editions and were translated into foreign languages, and she was especially honored in Denmark for her writing on the Schleswig-Holstein question. Surely her life cannot be properly described as a "protracted tragedy." Nor is there any reason to question the account she gave in old age of her emotional interview. Ibsen was very attached to his "skylark" and would be naturally upset by her entreaties. As for Ibsen's cowardice, it is notoriously true that he was braver in print than in life.

44 See especially Joan Kelly's essential essay, "The Doubled Vision of Feminist Theory," *Women, History and Theory* 51–64.

45 *Sesame and Lilies* (Chicago: Homewood, 1902) 143–44.

46 *Paradise Lost* IV: 636–38; *John Milton: Complete Poems and Major Prose,* ed. Merritt Hughes (New York: Odyssey, 1957) 293.

47 Chevrel's excellent short monograph is a welcome exception to the ruling backlash; for Chevrel, the play is both feminist and literature.

48 *Seduction and Betrayal: Women and Literature* (New York: Vintage, 1975) 48–49.

49 The English translation of Badinter's *L'Amour en plus* (Paris: Flammarion, 1980; New York: Macmillan, 1981).

6 MRS ALVING'S GHOSTS

1 "Ibsen and Shakespeare as Dramatic Artists," *Edda* 56 (1956) 371.

2 Eric Bentley: "When she tells Oswald – at the end – that she shared the blame, because, in her prudishness, her fear of sexuality, she had not welcomed Alving's joy of life, she is also telling herself" ("Henrik Ibsen: A Personal Statement," *Ibsen: A Collection,* ed. Fjelde, 13). Derek Russell Davis: ". . . she could not accept his sexuality, for reasons which are not known . . . She was not emancipated in her attitudes toward marriage" ("A Reappraisal of Ibsen's *Ghosts,*" *Henrik Ibsen: A Critical Anthology,* ed. McFarlane, 377). Davis argues that Oswald's condition is not syphilis but schizophrenia, a result of his mother's smothering love. Davis is alone in his bizarre diagnosis, but in insisting on Mrs. Alving's sexual failure, he is typical of her other detractors. Daniel Haakonsen: "[Mrs. Alving] clearly sees that, without realizing it, she herself had been instrumental in triggering the calamities in her husband's life" ("'The Play-within-the-Play' in Ibsen's Realistic Dramas," *Contemporary Approaches to Ibsen* 2 [1970–71] 115). Brian Johnston: "Alving's law – *livsgleden* [joy of life] – inevitably offends the laws of those pieties for which Helene stands." Mrs. Alving's "very obvious inadequate sexuality" represents an "inadequacy destructive of a whole cultural tradition in the West" (*The Ibsen Cycle: the Design of the Plays from 'Pillars of Society' to 'When We Dead Awaken'* [Boston: Hall, 1975] 100; 172–73). Evert Sprinchorn: "Mrs. Alving has repressed the sexual side of her nature. It is not until she hears Oswald's warm espousal of the joy of life that she realizes how blind she has been" ("Science and Poetry in *Ghosts:* A Study in Ibsen's Craftsmanship," *Scandinavian Studies* 51 [1979]: 363). Even Shaw, who reads *Ghosts* as an attack on society's ideals and not on Mrs. Alving, believes in her "injustice to the unfortunate father" (*Quintessence* 89).

3 Sverre Arestad, in "Ibsen's Concept of Tragedy," also views *Ghosts* as a thesis play, written to prove that "a marriage of convenience is an evil tyranny" (*PMLA* 74 [1959] 290). Perhaps the classic reading of *Ghosts* as failed tragedy is Joseph Wood Krutch's, in which the play is named as an example of the modern theatre's denial of human

nobility and its consequent failure to produce tragedy ("The Tragic Fallacy," *Atlantic* 142 [1928] 608).

4 Fergusson also mistakenly notes that "Captain Alving has just died . . . and his wife is straightening out the estate" (149); Alving died ten years ago.

5 The phrase comes from the last stanza of Joyce's poem "Epilogue to Ibsen's *Ghosts*," whose speaker is the ghost of Captain Alving: "Nay, more, were I not all I was, / Weak, wanton, waster out and out, / There would have been no world's applause, / And damn all to write home about" (*The Critical Writings of James Joyce*, ed. Ellsworth Mason and Richard Ellmann [New York: Viking, 1964] 273).

6 In Ibsen's day, it was believed that syphilis could be transmitted by smoking an infected pipe; whether Ibsen meant us to think that Oswald caught the disease in this fashion is a point of contention. For an interesting discussion of this point, see Sprinchorn, "Science" 366, note 4.

7 Manders has a defender in Charles Leland, who maintains that in living by his principles, the pastor is obeying what for him is religious truth; rejecting the woman he loves, refusing to read certain books, and deferring to Divine Providence in not insuring the orphanage are not necessarily actions to be criticized ("In Defense of Pastor Manders," *Modern Drama* 21 [1978]: 405–20). This analysis requires us to accept the notion that Ibsen could regard with equanimity or even approval someone who lived by principles he himself ridiculed.

8 *Selected Plays*, trans. Evert Sprinchorn (Minneapolis: University of Minnesota Press, 1986) 1:174, 2 vols. Strindberg hated what he perceived as Ibsen's monstrous championing of women, but even in his most anti-Ibsen phase, he always admired *Ghosts*; he appreciated its general radicalism, its importance as a landmark in the struggle of modern drama to be taken seriously, and, especially, its attack on the sacrosanctity of marriage.

9 "Director's Diary, 1905: The MAT Production of Ibsen's *Ghosts*," trans. Elizabeth Reynolds Hapgood, *Tulane Drama Review* 9 (1964) 26, 36. One of the legendary performances of the modern theatre was the great Swedish actor/director August Lindberg's Oswald. William Archer, who was lucky enough to be in Oslo for the Norwegian premiere on October 17, 1883, describes Lindberg in a letter: "You couldn't look at him without seeing that he was more than a smule bedævert indvendig [slightly damaged inside] . . . a very pale face, and those blinking, uneven, sort of lysræd [light-shy] eyes one so often sees in broken-down debauchees [sic], one or other of the eyebrows having a tendency to rise now and then" ("Ibseniana," *Edda* 31 [1931] 458). *Ghosts* shows an interesting *fin de siècle* side of Ibsen's genius, insufficiently appreciated except by one of his greatest admirers, Edvard Munch, who saw a kindred soul in painter Oswald, ravaged by disease and longing for the sun.

10 We now know, of course, that congenital syphilis cannot be inherited from the male parent. Neither did Bohemia have a seacoast. It was not until the early years of the twentieth century that physicians were able to establish with any certainty the etiology of syphilis.

11 Both Northam and Weigand note the contradiction. Weigand has an interesting remark on the new version; it is "true, no doubt, that the severity of her early ways was not calculated to win Alving. Yet there is a world of difference between admitting this, and picturing Alving, as she does, as a victim of circumstances" (89). Northam reads Mrs. Alving's speech to Oswald as her attempt to "shift her responsibilities," to avoid facing her responsiblity for Oswald's condition by taking the blame for her husband's unhappiness (*Ibsen's Dramatic Method* 71).

12 "Note on *Ghosts*," Egan, *The Critical Heritage* 185. Moore was describing Antoine in the landmark Théâtre Libre production of 1890 that introduced the play to France.

13 Munch designed the sets for Rheinhardt's 1906 Berlin production in a series of thirteen drawings, and in 1920 he made two lithographs of the last scene of the play. Seven of the drawings and the two lithographs are in the Munch Museum in Oslo.

14 "Die Aufzeichnungen des Malte Laurids Brigge," *Sämtliche Werke* (Frankfurt: Insel, 1966) 785.

7 A NEW WOMAN AND THREE HOUSEWIVES

1 The later reception in England was very different; *Ghosts* caused an immense public scandal, the worst of Ibsen's career. In "Ghosts and Gibberings" (*Pall Mall Gazette*, April 8, 1891), William Archer compiled a "lexicon" of the curses heaped on *Ghosts*, and followed this with the equally clever "The Mausoleum of Ibsen" (*Fortnightly Review* 54, n.s. [1893] 77–91), in which he quoted vicious attacks on Ibsen from reviews of *A Doll House*, *Ghosts*, *Rosmersholm*, and *Hedda Gabler*, and then pointed out that Ibsen's large book sales and strong stage successes suggested that it was premature to bury him.

2 Ibsen has invented wonderfully analytical malapropisms for his unlettered housewife. I have deviated from usual ways of translating Gina's "dividere" ("to divide") for Hjalmar's "divertere" ("to divert"), for example, Archer's "perversities," Le Gallienne's "divergence" and Fjelde's "diversities." I have kept the literal meaning because Gina's "divide themselves" is what Gregers and Hjalmar do. Because of its aptness in characterizing Gregers' meddling, I have also translated Gina's act-four curtain line literally: "That's what happens when crazy people come around with the claim of the complication" (139).

3 It is important to note here that Gregers' "på havsens bund," usually translated in English as "the depths of the sea" and frequently cited

as evidence of the attic's profound mysteriousness, is a set term in Norwegian ballads; as Einar Haugen explains, the phrase is "an old-fashioned way of saying 'on the seabottom' . . . In *his* [Gregers'] usage it seems rhetorical, revealing that he thinks in stereotypes" (*Ibsen's Drama: Author to Audience* [Minneapolis: University of Minnesota Press, 1979] 85).

4 One of the most commented-on aspects of *The Wild Duck* is the duck's function as governing symbol for the characters; an interesting addendum to Gregers' metaphor of Hjalmar as trapped wild duck is that Hjalmar, like the duck in captivity, has grown fat from over-eating.

5 *The Open Vision* (London: Athlone, 1982) 123.

6 John Chamberlain points this out in *The Open Vision* (113). He praises Gina for her motherliness and Christian charity, but in keeping with his thesis that the meaning of Ibsen's plays is ultimately ambiguous, claims that Gina "may be one of Ibsen's truly 'honest workmen,' unpretentious, devoted, sticking to her last" or she may be seen "as just doing what comes naturally and unremarkably – responding to environmental stimuli as a simple mind . . . dictates" (114–15). I would argue that Gina's simple mind does not prevent her from making apt moral judgments.

7 For Gina's mistakes, see Else Høst, *Vildanden av Henrik Ibsen* [*Henrik Ibsen's The Wild Duck*] (Oslo: Aschehoug, 1967): 76–78. Høst claims that Gina's incapacity to understand figurative language and malapropisms make her a comic figure, but as Thomas Van Laan points out, Gina "is not the sort of comic figure that gets deflated but the sort that deflates the pomposity of others . . . [Gina] can't speak Gregers' language, but she can recognize it when she hears Hjalmar speaking it, and she can realize that his speaking it constitutes a calamity" ("Language in *Vildanden* [*The Wild Duck*]" 54–55).

8 Inga-Stina Ewbank cites Gina's reply as an example of Ibsen's thematic use of language: "The language here enacts a kind of discrediting of metaphorical subtleties, and implicitly of idealistic theories – "den ideale fordring" ('the claim of the ideal') – as against common humanity" ("Ibsen's Dramatic Language" 115).

9 For a discussion of the *eiron*, see Northrup Frye, *Anatomy of Criticism: Four Essays* (Princeton University Press, 1957) 171–74.

10 Ibsen's model for Hedvig's external characteristics was the daughter of a German sculptor he met in his favorite summer residence, Gossensass. Ibsen wrote to his son that the thirteen-year-old Fraulein Kopf "is as nearly perfect a model for Hedvig in my play that I could hope for. She is pretty, has a serious face and manner, and is a little *gefrässig* [greedy]" (*LS* 235).

11 Having gone into the attic to shoot the duck, Hedvig shoots herself. As several commentators have pointed out, we cannot be sure how

much, if any, Hedvig hears of her father's speech and whether she kills herself accidentally, trying to shoot the duck, or intentionally. Ibsen's deliberate vagueness insists on the insignificance of what are finally only the details of an event of terrible senselessness.

12 See, for example, Valency: Relling is "the raisonneur of the play" despite his being a "drunkard and a disgrace to his profession" (*The Flower and the Castle* 171;174). Several textual studies have revealed the naivete of taking Relling to be Ibsen's raisonneur. Thomas Van Laan, in a ground-breaking essay, "The Novelty of *The Wild Duck*: The Author's Absence," notes that Ibsen "goes out of his way to give Relling a history [his love affair with Berta Sørby] and a seeming personal stake in the action," summarizes prior commentators' notes on "Ibsen's efforts to disassociate himself from Relling," and concludes: "Once we recognize these efforts to undermine Relling's authority and to establish him as a character in his own right, rather than as a detached, autonomous observer, it is fairly easy to realize that Relling's commentary is itself always suspect" (20).

13 "*The Wild Duck*: A Study in Ambiguity," *Milestones of Modern Norwegian Literature* (Oslo: Tanum, 1967) 113.

14 For example, see Downs (*Six Plays* 172); Northam (N 143); E.M. Forster, "Ibsen the Romantic," *Ibsen: A Collection*, ed. Fjelde, 174.

15 The most extreme of the "positive" readings of *The Wild Duck* is that of Jens Kruuse, who argues that Hedvig's death is a Christ-like atonement in "Tragedie og Komedie – Studie in *Vildanden*," *Ibsen Årboken* 4 (1955–56): 29–37.

16 *In A Different Voice: Psychological Theory and Women's Development* (Cambridge: Harvard University Press, 1982).

17 Linda Kerber, et al., "On *In A Different Voice*: An Interdisciplinary Forum," *Signs* 11 (1986): 326. This recalls the theory of dichotomous feminine/masculine behavior noted by Ibsen as he thought out *A Doll House*; Nora's attempt to save Torvald, which she deems right, would be judged wrong by "a male society with laws drafted by men, and with counsels and judges who judge feminine conduct from the male point of view" (*OI* 5:436). Gilligan presents her findings without offering a theory for women's choice of relationships over abstract right, but like Ibsen, she is no essentialist, positing as the highest stage of women's development the achievement of a sense of responsibility toward self as well as toward others, a notion Nora voiced a hundred years earlier.

8 TAMING WILD WOMEN

1 Bonnie Kime Scott notes that Cicely Fairchild chose her pen name because Rebecca West was initially interpreted as representing the "fresh, rebellious spirit of the new woman," but later regretted her

choice; she once remarked that she was not at all like the "gloomy" Rebecca (*The Gender of Modernism*, ed. Scott [Bloomington: Indiana University Press, 1990] 560).

2 Koht claims that Ibsen also based Rebecca West on the most famous Norwegian actress of the nineteenth century, Laura Gundersen, whose "tempestuous acting taught him much about feminine pyschology" (K 373). In fact, Ibsen vigorously opposed casting Gundersen as Rebecca on the grounds that "complex personalities" were not her forte and that with her "large, declamatory speech," she could not manage his "seemingly light, but weighty dialogue" (Anker, *Henrik Ibsen: Letters, 1845–1905* 1:301).

3 Rebecca comments that Dr. West's health was broken by "those dreadful ocean voyages" (502), but surely even a ship doctor's most onerous duties do not cause paralysis. Is Ibsen hinting through this symptom that Dr. West suffered from the same disease that plagued Dr. Rank and Oswald Alving?

4 In his study of *Rosmersholm*'s symmetry, Marvin Carlson notes that "Every act but the second begins with a dialogue between Madame Helseth and Rebecca and every act but the second closes in the same way until Madame Helseth, left alone at last, reports Rebecca's death" ("Patterns" 269).

5 Answering a letter from Georg Groddeck, now lost, Freud noted: "Rosmer's impotence can certainly be established" (Georg Groddeck, *The Meaning of Illness. Selected Psychoanalytic Writings Including his Correspondence with Sigmund Freud*, selected Lore Schacht, trans. Gertrud Mander [London: Hogarth Press, 1977] 44).

6 Rosmer's summary of his objectives reads like a caricature of classical economics: "Only friendly competition. All eyes converging on the same goal. Every will, every mind striving onward and upward – each following out its own natural path" (553). Ibsen no doubt enjoyed parodying aspects of Smith's and Mill's political philosophy that he considered especially naive.

7 In the essay "Some Character-Types met with in Psychoanalytic Work," Freud pointed out that this is the only explanation for Rebecca's violent objection to Kroll's charge. Freud bases his analysis of Rebecca as a classic Œdipal type on the assumption that West is Rebecca's father: "Rebecca's feeling of guilt has its source in the reproach of incest ... When she came to Rosmersholm, the inner force of this first experience drove her ... into getting rid of the wife and mother, so that she might take her place with the husband and father" (*The Complete Psychological Works of Sigmund Freud*, ed. and trans. James Strachey, [London: Hogarth, 1957] 14:330. 24 vols).

8 *Iconoclasts* (New York: Scribner's, 1919) 88.

9 The ballad is "Agnete and the Merman." See Maurice Gravier, "Le

Drama d'Ibsen et la Ballade Magique" 153. In the first draft of *Rosmersholm*, Beata was called Agnete; later, Ibsen removed this too blatant indication of Rosmer's collusion in his wife's disappearance. In the third draft of *Rosmersholm*, Brendel says to Rebecca: "For you there is no danger lurking. He's not likely to lure *you* into deep water" (*OI* 6:422).

10 Marvin Carlson points out that Rebecca's actions precisely repeat Beata's: Rebecca, like Beata, wants to expose Rosmer's apostasy to Kroll; Rebecca's letter to Mortensgaard, like Beata's, requests his help against Rosmer's enemies; Rebecca, like Beata, reveals her relationship with Rosmer to Kroll; Rebecca follows Beata into the mill-race ("Patterns" 273–74).

11 *Love and Will* (New York: Norton, 1969) 29.

12 The phrase is Errol Durbach's in *"Antony and Cleopatra* and *Rosmersholm:* 'Third Empire' Love Tragedies," *Comparative Drama* 20 (1986): 4.

13 After seeing *The Lady from the Sea*, Camilla Collett wrote to Ibsen expressing her admiration for the play and noting the similarity between her own and Ellida Wangel's "blind love . . . this monster, this dragon" (*H* 11:31). She was alluding to her long, fruitless passion for the poet Welhaven. Ibsen answered his friend kindly but evasively. While agreeing that there were "suggestive resemblances" between Collett's life and his protagonist's, he pointed out that he could have had only "vague premonitions" of them (*LS* 278). Characteristically, Collett continued to think what she liked, insisting until she died that she was the model for Ellida Wangel.

14 For the merfolk in Nordic tradition, see Gwen Benwell and Arthur Waugh, *Sea Enchantress: The Tale of the Mermaid and her Kin* (London: Hutchinson, 1961); Maurice Gravier, "Le Drama d'Ibsen et la Ballade Magique" 153–60; Reimund Kvideland and Henning K. Sehmsdorf, eds., *Scandinavian Folk Belief and Legend* (Minneapolis: University of Minnesota Press, 1988); Jacqueline Simpson, *Icelandic Folk Tales and Legends* (Berkeley: University of California Press, 1972).

15 The phrase is Fjelde's in *"The Lady from the Sea:* Ibsen's Positive World-View in a Topographic Figure," *Modern Drama* 21 (1978) 88. Fjelde does not treat the sub-plot.

16 At the matriculation ceremony, Cecilia Thoresen was the sole woman in a hall of two hundred and sixty men. The gallery was packed with women. (Camilla Collett, "Norway," *The Woman Question in Europe*, 192–93).

17 In Zucker's terms, Ibsen stopped trying "to influence conduct" and began the "study of souls" (Z 206); for Weigand, Ibsen stopped writing to reform and "bent his efforts to the task of studying life as it is" (*The Modern Ibsen* 132).

9 THE DEVIANT WOMAN AS HERO: *HEDDA GABLER*

1 December 21, 1890.
2 December 20, 1890.
3 Oswald Crawford, "The Ibsen Question," *Fortnightly Review* 55 (1891): 737–38.
4 April 21, 1891.
5 *Ibsen's Heroines* (an English translation and adaptation of *Henrik Ibsens Frauengestalten* [1892]), ed. and trans. Siegfried Mandel (Redding Ridge, Conn.: Black Swan Press, 1985) 129–31. Salomé's effusive, sentimental book, which treats Nora, Mrs. Alving, Hedvig, Rebecca, Ellida, and Hedda, is a surprisingly conventional work by an unconventional woman. Salomé admires Hedvig, Helene Alving, and Rebecca West as model heroines of self-sacrifice and suffering and seems determined to make Ibsen into a sentimental optimist; at the end of *Ghosts*, she writes, Mrs. Alving achieves "tranquility and peace . . . She lifts her face and hands toward the great transformation that breaks into her life, toward the truth – toward the sun" (66). Salomé is best on *A Doll House* in her blow-by-blow analysis of Nora's growing awareness of her husband's character.
6 *Seduction and Betrayal: Women and Literature* (New York: Random, 1974) 50.
7 *The Western Canon* (New York: Harcourt, 1994) 350–51.
8 Hjalmar Boyeson, *A Commentary on the Writings of Henrik Ibsen* (New York: MacMillan, 1894) 293.
9 *A History of Norwegian Literature*, ed. and trans. Einar Haugen (New York: New York University Press, 1956) 214.
10 F.L. Lucas, *The Drama of Ibsen and Strindberg* (New York: Macmillan, 1962) 240.
11 "Hundrede Aar: Fra Jane Austen til Henrik Ibsen" ["A Hundred Years: From Jane Austen to Henrik Ibsen"], *Tidens Tegn* (April 15, 1917).
12 *Vildanden [The Wild Duck], Rosmersholm, Hedda Gabler* (1931; Oslo: Aschehoug, 1973) 80–81.
13 *Women in Modern Drama: Freud, Feminism, and European Theater at the Turn of the Century* (Ithaca: Cornell University Press, 1989) 151.
14 *The Flight from Woman* (New York: Farrar, 1965) 28.
15 See Stein Haugom Olsen, "Why Does Hedda Gabler Marry Jørgen Tesman?" *Modern Drama* 28 (1985): 591–610. The essay defends the "tesmanesque ethos" of ordinary, everyday life, represented by the Tesmans and Thea, against the morally vacuous Hedda (593). Else Høst earlier made the same argument in *Hedda Gabler* (Oslo: Aschehoug, 1958).
16 See Weigand (252) and Finney (160).
17 "Ibsen and Modern Drama," *Ibsen and the Theatre*, ed. Durbach 79.

18 *Mythic Patterns in Ibsen's Last Plays* (Minneapolis: University of Minnesota Press, 1970) 82.

19 Later, however, Valency claims that "Eilert is not central in the play" and names Hedda the protagonist (196–97).

20 "Why Does Hedda Gabler Marry Jørgen Tesman?" 597.

21 This is Fjelde's apt American rendering of "Hva?" In British English, a literal translation of Tesman's terminal punctuation works marvellously: "What?"

22 "*Hedda Gabler*: The Play in Performance," *Ibsen and the Theatre*, ed. Durbach 84. Suzman's account of Hedda and how she played her is a fascinating and perceptive essay.

23 Hedda's objection has led a number of commentators to accuse her of not liking flowers, and thus life. The fresh air Hedda calls for is more suggestive of life than these perfumed bouquets, which recall those in a funeral parlor. Hedda is suffocating in Tesman's house.

24 One of Ibsen's working notes reads: "Hedda: – had no prospects. Or perhaps you'd like to see me in a home for old maids" (*OI* 7:478).

25 In one of Ibsen's drafts, Hedda says: "I had no other capital. Getting married – it seemed to me like buying an annuity" (*OI* 7:478).

26 For a good discussion of this ideal woman of the nineteenth-century bourgeois world, see Françoise Basch, *Relative Creatures: Victorian Women in Society and the Novel*, trans. Anthony Rudolf (New York: Schocken, 1974).

27 Hedda is also briefly alone at the beginning of act two, when she loads her revolver, and in three instances in act three when Ibsen is getting characters off and on stage: Hedda arranges her hair after Thea's exit, puts wood on the fire before Tesman's entrance, picks up Løvborg's manuscript after Brack's exit, then locks it in the drawer as she hears Løvborg arriving.

28 Weigand notes that critics who regard Tesman as his wife's innocent victim ignore his character; persuading himself that he dare not return the manuscript to the unstable Løvborg, Tesman lets the day pass, and upon hearing Hedda's explanation for her act even gets off a pun (*The Modern Ibsen* 271).

29 For a sympathetic reading of Hedda as a Romantic hero, see Errol Durbach, "*Ibsen the Romantic*" 34–52. Durbach wants to rescue Hedda from "the toils of Women's Liberation and restore her to the predicament from which there can be no liberation in this life. Her agony is not that of a thwarted power-hungry politician" (34). This is a strikingly reductionist view of feminism, and one wonders, given the criticism of Ibsen's play, why Durbach believes that Hedda needs rescuing from feminism. While Durbach's heroic Hedda, whose "view of history is consistent with her own most intense Romantic longing: to burst out of time" (39), represents a welcome change from the normative moralistic criticism, it is difficult to accept Hedda's

repugnance at her pregnancy as evidence that she believes that "nature itself" is deficient; Hedda is no philosopher. It is equally difficult to grant Hedda a "view of history," given her boredom with "listening to the history of civilization morning, noon, and –" (724), and her complete indifference to Løvborg's book, which is, precisely, a "view of history."

30 Brandes noted that "it is not very probable" that Thea "should go about with the whole rough draft of Løvborg's great work in her pocket" (B 108). It may be that Ibsen strained his realistic frame to achieve the comic irony he wanted. It could also be argued, however, that Thea Elvsted is the sort of woman who would carry on her person her male mentor's sacred writings.

31 *Tilskueren* (October 1892) 838. In an analysis remarkably similar to Tolstoy's in *The Kreutzer Sonata*, Bang argues that men have turned women into objects of desire and thus made self-admiration their only goal. While Bang was sympathetic to Hedda, the liberal critic could go only so far; like Hedda's detractors, he named her repugnance at bearing Tesman's child the ultimate expression of her egotism. Even John Northam, whose consideration of Hedda as both victim and hero constitutes the most sympathetic treatment of her to date, comments that to "hate pregnancy, as she seems to, suggests a radical abnormality" (N 150).

32 See Margaret Higonnet, "Suicide: Representations of the Feminine in the Nineteenth Century," *Poetics Today* 6 (1985) 103–18.

33 See my "Fallen Women and Upright Wives: 'Woman's Place' in Early Modern Tragedy," *Reconfigured Spheres: Feminist Explorations of Literary Space*, ed. Margaret Higonnet and Joan Templeton (Amherst: University of Massachusetts Press, 1994) 60–71.

34 Robins, who played Hedda, and her friend Marion Lea, who played Thea, pawned their jewelry as collateral for this landmark performance, after which they "jeered" at the press notices, Robins writes, "with anxiety in our hearts" (18). While the play was almost universally damned, the acting was praised. Robins went on to become one of the most important of the early Ibsen actresses.

35 "Fictional Consensus and Female Casualties," *The Representation of Women in Fiction*, ed. Carolyn Heilbrun and Margaret Higonnet (Baltimore: Johns Hopkins University Press, 1982) 10.

10 THE GLORIES AND DANGERS OF THE REJUVENATING FEMININE

1 "Part One: A Drama from the Life of a Dramatist" and "Part Two: The May Sun of a September Life," *The Century Magazine* 106 (October 1923) 803–15; 107 (November 1923) 83–92.

2 Brandes included the quotation from *Faust* and the dedication, the

latter in facsimile, in his chatty little German monograph *Henrik Ibsen. Mit zwölf Briefen Henrik Ibsens* [*With Twelve Ibsen Letters*] (Berlin: Bard-Marquardt, 1906). Bardach showed Brandes the quotation in her album (her "Stammbuch," not to be confused with "Tagebuch" [diary]), along with the dedicated photograph, and their authenticity is not in question.

3 "Le Mémorial inédit d'une amie d'Ibsen," *Mercure de France* 205 (July 15, 1928): 257–70.

4 "Meine Freundshaft mit Ibsen," *Neue Freie Presse* no. 15304 (March 31, 1907).

5 Meyer, who accepts the *Century Magazine* diary extracts as authentic, notes that if "one substitutes 'got to know him' for 'made his acquaintance' [in the translation of the German], the problem disappears" (M 612). McFarlane, skeptical of the King/Bardach account, which he believes shows signs of "very heavy retouching," wonders whether the discrepancy between the two versions means that Bardach took liberties with the truth or that King took liberties with her journal (*OI* 7:545). It is worth pointing out here that we do not know who did the translations of a supposed original German diary. Bardach was fluent in English.

6 I have been unable to trace the original typescript, but the Royal Library in Copenhagen possesses a photocopy of it, and the University Library in Oslo has a photocopy of this photocopy.

7 May 8, 1928. MS 7884.188, Série Rouveyre, Bibliothèque Littéraire Jacques Doucet, Paris. The Bardach/Rouveyre papers consist of the German manuscript of her memoir that Rouveyre included in French in "Le Mémorial inédit d'une amie d'Ibsen," and eight manuscript letters from Bardach to Rouveyre, written from March 15 to June 26, 1928, in fluent, occasionally flawed French.

8 Photocopy of a typescript mislabelled "'Tagebuch.' Gossensass 1.aug. 1889 – Wien 11.april 1890," 15. MS Folio 3648, University Library, Oslo.

9 *Nova über Henrik Ibsen und sein Alterswerk. Das "Tagebuch" der Emilie Bardach* [*New Light on Henrik Ibsen and his Last Work. The "Diary" of Emilie Bardach*] (Oslo: Edizione "a", 1977) 25–26. Basil King's daughter told Meyer that her father had returned the diary to Bardach, whose effects went to a cousin after her death. Meyer was unable to trace her (M 611–12; note).

10 *Henrik Ibsen* (Oslo: Cappelens, 1996), 10. Ferguson's further claim that the newly discovered diary allows him to shed light on Bardach's relation with Ibsen is not borne out; what he writes adds nothing to previous knowledge and speculation. Ferguson also maintains, without giving any evidence, that Bardach was not eighteen but rather twenty-seven when Ibsen met her.

11 I discuss this in more detail in "New Light on the Bardach Diary,

Studies, "New Light on the Bardach Diary, with Eight Unpublished Letters from Ibsen's Gossensass Princess" (Bardach's letters to Rouveyre).

12 Twelve original letters Ibsen wrote to Bardach are in the University Library, Oslo, as well as three original letters from her to him.

13 Ibsen died on May 23. Brandes could not wait to produce his coup; he published the letters in Danish translation in the Copenhagen newspaper *Politiken* (June 28 and 29), before including them in his German monograph *Henrik Ibsen*.

14 Rouveyre had published a French translation of the letters in a sentimental article in the *Mercure*, "Un amour du vieil Ibsen" (vol. 205, April 1, 1928). It was after reading this article that Bardach wrote to ask him if he would be interested in publishing her diary.

15 "Innlegg ved Else Høsts Doktordisputatus" "[Commentary on Else Høst's Doctoral Defense]", *Edda* 60 (1960) 5. Skard's informants were two women in Berne and another in Berlin, and Basil King's daughter and son-in-law.

16 Bardach's hopes for a French publication of the typescript went unrealized. In the article in which he published her memoir, Rouveyre wrote that the Gossensass account was "childish," with "a few exalted passages, rather artificial and puerile" (267), and that the banalities of the Vienna account helped to explain why Ibsen tired of Bardach so quickly (270). Since Rouveyre had flattered Bardach on her memoir and encouraged her to send him her diary, his harshness seems cruel. After the article appeared, Bardach never wrote to Rouveyre again; one can imagine how surprised and hurt she must have been.

17 See, for example, Lamm (*Modern Drama* 126) and Else Høst (*Hedda Gabler* 89–90), who notes that Ibsen's description of Hedda – her aristocratic face, fine skin, and veiled expression – bears a strong resemblance to Bardach's photograph in Brandes' 1906 book; as Meyer points out, "The same characteristics could, however, be found in the photograph of almost any well-born young lady of the period" (M 648).

18 Meyer calls his chapter on *Hedda Gabler* "A Portrait of the Dramatist as a Young Woman" (M 628). He claims that creating Hedda demanded of Ibsen "the most searching and agonizing self-analysis" (M 633); later, he notes that "if Hedda is a self-portrait, it is almost certainly an unconscious one" (M 648).

19 Elias was Ibsen's avid champion in Germany. He gave readings of Ibsen's plays in Munich before they were published in German, helped to make possible the Berlin performance of *Ghosts* by the Freie Bühne, which brought Ibsen wide recognition in Germany, and supervised the authorized German edition of Ibsen's collected works. Along with Halvdan Koht, he was Ibsen's literary executor.

20 "Christiania Journey: Reminiscences" ["Christiania-fahrt: Erinnerungen,"] *Neue Deutsche Rundschau* 17 (1906) 1462.

21 The "Ibsentagebuch" is lost; several typwritten extracts are in the University Library, Oslo. McFarlane includes them in *OI* 7:563–70.

22 Francis Bull, "Hildur Andersen og [and] Henrik Ibsen," *Edda* 57 (1957) 48. Bull's article is the fullest account to date of the relation between Andersen and Ibsen.

23 My summary of Andersen's career is based on accounts in *Norsk Kvinder: En Oversigt over Deres Stilling og Livsvilkaar i Hundreadeaaret 1814–1914* [*Norwegian Women: A Survey of Their Occupations and Living Conditions Between 1814–1914*], ed. Fredrikke Mørck (Christiania: Berg and Høgh, 1914); *Norsk Biografisk Leksikon* [*Dictionary of Norwegian Biography*], ed. Edvard Bull, Anders Krogvig, Gerhard Gran (Christiania: Aschehoug, 1923); *Cappelens Musikk-leksikon* [*Cappelens' Dictionary of Music*] (Oslo: Cappelens, 1978).

24 I owe my knowledge of this interview to Øyvind Anker's note in *Brev: Ny Samling*, bind 2, *Kommentarene* [*Letters: New Collection*, vol. 2, *Commentaries*], *Ibsen Ärbok* (1979) 121–23. Anker notes that neither Koht in his biography nor Seip in the *Centenary Edition* of Ibsen's works wrote about the interview even though both were familiar with it. Anker suggests that this was to spare the Ibsen family, which had been extremely distressed by Brandes' publication of Ibsen's letters to Bardach. Meyer does not mention the interview.

25 This is probably a sarcastic reference to Ibsen's letters to Bardach, published four years earlier.

26 David Grene, *Reality and the Heroic Pattern: Last Plays of Ibsen, Shakespeare, and Sophocles* (University of Chicago Press, 1967) 2.

27 Michael Meyer, "Ibsen: A Biographical Approach," *Ibsen and the Theatre*, ed. Durbach, 25–26. Suzannah Ibsen is sometimes said to have influenced the portrait of Aline Solness. As Zucker points out, however, even if Mrs. Solness' jealousy of her husband's relations with young women reflects Suzannah Ibsen's, the "vigorous" Suzannah is the opposite rather than the semblable of the "anemic" Aline (246). Downs makes the same point (*Six Plays* 186–87).

28 The minor character Aslasken appears in both *The League of Youth* and *An Enemy of the People*, but the plays' actions are unconnected. Rørlund, the schoolmaster of *Pillars of Society*, does not appear but is mentioned in *An Enemy of the People* by one of the Stockmann boys, whose teacher he now is.

29 Weigand uses the term "abnormal infantalism" (289). He argues that Hilda remains fixed in an "autoerotic" stage of sexuality; having experienced an orgasm as she watched the master builder climb the tower, she seeks him out ten years later in order to experience another one (294). It is curious that Freud, who uses a good bit of ingenuity to argue Rebecca West's "female œdipus complex", ignored Hilda Wangel.

30 In this respect, *The Wild Duck* and *Rosmersholm* are similar to *The Master Builder*, with the important difference that Ibsen does not privilege the self-deceptions of Gregers and Hjalmar and Rebecca and Rosmer.

31 Hilda's theory of the "robust conscience" seems an echo of Nietzsche, whose ideas were widely debated in Scandinavia. Following his usual response when he was asked about other authors' influence on him, Ibsen said that he did not know much about Nietzsche, but when Nietzsche died, Ibsen made the comment that the philosopher was a gifted thinker (K 436). In "Individualism in *The Master Builder*," Egil Törnqvist convincingly argues that Hilda's and Aline's philosophies are reflections of Nietzchean self-assertion and Christian selflessness (*Contemporary Approaches to Ibsen* 3 [1977]: 134–45.

32 Sandra Saari, in "Of Madness or Fame: Ibsen's *Bygmester Solness*," elucidates the opposition between Hilda and Aline as a quarrel between the Viking and Christian ethics (*Scandinavian Studies* 50 [1978]: 1–18).

33 The Norwegian word for duty is the harsh sounding "plikt."

34 This scene between Hilda and Solness is a counterpart to the scene in *Rosmersholm* in which Rosmer anguishes over the burden of his dead wife and asks Rebecca to marry him. Hilda, affected only temporarily by the suffering of the wife she is supplanting, agrees to stay with Solness, while the guilt-ridden Rebecca refuses Rosmer's proposal.

35 I depart from Fjelde's translation – "now, now it's fulfilled" (858) – to quote the English Bible; Hilda's words – "Nu er det fuldbragt" – are those of Christ in the Norwegian Bible.

36 Ernst Motzfeldt, "Af Samtalen med Henrik Ibsen" ["From A Conversation with Henrik Ibsen"], *Aftenposten* (April 23, 1911).

11 WOMEN WHO LIVE FOR LOVE

1 The line comes from Welhaven's poem "The Republicans." Rita's unabashed sexuality made contemporaneous critics abhor her. For Gosse, Rita was "the most repulsive of Ibsen's feminine creations" (A 13:176). William Dean Howells wrote that in "the wife and mother [who] vainly hopes to perpetuate the passion of her first married years . . . we have something intolerably revolting . . . Obsession is an easy name for the state of such women, but if it is the true name then it is time men should study the old formulas of exorcism anew" (Egan, *The Critical Heritage* 450–51). Muriel Bradbrook echoes these earlier criticisms, referring to Ibsen's "savage analysis of a predatory woman" (*Ibsen* 135). The case for Rita's abnormal sexuality is based on an uncritical acceptance of her husband's charges against her.

2 Ibsen said that the Rat Wife was drawn from a Skien childhood memory. Kirstine Ploug, Ibsen's great-aunt, a young widow with children, fell in love with a sea captain and became half mad when he abandoned her. Her children were taken away from her, and Ibsen's mother took her aunt into her home. "Faster" ("Aunt") Ploug wore strange clothes, and had an eccentric way of speaking. In the evenings, she would stand outside the Venstøp farmhouse and call for her children. She died at the age of seventy-six when Ibsen was nine. (See Mosfjeld, *Ibsen and Skien* 233.) One of Aunt Ploug's dresses is preserved in a case in the Telemark Folk Museum; it is of faded cotton, with a pattern of small, geometric brown–grey designs. When I went there, the guide excitedly informed me: "This is the Rat Wife's dress."

3 Northam writes: "The fiction was a device, unconsciously adopted, to control an affection that they show no signs of ever having identified, a protection against innocent incest" (N 197). Durbach interprets similarly: "As if to repress any incipient adolescent sexuality between the children, they oblige Asta to wear boys' clothes and call her 'Eyolf,' carefully concealing the true nature of their relationship" (*"Ibsen the Romantic"* 119).

4 See also Jacobs ("Ibsen's *Little Eyolf*" 613) and Seip (*H* 12:183).

5 Esslin goes on to write that "Eyolf ultimately dies because his mother wishes him dead" and considers the conflict of the play to be "between motherhood and uninhibited female sensuality." He also notes, somewhat contradictorily, that Rita's "exaggerated sexual drive" may result from Alfred's "equally disproportionate commitment to his ideal, his work as a philosopher" ("Ibsen and Modern Drama," *Ibsen and the Theatre*, ed. Durbach, 79).

6 "Gold and green forests" is a set term for wealth in Norwegian folklore, and Alfred's allusion may be a witty innuendo connecting the seductive Rita with the hulder, the temptress of the troll world; trolls inhabit the wild and are notorious hoarders of gold.

7 Rita's accusation recalls Ibsen's working note for *Ghosts*: "Nemesis is invited upon the offspring by marrying for extrinsic reasons, even when they are religious or moral" (*OI* 5:467).

8 Asta whispers to Alfred that she is "running away" from him and from herself (926), a confession that is usually taken to mean that she is afraid that if she stayed, she and Alfred would inevitably make love. As Jacobs points out, Asta has nothing to fear from Alfred. Jacobs sees "a deep irony in [Asta's] panicked flight from a danger that exists only in her own mind" ("Ibsen's *Little Eyolf*" 611).

9 McFarlane comments on the conventionality of their marriage; Borgheim's "natural promptings are to see the wife as helpmeet, as sharer of *his* joys and *his* sorrows: 'Nobody to help me in it . . .' he says in his unhappiness to Asta, 'Nobody. Nobody to share the joy

of it'. It is a role which Asta too would find wholly acceptable" (*OI* 8:12).

10 Edvard Beyer, *Ibsen: The Man and his Work*, trans. Marie Wells (London: Souvenir, 1978) 179. Beyer's objection is typical of much of the scant criticism of the play.

11 Arnold Weinstein has a good discussion of the tentativeness of the play's ending ("Metamorphosis" 313). McFarlane notes that it is the failure to understand Ibsen's irony that causes critics to mistake brilliance for ineptitude; thus, "the final moments of *Little Eyolf* are taken not as a penetratingly observed and resolved portrait of a falsely sentimental man but only as a passage itself inherently marred by false sentimentality" (*OI* 8:33). Critics who want to take the ending of *Little Eyolf* as baldly ironic like to cite Ibsen's remark to his doctor's wife, Caroline Sontum. After attending the Oslo premiere of the play, Ibsen dined with the Sontums. He was exhausted, and the food and wine revived him. When Mrs. Sontum remarked, "Poor Rita, now she has to go to work with all those mischievous boys," Ibsen replied: "Do you really believe so? Don't you rather think it was more of a Sunday mood with her?" (M 730). This reply is typical of Ibsen's teasing responses to people who tried to make him talk about his plays.

12 Kenneth Muir, *Last Periods of Shakespeare, Racine, Ibsen* (Detroit: Wayne State University Press, 1961) 105–6.

13 *Reality and the Heroic Pattern: Last Plays of Ibsen, Shakespeare, and Sophocles* (University of Chicago Press, 1967) 26.

14 Ibsen had heard Hildur Andersen play Saint-Saëns' popular "Danse Macabre." The hoped-for future of Frida Foldal, who goes abroad to develop her talent, is a private allusion to Andersen's own years of study on the continent and her later successful career.

12 THE REVOLT OF THE MUSE: *WHEN WE DEAD AWAKEN*

1 *The New Century Classical Handbook*, ed. Catherine B. Avery (New York: Appleton-Century Crofts, 1962) 728–29.

2 See Gilbert Highet, *The Classical Tradition: Greek and Roman Influences on Western Literature* (Oxford University Press, 1949) 155–56.

3 *The White Goddess: A Historical Grammar of Poetic Myth* (New York: Creative Age Press, 1948) x. Graves recommends A.E. Houseman's sure test of a Muse-inspired and thus true poem: "Does it make the hairs of one's chin bristle if one repeats it silently while shaving?" (7).

4 Graves adds that this does not mean that a woman should not write poetry, and explains: "A woman who concerns herself with poetry should, I believe, either be a silent Muse and inspire the poets by her womanly presence, as Queen Elizabeth and the Countess of Derby did, or she should be the Muse in a complete sense; she should be

in turn Arianrhod, Bloudeuwedd and the Old Sow of Maenawr Penardd who eats her farrow, and should write in each of these capacities with antique authority" (372).

5 De Beauvoir adds that belief in "female intuition" is also found in business and politics, where "Aspasia and Mme. de Maintenon continue to have flourshing careers" (290). It goes without saying, she adds, that these women possess intellectual qualities identical to those of men.

6 "Life and Creation," *Art and Psychoanalysis*, ed. William Phillips (New York: World, 1963) 306–33.

7 In a ground-breaking essay on Rubek's deficiencies as artist and man, Jørgen Dines Johansen relates Rubek's sexual rejection of Irene to ancient, transcultural superstition: "In many religions, male abstinence is a strong kind of magic. From Greenland to Africa the hunter before going to hunt big and dangerous game may abstain from sleeping with his wife or any other woman" ("Kunsten Er [Ikke] en Kvinnekropp: Kunst og Seksualitet i Ibsen's *Når vi døde vågner*" ["Art Is (Not) A Woman's Body: Art and Sexuality in Ibsen's *When We Dead Awaken*]" 12).

8 French sculptor Camille Claudel's biographer Reine-Maris Paris insists that Irene's mental breakdown "takes as its source the liaison between Auguste Rodin and Camille Claudel" (*Camille Claudel, 1864–1943* [Paris: Gallimard, 1984] 105). Paris claims that Ibsen knew about Rodin's exploitation of Claudel on the grounds that Rodin was well known in Norway and that Rodin's and Ibsen's "friend" the painter Fritz Thaulow would have told him about it (105). Paris' widely accepted claim (see, for example, the program of the Norwegian National Theater's 1994 production of *When We Dead Awaken*) cannot be substantiated. There is no reason to believe that the genial Thaulow believed that Rodin exploited Claudel, or that he would have gossiped about it to Ibsen, who was not, in any case, his "friend." More importantly, in 1899, when Ibsen wrote *When We Dead Awaken*, Claudel had not experienced her breakdown; Paris tries to circumvent this contrariant fact with the unconvincing argument that Irene's breakdown is a "prophecy" of what would happen to Claudel (105). It is also important to note that Claudel's mental condition had other sources besides her relation with Rodin, a fact that Paris herself points out, quoting medical authorities.

9 "Ibsen's New Drama" (Joyce's review of *When We Dead Awaken*), Egan, *The Critical Heritage* 388. Joyce comments: "However perfect Ibsen's former creations may be, it is questionable whether any of his women reach to the depth of soul of Irene. She holds our gaze for the sheer force of her intellectual capacity" (388). Joyce's essay, written when he was nineteen, remains one of the most laudatory appreciations of Ibsen's play and of his work as a whole.

10 In one respect, Rubek's and Irene's love death can be viewed as a
traditional liebestod, in which the lovers die rather than live apart;
Rubek chooses death rather than a life without Irene. But the basis
of Ibsen's love death is not only erotic, but moral, celebrating both
passion and *caritas*. (For an account of the liebestod tradition, see
Maya Bijvoet, *Liebestod: The Function and Meaning of the Double Love-
Death* [New York: Garland, 1988]).

11 *Webster's Ninth New Collegiate Dictionary* (Springfield: Merriam-
Webster, 1986) 418.

12 Ibsen's state probably accounts for the inconsistencies in the play's
plot, all of which have been painstakingly noted by Weigand (*The
Modern Ibsen* 380–87).

13 Other famous modern examples are Zola's *The Work*, Mann's *Death in
Venice*, and Kafka's *The Hunger Artist*.

14 The reading of *When We Dead Awaken* as Ibsen's confession of a failed
life is widespread even in analyses that are not primarily biographical; three examples follow: for Martin Lamm, Ibsen felt that his
happiness "was too high a price to pay for his life's work" (*Modern
Drama* 96); for Muriel Bradbrook *When We Dead Awaken* is a condemnation of everything Ibsen wrote after he left Norway (*Ibsen* 147);
Stephen Whicher asks rhetorically: "What had the great work
amounted to, each [of the last four plays] asks over again, to which
he had sacrificed so much? 'Nothing, nothing! The whole is nothing.' And the price! Happiness, love, life itself" ("The World of
Ibsen," *Ibsen: A Collection*, ed. Fjelde, 172).

15 See, for example, Kenneth Muir, who quotes the following lines from
Yeats' poem "The Choice" to explain Ibsen's play: "The intellect of
man is forced to choose / Perfection of the life, or of the work" (*Last
Periods of Shakespeare, Racine, Ibsen* [Detroit: Wayne State University
Press, 1961] 92).

IN CONCLUSION: IBSEN'S WOMEN AND IBSEN'S MODERNISM

1 *Modernism: A Guide to European Literature, 1890–1930*, ed. Malcolm
Bradbury and James McFarlane (1976; London: Penguin, 1991)
499. As Martin Lamm notes, "Ibsen's work is the Rome of modern
drama; all roads lead to it or from it" (*Modern Drama* 75).

2 *The Playwright as Thinker: A Study of Drama in Modern Times* (1946;
Cleveland: World, 1965) 92.

3 *The Theatre of Revolt: An Approach to the Modern Drama* (Boston: Little,
1962) 38.

4 *Inferno, Alone and Other Writings*, ed. and trans. Evert Sprinchorn
(Garden City: Doubleday, 1968) 189. The quotation comes from the
Inferno.

5 For an excellent discussion of Hauptmann's and Wedekind's treat-

ment of women, see Gail Finney, *Women in Modern Drama: Freud, Feminism, and European Theatre at the Turn of the Century* (Ithaca: Cornell University Press, 1989).

6 For the crucial connection between gender and genre in the development of modern tragedy, see my "Fallen Women and Upright Wives: 'Woman's Place' in Early Modern Tragedy: Hebbel, Ibsen, and Strindberg," *Reconfigured Spheres: Feminist Explorations of Literary Space*, ed. Margaret Higonnet and Joan Templeton (Amherst: University of Massachusetts Press, 1994) 60–71. The relation between feminism and modernism has recently emerged as a topic of inquiry, mostly among feminist critics of fiction and poetry; see Bonnie Kime Scott, ed. *The Gender of Modernism*, (Bloomington: Indiana University Press, 1990); Marianne De Koven, *Rich and Strange: Gender, History, Modernism* (Princeton University Press, 1991); Sandra Gilbert and Susan Gubar, *Letters from the Front* (vol. 3 of *No Man's Land: The Place of the Woman Writer in the Twentieth Century*) (New Haven: Yale University Press, 1994). Feminism is fundamental to the progressive modernism of writers like Ibsen, Meredith, and Woolf, but, as Gilbert and Gubar show, much of the rhetoric of the modernist *avant garde*, for example, Pound's "make it new," camouflaged "regressive or nostalgic sexual ideologies" (xiv).

7 The phrase "true universals" is Sherry Ortner's in her essay "Is Female to Male as Nature is to Culture?" 67.

8 My account of permanent inequality is drawn from Jean Baker Miller, *Toward A New Psychology of Women* 6–13.

9 See I.K. Broverman, et. al., "Sex-Role Stereotypes and Clinical Judgments of Mental Health," *Journal of Consulting Psychology* 34 (1970) 1–7; I.K. Broverman, et al., "Sex-Role Stereotypes: A Current Appraisal," *Journal of Social Issues* 28 (1972) 59–78.

10 Ibsen's androgynous characters outraged his conventional contemporaries and gave Shaw the comic capital for *The Philanderer*, whose second act takes place in the Ibsen Club, where a bust of the master looks down on a trousered woman reading an Ibsen play. To become a member of the club, one has "to be nominated by a man and a woman, who both guarantee that the candidate, if female, is not womanly, and if male, not manly" (*Plays Unpleasant* [London: Penguin, 1975] 118).

11 To argue that the "woman as individualist" in Ibsen represents both men and women, as Inga-Stina Ewbank does, is to ignore this vital difference: "Ibsen came to see the predicament of modern man (in the sense of 'human being') as most acutely realized in the predicament of modern woman" ("Ibsen and the Language of Women," "*Women Writing and Writing About Women*," ed. Mary Jacobus [New York: Harper, 1979] 131.) As Gerda Lerner points out, women's search for the authentic self has had to take different forms from that

of men because for men, "authority was assumed, while for women it was utterly denied" (*The Creation of Feminist Consciousness* 47).

12 In characterizing Ibsen's theatre of revolt as the quintessential modern drama, Robert Brustein claims that Ibsen's "enemy" is "domesticated man . . . who identifies his needs with the needs of the community as determined by the compact majority: Karsten Bernick, Torvald Helmer, Pastor Manders. The individual is revolutionary man, superior to all confining social, political, or moral imperatives . . . Brand, Doctor Stockmann, Master Builder Solness" (*The Theatre of Revolt* 38). Far from being above "all confining social, political, or moral imperatives," Brand, Stockmann, and Solness are thoroughgoing traditionalists on women; respectively, each demands that a woman serve him as nurturer, housewife, and inspirer. And if Bernick, Helmer, and Manders represent the enemy in Ibsen, it is to a great extent because of their conviction that women are put on earth to serve them. These domesticated men are challenged by revolutionary women: Lona, Nora, and Mrs. Alving.

13 *Samlede Skrifter* [*Collected Works*] (Copenhagen: Gyldendal, 1899–1910) 12:51. 18 vols.

Select bibliography

1. PRIMARY SOURCES

Henrik Ibsen: Brev, 1845–1905, Ny Samling [*Henrik Ibsen: Letters, 1845–1905, New Collection*]. Ed. Øyvind Anker. 2 vols. *Ibsenårbok.* Oslo: Universitetsforlaget, 1979.

Hundreårsutgave. Henrik Ibsens Samlede Verker [*Centenary Edition. Henrik Ibsen's Collected Works*]. Ed. Francis Bull, Halvdan Koht, and Didrik Arup Seip. 21 vols. Oslo: Gyldendal, 1928–57.

Ibsen. The Complete Major Prose Plays. Trans. Rolf Fjelde. New York: New American Library, 1978.

Letters and Speeches. Ed. and trans. Evert Sprinchorn. New York: Hill, 1964.

The Oxford Ibsen. Ed. James Walter McFarlane and Graham Orton. Trans. McFarlane et. al. 8 vols. London: Oxford University Press, 1960–77.

Peer Gynt. Trans. Rolf Fjelde. 2nd edn. Minneapolis: University of Minnesota Press, 1983.

2. BIOGRAPHIES

Due, Chrisopher. *Erindringer fra Henrik Ibsens Ungdomsaar* [*Reminiscences from Henrik Ibsen's Youth*]. Copenhagen: Græbes, 1909.

Ebbell, Clara Thue. *I Ungdomsbyen med Henrik Ibsen* [*In The Town of Henrik Ibsen's Youth*]. Grimstad: Ibsenhouse and Grimstad City Museum, 1966.

Eitrem, Hans. *Ibsen og [and] Grimstad.* Oslo: Aschehoug, 1940.

Heiberg, Hans. *Ibsen: A Portrait of the Artist.* Trans. Joan Tate. Coral Gables: University of Miami Press, 1969.

Ibsen, Bergliot. *The Three Ibsens.* Trans. Gerik Schjelderup. London: Hutchinson, 1951.

Jæger, Henrik. *Henrik Ibsen, 1828–1888. A Critical Biography.* Trans. William Morton Payne. Chicago: McClurg, 1890.

Koht, Halvdan. *Life of Ibsen.* Trans. Einar Haugen and A.E. Santaniello. New York: Blom, 1971.

Meyer, Michael. *Ibsen.* New York: Doubleday, 1971.

Mosfjeld, Oskar. *Ibsen og [and] Skien.* Oslo: Gyldendal, 1949.

Paulsen, John. *Samliv med Ibsen [Living with Ibsen].* 2 vols. Christiania: Gyldendal, 1906, 1913.

Zucker, A.E. *Ibsen the Master Builder.* 1929. New York: Farrar, 1973.

3. BOOKS

Aarnes, Sigurd Aa, ed. *Søkelys på Amtmandens Døtre [Searchlight on "The District Governor's Daughters"].* Oslo: Norwegian University Press, 1977.

Abrams, M.H. *Natural Supernaturalism: Tradition and Revolution in Romantic Literature.* New York: Norton, 1971.

Agerholt, Anna Caspari. *Den Norske Kvinnebevegelses Historie [A History of the Norwegian Women's Movement].* Oslo: Gyldendal, 1937.

Ashbjørnsen, P.C., and Jørgen Moe. *Norwegian Folk Tales.* Trans. Pat Shaw Iversen and Carl Norman. Oslo: Dreyers, 1960.

　A Time for Trolls. Fairy Tales from Norway. Trans. Joan Roll-Hansen. Tanum: Oslo, 1962.

Bradbrook, M.C. *Ibsen the Norwegian.* London: Chatto, 1966.

Brandes, Georg. *Henrik Ibsen and Bjørnstjerne Bjørnson.* Trans. Jesse Muir. Rev. trans. William Archer. London: Heinemann, 1899.

Byock, Jesse, trans. *The Saga of the Volsungs.* Berkeley: University of California Press, 1990.

Chevrel, Yves. *Henrik Ibsen. Maison de poupée.* Paris: Presses Universitaires de France, 1989.

Collett, Camilla. *Samlede Verker. Mindeudgave [Complete Works. Commemorative Edition].* 3 vols. Christiania: Gyldendal, 1913.

Cunningham, Gail. *The New Woman and the Victorian Novel.* New York: Macmillan, 1978.

de Beauvoir, Simone. *Le Deuxième Sexe [The Second Sex].* 2 vols. Paris: Gallimard, 1949.

Downs, Brian. *A Study of Six Plays by Ibsen.* 1959. New York: Farrar, 1978.

Durbach, Errol. *"Ibsen the Romantic": Analogues of Paradise in the Later Plays.* Athens: University of Georgia Press, 1982.

Durbach, Errol, ed. *Ibsen and the Theatre: The Dramatist in Production.* New York University Press, 1980.

Egan, Michael, ed. *Ibsen: The Critical Heritage.* London: Routledge, 1972.

Engelstad, Irene, et. al. *Norsk Kvinnelitteraturhistorie [A History of Norwegian Women Writers].* 3 vols. Oslo: Pax, 1988.

Fjelde, Rolf, ed. *Ibsen: A Collection of Critical Essays.* Englewood Cliffs: Prentice-Hall, 1965.

Goethe, Johann Wolfgang von. *Faust.* Trans. Anna Swanwick. 2 vols. 1850, 1878. London: Bell, 1928.

Gilbert, Sandra and Susan Gubar. *The Madwoman in the Attic: The Woman*

Writer and the Nineteenth-Century Literary Imagination. New Haven: Yale University Press, 1979.

Gilman, Charlotte Perkins. *Women and Economics*. Ed. Carl Degler. 1898. New York: Harper, 1966.

Goulianos, Joan, ed. *By A Woman Writ: Literature from Six Centuries By and About Women*. New York: Bobbs, 1973.

Gravier, Maurice. *D'Ibsen à Sigrid Undset. Le Féminisme et l'amour dans la littérature norvégienne, 1850–1950* [*Feminism and Love in Norwegian Literature, 1850–1950*]. Paris: Minard, 1968.

Hagstrum, Jean. *Sex and Sensibility: Ideal and Erotic Love from Milton to Mozart*. Chicago University Press, 1980.

Heilbrun, Carolyn. *Toward A Recognition of Androgyny*. New York: Knopf, 1973.

Holberg, Ludvig. *Jeppe of the Hill and Other Comedies*. Ed. and trans. Gerald Argetsinger and Sven Rossel. Carbondale: Southern Illinois University Press, 1990.

The Journey of Niels Klim to the World Underground. [n. trans.] Ed. James I. McNelis, Jr. Lincoln: University of Nebraska Press, 1960.

Høst, Else. *Hedda Gabler*. Oslo: Aschehoug, 1958.

Jones, Gwyn, trans. *Eric the Red and Other Icelandic Sagas*. London: Oxford University Press, 1961.

Kofman, Sarah. *Le Respect des femmes (Kant et Rousseau)*. Paris: Galilée, 1982.

Lamm, Martin. *Modern Drama*. Trans. Karin Elliott. 1948. New York: Philosophical Library, 1953.

Lavrin, Janko. *Ibsen: An Approach*. 1950. New York: Russell and Russell, 1959.

Lerner, Gerda. *The Creation of Feminist Consciousness: From the Middle Ages to 1870*. New York: Oxford University Press, 1993.

Logemann, Henri. *Commentary, Critical and Explanatory, on the Norwegian Text of Henrik Ibsen's* Peer Gynt. The Hague: Nijoff, 1917.

Magnusson, Magnus and Hermann Pálsson, trans. *Njal's Saga*. London: Oxford University Press, 1960.

McFarlane, James, ed. *Henrik Ibsen: A Critical Anthology*. London: Penguin, 1970.

Miller, Jean Baker. *Toward A New Psychology of Women*. 1976. London: Penguin, 1978.

Northam, John. *Ibsen: A Critical Study*. Cambridge University Press, 1973. *Ibsen's Dramatic Method: A Study of the Prose Dramas*. London: Faber, 1953.

Rich, Adrienne. *Of Woman Born: Motherhood as Experience and Institution*. New York: Norton, 1976.

Robins, Elizabeth. *Ibsen and the Actress*. London: Hogarth, 1928.

Rossi, Alice, ed. *The Feminist Papers: From Adams to De Beauvoir*. New York: Columbia University Press, 1973.

Shaw, George Bernard. *The Quintessence of Ibsenism: Now Completed to the Death of Ibsen.* 1913. New York: Hill, 1957.

Simmel, Georg. *On Women, Sexuality, and Culture.* Ed. and trans. Guy Oakes. New Haven: Yale University Press, 1984.

Thoresen, Magdalene. *Livsbilleder* [*Life's Images*]. Copenhagen: Gyldendal, 1877.

Valency, Maurice. *The Flower and the Castle: An Introduction to Modern Drama.* 1963. New York: Schocken, 1982.

Veblen, Thorstein. *The Theory of the Leisure Class.* 1899. New York: Modern Library, 1934.

Weigand, Hermann. *The Modern Ibsen.* New York: Holt, 1925.

4. ARTICLES AND PARTS OF BOOKS

Arup, Jens. "On *Hedda Gabler.*" *Orbis Litterarum* 12 (1957): 4–37.

Auden, W.H. "Genius and Apostle." *Henrik Ibsen.* Ed. McFarlane. 331–45.

Bardach, Emilie. Eight manuscript letters to André Rouveyre. MS7884.188, Série Rouveyre, Bibliothèque Littéraire Jacques Doucet, Paris.

"Meine Freundschaft mit Ibsen." *Neue Freie Presse* (March 31, 1907). No. 15304.

Photocopy of a typescript mislabelled "Tagebuch: Gossensass, 1 aug. 1889 – Wien 11 april 1890." Folio 3648, University Library, Oslo.

Baruch, Elaine Hoffman. "Ibsen's *Doll House*: A Myth for Our Time." *Yale Review* 69 (1979): 374–87.

Brandes, Georg. "Inaugural Lecture, 1871." Trans. Evert Sprinchorn. *The Theory of the Modern Stage.* Ed. Eric Bentley. London: Penguin, 1968. 383–97.

Bull, Francis. "Henrik Ibsen." *Norsk Litteratur Historie* [*A History of Norwegian Literature*]. Ed. Bull, Fredrik Paasche, A.H. Winsnes, Philip Houm. Rev. edn. Oslo: Aschehoug, 1960. 6 vols. 4: 267–465.

"Hildur Andersen og [and] Henrik Ibsen." *Edda* 57 (1957): 47–54.

"Introductions." *Hundreårsutgave.* Ed. Bull, Halvdan Koht, and Didrik Arup Seip.

Carlson, Marvin. "Patterns of Structure and Character in Ibsen's *Rosmersholm.*" *Modern Drama* 17 (1974): 267–75.

Collett, Camilla. "Norway." *The Woman Question in Europe.* Ed. Theodore Stanton. New York: Putnam's, 1884. 189–98.

Durbach, Errol. "Sacrifice and Absurdity in *The Wild Duck.*" *Mosaic* 7 (1974): 99–107.

Ellmann, Richard, and Charles Feidelson, Jr. "Preface." *The Modern Tradition: Backgrounds of Modern Literature.* Ed. Ellmann and Feidelson. New York: Oxford University Press, 1965. v–ix.

Ewbank, Inga-Stina. "Ibsen on the English Stage: 'The Proof of the

Pudding is in the Eating.'" *Ibsen and the Theatre.* Ed. Durbach. 27–48.

"Ibsen's Dramatic Language as a Link Between his 'Realism' and his 'Symbolism.'" *Contemporary Approaches to Ibsen* 1 (1965): 96–123.

Fergusson, Francis. "*Ghosts* and *The Cherry Orchard*: The Theater of Modern Realism." *The Idea of a Theater.* 1949. Princeton University Press, 1972. 146–77.

Fjelde, Rolf. "Foreword" and "Appendix One." *Peer Gynt.* Trans. Fjelde. 2nd edn. Minneapolis: University of Minnesota Press, 1983. ix–xxvi; 231–70.

"Introductions." *Ibsen: The Complete Major Prose Plays.* Trans. Fjelde.

Freud, Sigmund. "On the Universal Tendency to Debasement in the Sphere of Love." *The Standard Edition of the Complete Psychological Works of Sigmund Freud.* Ed. and trans. James Strachey. 24 vols. London: Hogarth, 1953–74. 11: 179–90.

Fuchs, Elinor. "Marriage, Metaphysics, and *The Lady from the Sea* Problem," *Modern Drama* 33 (1990): 434–44.

Garton, Janet. "The Middle Plays." *The Cambridge Companion to Ibsen.* Cambridge University Press, 1994. 106–25.

Gay, Peter. "Offensive Women and Defensive Men." *The Education of the Senses.* New York: Oxford University Press, 1984. 169–225.

Gosse, Edmund. *Henrik Ibsen. The Works of Henrik Ibsen.* Ed. and trans. William Archer. New York: Scribner's, 1917. 13 vols. 13: 7–216.

Gravier, Maurice. "Le Drame d'Ibsen et la ballade magique." *Contemporary Approaches to Ibsen* 2 (1971): 140–60.

Haaland, Arild. "Ibsen og [and] Hedda Gabler." *Samtiden* 67 (1958): 566–77.

Hanson, Katherine. "Ibsen's Women Characters and Their Feminist Contemporaries." *Theatre History Studies* 2 (1982): 83–91.

Horney, Karen. "The Overevaluation of Love." *Feminine Psychology.* Ed. Harold Kelman. New York: Norton, 1967. 182–213.

Huneker, James. *Henrik Ibsen. The Works of Henrik Ibsen.* Ed. and trans. William Archer. New York: Scribner's, 1917. 13 vols. 13: 259–92.

Jacobs, Barry. "Ibsen's *Little Eyolf*: Family Tragedy and Human Responsibility." *Modern Drama* 27 (1984): 604–15.

James. Henry. "On the Occasion of *Hedda Gabler*, 1891." *The Scenic Art.* Ed. Allan Wade. 1949. New York: Hill, 1957. 243–56.

Johansen, Jørgen Dines. "Kunsten Er (Ikke) en Kvinnekropp: Kunst og Seksualitet i Ibsens *Når vi døde vågner*" ["Art Is (Not) A Woman's Body: Art and Sexuality in Ibsen's *When We Dead Awaken*"]. *Agora* 2–3 (1993): 1–15.

Jones, David. "The Virtues of *Hedda Gabler*." *Educational Theatre Journal* 29 (1977): 447–62.

Joyce, James. "Ibsen's New Drama." *The Critical Heritage.* Ed. Egan. 385–91.

Kelly, Joan. "The Doubled Vision of Feminist Theory." *Women, History, and Theory: The Essays of Joan Kelly.* University of Chicago Press, 1984. 51–64.

Kinck, B.M. "Henrik Ibsen og [and] Laura Kieler." *Edda* 35 (1935): 498–543.

King, Basil. "Ibsen and Emilie Bardach." *The Century Magazine* 106 (October 1923): 803–15; 107 (November 1923): 83–92.

Kittang, Atle. "*The Pretenders* – Historical Vision or Psychological Tragedy?" *Contemporary Approaches to Ibsen* 3 (1977): 78–88.

Koht, Halvdan. "Introductions." *Hundreårsutgave.* Ed. Francis Bull, Koht, and Didrik Arup Seip.

La Chenais, Pierre Georget. "Introductions." *Œuvres complètes d'Henrik Ibsen.* Ed. and trans. La Chenais. 16 vols. Paris: Plon, 1930–45.

Lervik, Åse Hiorth. "Mellom Furia og Solveig" ["Between Furia and Solveig"]. *Contemporary Approaches to Ibsen* 3 (1977): 68–77.

Lukács, George. "The Sociology of Modern Drama." Trans. Lee Baxandall. *The Theory of the Modern Stage.* Ed. Eric Bentley. London: Penguin, 1968. 425–50.

McFarlane, James Walter. "Introductions." *The Oxford Ibsen.* Ed. and trans. McFarlane et. al.

Merivale, Patricia. "*Peer Gynt*: Ibsen's *Faustiad.*" *Comparative Literature* 35 (1983): 126–39.

Ortner, Sherry. "Is Female to Male as Nature is to Culture?" *Woman, Culture, and Society.* Ed. Michelle Zimbalist Rosaldo and Louise Lamphere. Palo Alto: Stanford University Press, 1974. 67–87.

Rasmussen, Janet. "'The Best Place on Earth for Women': The American Experience of Asta Hansteen." *Norwegian American Studies* 31 (1986): 245–67.

Rouveyre, André. "Le Mémorial inédit d'une amie d'Ibsen". *Mercure de France* 205 (July 15, 1928): 257–70.

Scott, Joan. "Gender: A Useful Category of Historical Analysis." *American Historical Review* 9 (1986): 1053–75.

Seip, Didrik Arup. "Introductions." *Hundreårsutgave.* Ed. Francis Bull, Halvdan Koht, and Seip.

Suzman, Janet. "*Hedda Gabler*: The Play in Performance." *Ibsen and the Theatre.* Ed. Durbach. 83–104.

Templeton, Joan. "The *Doll House* Backlash: Criticism, Feminism, and Ibsen." *PMLA* 104 (1989): 28–40.

  "New Light on the Bardach Diary: Eight Unpublished Letters from Ibsen's Gossensass Princess." *Scandinavian Studies* 69 (1997): 147–70.

  "Of This Time, Of *This* Place: Mrs. Alving's Ghosts and the Shape of the Tragedy." *PMLA* 101 (1986): 57–68.

  "Sense and Sensibility: Women and Men in *Vildanden* [*The Wild Duck*]." *Scandinavian Studies* 63 (1991): 415–31.

Trilling, Lionel. "Of This Time, Of That Place." *Partisan Review* 10 (1943): 72–103.

Van Laan, Thomas F. "Introduction to *Catiline*." *Catiline* and *The Burial Mound*. Trans. Van Laan. New York: Garland, 1992. 3–121.

"Language in *Vildanden* [*The Wild Duck*]." *Ibsen Årbok* (1974): 41–63.

"The Novelty of *The Wild Duck*: The Author's Absence." *Journal of Dramatic Theory and Criticism* 1 (1986): 17–33.

Weinstein, Arnold. "Metamorphosis in Ibsen's *Little Eyolf*." *Scandinavian Studies* 62 (1990): 293–318.

Index

Where several of Ibsen's plays appear in the same entry they are listed in the order in which they were written.

Aase (of *Peer Gynt*), 8, 10–12, 91–3, 94, 98, 100, 104

Achurch, Janet, 113

Adlesparre, Sophie, 146

Agnes (*of Brand*), 8, 22, 80–90, 109, 179, 328

Alfhild (of *The Grouse at Justedal* and *Olaf Liljekrans*), 31–2, 38

Aline Solness (of *The Master Builder*), 22, 28, 265, 267, 269, 270–4, 328, 329, 332

Andersen, Hans Christian: *The Little Mermaid*, 196

Andersen, Hildur, 247, 368; career, character, tastes, 249–51, 252–3; Ibsen's writings to, 252–6; influence on Ibsen's work, 254, 261, 262–3; relation with Ibsen, 250–7, 261–3, 319

Andréas-Salomé, Lou, 126, 206, 209, 360

androgyny, *see* gender, subversion of binary notions of

Anitra (of *Peer Gynt*), 102–3, 104

Anna Karenina, 230

Anne (of *St. John's Night*), 30

Antigone, 121

Archer, William, 23, 348, 355

Ariosto, 330

Aristotle, 161, 162, 329

art, and feminism, 118–24, 141–5; and life, 312–15, 318–22, *see also* love, and vocation; as male domain, 201–2, 303–9

Asta Allmers (of *Little Eyolf*), 29, 278–80, 282–3, 285–6, 328, 329

Auden, W.H., 11, 87

Aurelia (of *Catiline*), 23, 24, 25–8, 30, 35, 80, 271, 329

Bang, Herman, 229–30, 362

Bardach, Emilie, 247, 250, 253, 254, 255; Ibsen's letters to, 237–41, 246; influence on Ibsen's work, 243–6, 261–2; relation with Ibsen, 233–47, 256–7, 261–2, 319; writings on Ibsen, 234–7, 241–3

Beata Rosmer (of *Rosmersholm*), 185–8, 189, 190, 191, 192–4

Beaumarchais, Pierre-Augustin Caron de, 172

Berner, H.E., 127

Berta (of *Hedda Gabler*), 211, 230

Berta Sørby (of *The Wild Duck*), 167, 168–9, 172, 176, 179, 330

Betty Bernick (of *Pillars of Society*), 28, 132, 133, 134, 329

Bie, Hemming, 18, 20–1

Bjørnson, Bjørnstjerne, 10, 42, 47, 127, 241, 341

Bjørnson, Karoline, 44, 59

Blake, William, 304

Blanka (of *The Burial Mound*), 30

Bolette Wangel (of *The Lady from the Sea*), 22, 195, 199–202, 203, 334

Bradamant, *see* Ariosto

Brand, 8, 14, 22, 34, 47–8, 52, 58, 80–90, 129, 135, 147, 179, 289, 301, 321, 328, 331, 340

Brand's Daughters, see Kieler, Laura

Brand's mother (of *Brand*), 82–3

Brandes, Edvard, 251

Brandes, Georg, xvi, 23–4, 42, 43, 125, 126, 127, 128, 207, 231, 241, 242, 251, 262, 333; influence on Ibsen, *Main Currents in Nineteenth-Century Literature*, 325–6

Bremer, Fredrika, 65, 121

Brieux, Eugène: *Damaged Goods,* 324;
　Maternity, 324; *Three Daughters of
　Monsieur Dupont, The,* 324
Britomart, *see* Spenser, Edmund
Brynhild, 229, *see also The Volsung Saga*
"Building Plans," 33
Bull, Ole, 30
Burial Mound, The, 30, 31, 33
Byron, George Gordon, Lord, 304; *Don
　Juan,* 106

Candida, *see* Shaw, George Bernard
Catiline, 23–9, 30, 35, 321; as precursor
　of later plays, 23–5, 28–9, 55, 57, 80,
　229, 270–1, 290, 327, 329
Child Wife, The, 113
Christiania Theatre, 30, 47
Cicero, 25, 351
Cleopatra (see Shakespeare, William)
Coleridge, Samuel Taylor, 206
Collett, Camilla Wergeland, 114, 121,
　359; career, 68–70; friendship with
　the Ibsens, 69–70, 129; *From the Camp
　of the Dumb,* 69; *District Governor's
　Daughters, The,* 68, 70–2; Ibsen's
　indebtedness to, 70–2, 129, 132;
　Ibsen's praise of, 70, 128; "Women in
　Literature," 69
comedy, Roman, Renaissance, 172–3; in
　The Wild Duck, 170–3
Crawfurd, Georgiana, 16

Dagny (of *The Vikings at Helgeland*), 28,
　35, 54, 55, 57, 329
Dante, 304
De Beauvoir, Simone de: *The Second Sex,*
　304–5, 350–1
Diana (of *Hedda Gabler*), 224, 230
Dickens, Charles, 16
Dina Dorf (of *Pillars of Society*), 30, 133,
　134, 163, 201, 250
Doll House, A, 7, 22, 30, 34, 58, 65, 67,
　103, 109, 110–28, 129, 135–45, 146,
　147, 159, 163, 166, 169, 199, 201,
　205, 269, 278, 289, 301, 308, 316,
　321–2, 324, 325, 326, 327, 328, 330,
　331, 333, 334, 335, 340
Dowden, Edward, 205–6
Due, Christopher, 13, 14, 16, 18

Ebbell, Marthe Clarine, 18–22, 30, 32, 33;
　Ibsen's poems to, 18, 20, 21
Egeria, 305
Elias, Julius, 244–5, 262, 321, 364
Ella Rentheim (of *John Gabriel Borkman*),
8, 22, 291, 292–301, 322, 332
Ellida Wangel (of *The Lady from the Sea*),
　22, 37, 194–9, 201, 203, 327, 328,
　334
Ellis, Havelock, 127
Emma Bovary, 230, 267
Emperor and Galilean, 108–9, 129, 308
Enemy of the People, An, 38, 109, 163–6,
　269, 301, 316, 330
Eve, *see* female archetypes, fatal woman

Fairchild, Cicely, 181
Fanny Wilton (of *John Gabriel Borkman*),
　295, 298
Feast at Solhoug, The, 8, 22, 29, 35–8, 44,
　53, 54, 196, 229, 328
female archetypes, xvi; active, "masculine"
　woman versus passive, "feminine"
　woman, 23–5, 329 – in *Catiline,* 23–4,
　25–9 – in *The Feast at Solhoug,* 35, 36
　– in *The Vikings at Helgeland,* 28, 55,
　57, 329 – in *Brand,* 80–1 – in *Pillars
　of Society,* 28, 134, 329 – in
　Rosmersholm, 28, 189, 190–4 – in
　Hedda Gabler, 29, 209–10, 219–20,
　229–32, 329 – in *The Master Builder,*
　29, 270–4, 329 – in *Little Eyolf,* 29,
　286–7, 329 – in *John Gabriel Borkman,*
　292 – in *When We Dead Awaken,* 29,
　329; eternal feminine, 84–5, 102–4,
　106–7, 304; Norwegian fairy-tale
　princesses, 95–7, 101; fallen woman,
　94, 101, 106, 154, 168, 171–2, 179,
　190–1, 230–1; fatal woman, 25–9,
　188, 270–1, 276–7, 281–2, 284, 286,
　304 – Eve, 101, 102, 103, 115, 138,
　284, 303 – hulder, 31–2, 36, 54, 95,
　276 – seter girls, 94–5, 101, 346 –
　sirens, 304, 306; Galatea, 102, 303;
　mermaid, 195–7, 198; muse, 62–3,
　109, 304–9, 312–15; Penelope, 104;
　pure versus sexual woman, 100–4,
　108–9, 230; redemptive woman, 106–
　7, 309–10 – Mary, 101, 106, 107;
　sacrificial woman – in *Brand,* 82, 83–
　4, 86–7 – in *Rosmersholm,* 181, 183–4,
　189, 191–4 – in *Hedda Gabler,* 211,
　212–13 – in *When We Dead Awaken,*
　310, 312; warrior's repose, 28, 84–5
female autonomy, 202–3, 308–9, 324–9,
　332–5; in *Pillars of Society,* 131–5, 333;
　in *A Doll House,* 140–3, 145, 333,
　335; in *Ghosts,* 156–9, 333–4, 335; in
　The Lady from the Sea, 196–203, 334;
　in *Hedda Gabler,* 227–32, 334; in *Little*

female autonomy (*Contd.*)
  Eyolf, 278, 286–91, 334–5; in *When We Dead Awaken*, 308–9, 310, 311–12, 314–15, 335
female-centered triangle, xvi, 29, 328, 340; in *The Feast at Solhoug*, 35–6, 37–8; in *The Vikings at Helgeland*, 53–4; in *Love's Comedy*, 63–5, 70–2; in *Ghosts*, 148, 152–4; in *The Lady from the Sea*, 196–9; in *Hedda Gabler*, 220–2
female sexuality, 29, 31, 36, 41, 54, 94–6, 197–8, 221–2, 267, 268, 275–7, 304–6; refused by male characters, 122, 132 – in *Peer Gynt*, 98, 100–2, 106–8, – in *Emperor and Galilean*, 108–9 – in *Rosmersholm*, 107, 186–7, 190–4 – in *Little Eyolf*, 107, 280–1, 282–3, 284–6 – in *When We Dead Awaken*, 107, 306–9
feminism, xv, xvi, 16; American, 131, 134–5; European, 67, 120–1, 181; Japanese, 114; Norwegian, 68–9, 127, 129–31, 134–5, 181, 199; Ibsen's support of causes of, 125–8; in *Love's Comedy*, 65, 70–2; in *Pillars of Society*, 129–35; in *A Doll House*, 110–28, 137–45; and art, *see* art, and feminism; and the origins of modern drama, 323–5
Fibiger, Mathilde, 65, 67
Fitinghof, Rosa, 351
Freud, Sigmund, 305–6, 329, 346, 358, 365
Frida Foldal (of *John Gabriel Borkman*), 295, 368
Fuller, Margaret, 120
Furia (of *Catiline*), 23–9, 30, 35, 57, 80, 229, 271, 329, 330

Galatea, *see* female archetypes
gender, in *Lady Inger of Østråt*, 29, 33–5, 128; subversion of binary notions of, xvi, 21–2, 329–35 – in *The Vikings at Helgeland*, 57–8, 129 – in *The Pretenders*, 74–80, 129 – in *Brand*, 84–6, 89–90, 129 – in *Pillars of Society*, 129–31, 133–5 – in *A Doll House*, 129, 137–45 – in *An Enemy of the People*, 165–6 – in *The Wild Duck*, 166–73 – in *Hedda Gabler*, 229–32 – in *Little Eyolf*, 289–90 – in *John Gabriel Borkman*, 296–8, 300–1
Gerd (of *Brand*), 14, 80, 81, 83, 86, 87, 89
Ghosts, 8, 14, 17, 22, 34–5, 58, 82, 109,

120, 139, 146–62, 163, 166, 182, 183, 190, 196, 204, 208, 211, 246, 255, 266, 269, 301, 308–9, 315, 316, 322, 324, 326, 327, 328, 330, 333–4, 335
Gilman, Charlotte Perkins: *Women and Economics*, 139
Gina Hansen Ekdal (of *The Wild Duck*), 167, 169–73, 175, 177, 178–80, 283, 330
Gissing, George, 329
Goethe, Johann Wolfgang von, 251, 262, 346; *Faust*, 84, 89, 93, 102, 106, 234, 240, 347; *Götz von Berlichingen*, 27; *The Natural Daughter*, 340; *Wahrheit und Dichtung*, 321; *Werther*, 18
Gosse, Edmund, 8, 80, 112, 246
Granville-Barker, Harley: "On the Coming of Ibsen," 113–14
Graves, Robert: *The White Goddess*, 304–5
Gretchen (of *Faust*), *see* Goethe, Johann Wolfgang von
Grieg, Edvard, 103
Grouse in Justedal, The, 31–2, 38
Gunhild Borkman (of *John Gabriel Borkman*), 8, 22, 292–5, 296, 297, 298–9, 300–1, 303, 332
Gyldendal Norsk Forlag, 41

Hallgerd, *see Njal's Saga*
Hamlet, 101
Hamsun, Knut, 151, 250
Hansen, Peter, 10, 11, 61
Hansteen, Asta, 129–31, 134–5
Harryson's History of London, 12, 337
Hauptmann, Gerhart: *Before Sunrise*, 324; *Lonely Lives*, 324; *Rose Bernd*, 324
Hebbel, Friedrich: *Maria Magdalena*, 231
Hedda Gabler (of *Hedda Gabler*), 8, 22, 24, 29, 37–8, 203, 204–11, 213–32, 243–4, 309, 317, 322, 326, 328, 329, 330, 334
Hedda Gabler, 7, 8, 22, 24, 37–8, 109, 203, 204–32, 239, 240, 243–5, 246, 269, 309, 317, 322, 326, 327, 329, 330, 334, 340
Hedvig Ekdal (of *The Wild Duck*), 12, 167, 168, 169, 171, 172, 173–6, 177–9
Heiberg, Johan, 67
Heiberg, Johanne Luise, 67
Helena (of *Emperor and Galilean*), 108–9
Helene Alving (of *Ghosts*), 8, 22, 34–5, 146–62, 163, 201, 208, 315, 326, 328, 330, 334, 335
Hennings, Betty, 112, 127

Henriksen, Hans Jacob, 15, 17, 337
Hilda Wangel (of *The Lady from the Sea*
    and *The Master Builder*), 28, 29, 245,
    248, 250, 252, 261–77, 302, 328, 329
Hjørdis (of *The Vikings at Helgeland*), 8,
    22, 28, 29, 35, 37, 39, 45, 53–8, 61,
    80, 84, 182, 193, 229, 274, 328, 329,
    330, 333
Holberg, Ludvig, 16, 27, 346; feminism of
    – in *Comparative Histories of Heroines*,
    65 – in *Introduction to the Science of
    Natural Law and the Law of Nations*, 65
    – in *Jean de France*, 65 – in *The Journey
    of Niels Klim to the World Underground*,
    65–6 – in *The Transformed Bridegroom*,
    65 – in *The Weathercock*, 65, 67 – in
    "Zille Hansdotter's Defense of the
    Female Sex," 65
Holst, Henrikke, 32–3
Horney, Karen: "The Overvaluation of
    Love," 332
Howe, Julia Ward, 134
Huneker, James, 24, 171, 190, 206, 325

Iago, *see* Coleridge, Samuel Taylor
Ibsen, Bergliot Bjørnson, 8, 43, 47, 53,
    124, 253
Ibsen, Hedvig, 7, 8–10, 12, 241
Ibsen, Henrik: appearance, 13, 48–9, 51;
    character, 5–14, 16, 22, 30–1, 32,
    47–8, 51–2, 90–1, 125–6, 127–8,
    146, 163, 244–5, 253, 318–20;
    devotion to work, 47–8, 318–21;
    disassociation with father, 4–5, 7–8,
    11–12, 14; fathering of illegitimate
    child, 15–18; feminist influences on,
    65–72 (Johanne Luise and Johan
    Heiberg, Ludvig Holberg, Camilla
    Collett), *see also* Hansteen, Asta;
    Ibsen, Suzannah; and Thoresen,
    Magdalene; influence of
    Mediterranean culture on, 80;
    marriage to Suzannah Thoresen, 44–
    53, 58–63, 72–3, 248–9, 251–2, 257,
    261–2, 319; reading, 16, 18, 25, 27,
    35, 53, 65–7, 131, 194–5, 347;
    relation with Clara Ebbell, 18–22;
    relation with Emilie Bardach, 233–
    46, 250, 256–7, 261–2; relation with
    Helene Raff, 247–8; relation with
    Hildur Andersen, 249–63; relation
    with Laura Kieler, 135–7; relation
    with mother, 4–6, 7–13, 241; relation
    with Rikke Holst, 32–3; relation with
    sister, 7, 8–10, 12–13, 241; self-

judgment, 12–13, 47–8, 62–3, 318;
    support of feminist causes, 125–8
Ibsen, Knud, 1, 3–5, 7, 8, 11–12, 14, 22,
    336, 337
Ibsen, Marichen Altenburg: appearance,
    character, tastes, 1, 5, 7–8; influence
    on Ibsen, 5, 7–8, 21–2, 71, 336–7;
    marriage, 1, 3–5, 7–8, 21–2; model
    for Aase and Inga, 10–12; relation
    with Ibsen, 4–6, 8–13, 241
Ibsen, Sigurd, 44, 47, 48, 52, 59, 249, 253
Ibsen, Suzannah Thoresen, 39, 40, 43,
    124, 135–6, 239, 240, 241, 250, 341;
    appearance, character, tastes, 44–8,
    50–3, 59–63, 182, 194; devotion to
    Ibsen's work, 46–8, 51–3, 261;
    Ibsen's letters to, 261–2; Ibsen's
    poems to, 45, 46, 52; Ibsen's praise
    of her, 45, 52, 61, 182; influence on
    Ibsen, 45–6, 52, 129, 320; influence
    on *Love's Comedy*, 61–3, 65, 72–3;
    model for Hjørdis and Svanhild, 45,
    53, 61–3, 72–3; reaction to Ibsen's
    relations with other women, 248–9,
    251–2; refusal to have more children,
    59–60; translator of German plays,
    60; *see also* Ibsen, Henrik, marriage
Inga (of *The Pretenders*), 10, 75, 76–7
Ingebjørg (of *The Pretenders*), 77, 344
Ingeborg (of *Olaf Liljekrans*), 38
Inger (*of Lady Inger of Østråt*), 22, 33–5,
    45, 330, 332, 333
Ingrid (of *Peer Gynt*), 93, 94, 95, 96, 97,
    101, 102, 106
Irene (of *When We Dead Awaken*), 8, 22,
    28, 303, 306–15, 317–18, 321, 326,
    327, 328, 329, 332, 335

James, Henry: "On the Occasion of *Hedda
    Gabler*," 206, 210
Jensdatter, Else Sofie, 15–16, 17–18
John Gabriel Borkman, 7, 8, 22, 58, 107,
    109, 203, 246, 291–301, 309, 317,
    322, 328, 331–2
Jones, Henry Arthur: *Breaking A Butterfly*,
    113
Joyce, James, 150, 315
Juliana Tesman (of *Hedda Gabler*), 22,
    211–14, 225–6, 228, 230, 231, 328
Julie (of *Miss Julie*), *see* Strindberg, August

Kaja Fosli (of *The Master Builder*), 264,
    265, 268, 270, 328
Katherine Stockmann (of *An Enemy of the
    People*), 163–6, 167, 330

Keats, John, 92
Kieler, Laura, 135–7, 352
Kieler, Victor, 135–7
Kielland, Alexander, 127
Kierkegaard, Søren, 64, 81, 305–6, 343, 345
Knudsen, Tormod, 1, 14, 337
Kristine Linde (of *A Doll House*), 139, 169
Krog, Gina, 135, 181

Lady Inger of Østråt, 17, 22, 29, 32, 33–5, 45, 128–9, 321, 330
Lady from the Sea, The, 17, 22, 41, 109, 194–203, 263–4, 269, 286, 301, 317, 327, 328, 334
Lammers, G.A., 9, 345
League of Youth, The, 67, 128, 250
Legouvé, Ernest: *Bataille de Dames*, 67
Lie, Jonas, 127
Little Eyolf, 8, 22, 29, 58, 107, 109, 189, 203, 246, 278–91, 301, 303, 309, 317, 321, 328, 329, 330, 331–2, 335
Little Helga (of *Peer Gynt*), 93, 97, 98
Livermore, Mary, 134
Lofthus, Christian, 15–16, 17–18
Lona Hessel (of *Pillars of Society*), 22, 28, 67, 129–35, 182, 266, 329, 330, 333, 334
love, and vocation, 318–22; in *Catiline*, 25–8, 321; in *Lady Inger of Østråt*, 33–4; in *The Vikings at Helgeland*, 28, 55, 57–8, 321; in *Love's Comedy*, 61–4, 321; in *The Pretenders*, 74–80, 321; in *Brand*, 80–90, 321; in *Peer Gynt*, 28, 104–8, 321; in *Pillars of Society*, 132–3, 321; in *A Doll House*, 137–40, 143–5, 321–2; in *Rosmersholm*, 28, 187–8, 191–4; in *The Master Builder*, 28, 274–7, 321; in *Little Eyolf*, 28, 287–91, 321; in *John Gabriel Borkman*, 291–2, 295–8, 299–301, 321, 322; in *When We Dead Awaken*, 28, 305–8, 314–15, 321–2
Love's Comedy, 21, 22, 34, 37, 45, 53, 60–5, 70–3, 129, 133, 196, 200, 318, 321, 327, 328
Lukács, George: "The Sociology of Modern Drama," 332

Macrina (of *Emperor and Galilean*), 109
Maja Rubek (of *When We Dead Awaken*), 29, 312–13, 315, 319, 321, 329
male-centered triangle, xv–xvi, 55, 57, 134, 327, 329; in *Catiline*, 25–9; in *Brand*, 80–2; in *Rosmersholm*, 186–8,

189–94; in *The Master Builder*, 267, 270–4; in *Little Eyolf*, 278–80, 285–7; in *John Gabriel Borkman*, 292–5, 298–99, 300–1; in *When We Dead Awaken*, 312–14
Margit (of *The Feast at Solhoug*), 8, 22, 35–8, 53, 54, 200, 229, 328, 330, 333, 341
Margrete (of *The Pretenders*), 75–7, 78–80
marriage, 138–42, 196–9; attack on, in *Love's Comedy*, 61–5; of convenience, 21–2, 34, 35–8 – in *Love's Comedy*, 37, 63–5, 70–2 – in *Brand*, 82–3 – in *Ghosts*, 34–5, 37, 82, 147–51, 152, 154–5, 159–62 – in *The Lady from the Sea*, 37, 200–3 – in *Hedda Gabler*, 37–8, 203, 214, 216–18, 220–2, 229; woman's role in, *see* motherhood, and woman, as man's servant
Martha Bernick (of *Pillars of Society*), 22, 132–3, 213
Martineau, Harriet, 121
Masha (in Chekhov's *The Sea Gull*), 225
Master Builder, The, 17, 22, 25, 28, 32, 58, 109, 246, 248, 250, 252, 254, 261, 262, 263–77, 278, 290, 302, 321, 328, 329, 331–2
Maugham, Somerset: *Of Human Bondage*, 112
McCarthy, Mary, 115
Medea, 112
merfolk, 195–6
Mill, John Stuart: *The Subjection of Women*, 68, 125, 333
Milton, John: *Paradise Lost*, 31, 87, 138
Miss Julie, see Strindberg, August
modernism, 323–7, 332–3; in drama, 323–4, 332; embodied by Ibsen's women characters, 325–35; Ibsen as creator of, xv–xvi, 323–6
Molière, 346
Moore, George, 157
motherhood, in *Lady Inger of Østråt*, 34–5, in *A Doll House*, 143, 145; in *Ghosts*, 34–5, 152, 156–60; in *Hedda Gabler*, 217–18, 225–6, 227, 230–1; in *The Master Builder*, 271–3; in *Little Eyolf*, 280–1, 283–4, 287, 289; in *John Gabriel Borkman*, 292–5, 296–9, 300–1
Munch, Edvard, 158–9, 301, 354

National Romanticism, 29–32, 33, 38
Nazimova, Alla, 126, 142
New and Universal History of the Cities of London and Westminister, A, 7

"New Woman," the, 67, 131, 133, 163, 181, 207, 324

Njal's Saga, 54

Nora Helmer (of *A Doll House*), 22, 30, 67, 111–24, 127, 128, 137–45, 146, 163, 182, 200, 207, 289, 321–2, 325, 326–7, 328, 330, 333, 335

Norma, 340

Normans, The, 30

Norwegian Fairy Tales, 95–7, 346

Norwegian National Theatre of Bergen, The, 30

Norwegian Theatre of Christiania, The, 58

Norwegian Women's Rights League, The, 110, 127, 135

Œdipus the King, see Sophocles

Oehlenschläger, Adam, 16, 18, 20; *Stærkodder, The Vikings at Byzantium*, 27

Olaf Liljekrans, 38

Pater, Walter, 304

patriarchy, 142, 183–4, 230–1, 303–6, 323–4, 330–1; and violence, in *The Pretenders*, 74–80

Peer Gynt, 7, 8, 10–13, 14, 17, 28, 32, 58, 81, 90–108, 128, 129, 255, 282, 301, 321, 328

Penelope, *see* female archetypes

Petersen, Clemens, 60

Petra Stockmann (of *An Enemy of the People*), 38, 163–6, 250

Petrarch, 304

Phaedra, *see* Racine, Jean

Piper, Ebba, 181–2

Pillars of Society, 7, 22, 30, 34, 58, 65, 67, 109, 129–34, 147, 149, 163, 201, 203, 213, 269, 292, 308, 321, 324, 327, 328, 329, 330, 333

Pretenders, The, 8, 10, 17, 58, 74–80, 81, 129, 134, 321, 331

Prisoner at Akershus, The, 17–18

Racine, Jean, 119

Raff, Helene, 247–8, 251, 256, 257, 262

Ragnhild (of *The Pretenders*), 75, 78

Raicho, Hiratsuka, 114

Rank, Otto, 306

Raphael, Clara, *see* Fibiger, Mathilde

Rat Wife, the (of *Little Eyolf*), 189, 281–2, 287, 367

Ravnkilde, Adda, 194–5

Rebecca West (of *Rosmersholm*), 14, 22, 28, 29, 181–94, 229, 274, 330, 334

Regine Engstrand (of *Ghosts*), 14, 151, 152, 154, 160–1

Reimers, Karoline, *see* Bjørnson, Karoline

"Rhyme Letter to Fru Heiberg," *see* Heiberg, Johanne Luise

Rilke, Rainer Maria, 162

Rina Tesman (of *Hedda Gabler*), 213, 225, 228, 230

Rita Allmers (of *Little Eyolf*), 8, 22, 28, 29, 278–91, 303, 321, 328, 329, 330, 332, 334–5

Robins, Elizabeth: *Ibsen and the Actress*, 231–2

Rodin, Auguste, and Camille Claudel, 369

Romantic tragic drama, women in, 26–7

Rosmersholm, 14, 17, 22, 58, 107, 109, 132, 181–94, 202, 211, 243, 246, 250, 290, 301, 309, 317, 330, 334

Rousseau, Jean-Jacques, 329

Ruskin, John, 138

sagas, 35, 44; women in, 51, 53–4, 275, 342, *see also Njal's Saga* and *The Volsung Saga*

Sallust: *Catilinae Coniuratio*, 25

Sand, George, 41, 44

Sayers, Dorothy: "The Human-Not-Quite-Human," 119

Schiller, Johann Friedrich von, 27, 74; *Conspiracy of Fiesco at Genoa, The*, 27; *Maid of Orleans, The*, 340; *Maria Stuart*, 340; *Robbers, The*, 27, 44; *William Tell*, 27, 106

Schulerud, Ole, 16, 124

Scott, Clement, 114

Scott, Sir Walter, 16

Scribe, Eugène: *Bataille de Dames*, 67

Selma Brattsberg (of *The League of Youth*), 128

Shakespeare, William, 79, 94, 344; *Antony and Cleopatra*, 119; *Macbeth*, 211, 346

Shaw, George Bernard: *Candida*, 119, 324; *Philanderer, The*, 324, 371; *Mrs. Warren's Profession*, 324; *The Quintessence of Ibsenism*, 111, 158

Signe (of *The Feast at Solhoug*), 35, 36, 341

Sigrid (of *The Pretenders*), 75, 79

Simmel, Georg: *On Woman, Sexuality, and Culture*, 327, 332

Snoilsky, Carl, 181–2

Solveig (of *Peer Gynt*), 91, 93–4, 97, 98–102, 103–8, 202, 308, 321, 328

Sontum, Christian, 252

Sontum, Helene, 249
Sophocles, 149; *Oedipus the King*, 147, 161
Spenser, Edmund: *The Færie Queen*, 31, 330
St. John's Night, 30–1, 32
Stanislavsky, Konstantin, 156
Stone, Lucy, 134
Storm and Stress drama, women in, 27
Stousland, Hedvig, *see* Ibsen, Hedvig.
Strindberg, August, 127, 354; *Comrades*, 324, 351; *Creditors*, 324; "A Doll House," 351; *The Father*, 155, 324; *A Madman's Defense*, 351–2; *Miss Julie*, 117, 119, 231, 324
Sumako, Matsui, 114
Svanhild (of *Love's Comedy*), 21, 22, 37, 45, 53, 61–5, 70–3, 133, 201, 327, 328, 333

Thea Elvsted (of *Hedda Gabler*), 22, 25, 29, 209–10, 218–20, 222, 223, 224, 227, 230, 327–8, 329
Thomsen, Grímar, 41
Thoresen, Hans Conrad, 41
Thoresen, Magdalene Kragh, 40–4, 336, 341; *My Grandmother's Story*, 41–2, 72; *Pictures from the Land of the Midnight Sun*, 41; *Poems of A Lady*, 41; *A Witness*, 40; model for Ellida Wangel, 41, 195; relation with Ibsen, 40, 42–4, 65, 251
Thoresen, Marie, 44
Thoresen, Suzannah Daae, *see* Ibsen, Suzannah
"To Autumn," 33
tragedy, Greek, 147, 148–9, 158, 161–2, 269; tragic form in *Ghosts*, 147–62
trolls, 95–8, 101, 105, 367

Undset, Sigrid, 207

Veblen, Thorstein: *The Theory of the Leisure Class*, 121, 139
Vikings at Helgeland, The, 8, 22, 28, 30, 34, 35, 37, 39, 45, 53–8, 61, 62, 80, 84,
102, 129, 193, 196, 229, 290, 292, 300, 308, 321, 328, 329, 330, 331
Volsung Saga, The, 54–5, 70–1
Voltaire, 16, 345

Wagner, Richard, 193, 197, 307
Wedekind, Frank: *Earth Spirit*, 324; *Pandora's Box*, 324; *Spring's Awakening*, 324
Wergeland, Henrik, 18
West, Mae, 103
West, Rebecca, *see* Fairchild, Cicely
When We Dead Awaken, 8, 22, 24, 25, 29, 58, 107–8, 109, 203, 246, 302–22, 327, 328, 329, 331–2, 335
Whitman, Walt, 304
Wild Duck, The, 12, 14, 17, 109, 148, 166–80, 202, 212, 246, 283, 289, 301, 309, 317, 327, 330
Wilde, Oscar: *Ideal Husband, An*, 324; *Importance of Being Ernest, The*, 324; *Lady Windemere's Fan*, 324
Wollstonecraft, Mary: *Vindication of the Rights of Women, A*, 120
Woman in Green, the (of *Peer Gynt*), 95–7, 101, 282
"woman question," the, 120, 163; and modern drama, 323–5
woman, male reification of women into, 108–9, 286–7, 304–9, 312–15; *see also* female archetypes, motherhood, and woman, as man's servant
woman: as man's servant, 84–6, 131–3, 142, 143, 145, 229–30, 302–3, 327–9 – housewife, 164, 165, 168–73, 179, 199–200 – man's disciple, 80–2, 83–4, 102–3 – man's helpmate, 201–2, 219–20, 227, 231 – man's intercessor, 84–6, 98, 105–8 – man's rejuvenation, 266–71, 274–7; *see also* female archetypes: eternal feminine, muse, redemptive woman, sacrificial woman
"woman's sphere," the, 137–45, 331
women's rights, *see* feminism